Thomas Wright Blakiston

Five Months on the Yang-Tsze

With a Narrative of the Exploration of its Upper Waters

Thomas Wright Blakiston

Five Months on the Yang-Tsze
With a Narrative of the Exploration of its Upper Waters

ISBN/EAN: 9783337212742

Printed in Europe, USA, Canada, Australia, Japan

Cover: Foto ©Andreas Hilbeck / pixelio.de

More available books at **www.hansebooks.com**

FIVE MONTHS

ON

THE YANG-TSZE;

WITH A NARRATIVE OF THE EXPLORATION OF
ITS UPPER WATERS,

AND

NOTICES OF THE PRESENT REBELLIONS IN CHINA.

By THOMAS W. BLAKISTON,
LATE CAPTAIN ROYAL ARTILLERY.

ILLUSTRATED FROM SKETCHES

By ALFRED BARTON, M.R.C.S., F.R.G.S.

WITH MAPS BY ARROWSMITH.

LONDON:
JOHN MURRAY, ALBEMARLE STREET.
1862.

PREFACE.

THE following pages were prepared for the press some months since; but the publication of the work has been delayed till the autumn season, at the request of Mr. Murray.

Late events in China, and the policy adopted by the present Government, have changed our attitude towards the Taiping rebels; but as that of the Imperial power remains the same, both with respect to the Taipings and to other insurrectionists in the interior, any remarks on the state of the rebellion are as applicable now as when they were written.

In offering to the reading public a narrative of the "Upper Yang-tsze Expedition," I must in justice remark that the undertaking was a private enterprise of Lieut.-Colonel H. A. Sarel, 17th Lancers, Dr. Alfred Barton, and myself; while the fourth member of the expedition, the Rev. S. Schereschewsky, of the "American Episcopal Board of Foreign Missions," afforded his assistance gratuitously. To each of these gentlemen I am indebted in one way or another for information and assistance, which I have acknowledged more particularly in the body of the work. Dr. Barton, however, having undertaken the illustration of the book, is entitled to any credit which may be due on that score; while at the same time he wishes me to state the obligations he is under to Messrs. H. G. Hine and J. W. Whymper, for the manner in which they have executed the drawings on wood.

It will be observed that most of the information concerning the Taiping rebels is from the pen of Mr. R. J. Forrest, than whom I know no one more competent to handle the subject. My best thanks are due for the valuable matter which he so kindly placed at my disposal, to which at the present juncture I would particularly direct the attention of the reader.

The names of Sir William Hooker, Professor Morris, Professor Ramsay, Mr. John Riddle, and others, are sufficient guarantees for the accuracy of such portions as rest on their authority, and I am glad to express my thanks for their readily afforded aid.

The Maps attached to this volume are by Mr. John Arrowsmith, and may therefore be considered as accurate as our present knowledge of the country will allow. That of the Yang-tsze Kiang above Hankow is a reduction, in which many details are omitted, of a Chart* prepared from our survey, which it is hoped will be found of service to those interested in the geography or navigation of the Upper Yang-tsze.

Lastly, I have to acknowledge the valuable assistance of my friend Mr. F. Lawrence in passing these pages through the press.

Rather than encumber the narrative with matter of a

---

* The Yang-tsze Kiang, from Hankow to Ping-shan, from the Survey of Captain Blakiston, R.A., in 1861, by John Arrowsmith. London: published by John Arrowsmith, 35, Hereford Square, South Kensington.

scientific nature, some details of that description will be found in the Appendix and in a chapter (Chap. XVII.) devoted to the physical geography of the region passed through.

The object, equipment, and assistance rendered the "Upper Yang-tsze Expedition," are sufficiently explained in the body of the work to relieve me from trying the reader's patience by protracting the prefatory part of a production pretending only to accuracy, simplicity, and impartiality; and as no apology is required at the present time for the publication of any reliable information concerning China and its inhabitants, particularly with respect to the state of the disturbed districts, I humbly but unhesitatingly submit to the reader this record of a private expedition, which, principally by means of its own resources, ascended one of the greatest rivers in the world a distance of eighteen hundred miles, and by the care of Divine Providence was permitted to return the same distance to the coast after an absence of five months.

London, October, 1862.

CONTENTS.

CHAPTER I.

UP TO NANKING.

Start from Shanghai — Admiral Hope's squadron — The *Centaur* and *Couper* run ashore — A sham battery — Proceed to Chin-kiang — Shooting — Installation of a consul — Silver Island and the city — Voyage to Nanking — Imperialist and Rebel outposts — The Taipings at Nanking — The steamer *Yang-tsze* — Sight-seeing .. .. Page 1

CHAPTER II.

THE MING TOMBS.

Way to get to the tombs — A Taiping chief — A scene of desolation — Taiping slaves — The Golden Pearl mountain — Siege of Nanking — Devastated country — The tombs — The Manchoos and the Mings — Effects of civil war — Porcelain pagoda — The South Gate of Nanking 17

CHAPTER III.

THE TAIPINGS AT THEIR CAPITAL.

Sketch of the Taiping rebellion — Enter the Heavenly capital — Misery of Taiping life — Palaces — Visit to the Prince of Praise — The Sacred Palace — Tien-wang — Taiping religion — Dinner with a king — A night in a palace — Interview with the Kan-wang — Interior of his palace — The Taipings — The Mantchous — Christianity — Commerce — and the future 31

CHAPTER IV.

A NAVAL SQUADRON INLAND.

Voyage above Nanking — Scenery on the river — Desolation at Wu-hoo — Foraging excursion — An-king besieged — Outlet of the Poyang lake — Kiu-kiang — Voyage to Hankow — Hankow described — Its trade — The river Han — Our position at Hankow 56

CHAPTER V.

ADMIRAL HOPE'S EXPLORATION.

Transfer to a junk — Farewell dinner — Voyage continued — Commissariat arrangements — A low couutry — The Great Bend — Fleet of junks — Naval surveying — Chinese fishing-nets — Rafts — A singular fish — Names for the Yang-tsze — Collision with the *Coromandel* — Our skipper — Town of Sing-ti — Inundations — Outlet of Tung-ting lake — Yo-chow — The Tung-ting lake — Parting with the naval squadron .. Page 70

CHAPTER VI.

JUNK TRAVELLING IN HOO-PEH.

Organization of the expedition — Description of junk — Leaving Yo-chow — Expedition not a government undertaking — Our mandarin — Outlet of Tung-ting lake — Huc's Reach — St. Patrick's Bend — Catering and foraging — The Nan-tsuin hills — Flood — Boulder shoal — Low country and agriculture — Tortuosity of the river — Tiau-hien range — Astronomical observations — Waterfowl and game — Agricultural population — Shi-show — British law in China 84

CHAPTER VII.

SHI-SHOW TO I-CHANG.

Continuation of voyage — Hints for future navigators — Ho-hia narrows — Birds — A storm — Level of the land and river — Sha-szo and Kin-chow — Taiping Creek — The junk trade — Exports and imports — Coal — View from the pagoda — Visits from mandarins and ladies — Taiping Canal — Land-route from Hankow — Nearing the mountains — Effects of a flood — Approach to I-chang — Beautiful scenery — A day's halt — Rebels — I-chang — Show beasts — Loss of boat fixings — Country around I-chang 102

CHAPTER VIII.

GORGES AND RAPIDS.

Last porpoises — Sz'chuan *voyageurs* — Enter the mountains — I-chang gorge — Braves — Sz'chuan junks — Scenery — Rapids — Ascent of a rapid — Rapids as influencing future navigation — Lu-kan gorge — Village and rapid of Tsing-tan — Mi-tan gorge — Kwei — Coal-mines — Fishing in the rapids — Wu-shan gorge — Boundary between provinces — Wu-shan — Chinese measure of distance — A poisoning case — Wind-box Gorge — Arrival at Quai-chow 119

CHAPTER IX.

EASTERN SZ'CHUAN.

Interview with the prefect at Quai-chow — Treaty of Tien-tsin not promulgated — Antipathy to Europeans travelling by land — Return of our mandarin — Government corruption — Substitutes for soldiers — A second escort — The Yang-tsze below Quai-chow described — A new flag — Quai-chow — Pagodas — Affixes to the names of towns — Our money — Exchange — Cultivation — The poppy and opium — Start from Quai-chow — Break-down — Chinese ignorance of other nations — Leaky junk in the rapids — Physical features — Coal — Tung-yan Rapid — Yung-yan — Medical aid — Towers on the hill-tops — Beauty of Sz'chuan — Curiosity of the people — Rock flats — Gold-washing — Arrival at Wan .. .. Page 138

CHAPTER X.

VISITS AND CEREMONIES.

Situation of Wan — False notions of China — Reception of a general — Our costumes — Our troops — The procession — Entertainment — Arrangements for a campaign — Embarkation — Visit to the prefect — Evils in the Mantchou system of local government — Huc's '*Journey through the Chinese Empire*' — The prefect's advice and civility — Peculation by Chinese servants — Arrangements for farther voyage — Indefinite information — Generalization on China — Huc's Chinese in Europe — Thriving appearance of the people and country — Coal and other products — The weather — Expedition records — Assistance in preparing this narrative — Chart of the river — Chinese Christians — Missionaries in China 162

CHAPTER XI.

THE GOLD-SAND RIVER.

Leave Wan — Chinese names — Sandstone country — Rock temple and pagoda of Shi-pow-chai — Roman Catholics — Islands, reefs, and rapids — Town of Chung — Frogs — Obstructions in the river — Ranges of mountains — Fung-tu a pretty place — Black and white houses — Huc's description of Sz'chuan — Appearance of the people — Shyness of the fair sex — Bathing — St. George's Island — Town of Fu — Maps of China — Mode adopted in spelling Chinese names — Redoubts erected by the natives — The Kung-tan river — Business and agriculture 181

CHAPTER XII.

CROSS RANGES.

Departure from Fu — Our boat's crew — An opium-smoker — Boatmen's songs — The bowsman and his son — The one-eyed cook — Boatmen's faro and wages — Fortified hills — Vegetable productions — Ranges of hills —

Small feet of the women — Snipe-shooting under difficulties — Effects of the hot weather — Course of the river — Climate of Sz'chuan, and agriculture — Troops of tame ducks — A pretty temple — Roads in China — The latter days of the Sing dynasty — Chinese easily governed — What is to become of China? — Arrival at Chung-king .. .. .. Page 198

CHAPTER XIII.

CHUNG-KING.

Importance of Chung-king — Size and population — The Yang-tsze and Ho-tow — Coal, limestone, and sandstone — Visit to a pagoda — Gratuitous refreshment for travellers — Extensive view — A hermit — The dog "Bill" — Civility of the country people — Inscriptions and mottoes — Invitation from the French missionaries — Independent soldiers — Threatened attack on our party — Preparations for defence — Standing on our dignity — Reasons for the hostility — Visit to the governor — Dinner with the French missionaries — State of the country — Guarding the junks — Engage for farther voyage — Rise of the river — Chinese bamboo structures — Trade of Chung-king — Freight and time of transit — Letter concerning our progress 211

CHAPTER XIV.

THE FOUR VALLEYS.

Departure from Chung-king — Change in our junks — Curiosity of the boatmen — Nature of the river — Island and temple of Kin-tin-tsze — Coke — Mosquitoes — Hot weather — Pagodas at Kiang-tsze — Nature of the country — Gold on the Yang-tsze Kiang — Outlooks — Rafts — Farming operations — Pink buffalo — River junks — Ho-kiang — A cottage scene — Continuation of the voyage — Productions of the country — Shells — Town of Lu — Reports of rebels — Rainy season — Wreck of our mandarin's junk — Number of towns — Poorer appearance of the country and people — A Chinese picket — Foraging — Kiang-an — Barton Island — Nan-ki — Arrival at Sü-chow 231

CHAPTER XV.

SÜ-CHOW AND THE WESTERN REBELS.

Reports of rebels — Inhabitants combine for their own protection — Depredations of imperial and rebel troops — Four kinds of rebels in China — Mussulman rebels — Towns held by the Sz'chuan rebels — Headless bodies — Boatmen refuse to ascend the Min — Country around Sü-chow — Jesuit maps of China — Situation of the city — Trade and products — Coal-mines — Future use for the coal — Navigation of the Min and Yang-tsze — Sudden changes in the water — Correspondence with the prefect — Annoyance by the braves — Difficulty in proceeding — Determine to proceed farther up the Yang-tsze — Refugees — A battle between braves 247

CHAPTER XVI.

PING-SHAN — OUR FARTHEST.

Voyage above Sü-chow — Accident at a rapid — Mode of working coal — Mountainous region — Arrival at Ping-shan — Boundary of the province of Yu-nan — Name of Ping-shan — Productions of the country — The Yang-tsze above Ping-shan — Interview with the prefect — No transport procurable — Independent tribes — Miau-tze — Intention to live in the city — Gates closed against us — A reconnaissance — Ruined suburbs — Select a temple for quarters — Endeavours to get the boatmen to move — Our junks fired on — Quieting the boatmen — The prefect's advice — A night alarm — City attacked by rebels — Panic among the Chinese — Our junks become separated — An anxious night — Search for the Doctor — The Doctor's adventure .. .. Page 264

CHAPTER XVII.

THE UPPER YANG-TSZE.

PHYSICAL FEATURES OF THE RIVER: Course of the Yang-tsze. *The Hoo-peh plain:* Alluvial country. *The Hoo-peh and Sz'chuan mountain district:* First gravel and rock — Conglomerate region — The gorges — From Quai-chow to Wan — Sandstone of the Upper Yang-tsze coal-fields. *Sz'chuan and its cross ranges:* Change in the character of the river — Shingle-beds and gold — Grey sandstone — Run of the mountains and their composition — Change in the bed of the river — Coal from the mines near Sü-chow — Mountainous country. *Fall, discharge, and course:* Fall for different parts — Comparison with other rivers — Velocity of the current — Summer floods — Amount of water discharged — Basin area — Depth in the gorges — Winding of course and direct distances compared — Excuse for want of scientific details. REMARKS ON THE NAVIGATION: Admiralty chart — Chart published by Mr. Arrowsmith — Directions for the tortuous part — The least soundings — Navigation of the gorges — The river as suited to steamers. COMMUNICATION BETWEEN INDIA AND CHINA: Schemes to open a commercial route — Difficulty of land-transport underrated — Upper Yang-tsze Expedition had no intention of opening a route — Proposed route from the Bramapootra to the Yang-tsze Kiang 285

CHAPTER XVIII.

DOWN THE KIN-CHA KIANG.

Narrative resumed — Commence our return voyage — Settling the difficulty about boat-hire — Rate of travelling and the current — Halt at Sü-chow — Un-Chinese features — Sport on the Yang-tsze — Rainy weather — Barton Island — Effects of change of air — Odour of live Chinaman — Visitors to our junks at Chung-king — Appearance of the country — A Chinese angler — Clearing muddy water — Exorbitant charges for boat-

xiv   CONTENTS.

hire — Dragon-boat festival — Summer in Sz'chuan — Christians and Mussulmans — Letter in Latin — Reports of rebels — Departure from Chung-king — River's course and range of the hills — Rope manufacture — Religious ceremony of the boatmen — The missionary cause in China — Change in the crops — St. George's Pass — Height of the water — Pass Wan — Cotton-growing — Unfavourable weather — Wrecked junks — Fung-siang and Wu-shan gorges — Temperature — More gorges — The scenery — Return to I-chang   .. .. Page 304

CHAPTER XIX.

RETURN FROM THE INTERIOR.

I-chang as a port for foreign trade — Weather — Change of mandarins — Engage a large junk — Leave I-chang — Sounding — Stormy weather — Pass Sha-sze — Night travelling — Rise of the water — Arrival at the outlet of the Tung-ting Lake — Other expeditions — Yo-chow and the rebels — Progress down the river — Native craft — Crossing the neck of the Great Bend — Wind-bound — Arrival at Hankow — Commerce — Height of the river ;— Instances of pilfering — Embark in the *Hellespont* — H. M. consulate at Kiu-kiang — The Poyang Lake — Navigation of the lower river — An-king still besieged — Arrival at Nanking — Walk on shore — Mr. Forrest — His Celestial Majesty's customs — Visit of the *Pluto* to Nanking — Intense heat — End of our cruise   326

APPENDIX.

I. Itinerary of Distances on the Upper Yang-tsze 353
II. Trade of Chung-king 355
III. Form of Passport 357
IV. Two Letters (in French) from the Roman Catholic missionaries .. 358
V. Geological specimens from the Yang-tsze Kiang 359
VI. List of Ferns collected by Lieut.-Colonel Sarel 361
VII. Geographical Positions 368
VIII. Meteorological Register 369
IX. Specimen page of Log-book 379
X. Ditto of Field-book (Woodcut) 380

LIST OF ILLUSTRATIONS.

ENTRANCE OF LU-KAN GORGE, UPPER YANG-TSZE	*Frontispiece.*
THE CENTAUR ASHORE	*to face page* 3
TORTOISE AND COLUMN CUT FROM ONE BLOCK OF STONE, MING TOMBS, NANKING	16
TOMBS OF THE MING DYNASTY, NANKING	*to face* 24
DIP NET FOR FISHING	30
YO-CHOW	*to face* 81
SINGULAR FISH	83
A MID-DAY HALT	*to face* 98
OUR SKIPPER AND MANDARIN	101
FIRST RAPIDS ON THE YANG-TSZE	*to face* 125
PART OF WU-SHAN GORGE	*to face* 134
BOUNDARY BETWEEN HOO-PEH AND SZ'CHUAN	*to face* 135
NATURAL ARCH NEAR I-CHANG	161
SHI-POW-CHAI	*to face* 182
SZ'CHUAN HOUSES	*to face* 188
SHA-SZE	197
CHUNG-KING, AS SEEN FROM THE RIVER ABOVE. EXPEDITION JUNKS IN THE FOREGROUND	*to face* 211
KIN-TIN-TSZE ISLAND	*to face* 233
COAL GORGE	*to face* 265
PING-SHAN	*to face* 267
MIAU-TZE	284
MOUTH OF THE FUNG-SIANG GORGE BELOW QUAI-CHOW	*to face* 323
THE YANG-TSZE IN FLOOD	*to face* 336
SPECIMEN PAGE OF FIELD-BOOK	380
TWO MAPS BY ARROWSMITH	*at the end.*

FIVE MONTHS ON THE YANG-TSZE.

CHAPTER I.

UP TO NANKING.

DEEP in mud and deluged with rain, Shanghai hardly presented on the 11th of February, 1861, an appearance to justify the appellation of "The Model Settlement," which it, nevertheless, so well merits in the far East. Its princely mercantile residences and extensive Consular buildings looked desolate and dripping. The "Bund"—that promenade of which the residents may well be proud—was deserted, save by a chance pair or two of coolies trotting along under heavy burdens, with their monotonous "ho-ha, ch-ho." The Chinese city was but dimly visible beyond the forest of junk-masts above the foreign shipping; and one would have almost doubted that an immense mass of human life existed at all in the dismal scene, but for occasional explosions of crackers, with which the natives were propitiating the new year, or "chin-chinning joss," as it is familiarly called—for it was the second day of the first moon and holiday-time among the Celestials.

But on the river, notwithstanding the incessant rain, there were signs of movement apparent among the vessels of war lately arrived from the Gulf of Pecheli; and during the day one by one they dropped down stream, forming by evening a respectable little fleet at Woosung.

By nine on the following morning Vice-Admiral Sir James Hope had assembled his squadron outside the mouth of

Woosung or Shanghai river; and at ten, each vessel being in its allotted position, the Expedition began to stem the muddy current of the great Yang-tsze. The sailing order was in three parallel lines, headed by the smaller craft. The centre column was composed of H.M.SS. 'Centaur,' 'Waterman,' and 'Attalante,' headed by No. 95, the 'Bouncer' gun-boat. On the starboard hand the Admiral's vessel, the 'Coromandel,' was followed by the gun-boat 'Havoc;' while Commander Ward led the left or port line in the 'Couper' surveying vessel, with No. 90, the 'Banterer,' astern. Thus started the Yang-tsze Expedition of 1861, the object of which was to open the Yang-tsze Kiang to foreign trade.

It was a pleasing sight to witness the vessels steaming steadily onwards in the broad expanse of estuary, prevented only from appearing like the ocean itself by the island of Tsung-ming, and its smaller companion Bush Island; and, as there was nothing of interest in those low flat shores or the equally monotonous line of the mainland, where a few house-tops and trees alone showed over the embankment which keeps the country from inundation, the doings of the squadron naturally attracted all attention. Flags and pendants which, in the leading vessels, were signals for the depth of water as shown by the lead, in the flag-vessel orders or questions, and in the others answers to the same, were continually being hauled up and down; and it would have been a superior kaleidoscope that could have exhibited such combinations and changes of colours. The squadron kept perfect order.

However, in the best-regulated—or may we say, over-regulated?—families or fleets, accidents will sometimes happen, and "running ashore by Act of Parliament," as it is called, was not to be avoided, notwithstanding such regulations. Thirty-three miles only had been made, we were not quite up to Plover Point, whence Lang-shan Hill (the first high land on the river) is visible with its pagoda, when bump goes the

THE CENTAUR ASHORE.

'Centaur' on a shoal, and the 'Waterman'—which vessel she had been obliged to take in tow shortly before—smashes into her quarter. "Ahead" or "astern" full speed is of no avail; sails are set, but she does not move; so the squadron is ordered to anchor, and thus ends the first day.

In H.M.S. 'Attalante,' which accommodated amongst others the members of what was then called the "Overland Expedition," we for three days watched the unsuccessful endeavours at each succeeding high tide to get the 'Centaur' off, which one may imagine to us inactive folks was not particularly interesting. Then we were anchored so far from the shore, and the weather was so unseasonable, that we had no opportunity of making a more intimate acquaintance with the country in the neighbourhood of Plover Point. This caused us to pace the decks with impatience, especially those of us who had visions of the high-lands of Tibet and the Himalayas; and walking up and down the twelve or fifteen feet of deck not obstructed by ropes, hen-coops, or other obstacles, could be compared only to the constant motion of the hyæna in the Zoological Gardens: the simile, if not exactly true, was ludicrous, and this nautical exercise became henceforth known as "doing the hyæna."

At last, on the 15th, after all the devices which come under the list sanctioned by the Lords Commissioners of the High Court of Admiralty had been tried and had failed, it was decided that a gun-boat should go back to Woosung for assistance, and that the remainder of the squadron should proceed. Twenty miles farther up we anchored that evening, having, under the skilful pilotage of Commander Ward, passed the bugbear of Yang-tsze navigation known as "Lang-shan Crossing;" only one vessel touched the ground, and she was quickly towed off again.

Starting early on the following morning, the unprecedented distance of four nautical miles—they are longer, it must be recollected, than ordinary terrestrial miles—was made without accident; but, that distance accomplished, the leading vessel, the 'Couper,' having been feeling on the left bank a little too eagerly, went right up on a sandbank, and all endeavours to get her off proved unavailing; the receding tide leaving her with only two feet of water alongside. The 'Couper' was a vessel which had been built in China as a river steamer, and fitted up with a good saloon for passenger accommodation; she had therefore been specially set apart by Sir James Hope to carry, besides the surveying staff, a number of mercantile and other gentlemen whom his liberality had granted the means of ascending the Yang-tsze on this occasion. Her commander, Lieutenant Broad, R.N., who has since received promotion, had done everything in his power to provide for the comfort of those on board, until she had obtained the *sobriquet* of a "floating hotel." But now, as she lay hard and fast, we of the other vessels jeered at her as a "shore-going craft."

This time our anchorage was more convenient, and, getting ashore with our guns, we were rewarded by a shot or two at pheasants and teal, and a few geese. The place where we landed had the appearance of a heavy earthen battery; and, being uncertain whether Imperialists or Rebels held this part of the country, we approached the shore with caution. We found, however, on landing, that we need have had no apprehensions, for the impressive-looking battery turned out to be merely the river embankment heightened by the addition of earth on its top, and of so weak a profile that I doubt if a matchlock-ball would not have penetrated it, and without even a wooden gun mounted; while the gallant defenders, as we had supposed them, were quiet farm labourers hoeing beans. It was one of those shams so constantly seen in China, from the government down to the religion, or from the religion down to the government, whichever way one puts it, since it is impossible to say which is the more corrupt. In every institution, in the daily affairs of life, in business, in common conversation, is there not a vein of deception running through the whole? Go into a temple, we see the boots, clothes, and valuables of the deceased being burned;—but they are imitations in paper. We visit the grave on the mountain-side, and find relations, actuated by a spirit of "filial piety," offering sweetmeats and dainties to the dead;—but they carry them all home afterwards to be devoured at their own supper. A general writes, that his brave legions are numberless;—he has perhaps at most two or three hundred wretches, deficient in arms, ammunition, and courage. " Sedan-chairs will be at once placed at your Excellency's disposal," means, that most uncomfortable hencoops will not be forthcoming for the "foreign devil" until he has badgered the official half-a-dozen times more. A myriad means 365, a Celestial is a liar, and the Central Flowery Land a myth.

After our run on shore we were not sorry to get again alongside the cabin-fire of the 'Attalante.' By the way, this same fireplace was a very comfortable one, the ship having been built for a Dutch company—and Old Schnapps knows what being comfortable is—and we found it really welcome, for the cold weather we experienced at this season was calculated to make one's teeth chatter, after the broiling of a summer in Southern China. The thermometer at sunrise usually stood about freezing-point, and one day it did not rise at all over 32°; yet with such weather, that, to an unfortunate landsman, most detestable operation known as washing decks, but which might with far more propriety be called flooding ship and wearing away the upper surface of the deck-planks, was daily carried out. He who has tried to sleep with half-a-dozen holystones grinding away immediately above his head, or who has fallen heavily on his first step on the deck of a morning when it is one sheet of ice, will understand my full meaning. But we had no cause to grumble, for it was only carrying out the regulations; and I will say, once for all, that I believe, what with the kindness of Mr. Swain and his officers, and the help of the fireplace before mentioned, we of the 'Attalante,' although somewhat crowded, were more jolly and comfortable than any others of the squadron.

We lay still another day at this anchorage; it was Sunday, and no work was done. On Monday, the 'Waterman' being left to take care of the 'Couper' in her awkward situation, the Admiral's vessel, attended by the 'Attalante,' " proceeded under steam "—to take an expression from the log-book; made a good run of forty-eight miles, passing Kiang-yin, the gate of the Yang-tsze, and anchored above Starling Island. The country retained the same low character, and but little high land was seen, until on the following day when we came up to Kiun-shan, and soon after to Chin-kiang, 155 geographical or nautical miles from Shanghai or the sea. Mr. Oliphant, in his 'Narrative of Lord Elgin's Mission,' has described the scenery on this part of the river in such striking language, that I will not recapitulate anything concerning Silver and Golden Islands or the surrounding country: but as it is near evening, we will go ashore and look around us.

There was a race to get to the top of a hill overlooking the once populous city of Chin-kiang, the great entrepôt of the commerce of the Grand Canal. A long residence in China usually induces some weakness in the lower limbs, but still there was little difference between the first and last of a numerous party. A French officer who wore spurs—which he also wore on board ship—was among the foremost, and I expected to see a little tricolor flag issue from his bosom and wave from the end of his sword; but it was not suited to the occasion, so, forgetting the Emperor and France altogether, he sat down, as most of us did, to regain breath. But what a scene was below us!—Chin-kiang in ruins. Within the large extent of city wall, or among the heap of *débris* which marked the site of a once populous suburb, hardly a roof was to be seen. A pheasant rose at our feet, out of a ditch which had formed part of one of the numerous entrenched camps used in the successive sieges, the remains of which may be seen crowning the top of every rising ground around the place; and as we descended to get a nearer view of this desolation, we disturbed a hare and some quail, where human life ought to have been buzzing in jostling crowds. Passing a fine triumphal arch, erected no doubt to some benefactor of his species, but now partly destroyed, we walked for near a mile through the ruined suburb before we reached one of the city gates. The Imperialists at this time held the place, and the presence of our ships of war in the river gained us ready admission. The only difference between the inside and outside of the walls was, that, while the latter was deserted, and had the appearance of a number of Irish villages after the famine clustered together, the former, although in ruins, was inhabited in part by refugees. Reed huts and brick hovels held these starving wretches; everywhere filth abounded, and I had never seen anything so horrible and revolting. After vainly endeavouring to purchase some fowls or a sheep, we left the city by a gate nearer the water, where a party of half-starved soldiers with gaudy banners were on guard, and made our way to our respective vessels. That night, I fancy, with each and every one of the party the subject uppermost in his thoughts was the scene I have given a faint idea of: it was so in mine. I had often thought of civil war, of the glory of battle, and the satisfaction of serving in a patriotic cause. I had looked on the Wars of the Roses, and the struggle of the Commonwealth, as rather fine times to have lived in: but if this scene was the necessary effect of internecine strife, we had need pray in the words of our Liturgy, and pray earnestly, "That peace and happiness, truth and justice, religion and piety, may be established among us for all generations."

Without waiting for the remaining vessels of his fleet, which had been disposed of as already mentioned, Sir James Hope decided on going up to Nanking with the 'Coromandel' alone, leaving the 'Attalante' at Chin-kiang for the present. Some of us were hardly well pleased with this delay, but consoled ourselves with the reflection that lying at anchor, even at Chin-kiang, was better than being high and dry on a sandbank. The weather, although it was February, was all that could be desired—bright, clear, and bracing; while the whole surrounding country, having been for years overrun alternately by Rebels and Imperialists, who had effaced all traces of cultivation, was rapidly regaining a state of nature, and was most favourable for sporting purposes. Consequently, during the few days we were here, each morning one or two parties of sportsmen left the vessel, and were invariably well rewarded after a healthy day's exercise by tolerable bags of pheasants, quail, and waterfowl. Besides these, there were many of the small hog or musk deer, one of which fell to the gun of a fortunate sportsman. The number of ducks which congregated on the river was immense, and they would at first float down within shot from the steamer; but afterwards they seemed to find out that we had some mysterious mode of dealing death among them, and they became more cautious.

Our walks into the country showed us that the work of destruction had not been confined to the city, for not a village or hamlet was to be seen except in ruins; but what struck me most was the entire absence of trees. An extensive view that could be gained from Golden Island Pagoda, Silver Island, or any of the heights overlooking Chin-kiang, showed nothing but a treeless country, on the city side of the river hilly and undulating, and opposite an extensive plain as far as the eye could reach; but, saving on Silver Island, whose temples and groves had in some way or another escaped the general ruin, not a tree was visible. This accounted for the general assembly of rooks and jackdaws which took place every evening about sunset, when in dense clouds these birds hung over the summit of the beautiful island, circling round and round as is their wont before settling themselves for the night's repose. Then again with the first rays of light and heat, before separating, each flock for its favourite feeding-ground, they went through a similar performance. The number was so enormous that I should not have been loth to believe that all the *corvidæ* of China had here assembled. Their doings interested me; and as I watched them repair to their chosen resting-place each evening, and depart again in early morning, I reflected that while they carried on their duty in the great theatre of nature in peace, under the same sun thousands of beings of what we call a higher order, and endowed with reasoning faculties, were cutting one another's throats. But then I thought it was not such a bad thing for the rooks either, and I was just fancying what a fine thing it would be to be a Kiang-su rook, able to breakfast off a dead rebel, and sup on a headless Imperialist, when—" Eight bells, sir." " Thank you." That means grog in the cabin.

But I was almost going to leave Chin-kiang without establishing a Consul at this the first port opened to foreign trade by the late treaty. The gentleman who had been selected to act *pro tem.* as Her Majesty's representative, had already placed himself in communication with the chief mandarins of the place, and a position had been agreed on for the British Consulate. It was a temple, or rather I should say, had been one, on the summit of a bluff just within and overlooking the city. The position was imposing, but particularly airy, which however it then required to be to render it habitable, such an amount of filth lay scattered on all sides. It was situated just at that part of the river where no vessel could possibly anchor, as is not unusual with British enterprises of this kind; however, it had the advantage of the later concessions at the upper ports, in not being likely to be under water the whole summer.

A flagstaff had been rigged by the ship's boatswain, and at a certain hour—I forget which exactly, but it was some time in the morning—the British jack was seen to break from the truck. At that instant the first gun of the 'Attalante' went "puff;" the second went "puff"—hang those old Dutch popguns, they are three times as wide at the muzzle as they should be; the third does not go off at all; a run is made with the red-hot poker to No. 4, feeling which No. 4 explodes with a tremendous bang, then topples over, and reclines carelessly on the deck. "I say, gunner, what did you put in that gun?" "Nothing, sir." Of course not, which is the reason, no doubt, it kicked so terribly. Nos. 5 and 6 are "let off," which make five guns of the salute, No. 3 not having exploded. No. 1 is loaded again, but this time objects to reply to the command "Fire." No. 2 is not ready. Try No. 3 again. No, it's no use, he won't go, the brute hangs in the breeching. Then a pause—certainly more than the orthodox interval for salute firing—after which, two others being got ready and fired, the seven guns are made complete—Her Majesty's Representative is established, and the British flag insulted. . . . I see two urchins looking for a piece of something—they have no knives—wherewith to cut away the spare portion of the haulyards; an old man gazes with longing eyes on the fir pole, for he has a fuelless and starving family in a hovel hard by; and another ruffian swears he'll have the bunting for a shirt.

During the Admiral's absence at Nanking Mr. Parkes arrived per 'Bouncer,' Lieutenant Creasy having run on all night from Woosung without stopping,—and, waiting only long enough to deliver our letters, he proceeded towards Nanking. About half way the Admiral was met returning, and by evening the 'Coromandel' and 'Bouncer' were again at anchor along with us. Next morning Sir James Hope started to go down and collect the squadron, and Mr. Parkes at once entered into negotiations with the principal mandarins at Chin-kiang concerning a piece of ground for the British concession; after which the Admiral's orders were that the 'Attalante' should proceed to Nanking and there await his arrival. The 'Bouncer' was told off as guard-vessel for the Consul at Chin-kiang; and when Lieutenant Creasy moved down to take up an anchorage off the new Consulate, he was kind enough to afford those who wished to avail themselves of it, a passage to Silver Island. It was most delightful weather, and we enjoyed a ramble over the beautiful island exceedingly.

After visiting the temples and making friends with the shaven-pated Bhuddist priests, we crossed in a boat to the south side of the river, and thence walked along the bank and into the city. On looking over the wall we observed the 'Bouncer' hard and fast on a rock close in to the shore. She had got into this position while trying to find an anchorage off the new Consulate: however, after we had been sitting a long time on the wall watching the different attempts to get her off, and chaffing her commander, she at last slipped quietly into deep water, proceeded up above the town, and again anchored near our vessel.

On the morning of the 24th of February the anchor was weighed, and at half-past eight the 'Attalante' left Chin-kiang under steam. Mr. Parkes was on board. The distance to Nanking is forty-five miles, but to which, in estimating the voyage, has to be added the force of a strong current. Immediately after starting we passed the principal mouth of the northern section of the Grand Canal, where a large fleet of Imperial junks was collected, besides a brig and schooner in the same employ. The southern entrance to the Canal is about eight miles below Chin-kiang, whence it passes through a gap in the range of hills between that place and Kiun-shan. It was said to be filled up in many places and altogether useless.

Above Chin-kiang the hills, trending to the westward some three or four miles from the river, are from 500 to 800 feet high, and connected with those in the neighbourhood of Nanking. On the north bank the first high land is met half way between the two places, and a pagoda or two serve as landmarks. Hitherto the country on both banks of the river had been in the hands of the Imperialists, but now we passed their last outpost, where a few war-junks, displaying numerous variegated banners and standards, lay in a small creek on the north bank. A short distance above, we found a similar position held by the Rebels, and on the point where the river makes a bend before forming the last curved reach below Nanking, and opposite a line of red sandstone cliffs, a large number of people were employed throwing up a heavy earthen battery. The position had been well selected for commanding the passage of the river, and the work itself would have done credit to other than Celestial engineers.

After stemming the yet pea-soup-like current for over ten hours, we arrived near the Heavenly city just at dark, and anchored for the night as best we could in the stream. On the following morning we shifted and took up a position out of the strength of the current, off Theodolite Point, the upper end of an island formed by a loop of the river, cutting off a considerable round; having plenty of water, though narrow, it will doubtless, notwithstanding the edict of the "Great Wang" to the contrary, be used by most vessels on the upward voyage.

Our stay at Nanking embraced the rest of the month of

February; and, as the weather was fine, the Taipings not quite so bad as they had been represented, and the country well stocked with game, we made daily excursions either within or without the walls, passing the time very pleasantly. The nearest point of the city is about a quarter of a mile from the river, the intervening space being occupied by moats, ruined temples, and the remains of a suburb. Under the Taiping rule part of this has been walled in, and some batteries thrown up on the river bank. An officer of rank, formerly a common coolie, acts as Chief of the Customs, and all trade is supposed to be carried on here, as no mercantile transactions are allowed within the city.

The first day we were ashore a large party of us made our way, through this stinking suburb, to the city. What struck every one most at first was of course the tremendous heads of hair, when we had been accustomed to see cleanly shaven pates. But next to that were the gaudy colours of the dresses of both men and women; being a striking contrast to the sombre blue and grey of the inhabitants of the settled districts. These colours, and the textures of the silks and satins from which they shone, told tales of plunder and robbery—of fire and the sword—of Soo-chow and Hang-chow; they showed why the waters of the Grand Canal cease to be ploughed by deep-laden craft; why China requires to be fed with the rice of Siam; and they scented of a government become rotten.

Proceeding towards the north-west gate of the city, we obtained admission only by making a rush just as the keepers were in the act of closing the doors against us, and by forcing them back. The consequence of which was, as we were officially informed from head-quarters, that these poor people were beheaded the same day. This we considered such summary justice, that we resolved to find out their widows, and do what we could in providing for the fatherless children. With these best of intentions, and resolving in our minds how they could be most satisfactorily carried out without the knowledge of the authorities, imagine our surprise on meeting these very same guards two or three days after, alive and kicking. Being ignorant of the language, we could not gain from them any knowledge of this miraculous mode of curing decapitation. Truly, we thought, wonderful things may be done in these heavenly regions! but on reflection we fancied it might be possible for a Wang to tell a lie.

On ascending a hill, just inside the gate already mentioned, a view is obtained of a considerable portion of the space enclosed by the twenty miles of wall, but no description that I know of gives any just idea of it. The extent is enormous, but, instead of being, as one would have supposed, covered with houses, Nanking in its best days must have been for a great part fields and gardens under cultivation, and now there is even wood and waste land. Hills of some elevation exist, particularly on the west side, where the scarped sides of the crooked line of heights form a natural wall of red sandstone. The height of the wall varies from fifty to seventy feet. Outside the north and west walls, an extensive moat, or rather series of ponds, extends; but farther on, its place is taken by a creek, which approaches the city at the west gate, and then continues round the south-west angle, towards the site of the famed Porcelain Pagoda. To the east is the Taiping Gate, where a large sheet of water is banked in with masonry. Thence towards the Yang-tsze the walls are regular, but the ditches are choked up with reeds, affording cover to immense numbers of pheasants. Beyond the Taiping Gate, and at the foot of a mountain which overlooks the city from the east, are the sepulchres of the Ming dynasty. Several of the other gates are now bricked up.

Within the city, the inhabited part of which is some miles

from the river, there is much desolation, ruin, and filth. There are some palaces, if such they deserve to be called, in a state more or less advanced towards completion, the residences of "Wangs," or kings. The walls are dotted with proclamations on imperial yellow paper, and the proportion of women is large, many being captives, and proving that the Taipings act on the adage that "All's fair in love and war."

On the 26th of February the steamer 'Yang-tsze,' belonging to the firm of Messrs. Dent and Co., arrived at Nanking, having on board the representative of that house at Shanghai; she was then sailing under American colours; and, as the time of those on board her was valuable, she only remained one day, and then proceeded up the river to establish agents at the new treaty-ports. She thus had the honour of being the first merchant-vessel at Hankow, and I believe Mr. Webb received from the Viceroy some of the favours which were intended for Admiral Hope.

Everything that ought to be seen at Nanking was visited by our party, and three gentlemen went so far as to pass a few nights within the walls of one of the palaces in company with a missionary who was living on the charity of the Taiping rulers; but our friends came rather short off for food in those heavenly regions, and were glad to get on board ship again. Powder and shot were liberally dispensed among the pheasants, hares, and waterfowl, and good bags invariably obtained. In fact, I doubt if any cover in England could exhibit pheasants so closely packed as in the reed-beds under the walls of Nanking.

An excursion to the Tombs of the Mings, including an afternoon's shooting, was as pleasant as anything I have ever enjoyed; and I should like to describe that day; but the account of a similar visit has been so happily penned by a friend, whose knowledge of the Rebels and their enemies is considerable, that I shall refer to the following chapter, the contents of which appeared originally in the columns of the 'North China Herald,' among several other interesting papers relating to the Taipings and Taipingdom, by Mr. R. J. Forrest, of Her Majesty's Consular Service.

Tortoise and Column cut from one block of Stone, Ming Tombs, Nanking.

See p. 25.

CHAPTER II.

THE MING TOMBS.

"EVERY one who has a little time to spare at Nanking should go and see the ruins of the Ming tombs. Tien-wang's palace may be interesting with its red and gold dragons and other moustrosities; the Porcelain Tower may be worth the trouble of a looting expedition among its bricks; but neither of them has such an interest attaching to it as the Golden Pearl Mountain, beneath which repose the remains of his Majesty Choo, first monarch of the Ming dynasty. The place is awkwardly situated for visitors; you cannot run thither, nor ride, nor walk, without going in a roundabout direction over a great extent of road. From the river it is ten miles as the path goes, six perhaps as the crow flies, by the moat around the city it is a good fifteen, and one has to walk four miles after leaving the boat. When Admiral Hope left Nanking the Celestial authorities closed the Taiping Gate, by going through which, after traversing the city, you could get to the tombs tolerably comfortably, rowing half the distance and walking the other half. The best way to go if you have a good crew to your boat is along the city moat as far as you can proceed, that is to say until the moat begins to wind out into the country away from the city walls; then put your chow-chow on some coolies' shoulders and walk to the foot of the hills. That is the way I am going. The bridge at the South Gate is crowded as usual by a noisy mob of soldiers, pedlers, women, and of course an unlimited number of small boys. The beating of drums and gongs, and the procession of some dozen mounted soldiers in parti-coloured garments, carrying in their hands very gorgeous and very large silken flags, tell you that a chief is about to enter the city. There he is, dressed in a long robe of brilliant scarlet silk, richly embroidered boots, a yellow silk cap on his head, and in his hand a tricoloured umbrella of large dimensions, but made after foreign pattern and of silk. Two slave-boys are following, dressed very meanly and looking very tired and dirty. One is carrying the chief's double-barrelled gun carefully sewn up in a well-fitting cover of red flannel trimmed with black braid, but the locks are left exposed, so as to be ready for use, as the rust would come off in his Excellency's hand had the weapon no cover. The other little fellow carries a Japanese sword with lots of silver about it, and a bamboo stick. I should not wonder if the sword has done good execution not alone in war, but among refractory soldiers and people, for the chief is a desperate-looking fellow, and evidently not to be trifled with. He has come from Soo-chow, and has been to sell some precious stones to a dealer near the Porcelain Tower. Strange that his jewels are all ornamenting articles of ladies' apparel. How came he by them?

"After South Gate Bridge the moat goes on winding and twisting through utter desolation and the abomination thereof. The huge walls rise at its side solid, strong, and lofty, but no soldiers or flags or sign of life can be observed. A couple of minas are inspecting a hole in the battlements for the purpose of therein building their nest, and so great is the stillness that their chatter sounds harsh and disagreeable to the ear, although they are a hundred yards from you; no wind disturbs the broad clear water, and a little swallow is fluttering tamely enough about the oars trying to pick up a large insect before a fish can get at it. There is a corner of the moat that I should much like to make a sketch of. It is where the wall shoots out a long stretch almost due east. In former days a gate existed here and a fine broad bridge. Here, too, are the remains of a large granite wharf and dock with water-gate leading into the city canal. The whole *was* magnificently made, but neglect soon ruins even granite walls. Roots of trees have raised the stone slabs from their places, Taiping rapacity has rudely forced away the iron rings and bolts, the bridge has been partially destroyed, the gate built up, and the entrance to the canal in the city choked up with stones, furniture, and mud, 'lest imps' should force their way into the Heavenly capital by that entrance. Not long ago—only twelve years—that particular corner was teeming with life. You can see the remains of what must have been a fine suburb; and the marks where large merchants' houses and temples were erected against the city wall are most plainly distinguishable. The high road to Tan-yang, Soo-chow, and the cities on the Grand Canal ran across that bridge, and across it were conveyed the silk to feed the city looms and the provisions for its inhabitants. Across it came and went the inhabitants, old and venerable, young and pretty, of fifty cities that have since melted before the horrors of war. Now a man on the wall stares with a weary look at a couple of foreign devils going by in one of their own boats. It is just the place to see when you are going to visit a tomb; it cannot fail to strike you and make you feel sad. Observe, gentle reader, if ever you go by that place, although you have a dozen friends in the boat, not a word will be spoken by any of you while passing it, nor for five minutes afterwards. You get out of your boat about a mile from the place and walk towards the Taiping Gate, having a series of large ponds between you and the city wall. A few country people, perhaps a dozen, are hanging about, but they are silent and sorrowful.

"There is a little watch station a few yards in the country, where soldiers are lolling about, smoking, gambling, and drinking samshoo in utter defiance of the commands of the

Heavenly king whose cause they are defending. They laugh violently at the foreigners and frown at the timid peasantry as they go by. I fancy the few miserable beings who are compelled to live outside the east side of Nanking must suffer considerably from the depredations of the insolent troops constantly coming and going along the way to the canal. Anon comes a file of labourers who have been to some ruins for the purpose of extracting tiles to build a house for some city magnate. A man accompanies them with a drawn sword to see that they are not lazy or mutinous, so they walk along sulkily and silent, having no hope of better days, getting no money and but indifferent rice. Speak to some of them, and you will perceive they are utterly cowed, scarcely daring to draw breath, and talking in a low suspicious tone of voice like people whose *lives* are in constant danger. All the chatter and laugh that so eminently distinguishes the coolie in other parts of China is wanting under the Taiping rule. The unhappy folk are compelled to work almost gratuitously for very hard taskmasters. Their homes are wretched to a degree. There is nothing anywhere to make them laugh at life, and their appearance can hardly fail to excite the sympathy of passing foreigners.

"There is a lofty hill which frowns over the city wall a mile or so below the gate. The storms and rains and changes of centuries have made its sides steep and rugged. Bleached rocks of limestone start boldly out from it, and stamp the impress of age on their parent mountain. The vegetation is scanty enough, for the rains pour down in torrents and the fiery sun sleeps on the hill-side; the one washes the soil from the limestone, and the other parches and kills the herbs that try to grow in the crevices. It would be a hard day's work to reach the summit, from which, however, can be seen most of the empire of Taiping. They say the White Dragon Hill at Soo-chow is visible from it. I distinguished that mountain while yet on the Grand Canal; during the long three days' walk over the dreary Nanking moors, it never seemed to approach nearer, and I thought that the Great River must surely float between me and its barren steep. The ten-thousand-li wall of Chang-kwo-liang, however, which runs over one of its spurs, convinced me that the river was beyond it, and I have since made intimate acquaintance with the hoary giant. On the summit of the spur over which the wall runs is a square spot enclosed by thick walls which look as though they had been whitewashed. His Excellency Ho-chên, the general of the Imperial besieging army, used to pitch his tent in this place, and from it view the city spread like a map beneath his feet, the inhabitants of which he had devoted to destruction. Tien-wang's palace is quite within range of a British 10-inch gun from this spot, and perhaps the day may come when his Heavenly Majesty will find that an Armstrong shell can carry even further. Tien-wang, during the siege of his capital, used to hang out the Sacred Heavenly flag on the city wall opposite this spot, and serenely behold his enemy from his minarets. To give him his due, I believe he does not know what fear is, and during the whole siege, down to the time when even his officers had but one bowl of rice a-day, he never failed to impress them with the conviction that deliverance was nigh, both by his conversation and example. At last he wrote a doxology, sonorous and musical enough, and ordered all his officers and soldiers to learn it by heart, promising that when they did so Heaven would give them manifest assistance. By day and night for weeks together might this doxology be heard. The guards on the wall were repeating it, the women and children were singing it in the streets. At last, down came celestial assistance in the shape of the Chung and Ying Wangs, who broke up the siege and set the horrors of war loose in the fair province of Kiang-su. Ho-chên is lying dead in a ditch somewhere near his camp, and Chang-kwo-liang has found his rest under the walls of Tang-yang. If the villagers at the anchorage can be believed, some of the green jade beads which formed the full-dress necklace of the Imperial Commissioner were in my possession the other day. *Quien sabe?*

"But where are the tombs? If I run on in this way, I shall be giving a most veracious history of the Taiping war from the relief of Nanking to the fall of Chapoo, and forget all about my subject-matter. As I before remarked, there is a hill outside the Taiping Gate. Well, beneath that hill are the remains of the Ming tombs. In the distance you can perceive a large red building, with a circular wall enclosing a space beyond it. The Golden Pearly Mountain, although within this wall, is not distinguishable, on account of the superior magnificence and shade of the ancient one at the back of it—in fact, it is absorbed in it. The drivelling efforts of man to oppose the magnificence of nature are signally defeated in this as in all other instances. You are walking along a country that was once smiling with happy villages and cultivated fields. See how the rice-grounds were terraced up to the hill-side that not a yard of ground should be lost, and behold how ruin on ruin encumbers the ground below us in the valley where once stood a village of three thousand inhabitants. But the inhabitants, houses, rice, and cultivation have left the place for a while, the black duck is preparing to nestle in that fish-stew, where ducks of a tamer nature once sported. Aim low at the roebuck standing in the ruins of that farmhouse, and try and hit him in the fore legs, or he will get away from you, oh dog-less one! although severely wounded. There, I told you so! Now go and ask that old man, who has been looking on, which way the 'Changtsze' has run. He will crouch and chin-chin, ay and kowtow too, if you will let him, when you stand before him, and stammer something out and call you 'Foreign Excellency,' and know nothing at all. The man is frightened, heartbroken, demented. The deer was standing on the ruins of what was once his homestead. He is labouring for others now, his sons have gone to war for a cause they little love, his daughters are in the city where he cannot see them, the spoil of masters they love even less, and all his life is a blank. He will be down in the ditch there before long, and his troubles will be over. I hate the stillness of the country near the Ming tombs, it is so utterly unnatural. Everything seems sleeping or going to decay. The half-dozen people one sees only make it worse. The crow of the pheasant is loud enough, and the petards resound from the distant palace of the Heavenly king, but the merry sounds of human happiness and comfort and business which ought to enliven that spot are missing, perhaps for ever. The tombs are apparently two in number, separated about a mile from each other. The one is much smaller than the other, consisting merely of two large square buildings, unsightly enough on the exterior, but elaborately finished within. A strong wall encloses those two buildings, but a paved road to Chin-kiang runs through the gates. As the sepulchre is situated on the crest of a range of low hills, every advantage has been taken to make it useful as an outwork. The Imperialist soldiers had guns on the wall, and barracks in the buildings. The land all around is honeycombed with little pits to prevent the advance of the Taiping cavalry up the slope. When I visited the place the planking on which the braves slept was still in its place, and Tien-wang had with foresight ordered up several loads of lime, to be thrown into the faces of any desperadoes who might take a fancy to come by that road to disturb his Great Peace. I said that the interiors were elaborately finished, but neglect and mischief have defaced the walls, and accumulations of filth conceal much from the sight. Huge slabs of polished limestone form the walls, supported at the bottom by a projecting base of highly carved stone; the roofs have likewise been polished, but I need hardly remark that, inasmuch as Chinese soldiers inhabited the place for the space of two years, the original flooring is invisible. The gateway to this enclosure is still standing, and from it to the city there was once a path lined on either side by monsters cut in stone. Tradition says that the great Ming's son was buried in the enclosure, and that priests dwelt in the stone houses to sing eternal requiems. The old barbaric pride is everywhere visible. The son of a great conqueror, torn from the earth and from the prospect of the universal throne, must be buried with no common pomp. The successor to the king's crown, having become a guest on high, must not go unattended; and stone camels, elephants, horses, dogs, and men, that stand and sit by the roadside, are the obedient slaves waiting to attend the spirit of the heir-apparent to his last and blissful abode. More ferocity and perhaps more sense were shown by other great conquerors—the corpses of the slaves who had dug the pit mingled with the returning flood of the Busentum when Alaric was entombed, and the mountain which enclosed the remains of Attila was reddened with the blood of those who raised it. *They* would have souls to go with them, the Ming prince was satisfied with effigies. These images will not last much longer, age and ruin are fast destroying them; some are already deep in the ground, the lion has lost a leg, one of the nondescripts is on his side, and a young tree is sprouting with vigour from the elephant's back; the men evince every sign of desiring to lie down, and will do so very soon, unless encouraged to hold up for a little longer.

"The Emperor's tomb must have been a fine structure in its day, but is a sad ruin at the present time. The imperial yellow and red with which the walls are stained look as

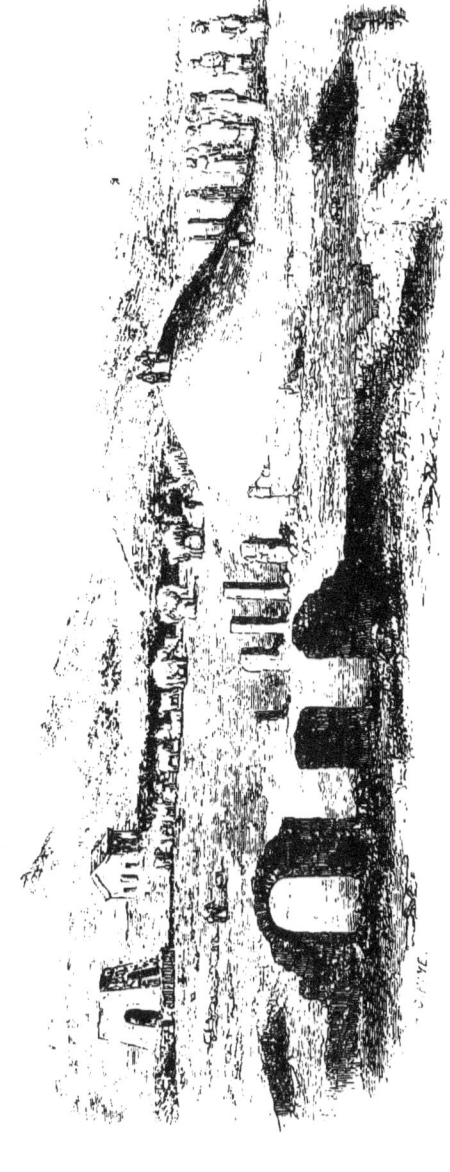

TOMBS OF THE MING DYNASTY, NANKING.

fresh to-day as they did centuries ago. You can pick up a yellow tile with a five-clawed dragon on it, and find the exact counterpart among the ruins of Yuen-ming-yuen. The mortar with which the place was built is so white, and laid on with such profusion, that all the ruins look white, and, if the glaring sun is resting upon them, almost dazzling. No inconsiderable number of priests must have droned away their lives in the immense houses which were once erected both over the gateway and the entrance to the tomb. The entrance is easier now through a gap in the wall than through the regular gateway, the stone steps of which are encumbered with the ruins of the several-storied house which was once erected above it. Proceeding along the broad paved way, the huge stones of which have all been more or less carved, you pass a series of tablets which, as I have read somewhere, were erected to commemorate the visit of a Tsing prince to the tomb of the founder of the race just extinguished by the Manchoos. Beyond the tablets you cross over a deep pond by the everlasting Chinese bridge, which is built in every Confucian temple, pleasure-garden, or park in China, exactly on one model. Beneath it once flowed a rivulet of pure water from the neighbouring mountain, but ruin has turned this aside now, and only a little stagnant rain-water remains in the reservoir, which filled with the clear stream would be a striking ornament. A huge square pile now rises before you on which formerly was erected a temple, a tunnel on a steep inclined plane goes directly through it, and the Golden Pearl Mountain, beneath which is the coffin, is immediately beyond. One cannot give a description of a great mass of ugly buildings such as these would appear were they described in print, or were they built anywhere else or for any other purpose. The whole ruin is impressive enough where it stands, in the silence of a hill-corner, with the old rugged mountain rising beyond it mocking at its insignificance.

The artificial "golden" mound must have taken the slaves no small trouble to make, for the rains and storms of centuries have swept over it and it is still a large hill. Although report speaks of much treasure deposited near the coffin for the departed monarch to pay his way with in the world of spirits, yet no avaricious hand has tried to break the sanctity of the tombs, knowing well the difficulties attendant on the enterprise.

"All in ruins! The Manchoos in their first irruption laid sacrilegious hands on everything belonging to the structure of any value, slew the priests, and destroyed the buildings. Wind and tempest have done even more than man to complete the devastation. The last abode on earth of both the emperor and his son is fast becoming a thing that was, bringing almost to pass the agonized wish of the hero in an old play—

> 'Yet overwhelm me with this globe of earth,
> And let a little sparrow with her bill
> Take but so much as she can bear away,
> That, every day thus losing of my load,
> I may again, in time, yet hope to rise.'

And perhaps the old Ming is wishing it literally, for he was very bloodthirsty in his career. Reclining on the golden mountain in all the warm luxury of a spring morning, we awoke the shade of the old monarch in the shape of a magnificent echo; a more perfect one I never heard in my life. The awful stillness makes it all the more striking. Sing a song, and old Ming does the same; whistle, and he will mock you like any ploughboy. A beautiful cock pheasant flew from among the rhododendrons and flashed its way in the sunshine. Its whirr was answered by the echo, and my double-barrel made the hills detonate, until the reverberation was too distant to be distinguished. What a change has come over the Celestial Empire! The tombs of one dynasty are lying around you, another is passing away, while away in the city through the moving haze of the sunlight can be seen the palace of him of Heaven, Hung-tsiu-tsuen, who lays claim to be the founder of a new race. All around are the signs of a sanguinary struggle, yet but half finished. The inviolability of the sacred empire is broken, and conquerors have trodden its soil with iron footsteps. Your dynasty is long passed, oh, Ming! but the citizens below there in Nanking are once more taking your dress and habits. Take comfort from that if you can; but start from your troubled grave, for foreign devils from the Western Seas are holding jubilee over your tombs, and the corks from their diabolical explosive water resound in the vaulted chamber. There are none there to keep them back—Peking and Nanking respect them as they go. Oh, Ming! how are the proud, the mighty fallen, and none so poor to do them reverence!

"In returning, you may make a détour and strike into the road from the Grand Canal. The country all the way from Paoying to Nanking is in a wretched condition. Ruined villages and burned houses mark the fury of last year's war. A small crowd of old women are generally to be met with at the entrance of each village, trying to eke out a living by the sale of tea and congee to the passers-by. All the able-bodied men are gone—some were killed, but more enlisted in the Taiping army, from whose ranks death alone will relieve them. They will never return to the home of their fathers, and their possessions are in the hands of new masters. All the old women we saw were left in contempt by the Taipings to till the fields; all had lost some relations, and two of them sat down on a bank and cried sadly, one for the loss of her husband and two sons, the other for her husband and father. 'They killed my husband,' said an old woman, 'because he was not strong enough to do their coolie work.'

'They carried off my daughter because she was pretty,' said another to me beyond the Great River. It is all one story—girls carried off, useful men compelled to go to the camps, old ones who perhaps might excite commiseration ruthlessly murdered! One great story of violence and wrong carried with a mighty hand throughout the land in the name of the Christian faith, by men as merciless as the stones they tread on! When and where it will stop Providence alone can tell; the land is threatened with depopulation; trade, industry, and manufacture are at an end, wherever Tien-wang's commands extend. The Tien-hai-kuan said to me, by way of a joke, that, when all were slain, then truly the reign of 'Great Peace' would have arrived. A ghastly joke truly; but I hope, before such a state of things is brought about, 13-inch shells will be exploding in the palace of the blasphemous impostor ruling at Nanking.

"Passing by a wall and strong stockade, you enter into a space formerly covered by the southern suburb, and in which rose the Porcelain Tower. How well we remember, 'in the days when childhood fleeted by,' reading in Pinnock's, or somebody else's Questions, of this splendid work; nay, every map or tract or chapter concerning China was prefaced by an illustration of the pagoda, one of the wonders of the world. Now it is a white hill of ruins. Two immense walls, divided by a narrow aperture, are the only portions of the tower now standing. I hope no one ever believed that the edifice was entirely built of porcelain, because brick and tile entered very largely into its composition, and merely the tiles on the slanting roofs were of the much-coveted material. Every ship that has touched at Nanking has made a looting excursion to the white heap, and boat-loads of porcelain bricks have been carried away in triumph. Now, unless by bribery among the little Maos who surround any foreign visitors, not a brick can be got. However, tradition asserts that at the bottom of the whole mass lies a stratum of rose-coloured bricks valuable in the extreme; perhaps I shall be at Nanking when this mine of wealth is disclosed, and then compensate myself for my present brickless condition.

"The portion of the suburbs in which this porcelain tower was situated was under the command of the Eastern King. Tien-wang, having occasion to doubt the fidelity of this gentleman, deputed the Northern King to cut off his head and quietly slaughter his followers. This was done to the number of 10,000. But now Tien-wang, to satisfy the minds of men, accused the Northern King of the wilful murder of Tung-wang (who was elected Saviour of the World, and afterwards the Holy Ghost), and slew him and his followers. After this, Tien-wang was told that Tung-wang boasted that from his porcelain tower he could command the city. Powder was ordered into the tower, and the whole building blown up. A gigantic iron basin is lying on the ruins, now perfect as ever, and beautifully wrought. What a splendid public drinking fountain it would make, even at Shanghai!

"The South Gate is pierced in a straight line through the enormous wall. A large crowd is always assembled here, for no trade is allowed in the city. Women's clothes, ornaments of all sorts, pistols, caps, and small tins of powder, marked Curtis and Harvey, but made at Ningpo, are exposed for sale. The loot of Soo-chow might some time ago have been bought here for a song. Vendors of fish, women on horseback, soldiers, flags, and chow-chow apparatus were crowded together in this motley scene. A man is lying with the cangue round his neck, on which is stated that he did not obey the celestial commands, and the head of another is hanging up in a basket. You pass under the walls through a long dark tunnel, then through three more gates and three more small tunnels, where brass guns are placed, and Nanking, the Heavenly Capital, stands revealed to your mortal eyes. But let us pause ere we describe it. On the gate is a proclamation from the Heavenly King, on which is written—'The Heavenly Father, Christ, Myself, and my Son are Lords for ever. The Heavenly Kingdom is established everywhere, and the effulgence of the Father, Brother, Myself, and the Young Lord is spread upon the earth for a myriad myriad autumns.' Let us pause before attempting to describe the heavenly effulgence, lest the description might dazzle mankind."

Dip-net for fishing. See p. 75.

CHAPTER III.

THE TAIPINGS AT THEIR CAPITAL.

In continuing Mr. Forrest's account, I should state that the matter of this chapter was originally published in the 'North China Herald,' in two papers, entitled 'Nanking and the Inhabitants thereof,' and 'The Taipings at Home.' My friend has so vividly portrayed what few have had the same opportunities of seeing, and none have so well described, that I make no apology for transferring his observations to these pages almost in full. As I do not pretend to give a history of the Taiping revolutionary movement, I will only preface this chapter by remarking that the Taiping (Peace) rebellion originated about 1850 in the southern province of Kwang-si. The founders belonged to a religious sect called God-worshippers, who in the autumn of that year came into collision with the authorities, and immediately started as regenerators of the empire; and there is reason to believe that they were sincere, and their motives pure—Christianity being their profession, but mixed with a good deal of error. Yung-an was the first city they captured; it remained in their hands from the 27th August, 1851, till the 7th April, 1852, when they left it and marched through the country in a united band, carrying all before them, ravaging and destroying many of the finest cities of Hoo-nan; and thence descending the Yang-tsze Kiang, visiting Hankow and other cities on its banks, they ultimately took possession of Nanking on the 19th March, 1853, where they established their head-quarters. Since that time they have sent forces in different directions, and have been within a hundred miles of Peking, but retired from there early in 1854. Nanking has also withstood a two years' siege by the Imperialists.

The country at the present time in the hands of the Taipings (for it must not be thought that the insurrections in other parts of the empire are connected with this movement) may be said to be the half of each of the provinces of Kiang-su and Chi-kiang, a district as fertile perhaps as any part of China, and estimated by Mr. Parkes at 60,000 square miles, and having formerly a population of 70,000,000 souls—an extent rivalling England and Wales taken together, and a mass of human life nearly equal to one-third the population of Europe.

The originator of the movement, or rather the one known to us as such, is Hung-tsiu-tsuen, the present "Tien-wang," or Heavenly king. He was originally educated at a Protestant missionary school in the south of China. His son, now about fourteen, is known as the "Junior Lord;" "Kan-wang" is his cousin, and the only one who has free access to him. There are several other wangs (kings), but Kan-wang, specially mentioned in the following account, is the most enlightened, according to our ideas. Late advices represent him to have been degraded, it is supposed on account of his partiality to foreigners. The Rev. I. J. Roberts, the former teacher of Hung-tsiu-suen, lived among the Taipings since the latter part of 1860; and although he was favourably received and cared for in the capital, his efforts to restrain the blasphemous tendency of the present religion of the Taipings proved unavailing, and he made his exit from Nanking on the 20th of last January. On that day he wrote a letter, which has appeared in the public press, in which he describes the murder of his boy, and the way in which he himself was treated by Kan-wang, acting under the orders of the arch-impostor. "I then," says Mr. Roberts, "despaired of missionary success among them, or of any good coming out of the movement—religious, commercial, or political—and determined to leave them."

A year or two ago the Taipings had many friends, particularly among Protestant missionaries, by whom they were looked on as Christians; but the bubble has burst on a nearer scrutiny, and now it is equally the fashion to abuse them. Foreign aid is solicited in destroying their power; but I think the light in which my friend has shown the case in the latter part of this chapter is the true one; and refraining from farther remarks in this place, I will say once for all that I entirely agree with his views.

The reader was left at one of the gates of Nanking; and here I shall again hand him over to the safe keeping of Mr. Forrest:—

"*Allons!* Entering the South Gate, a dirty man asks for the pass of His Foreign Excellency, while an admiring boy claws hold of your umbrella or coat-tails; and, having inspected you to his satisfaction, screams out that the Foreign Devil has arrived. Having satisfied the janitor, you must look sharp to get out of the way of two faggots of enormous reeds which are approaching you, apparently of their own accord, for no motive agency is visible. When alongside you find that a little donkey is propelling the bundles, or perhaps a little girl—boys do not seem to like the work. If you watch the donkey you will see that in China he loses nothing of his proverbial obstinacy. He will lie down in the middle of the gate with his bundle on the top of him, and defy all the powers that be to move him, until it is his good will and pleasure to resume his journey. All the passengers have little wooden billets tied round their waists, with a Heavenly seal impressed thereon. Did a Chinaman venture into Nanking without this badge, his head would be in the greatest danger. The street from the South Gate toward the North

D

is fine and broad. In its happier days great attention was evidently paid to the pavement thereof; in some places the stones were even fantastically carved; but now there are holes and gaps, little ponds and gutters reeking with filth, and on a wet day lakes impassable to any but the bare-legged inhabitants wandering about on their proper occasions. A man comes riding along dressed in scarlet or parti-coloured garments, with a yellow cap on his head; in his hand he holds a bright red umbrella of foreign make; two little boys run after him—one with a big rusty gun, holding on to the tail of the pony (who does not resent the insult as other ponies would), the other with a flag on a bamboo pole. The horseman scowls on you as he passes, but he is a chief. Those little slaves following were kidnapped by him during an expedition, and will never see home or parents more; but they call him 'Ta-jên' (Excellency), and follow him everywhere. He has a dozen more boys at home, likewise kidnapped; he can kill them if they run away or disobey him. It is a hard life, although they are well fed; but brighter days are in store for the urchins—they will grow old and strong, will themselves go to the war, and murder, kill, and destroy, until they in their turn are Ta-jêns, and can ride in the streets of the Heavenly City with slaves at their heels. But there is another side to this: you see a little boy throwing stones and calling you a devil, laughing with all his might; he has forgotten all about home, and is beginning to enjoy Taiping life and laziness; although only twelve years old he has got an ugly knife, and would fain run it into a Yao (foreigner) or anybody else, if only let loose to do so; but he has got an incipient skin disease, and will be a frightful object in a week or so; his master will kick him out into the street, and he will lie in a corner with a little bowl in his hand, begging for rice or cash to try and keep his life's lamp a little longer alight. Let us leave the city for a moment to follow this story to an end, and walk through the T'ien-hai-kwan village, where the starvelings have flocked together in hundreds; for there is the port, and foreign brethren are wont to give cash away, and eke rice from the neighbouring cookshop. There they lie or crawl; this one with his toes off from frostbite, that one too weak to speak. What! not take money when it is given to you? shut your hand on it, or it will be stolen. Alas! the hand can move no longer; not even a dollar would make a muscle start. The beggar is dead at his bowl, and the flaunting proclamation of the Heavenly King on the wall over his head tells us that Great Peace has gone out over the whole earth!

"We are in the city again, going along the street where the Tien-wang's brothers live. A large wall in a curved shape is erected opposite to a house redolent of red paint and gold. About three-fourths of the road passes between the wall and the house—I beg pardon, palace. People on horseback, nay even pedestrians, must go behind the wall *en passant*, or lictors will rush from the gilded doors and beat them. The guardians of the gate are however good-natured, and very lazy. People do go by in front, but no horsemen. Of course foreigners are exempted from all such nonsense, and pass by with much greeting from the soldiers at the gate. Two small cannon are placed at the door, pointed across the street; they are of course useless as a defence, but it looks something, and that is all a Chinaman cares about. The entrances to the palaces are all similar. It is the old familiar Yamên door, only brilliantly painted in red and gold. A board over the door announces the title of the owner. There is less taste displayed in the mixture of the various hues than I ever witnessed elsewhere in China. As long as there is plenty of red it pleases the owner; a lot of dirty ragged attendants imparts a neutral tint, and some of the palace-fronts are really not unpleasant to the eye. They are building a handsome palace for Ying-wang; and Chung-wang has boasted that his new abode shall be the handsomest in the Empire, after the Celestial Palace. We will just step into one of these gaudy buildings, and dig out the owner. Marching to the door, the attendants eagerly inquire your business, which of course you refuse to divulge to them. The portals, on which gigantic ugly dragons are painted, are thrown open, and you find yourself in a court in front of a tribunal. Every building is new, and the cunning of Chinese artizans is displayed in the curious windows, stonework, and tablets. Everything is painted with brilliant colours, red always predominating; and the walls of the tribunal are covered with long strips of yellow satin or paper with dragon margins, on which are inscribed compliments to the owner of the house. There are a couple written by Tien-wang himself, but the meaning of them is so transcendentally celestial and mystical that no Chinaman that I have met with could make them out. A couple of large earthen vessels support a miniature landscape, on which are growing beautiful dwarf trees and shrubs. A little porcelain city is among these trees, while a hill crowned with a pagoda rises abruptly at the back. Numbers of gold-fish flourish in the water around it, and the whole forms a very pretty drawing-room ornament, far prettier than aquaria or other clumsy contrivances of that kind used in England. Passing from this hall of judgment, which is always dirty and dark, through several passages, in one of which you observe a boy boiling the tea you will presently have to drink, you arrive at the Audience Chamber, and make your bow to His Excellency the Acting Prime Minister, Son of the Prince of Praise, and styled the successor to the dignity thereof. If you are a missionary he will grin a ghastly smile of welcome, because then he can narrate the history of Tien-wang's ascent to Heaven; if an official, he will frown a most killing frown to show his dignity, and then screw up the corners of his very large mouth into a kind of smile, to show that, notwithstanding all his magnificence, he has still mortal sympathies left. His dress is intended to be very magnificent. On his head he wears a gilt affair called a dragon hat. I cannot give a description of it, except that it is made of pasteboard, gilt, with amber beads and pearls suspended, and a little bird on the top. I always fancied that the Pope's tiara must look very like this Tsan-sze-keuen's crown, if a shell burst inside it. This cap is only assumed on great occasions. Generally you only see a kind of undress affair, something between a mitre and a fool's cap of olden time, on which is a space for the title of the owner. There is more paint than gilt about this, and it certainly cannot be called pretty. His dress consists of a long robe of yellow embroidered satin, covered with dragons, the sun, moon, and stars, and all kinds of curious things; embroidered yellow trowsers, and boots likewise ornamented. On one occasion, when he was obliged somewhat hurriedly and reluctantly to see some foreigners, he had occasion during the visit to get some document or seal, but was observed to be unable to leave his seat, in front of which is a large table covered with an embroidered cloth. You cannot see underneath it; and from the curious way in which His Excellency persisted in keeping his chair, it was basely whispered among the Western brethren that in the hurry of the moment he had forgotten his unmentionables. His appearance is dreadfully unprepossessing. The countenance is that of a young man utterly used up; you would fancy that he, instead of his kingly father the Tsan-wang, was dying. He can tell lies as well as any man I ever saw, and indeed never tells the truth if he can avoid it. In the conduct of public business he is a complete child, and has to be dealt with as such; but he has always a monitor with him to advise him. The rest of the officers present are the four city majors, who are tolerably intelligent people, to whose palaces we would go and have a cup of tea, had I time; and the grand admiral, whose fleet he will tell you is at Soo-chow, Hankow, or anywhere except Nanking. I should fancy this man eats a great deal, he is so slow and deliberate in all he does or says. He has a very large house near the Han-sze Gate, and, from a furtive peep I took one day into his quarters, some very pretty women. The rest are nobodies, who have been asked to impress the foreigners with the grandeur of the Minister. While I am doing a little business, will you, my friends, look round the room? Observe the mixture of blue, red, and gold, with which the rafters on the roof are painted, and the curious capitals to the wooden columns. Those paintings on the wall would not be admitted in the corridors of the House of Commons; for see the trees are red, the walls yellow, and the houses pea-green. The perspective is likewise a little defective, as the pheasant on the tree is fully fifty thousand times as big as the owner of the mansion, which is higher than the mountains fifty miles off; the boats, too, are of frightful size, and will be wrecked yet, against the bridge through which the artist intended them to pass, if the bridge, which looks rickety, does not come down. But never mind, every panel in this audience-room has its picture, and this gives it a far better appearance than if the place were hung with those horrible satin scrolls. All the chairs on which we have been seated were formerly the property of Hien-fêng's Viceroy; and if you inquire you will hear that the change of owners was effected through the immediate agency of Heaven. They are covered with embroidered satin, and are not inconvenient. On the various tables are pots planted with the most beautiful dwarf flowering trees. One, about a foot high, is covered with brilliant yellow flowers, and there is a lovely flowering peach by its side; then there are a couple of camelias and some flowers to me unknown. Every time I have been to this place new flowering trees were on the table and the old ones gone. In front of the Audience Chamber is a small court-yard, with a road and bridge across it made of limestone, and beyond is a little room for dining purposes; where, if you accept his Excellency's invitation, you may satisfy your hunger with sea-slugs, bamboo sprouts, rancid pork, and other delicacies. What is more, the unfortunate man, who during business has been making himself excessively uncomfortable by keeping up what he fancies is a dignified demeanour, now takes off his crown and robe, and sits down to meat with a smile. He will talk away for an hour in a very amiable way, and express his sorrow that he has no wine to give you, as in the Heavenly Kingdom no one drinks it. Poor fellow, I do not want to libel him; but what became of the case of gin that was bought and paid for by him? and as for his Celestial teetotalism, only yesterday I had as much stuff called Heavenly wine as I could drink in the residence of the Mayor hard by; and what is more, that wine had been made in the city.

"We will now take a stroll towards the Celestial residence of his very Celestial Majesty Hung-tsiu-tsuen. We cannot get in, but can see a good deal outside. This palace is of great size, enclosed in a yellow wall forty feet high, and very thick. Within you can see yellow and green roofs and a couple of not unhandsome minarets, but the mass of buildings is hidden from the curiosity of visitors by the wall aforesaid. The palace is only half completed, and is intended to cover twice its present area; but when His Majesty's devoted and loving subjects will have completed this project Heaven only knows; for only a dozen workmen or so are loitering about; hardly enough to keep the place clean. Near the palace in a ruined shed is a curious boat formed like a dragon with an immense head; it is fast going to decay, but was once evidently most gorgeous with paint and gilt. That is the Sacred Dragon Boat in which His Majesty descended the Great River from Han-yang to the siege and capture of Nanking. It was once kept inside the walls, but has now been turned out, and nobody takes much notice of it. There is a huge yellow wall about three hundred yards from the first gateway, whereon are painted the most ferocious-looking dragons possible. It is on this wall that Tien-wang posts his own peculiar proclamations. See, there they are, all on yellow satin, written in vermilion ink, in the straggling ill-looking handwriting of the King himself. He is most indefatigable in getting up these documents, and in them are to be found the most startling and infamous blasphemy the human mind can imagine. I have seen the wall half covered with yellow satin, and often wondered whence it all came from. In your front is a tall curious gateway, very handsome in its way, and, although unfinished, gilded with great taste. It is built on columns, painted in red and gold, and the top is formed of that curious combination of woodwork so familiar to us in the Yamên at Canton. Passing through this gateway and the outer door, you approach the grand door of the palace by a covered way supported by gilded columns. The roof is covered with dragons of all sizes and sorts doing all kinds of things, from eating the sun to pursuing a gigantic shrimp. Over the door, which is as gaudy as paint and gold can make it, is an inscription "of the True Shên, the Sacred Heavenly Door." On either side are two gigantic drums, which were you to beat you would create intense alarm. In the inner chambers gilded lanterns suspended on silken cords and ornamented with rich tassels are hung about in every direction; a very large and handsome glass one suspended in the centre once graced the Yamên of Ho-quei-ching at Soo-chow. To the right of the Sacred Heavenly Door is a space containing chairs and tables, where Heavenly soldiers are lying about in easy but not graceful positions. The arrival of foreigners does not create much sensation; and the old janitor, who told me that his age was great when he nursed Tien-wang, then a coolie child in a village near Canton, asks you to take a seat and cup of tea politely enough; and, as you cannot get any farther into the palace, you had better accept his invitation and rest after your long walk. There is a map called the 'Map of the Entire Territory of the Heavenly Taiping Dynasty to endure for a myriad myriad years.' It is an amusing document, or whatever you like to call it. A vast space of ground, almost square, and surrounded by seas, is China; a great square place, surrounded by apparently four walls, is the Heavenly Capital; Hongkong is nowhere, Japan a small speck; nor could I detect Peking in the part of the map where I should have supposed it to exist. Two little islands in the north-west are called England and France. Other European nations are, I suppose, suppressed by Heavenly command; and the whole of Asia, with the exception of China, is swallowed up, probably by a dragon. Now you would fancy that so much gold and red paint, lamps and flags, would make a very grand sight. Nothing of the sort; everything is dirty to a degree. The gilding is fast sinking beneath a brown coating put upon it by dirty hot hands, dust, and rain; the red and the blue, the white and green are badly laid on, and seem inclined to run together; the dragons on the ceiling will not be visible much longer unless repainted; the floor is covered with saliva and filth; the Heavenly troops lolling about are dirty, unkempt, and ragged; ruins that can be seen all round you look like misery in spite of Tien-wang; and you cannot help feeling that you are sitting in the centre of a vast system of human degradation and imposture.

"Presently there is a dreadful noise of drums, cymbals, and gongs, mingling with the roar of petards and the shrill notes of the wry-necked but celestial fife—Tien-wang is going to dinner, and that noise will continue until repletion comes to His Majesty. For some time previously the Sacred Gate has been partially open, and seedy-looking women have been entering and coming out with the plates, chopsticks, and other articles about to be used in the royal repast. Most of the articles are of gold. From the appearance of the chow-chow which was conveyed into the interior, I should opine that the celestial taste had a leaning towards cabbage. Although we cannot put our legs under the royal mahogany, we can listen to what the fellows outside tell us of the glories of the interior. His Sacred Majesty the Heavenly King is fifty-one years of age, tall, strong, and healthy. He will never die; but when tired of sublunar affairs, a dragon-car will descend, and he becomes a guest on high. He has had many interviews with the Almighty, and according to his own proclamations this favour has lately been extended to his wife—I cannot tell you which out of the hundred and eight, but probably the mother of the Junior Lord. None but women are allowed in the interior of the palace; and I have been told there are about a thousand of them. How they must talk! His Majesty has a crown of gold that weighs eight catties, a necklace of golden bosses of like weight; and his gold-embroidered dress is thickly studded with lumps of gold, something like and probably an imitation of foreign buttons. He is drawn from his distant apartments to the Audience Chamber in a gilded affair, called the Sacred Dragon Car, by his ladies, and is there seated on a throne to receive the prayers and flattery of his high officers. His son usually attends, but is rather a sickly youth by all accounts. He is very industrious, writes dozens of proclamations, receives and answers the letters from the Kings, and has a keen eye for business. I am not a missionary, and can consequently give only a lay opinion, which, however, is strong and well-founded, that Tien-wang's Christianity is nothing but the rank blasphemy of a lunatic, and the profession of religion by his followers a laughable mockery and farce. As a heretic, Tien-wang is the most incorrigible self-willed one I ever heard of. He has been talked to, written to, written at, memorialized, and addressed in all shapes and forms about the truths of Christianity, and he remains more stubborn than ever. Doses of orthodoxy have been carefully administered to him by foreign missionaries, but have not acted as was expected. Little doxologies and prayers have been furtively hurled at him, and he has swallowed them all. Dozens of Bibles have been presented to him without doing much good, although I believe he reads them. The opinions of the fathers and of the councils have been sent him, and he has learnt his lesson so pat that he will overwhelm the next clerical gentleman who enters the lists with him with the opinions of Cyril, Augustine, and the other ancient fathers. He is most baffling in his arguments. The Pope would have had him burnt long ago. One day he yields a point, and then says his instructor is wrong. He finds new translations of the Bible, and none of our commentators would meet with his approval. He would spoil your best edition of Scott by scribbling his celestial opinions in red ink down the margin thereof. When everything else fails, he will tell you that he has been to heaven and you have not, and so 'shuts you up.' Then he takes theological fits, and tells his people all kinds of curious things. The other day he ordered his chiefs to take unto themselves more wives against his next birthday. 'Adam was right in the beginning to take one wife,' says he, 'but I know better now and tell you to take ten.' He is equal to the Son according to his older documents, but more recently he always makes the Father, Son, Himself, and the Young

Lord, all equal. He has dismissed the Third Person of the Trinity, after vainly endeavouring to incarnate it in the person of Tung-wang, the most bloodthirsty of all the Kings. He seems to me to luxuriate in heterodoxy, flinging, while so doing, proclamations and books about like a wizard throwing flowers from a hat; when the fit is over he will correspond on yellow satin with any missionary, whether Churchman, Dissenter, or Papist, and perhaps accompany his missive with a bolt of silk, and be quite submissive. But the best of friends must part, and we will say good-bye to him, hoping to see him personally some day. We go out by a side door, where, according to the inscription, all nations enter to do homage. On our left hand is a low range of buildings where the chiefs put on the court robes previous to an audience. An important yellow satin proclamation there suspended is used to wipe the neighbouring lamp; the whole building is a tawdry, dirty, trumpery affair.

"Having, on my arrival at Nanking, resolved to see as much as possible of the chiefs and people, without becoming exactly familiar with them, I was very glad when a civil letter came one morning from the Chung-wang-tsun, the brother of the redoubtable conqueror of Soo-chow, inviting myself and my friends to come and take dinner with him. He sent ponies and an escort; and in a couple of hours we arrived at Chung-wang's palace, and were duly ushered in by crowds of fantastically dressed youths. Chung-wang's brother, by name Le (*anglicé*, Jones or Smith), is the exact counterpart of the great fighting king, who is at present away spreading Great Peace in Hupeh. About five feet four high, with a good-looking cunning countenance, always laughing, he is not at all a disagreeable man to spend a day with. His dress was of bright scarlet satin, with a yellow cap, to which is fixed a fine pearl as large as a hazel-nut. He led us through a good many rooms to a pretty little pavilion looking out on a miniature garden of rock-work and trees, where he gave us a very good Chinese dinner, keeping up a merry chat the whole time. The food came to his table in a series of nine porcelain dishes shaped like the petals of a rose, and all fitting into one another on the table. He said that Heaven had been kind enough to give this equipage to his brother at Soo-chow. The chopsticks, forks, and spoons were of silver, the knives English plated ware, and his wine-cups of gold fitting into cases of enamelled silver. After a couple of visits, I made a practice of going and talking to this man whenever I had time; and he has shown me some very curious things belonging to Chung-wang. This potentate is the only one after His Celestial Majesty who has a crown of real gold. It is to my idea a really pretty affair. The gold is beaten out thin enough, and then formed into leaves and filigree work like a tiger,— enormous as to tail in front and behind. On either side is a bird of what species you please, and on the top a phœnix. It is covered from top to bottom with pendent pearls and other gems. I put it on my head, and should guess the weight to be about three pounds. Chung-wang has likewise a very handsome yu-i or sceptre made of gold, and ornamented with large bunches of sapphires and pearls. Some peculating individual had picked out some of the stones at the time I saw it, and the wrath of His Excellency Le was wonderful to behold. There are some beautiful pieces of carved jade placed about the various apartments, as well as old bronzes and vases. The writing apparatus used by my friend is of great intrinsic value. The inkstone is of jade, and the vessel to contain the water is cut from a large pink stone like an amethyst. The stand for the golden pencils is a large sprig of pink coral, fixed in a cube of silver. Crystal and jade paper-weights lie about in abundance, and seven watches were keeping various and eccentric records of the time on the table. Every article on which silver could be expended is covered with that metal. The sword has a silver scabbard and silver belt; the umbrella has a silver stick; the whips, fans, and tails for mosquito-flappers have all silver handles; and his Excellency's arms are crowded with silver and gold bracelets.

"Being one day very late in the city, and a storm coming on, I resolved to accept Le's invitation to stay a night at his palace. He did his utmost to make me comfortable, and I certainly have been compelled to put up at worse places than Chung-wang's abode. A very nice supper was prepared at eight o'clock, consisting of fowls, mutton, and other such viands delightful to Western tastes. Two bottles of sherry— with paper rolls, however, instead of corks to stop them—and a large silver pot of hot Celestial wine, were passed round very briskly among the Ta-jêns who had been invited by Le to meet me. It was very evident that the more important chiefs pay but little attention to the absurd mandates of the Heavenly one who rules over them, for every one of my friends certainly appreciated sherry, and the Celestial wine-pot was replenished more than once during the evening. Nor was tobacco-smoke strange to the lips of these Maos, who have nevertheless strictly prohibited its use. I slept in Chung-wang's state bed, with a beautifully soft mat and with scarlet silk curtains all round. While dozing off, I was somewhat startled by the sound of Chinese boots in the room, and put my head through the curtains to see what was moving. Judge of my astonishment at seeing a couple of Celestial girls crossing the place with lanterns in their hands, and an old attendant with another. The moment they caught sight of my ugly foreign head, they screamed and made a most precipitate retreat, although I assured them that I was not in the least alarmed. They got to their quarters by another way, leaving a horrid dog snarling and barking about the door all night. I found in the morning that I had cut off the retreat of their Majesties the two Mrs. Chung-wangs, who had been out visiting the ladies of the double-eyed dog Ying-wang. They, little dreaming that a foreign devil was lying in state in the palace, had taken the usual road to the harem through the room in which I slept,—hence the adventure.

"These Celestials rise at most unconscionable hours. At dawn a deputation waited on me to know whether I would have a hot bath. Seeing that it was intensely hot already, I asked for a cold one, upon which much alarm was expressed, and the writer or secretary assured me that the use of cold water would certainly produce some malady or other. On my persisting, another Ta-jên came and remonstrated with me, but without effect. At last H. E. Le came himself, but left me despairing of prevailing against foreign obstinacy. So I had my bath, and was looked on during the day as a kind of wonder.

"After breakfast Le took me to see the new palace his brother was building, on a spot about a quarter of a mile from his old one. It is certainly going to be a vast affair, little less than the Yamên at Canton. Upwards of a thousand workmen were engaged—some building, some carving stone and wood, and not a few standing with a bundle of rattans in their hands ready to inflict blows on any one shirking his work. A great portion of the building is already completed, and the whole will be a good specimen of a Chinese Yamên of the old style, with its network of beams at the gables, its large wooden columns, and fantastic carvings. Asking what the workmen were paid, Le laughingly replied, —'You English pay for work; we Taipings know better. Is not ours a truly great empire?' About 11 o'clock Le told me that he, in common with every other chief, was going to sleep until about one; and to sleep he went, leaving me a pony, on which I rode round to such other friends of mine as could be found awake. I returned to dinner and found his Excellency learning to write, for, although brother to Chung-wang, and styled 'Heaven's Righteousness,' his fist cannot be called pretty. He soon gave up the work, and, curling himself up in a chair, ordered a couple of boys to fan him; and in this position he remained until dinner, after which I left him.

"And now we will go and have some chow-chow with perhaps the most eminent man connected with the Taiping movement —I mean Hung, the Kan-wang. I frequently pitied this man before I knew him, as from his knowledge of foreigners he has always been put prominently forward in everything connected with them, and has suffered not a little from the absurd way in which his Western friends have talked about him. I have seen a good deal of Kan-wang, and will proceed to give my lay opinion about him. Kan-wang told me some months ago that he was going to spread Great Peace towards Gan-hui. He did so, and the foreign ships saw the smoking and flaming villages that marked his course. Can we not therefore call him 'a burning and a shining light'?

"On arriving at the palace, which is very redolent of paint and gilding, you observe two box-like affairs on the opposite side of the street, in which bands of musicians keep up eternal discord, sometimes so low in tone as not to annoy you, but on other occasions so dreadfully loud as to be intolerable. I once lived four days in Kan-wang's palace, and the music never ceased for longer than half an hour. Between these two music-boxes, fixed to a wall covered with dragons, and peacocks, and asses, and even fishes, is a large board on which the character for happiness is painted in gold, and above it the Beatitudes from St. Matthew. Turning through the gate to the right through dirty courts, you come to a series of dirty dark chambers which are designated the Six Boards. Coolies are sometimes

visible in these rooms, and in the larger of them some three
scribes are for ever writing on yellow paper—these few men
combining in themselves, in all probability, the functions of
the whole Six Boards. The Board of Revenue contained
much coal when I was there; and the Board of Rites had
evidently been turned to a worse purpose. Above these
boards lives Mr. Roberts, who, at the back of all, has a shed
for a hospital. On a wall I espied an old account of the
success of British and French arms against Tientsin, ending
with the usual Celestial exhortation 'utterly to slay the
imps.' Kan-wang is pulling all these places down, and in-
tends to erect a handsome edifice on the ruins. Returning
to the front door, a pale-faced little boy, dressed entirely in
yellow, will, if you are known, come out and put his little hand
in yours, and lisp 'Good morning.' This is the Kan-wang's
only son, and a nice little lad he is. He has himself a crown
and title, even that of Kan-szü-keuen, *i.e.* successor to the
dignity of Kan. He knows how to talk to the servants in
great style, and is promptly obeyed. But now the great
gates open, and inside, seated in his Yamên, dressed in full
robes, is the Kan-wang. His attendants finely dressed stand
at his side. He will shake hands with you when you have
advanced, and say in English, 'How do you do?' and bid
you to be seated. Kan-wang is, I should say, about 45
years old, rather fat than otherwise, and has an open and
very pleasing countenance. He is an extremely pleasant
companion, can drink a glass of port wine, and, if necessary,
make a dinner off *bifstek à l'Anglais*, with a knife and fork.
I must confess that he is the most enlightened Chinaman I
ever saw. He is perfectly acquainted with geography, moderately so with mechanics, acknowledges the superiority of
Western civilization, has books of reference with plates on all
imaginable subjects, is generous, and very desirous of doing
good. *Per contra*, he is indolent, and consequently takes but

little trouble to see his theories put into practice. He is not a soldier, and the fighting kings are therefore very jealous of his perpetual stay at the capital. He was even compelled to go to the wars, but made a mess of it, and returned on being informed that certain foreign devils were making extravagant and insolent demands in Nanking. He told me that he hated war, and tried on his excursions to make it as little terrible as possible. 'But,' said he (and Kan-wang has some appreciation of truth), 'it is impossible to deny that this is a war of extermination: quarter or mercy is never shown to our men by Hsien Fêng's soldiers, and in revenge our people never give any. But men under my command never unnecessarily slay country people.' He also hinted at what I know to be a fact, that if the Taoutai at Shanghai would take it into his head to show mercy on runaway Taipings, instead of immediately ordering their execution, it would be a most difficult matter to keep the frontier Rebel armies together.

"I must now entreat the reader to walk with me round the interior of the palace, have dinner, and go back to the Tien-hai-kuan. Opening folding doors at the back of the tribunal, Kan-wang will lead you into a large dark Yamên, exactly like the one at Tsan-wang's, and thence through a side door, to one more cheerful, looking on to a small rock-work garden. The Yamên is hung round with satin scrolls, and is dreadfully dusty. I don't think it is ever used. In one corner are a dozen solar lamp glasses, and on the table two canisters of gunpowder in Curtis and Harvey flasks, the one made at Ningpo, the other in Britain. In a large press are a multitude of picture-books, done up in cloth covers. His Highness will take them down and show them to you, and you can't deny that some of the Soo-chow flower-paintings are exquisite. Turning through a small door to the left, you come into Kan-wang's own sanctum, which is quite a museum in its way. It is a large cheerful room facing a garden of flowers. The principal article of furniture is a large bed of Soo-chow manufacture, covered with jade and other ornaments, and hung with yellow curtains. The Wang takes a siesta in this now and then. Tables line the sides of the chamber, and support a most extraordinary conglomeration of different articles. There is a telescope on a moving pedestal (broken), a gun-box (gun gone), three Colt's revolvers (all useless from rust), a box of gun-caps, ditto of Vestas, two solar lamps that can't be made to light, and a cake of brown Windsor soap; the Woolwich Manual of Fortification, a book on military tactics, and the Holy Bible; any amount of Chinese books, comprising all those valuable works published by foreign missionaries; quires of yellow paper, five or six clocks, an alarum, broken barometer, heaps of proclamations, ink-stones, gold pencils, and dirty rags. On the other side piles of books suffering from moth, a hat-box with the dragon hat inside, fans mounted in silver, jade-stone drinking cups and saucers, gold and silver cups, platters, chopsticks and forks, three English port-wine bottles, and one ditto of Coward's mixed pickles. At various places are suspended an English naval sword, some dragon caps, a couple of Japanese knives, two French plates, and an old engraving of the Holy Well in Flintshire. Lying on the bed are a number of silver ingots tied up in cloth. Chairs and stools with marble seats are placed round a marble table, and an attendant dressed in spotless white crape, with blue jacket, pulls a punkah, and so keeps you beautifully cool. Here Kan-wang will give you a pretty good dinner and lots of wine. He told me that when Tien-wang prohibited wine he applied for a dispensation, asserting that unless he drank he could not eat; the dispensation was immediately granted. At dinner he will tell you what difficulties he has to encounter in introducing reforms; how

Tien-wang's 'head is in the skies, while his feet are on the earth,' and how little the other Wangs care for his authority. In fact, the central authority among the Taipings extends but little beyond the capital. I cannot help liking Kan-wang. Often as I have visited him, always on unpleasant business, as soon as business is finished he is as friendly and open as ever. I must now bid him good-bye, wishing him well out of the difficult position he occupies, where to attempt reform is to place oneself in enmity with all other chiefs. His ambition is counteracted by his indolence. Pride and the innate Chinese love of concealment and trickery but too often develop themselves in the man, and are made evident almost immediately by his openness and candour. If all Taipingdom was composed of such men, China would be theirs in a short time, but Kan-wang unfortunately stands perfectly unique among the chiefs of Nanking. He is a firm believer in the Christian religion, but accommodates his faith to his own peculiar habits. I fail to distinguish in him a most essential element of success in his peculiar station, namely, sagacity; his pride destroys what wisdom his experience should have given to him, and the flattery, fulsome enough, which has been so plentifully bestowed on him from all sides, has produced its inevitable result. I would remark that Kan-wang is waited on by females; but I must deny an insinuation which might have been and should have been rebutted from another source, that these women are either attractive, young, or pretty, or have any other employment in the palace than that of menial servants. I have possibly seen more of Kan-wang and the Taipings in general than any other Englishman, and can consequently be somewhat trusted in what I say.

"I could tell much more concerning the Taipings individually and collectively, but will now only add that it is impossible to live a long time among a set of people and not take an interest in them, and in a certain way to like them. I have met with not only civility, but actual courtesy from them, and shall never regret the time I have spent among them. Not being a clergyman, I have not looked at Taipingdom from its weakest side—its Christianity; but I must state that I see no hope of the Taipings becoming the dominant power in China, because they are simply unable to govern themselves, except by a species of most objectionable terrorism. But neither do I see any prospect of the Manchoos reinstating themselves in their former position. There is more or less rebellion (not always Taiping) in every province except one in China. Something will spring from this state of disorder to restore order, as has been the case a dozen times before in the empire. The greatest cause of the frightful disorder into which the nation has been plunged is the want of a sufficiency of civil officers—one man ruling over a place as big as Yorkshire, and knowing nothing of his district during his reign. The Taipings might remedy this, inasmuch as every other man is an officer of some kind or other, at all events a Ta-jên. As yet it is but the beginning of a chaos in which trade and commerce, prosperity and happiness, must for a time sink, but only to rise again more flourishing and glorious than ever. Heaven forbid that England, or France, should ever make confusion worse confounded by interfering in the internal struggle now raging! Things are governed in China by rules that we don't understand. The springs of vitality which have enabled China to trace her way through political convulsions as bad as the present, and to exist as a powerful empire through such a series of years as makes our European dynasties look small enough, are not yet exhausted. It will be well to look at the present crisis in a broader light than we are inclined to at present, and see in it merely Chinese fighting Chinese, righting, or attempting to right, their injuries in their own peculiar way. It will not do to look at it in the light of the spread of Christianity against Heathendom, as some people would have it, nor will it be well to consider altogether the individual and temporary damage done to foreign commerce. When serious political difficulties are being solved, such losses must stand in abeyance, and we must be witness to much human misery and tears—to the loss of much life and much property. In this 'Great Whole,' in the vortex of sublunary affairs, we in our own time have seen much of revolution and death, have seen dynasties overthrown and evil potentates cast out. In Western Europe we can look on such things according to the great principles actuating them, and not according to individual losses or interests. Why should it not be the same in China? The darkness in the land is undoubtedly thick and tangible, but is there no ray of hope? Most verily there is. What place can so be shut out from the brilliant sun shining over us, but that some furtive ray will come playing through, be it even from a keyhole or spider-crack? We of England are from our earliest years accustomed to hear a prayer that magnates, magistrates, mandarins, or what you will, may execute justice and maintain truth; and we know that veritable retribution will be exacted from those who fail, and from the nation to which they belong. Those who know anything of the Manchoo dynasty cannot but confess that it is a sad culprit against the above prayer; while those who have been never so little behind the scenes can testify to the mass of corruption which lies universally seething in high and low places. In such a national dysentery, nothing but the most vigorous remedies can be applied; and much actual cautery (after the manner of the Arabs) and bloodletting is being most vigorously administered. The disease is at present very intermittent, but by-and-by the patient will need repose, and will most indubitably find it without calling in to its aid Western soporifics—opium perhaps excepted. I pray my readers, when perusing of Chapoo fallings and other dismal records, to consider that the dreadful cruelty therein enacted is hardly a counterpart of Tsing atrocities. But the other day, at Ngan-king, the Imperialists enjoyed a three days' slaughter, and left neither man, woman, nor child in that unfortunate city. The Great River is crowded now with their headless victims. I have always had my opinion as to the brigand-like character of the Taipings, but after seeing a good deal of both I must confess that I have no better opinion of the other party. But I know this, that there is much hope; that order is doing valiant battle with disorder, and is conquering; that English prosperity and rule, manifested in many mercantile houses in Hankow, Kiukiang, Shanghai, and elsewhere, are silently becoming the umpires in the Celestial struggle; for round such beacons the tired Chinese will cluster and reform their strength. But this restoration will be fatal to both the Manchoo and Taiping dynasties sooner or later. In the mean time, looking on the mighty highway— the silvery track of the Great River, where the forerunners and pioneers of coming peace are going and returning—I anxiously await the time when the tide of disorder shall have flowed by. And now good-bye to Nanking, the city of the Coolie Kings."

CHAPTER IV.

A NAVAL SQUADRON INLAND.

THE squadron being reassembled at Nanking, 200 geographical miles from the sea, Admiral Hope left that place to continue his progress up the river on the 2nd of March, with the 'Coromandel,' 'Couper,' 'Snake,' 'Havoc,' and 'Attalante;' the 'Centaur' and 'Bouncer' (gun-boat) being left at anchor off the suburb. The same evening, being favoured by the wind and deep water—for we were now beyond tidal influence—we reached Wu-hoo, a town, or rather the remains of one, in possession of the Rebels. The day's run was fifty-six miles on a S.S.W. course, the average width of the river being about that of the Thames at Woolwich. On the way, a little above the town of Taiping, we passed between the East and West Pillars, but I am not able to endorse the pleasing description given of them by the historian of Lord Elgin's Mission; and as to this being the gate of the Yang-tsze, one might as well suppose a gate half-way up a carriage-drive. On this day, too, we passed from the province of Kiang-su into its inland neighbour, An-hoei; and the next few days showed us in it, and the little corner of Kiang-si, some of the finest scenery on the lower river.

Why China should ever have been called a "vast plain," or "enormous fertile valley," is to me inexplicable. More variation of surface perhaps does not occur in any country; and where we should be most inclined to look for such features, namely, on its great artery, there it is diversified enough to please the most exacting of tourists. Commencing at the mouth of the Yang-tsze Kiang, there is naturally a considerable extent of flat alluvial land, the delta of the river, where once no doubt the ocean held its sway; but soon we come to hills and high lands, and at Chin-kiang one is delighted with the steep and rugged cliffs. About Nanking the country is prettily broken into ridges and hills, and, before reaching far above this, mountains shut in the river on either hand. In fact, I think the scenery between Wu-hoo and An-king (usually spelt Ngan-king) equal to that of almost any part of the river. It is, of course, not such bold and near scenery as is found on the upper waters; but the fine ranges of mountains, well removed from the river, whose broad expanse is now broken by low islands, and now widens into lake-like form; the beautiful, partially wooded slopes of the mountains reaching down into the highly cultivated lower land; the occasional village; the collection of reed huts gathered on the immediate bank, as if in doubt whether the ground were as safe as the water; the distant pagoda, marking the site of a town approachable only by some narrow canal-like creek; and then, life made apparent by numerous boats with their white cotton wings; the fisherman attending his ingenious dip-net; some coolies trotting along an embankment which raises them above their fellows who are working away in the irrigated paddy-fields below, while two of a more favoured class are being wheeled along a paved pathway in those best of wheelbarrows;—the objects serve to remind one, —the country, of the lake scenery of the Old World,—the river, of the New; but the people, of China, and China only. And then the thought comes over one, that those peaceful and industrious people are doomed to destruction: the edict has gone forth, "kill and destroy;" that pagoda must fall; those villages will soon send dark volumes of smoke on high; such as have boats will flee, the rest must submit to slavery; fields will be laid waste, dams broken, and desolation will appear on every side; for the rule of the Taipings has begun. But the "Son of the Ocean" will remain ever ebbing on its course towards its parent; those mountains cannot move; the bright Eastern sky will be above; and, though governments and people should change, Nature will be Nature still.

Wu-hoo is situated at the mouth of a tributary stream of clear water falling in on the right bank of the pea-soup-coloured Yang-tsze, fifty-six geographical miles above Nanking; or, rather, a suburb with an old pagoda stands at the mouth of the creek, and the walled town itself is about a mile inland. The day following the evening of our arrival was Sunday, consequently the squadron remained at anchor, the Admiral being always careful that there should be no work on that day. It rained the whole day; but from necessity some of us were obliged to put on our oilskin coats and go ashore in search of provisions. The scene of desolation was as complete as at Nanking or Chin-kiang, and the whole distance from the suburb to the town was one heap of ruins. We walked around looking for provisions; but fish was the only thing to be found, and the population appeared to be in a starving condition. One square place—I think, the ruins of a temple—was literally filled with beggars lying in filth, and but partly covered by some cotton rags alive with vermin. One or two were lifeless, others breathing their last gasps of the noisome stench that pervaded the den. Most were affected with virulent skin disease, and all had the verdict stamped unmistakeably on their countenances, "Died from starvation."

After searching in vain for some time, we arrived at the Custom-house, where the people seemed inclined to be civil. But at no reasonable price could we obtain either eggs, fowls, or a goat; seven dollars were asked for a wretched apology for the last; and as for fowls, we offered ten dollars (about forty-two shillings) for a couple of dozen, and were refused. The only chance was one bullock known to be in existence in some part of Wu-hoo, and he was sent for accordingly for our inspection. I forget what we paid for this last of the Wu-hoo bullocks; but we ultimately succeeded, thanks to the Celestial distaste for beef, in striking a tolerably satisfactory bargain. We had a great job to get our purchase to the river, and harder work still to get him on board our vessel, which lay half a mile distant. We first put him in a sampan; but this craft, being unseaworthy, sank under him, which forced us to tow him the whole way astern of the cutter. The blue-jackets enjoyed the fun greatly, and the animal was at last hoisted on board by his horns, after being half-drowned on the passage. So ended our Sunday afternoon's foraging excursion; certainly not a right proceeding, but pardonable under the existing circumstances.

In the neighbourhood of Wu-hoo the country retained the same desolate appearance as we had observed below; the hilly ground on the right, or southern shore of the river, being equally devoid of trees with the low land which stretches away towards the distant hills to the northward. It seems to be a distinctive mark on all districts which have been overrun by the locust-like hordes of the belligerents.

Leaving Wu-hoo and its possessors on the 4th of March, sixty miles in a W.S.W. direction, and then fifty more on various courses, brought us on the day following to An-king, the capital of the province, which had for some time been in the hands of the Taipings, but closely besieged by the Imperial forces under Chin-koo-fang, one of the ablest generals left to the Emperor. The state of siege appeared to be pretty much as it was when the squadron of 1858 gave the batteries a dose of iron in return for a similar compliment. The lines of circumvallation were distinctly visible, and those of contravallation showed that the besiegers were apprehensive of danger from the field as well as the fortress. In fact, when we were at Nanking the "Coolie Kings" accounted for the smallness of their force at their capital by saying that an army had just left for the relief of this place; but, if I mistake not, the same story was told two years before, which we may charitably put down as a Celestial mistake, otherwise, were we accustomed to use unparliamentary language, a harder word would be substituted.

A considerable fleet of war-junks lay below, and another above the city, quite blockading the river against native craft, while the Rebels were devoid of any naval force. A few desultory shots at long range, and some rockets thrown towards the town by the Imperialists, showed us that the game was still being carried on. The walls, as we passed, were crowded with spectators, but the garrison was said to be in a very forlorn state. This place has since been captured.

I have already mentioned the beauty of the scenery on the river between Wu-hoo and An-king. Some twenty-five miles above the former place, high hills on the right bank are the commencement of a range, which, with a general direction of south-west, strikes the river much farther up, joining what are marked on the chart as "Wild-Boar Hills;" thence the range is taken up on the other side of the river also, and gains greater altitude with a westerly direction, and was at that time covered with snow.

Kieu-hien, a small place, we found to be in possession of the Imperialists, and thence up to An-king the people and country contrasted strongly with what we had seen below. Here were quiet villagers dressed as the ordinary Chinese are, in their blue cotton, and devoid of all the gaudy coloured silks the Rebels so much delight in, at the expense of others. The dwellings appeared in good order, and both by the craft which enlivened the river, and by the people quietly employed on shore in their daily avocations, an air of tranquil industry was manifested, and formed an agreeable relief in the great panorama.

It was just sunset as we passed by An-king. The walls seemed in good preservation, having apparently undergone considerable repairs of late. Some one, I should imagine, had given the Taipings a hint or two in military science, for they had carefully levelled a whole suburb, together with all detached buildings outside the walls which might afford shelter to an attacking force, while they had occupied the several eminences with redoubts, mostly of masonry. The "Pagoda Fort," close to the river-bank on the east side of the city, was strongly fortified, and the pagoda, *minus* its top, seemed in a tolerable state of preservation for anything in China. The city is about a mile square, as nearly as I could judge, and faces the cardinal points, the south side being on the river. Advantage has been taken of the ground in selecting the site—not always the case in Chinese fortresses—and the whole city stands on ground considerably raised above the neighbouring country A fine range of mountains, some two thousand feet high, rises at a distance to the north, and altogether it is a beautifully situated place. We anchored about four miles above, near Christmas Island.

It was a delightfully clear morning as we started on the 6th of March; flocks of geese were preparing for their northward journey, a few wild swans were seen, and a number of pelicans. Tung-lieu, where there was a large encampment of Imperial troops, was passed before noon, the fine ranges of mountains to the southward being seen to great advantage. A strong current, with eddies at "Dove Point," obliged the 'Couper' to cast off the 'Havoc,' which she had in tow, and we sighted the "Little Orphan Rock." Porpoises disported themselves in the still muddy current of the Ta-kiang, as the Yang-tsze is called at this part. The day was bright, with a warm sun and little or no wind; and we viewed the cliff and crags of this interesting pass in their best colours. The "Little Orphan Rock" is a great resort for cormorants, which we observed in immense numbers perched on its ledges, and much of the cliff was whitened with the dung of these birds. Completing seventy miles this day, we reached Hu-kow, a fortified temple at the outlet of the Poyang Lake, after dark. This point is 236 geographical miles above Nanking, and 436 from the sea.

As the sun rose next morning, we enjoyed a beautiful view of the entrance of the lake, the "Great Orphan Rock" standing in bold relief like a guardian to the passage, with Lieu-shan, a huge mountain mass which rises some four thousand feet above the lake, at that time with snow on its summit, in the background; Hu-kow temple, with its picturesque walls and cliffs, coming in in the left corner. We soon had some boats off from the shore, freighted with inquiring Celestials to "makey look see," as the Cantonese say; besides others offering for sale oranges, sweetmeats, and fowls, but the last at exorbitant prices. The people were in no way timid, although this was only the second time that any foreign vessels had ploughed their waters. They informed us that they had cattle on shore, but we had much trouble in making ourselves understood, using various devices to this end; as, for instance, eggs were indicated by rolling up a white pocket-handkerchief, and imitating the crow of a cock.

Overhead the day continued to be delightful, and sensibly warmer than we had yet felt on the river, the thermometer standing at 60° in the shade at a quarter past two, with a dead calm. Coaling, at no time a very pleasant occupation, was to us voyagers the more inconvenient, as, it having been ordered that the 'Attalante' should supply such of the vessels as required coal and then be left here, we were engaged packing and removing our baggage to the 'Couper.' Before evening all had been satisfactorily accomplished; we took our last dinner, and then bid farewell to the 'Attalante.' Our party, having been nearly a month on board, had become intimately acquainted with all hands, and it was not without regret that we left the vessel in which we had been so kindly treated and had spent so many pleasant days.

Starting at 7 A.M. on the 8th, a few revolutions of her engines ran the 'Couper' ashore on the end of a spit; but she did not remain there long, for, just as hawsers were being got ready to tow her off, she slipped into deep water of her own accord, and we proceeded to Kiu-kiang, fifteen miles higher up the Yang-tsze, arriving there by ten o'clock. This was the place selected for the second open port on the river, but first appearances were anything but encouraging. It is one of those towns which have been in the hands of the Rebels, but retaken by the Imperialists, and it has not yet had time to recover from the plague. It is situated on the right bank of the river, backed by Lieu-shan mountain to the southward, between which and the city walls lies an undulating and picturesque country. On the opposite side of the river the land is flat.

Another Consul was dropped here, the deputies of the Shanghai Chamber of Commerce visited the shore with their note-books, some pheasants were shot, and the next morning we were again steaming up the river, the squadron now sensibly reduced. The first day's route above Kiu-kiang was on a most beautiful and interesting portion of the river. High hills rise immediately from the bank, some prettily wooded, with others terraced and cultivated to a great height. The general formation is limestone, and we observed some extensive quarries. A little before noon we passed the "Split Rock," a peculiar feature which occurs at a narrow pass where the river alters its course from S.S.E. to an easterly direction, and we entered the province of Hoo-peh. The water-line was distinctly marked on the rocks, more than twenty feet above the present level. We made eighty-two miles this day, and anchored off Wu-chang, a *hien* or town of the second order on the right bank. Another place, called Hwang-chow, stands on the opposite side, and about three miles above; it contains a fine stone pagoda of recent date. Both these places were in the hands of the Imperialists at that time; but, as we subsequently learned, the latter fell to the Taipings shortly after. As we remained at anchor all the next day, which was Sunday, parties of the squadron visited both places, and in each they were mobbed and insulted; so that doubtless, as in many other cases in this rebellion, this town was captured from within rather than by a hostile force from without.

We had now but fifty miles to reach the highest point to which foreign vessels had ever ascended on the Great River, and to which by treaty British merchants could now transport their merchandise in British vessels. All eyes, therefore, were anxiously strained, on the 11th of March, to catch the first glimpse of the pagoda which marks the mouth of the Han. A number of timber-rafts were passed, usually in several sections joined together, with temporary abodes on each. The country generally was level, with some low isolated hills and a few ridges; and a new feature in the river was the existence of immense sand-points, flooded during summer, but now bare. Soon after passing Yang-lo, a small place with some red sandstone cliffs, we caught sight of the pagoda rising from the crest of a blue hill, showing over the long flat between us and Hankow; and by a few minutes after three in the afternoon we were at anchor between Hanyang and Wu-chang, and were immediately surrounded by innumerable sampans containing anxious gazers at our leviathan craft.

The immense number of river junks crowded together at the mouth of the Han, and lining its shores for a considerable distance up, and the fleet of white sails seen in the distance as one looked up the main river, at once convinced us of the commercial value of this port which the next few months were to prove. A walk on shore through the crowded streets of Hankow reminded us more of the western suburbs of Canton than anything we had seen since we left that city, and was a bright contrast to the wretchedness and misery which had almost invariably met our gaze on the lower portion of the river. The people too seemed more alive and stirring, and in appearance much more resembled the Southern Chinese than those of the seaboard at Shanghai. European articles were displayed in the shop-fronts, even to lucifer matches, while the numerous articles of native produce attested a large trade with the interior. These were salt, tobacco, hemp, opium and other drugs from Sz'chuan, and silk even from its western confines; coal and tea from Hoo-nan, and cotton from the neighbouring districts, with oil in abundance. Here was a feast for the eyes of the mercantile gentlemen, and I doubt not they profited by it.

Hankow as known to Europeans, but really Wu-chang (foo), the capital of Hoo-peh, Han-yang (foo), and Hankow—three towns only prevented from being one by the Yang-tsze and its tributary the Han—are situated just where an irregular range of semi-detached low hills crosses a particularly level country on both sides of the main river, in an east and west direction. Stationed on Pagoda Hill, a spectator looks down on almost as much water as land, even when the rivers are low. At his feet sweeps the magnificent Yang-tsze, nearly a mile in width; from the west, and skirting the northern edge of the range of hills already mentioned, comes the river Han, narrow and canal-like, to add its quota, and serving as one of the highways of the country; and to the north-west and north is an extensive treeless flat, so little elevated above the river, that the scattered hamlets which dot its surface are without exception raised on mounds, pre-

F

bably artificial works of a now distant age. A stream or two traverse its farther part and flow into the main river. This flat is completely covered during summer, and in fact the same may be said of all the low land around Hankow, so that a view at that season from this position presents an almost unbroken expanse of water. Carrying his eye to the right bank of the Yang-tsze, he sees enormous lakes and lagoons both to the north-east and south-east sides of the hills beyond the provincial city. To the south-west he may observe a hill or two in the far distance, whence the "Blue River" winds like a silver band, but still with large expanses of water on either side; then his glance is brought up to the hills again, and, passing these, he has completed the panorama by returning to the Han.

Speaking of Wu-chang, the capital of Hoo-peh (north of the lake), and the residence of the viceroy governing both that province and Hoo-nan (south of the lake), which are sometimes included together under the name of Huk-wang, one of the gentlemen deputed by the Shanghai Chamber of Commerce to accompany the naval expedition, who had more facilities for observation than our short stay allowed us, writes in the 'North China Herald' thus:—"A ridge of hill runs through it nearly in the centre, commanding the view of the whole space within the walls. In this hill there is a gap through which one of the chief streets runs, and near this gap is a belfry-tower under which the street passes. This was apparently mistaken by the first visitors for the tunnel under the hill spoken of in Mr. Oliphant's book, for nothing else in any way like a tunnel could be discovered. The chief buildings, besides the Yamuns, are a Confucian temple; the Examination Hall, with separate cells, each about four feet square, for 8000 candidates, who assemble from the two provinces once in three years; a powder manufactory; and a walled garden and house—the latter destroyed by the Rebels

made an expedition for five days up the Han, intending to run up some of the nearer tributaries towards the hills to the north, as time would not admit of their attempting to reach Seyang. The Fates and the Chinese boatmen, however, were adverse: whether the smaller streams were really deficient in water, or whether the boatmen could not realize the idea of men going up a small river when a larger one was before them, must remain a mystery. The trip, however, was not without interest, through a vast level plain from which the water has to be kept out by embankments. These were generally under repair, and a great deal of patient industry was being bestowed on them; much damage had been done by excess of water last year (1860), the crops being reduced to eight-tenths of an average, and much loss incurred by houses falling in. Probably a survey and works on a comprehensive plan would secure the whole of this magnificently fertile alluvial plain from the one evil which checks its prosperity. As an old Chinaman said—If they got no flood for ten years they got very rich, but when the waters rose they suffered much loss and misery. Wheat is largely grown. Millet-stalks also, ten or twelve feet long, were to be seen. The wheel for spinning cotton is in every cottage. The people, both in the country and towns, were quite civil and friendly; provisions were cheap and good. The villages are mostly built on the banks of the rivers or lakes, of which there are many on the raised Bunds. The fields are lower and perfectly level, looking as smooth as a billiard-table."

But what need I say more of this great emporium of commerce? When we visited it, not an European—excepting a disguised priest or two of the Romish Church—was within hundreds of miles of it; now, merchants and missionaries follow their avocations without secrecy, and a vessel of war lies off the town to remind the Celestials of the promise they made at Tien-tsin, of Yuen-ming-yuen, and of the barbarian force that has been within the walls of Peking.

CHAPTER V.

ADMIRAL HOPE'S EXPLORATION.

WE arrived at Hankow just one month after our departure from Shanghai. Hankow is 588 geographical or 676 statute miles from Shanghai.

On the following day, at a visit of ceremony which Sir James Hope paid to the Viceroy of Hoo-peh, our expedition was duly represented; and when Mr. Parkes intimated to His Excellency that our little party had the intention of penetrating into the interior, and that it might be as well for us, as the first Europeans travelling under the new treaty-rights, to be accompanied by some one having authority, the Viceroy at once nominated a military mandarin to accompany us to the limits of his jurisdiction. He, moreover, countersigned our passports,* which we had obtained from H. M. Consul at Shanghai, and promised to inform the Viceroy of the next province — Sz'chuan — concerning us, by letter to be sent overland.

The Admiral now decided on continuing his voyage with only one gun-boat, besides his own vessel the 'Coromandel,' but offered to take us in tow. We therefore hired a passage-boat capable of accommodating our party comfortably, making an agreement for forty-five dollars to I-chang.

It was some time before those who negociated the hire of the junk could bring the skipper to realize the fact that she must be alongside the steamer the same day, in order that we might shift our baggage into her; such a rapid proceeding was altogether beyond his Celestial comprehension. At

---

* See Appendix.

last, however, he agreed to do as was required, and during the afternoon, while most of the officers were with the Admiral on his visit, we made our transfer. The summary mode in which we proceeded to do it, however, did not suit our skipper; he protested that the junk was not ready, and became most irate, stamping and foaming like a madman, varying the performance occasionally by a good blubber. We were luckily without interpreters, and so took a practical method of settling the difficulty by lowering a heavy box on to the head of the old fellow, who had placed himself right in the gangway. This proved at once efficacious; so, getting the Chinese boatmen to work, and being assisted by some of the sailors and our Seikhs, we very soon got everything on board; and then finding out the old skipper, who had retired sulkily into his cabin, we gave him a good stiff glass of grog, which set matters all right in that quarter, and we saw no more of him for the day.

In the evening we were entertained on board the 'Couper' at a farewell dinner, where the wishes that success might attend us on our proposed journey were universal; in the midst of the jollity there was a sudden cry of "Man overboard!" The officers hastily left the table, boats were lowered, and immediate search made for the missing man; but the night being quite dark and the current strong, notwithstanding that some of the boats went a long way down the river, no trace was found of the poor fellow. He was one of the crew of Commander Ward's gig, and had been selected from among a number to fill that situation. Having shared in much hard service in China, he was now taken away while on almost a pleasure excursion. Such are the workings of the Almighty by which He shows His power, to convince us of our own littleness, and the frailty of all things mortal. This sad accident threw a gloom over the party. We separated earlier than we should otherwise have done; and having shaken hands with all our friends, we left the 'Couper' and her agreeable society, and went to take our night's rest in the junk, which was now secured by hawsers astern of the 'Coromandel.'

And here, as a preface to what follows in these desultory notes, let me observe that, proceeding as our small expedition did from the seaboard almost to the western confines of the empire, through seventeen degrees of longitude, or eighteen hundred miles from Shanghai as far as the country of the independent tribes, we passed through portions of six provinces; still I do not consider that I am more entitled to speak of "China and the Chinese"—so favourite an expression with pamphleteers and speech-manufacturers—than one who, shut up in the old factories of Canton, gained his personal knowledge of the interior from observations made during a picnic on the White Cloud Mountains, or a visit to Fatshan. No: having only touched upon some provinces, and merely seen others from steamers, all that I could narrate concerning them would be mere hearsay: I have therefore studiously avoided any generalizations. In these pages no attempt is made at anything beyond a simple record of facts—they contain our observations on the people and country as we saw them ourselves, and our deductions therefrom.

The morning of the 13th of March (a most inauspicious one by the way) found the now diminutive squadron ploughing against the wind and muddy current in a south-westerly direction, the 'Bouncer' with the surveying staff leading.

A good stock of provisions in the shape of fowls, eggs, and flour, with charcoal for cooking, had been laid in at Hankow; besides which, Lieutenant (now Commander) Broad of the 'Couper' had kindly supplied us, by the Admiral's order, with salt meat and biscuit from the ship's stores, and a number of other necessaries from the officers' mess, so that we made a pretty fair start in the eating way at our first breakfast on board the junk. One of the few drawbacks was the depth of our tin plates, which precluded the ordinary method of holding the knife and fork, the effect of which has been to force on me a habit which I have never got rid of to this day. We had selected plates of that form on account of their being able to serve for soup as well as meat; for having, as we expected, to travel a long distance overland, we were desirous of keeping our baggage within the smallest possible limits. We soon became accustomed to them however, and consoled ourselves with the reflection that we might "go farther and fare worse."

Our little party being now collected by itself, we began to look upon one another as fellow-travellers; and I doubt not that each revolved in his head over and over again the first impressions which he formed from the outward appearance of his companions. For my part, I did so, as I then placed some little, though not much, faith in such signs. I have now, however, quite given up such a belief; and should no more credit a person who would judge of others by the countenance, mode of speaking, or handwriting, than I could come to the conclusion that the moon is made of green cheese.

It was thickly overcast and raining all the forenoon, so that we saw little of the country except the immediate banks of the river; and it must have been very disagreeable for Commander Ward and his staff, who were continually surveying as we went along. At noon we passed the "Golden Hill," just below the town of King-kow on the right bank, and then entered an extensive plain which forms the valley of the Yang-tsze, and on its northern side is unbroken by a single eminence for some hundreds of miles. The riverbanks are low, and only prevented from being extremely monotonous by the occurrence of small villages and hamlets along them. Porpoises kept us company, seeming to delight in racing with the steamers, of which they must have formed all kinds of conjectures, being only accustomed to the slow-going native junks, for we were now in waters which had never before been cleft by the stem of a European-built vessel; we were above Lord Elgin's farthest in 1858, and, in fact, a greater distance into the interior than any undisguised foreigners had yet penetrated. Our skipper, too, seemed to fancy that we were moving at a tremendous rate, for he set to work and tied the old junk together with ropes in every imaginable way, lest the Admiral's vessel, astern of which we were towing, should tear the stem out of her.

The direct course of the river from Tung-ting Lake to Hankow is north-east, but at thirty miles above Hankow a great bend occurs, which, while it may be cut off by half a mile overland across the neck—and this was actually done by our expedition on its downward voyage, when the country was flooded—the circuit the curve makes is thirty miles. The vessels anchored for the first night in this bend.

When they first stopped and searched about for a good anchorage, it was most amusing to see the antics that our skipper went through, signalling to those on board the vessels to go over towards the other shore; and he gave a great many explanations why they should do so, evidently thinking all the time that they wanted to make fast to the bank, in the same way as he would have done with his junk.

We started at 6 A.M. on the 14th, and when we got beyond a large low island, which has been called "Ashby Island," near the upper part of the "Great Bend," we passed the villages of Lung-kow and Pai-chow, both on the right bank, and above this met with a great fleet of junks sailing down the river. Many of them were very clipper-looking craft, and we were informed that they were mostly from the Tung-ting Lake. The district from which a boat hails can be easily told by the peculiarity of its build or rig. Long strings of junks too were tracking, or towing, up against stream under the high alluvial banks; they seemed usually to travel in these companies or fleets, probably for mutual protection against pirates, although we did not hear of any of those river robbers.

At noon we came up to a point where Commander Ward went ashore for the purpose of determining the latitude, but the sky becoming clouded over he was not able to obtain a meridian observation. It must have been very annoying to him, because he had come all the way from Hankow without sights, and, no matter how carefully a running survey of this kind is conducted, the advantages of stations laid down by celestial observations cannot be overrated. Great credit is certainly due to the surveying staff for the way in which they laid down this 150 miles of river under such adverse circumstances. I am glad to be enabled to state that a very complete chart of it is now among other valuable records in the Hydrographical Office, and Admiral Washington has been kind enough to allow Mr. Arrowsmith to make use of it so as to bring mine down to a known point, Hankow.

Dip-nets were very common along the banks. They are large affairs very ingeniously contrived, so that they can be lowered into the water, where they remain until the China-man thinks there may be some fish over them, or has just finished his pipe, which he has been smoking during his time of watch, when by means of a lever the machine is lifted, and the net brought to the surface; when, if there happen to be a luckless perch in it, he is scooped out with a small kind of landing-net affixed to the end of a long bamboo, and the machine is lowered again. The watcher has usually a small hut built on the bank alongside, in which he is protected from the inclemency of the weather, or the too powerful rays of the sun. These same kind of nets are also rigged on boats, which is advantageous, as the fishing ground can then be frequently changed.

We observed a good many rafts on this portion of the Yang-tsze. They were usually some two or three hundred yards long, but being formed in sections they could be easily divided. Small huts or shanties were erected on them where those engaged in their navigation lived; and as we swept past, and the waves set in motion by the paddles washed up among the logs, the lumberers and their families came out and gazed in mute admiration and wonder. What seemed to astonish them most was the gun-boat being able to go along without any paddles, the screw being immersed in the water and not visible. We had seen at Hankow a great quantity of timber which had been brought down in these rafts, and a good deal of boatbuilding was going on at Han-yang. Since trade has been opened on the Yang-tsze very large rafts have been sent down from Hankow to Shanghai by European merchants, some as much as 600 feet long, but the timber is mostly small. This timber is said to come all, or nearly all, from the borders of Tung-ting Lake; and such is most probable, or rather it is brought down the rivers flowing into that lake, because on the lower portion of the Upper Yang-tsze we saw little or nothing in this way.

Above the "Great Bend" hills are soon seen in the distance to the south; and although the land in the immediate vicinity of the river retains its low and flat character, at a little distance one can discern an undulating country, in some parts tolerably wooded. Higher up a few outstanding bluffs approach the river, and the scenery becomes interesting. On the second night our anchorage was off the mouth of a creek which falls in on the right bank, called Shi-ta-kow, just above the ruined temple and village of Lo-gi-kow, in the district of Kia-yu.

When we anchored, numbers of boats came off from the

shore offering fish for sale at a low price, some of which we found very good eating. We only bought one, however, out of curiosity, as being of a very singular appearance. Dr. Barton's sketch will explain it better than I can in writing. It was three feet in length, with a large bell-shaped projecting mouth, and a snout or horn sticking out over twelve inches beyond the head. From these particulars naturalists may perhaps be able to recognise the species; it had somewhat the appearance of a dog-fish or shark.

With respect to the various English names under which the Yang-tsze Kiang is known, as "Son of the Ocean," "Great River," "Blue River," and "Gold Sand River," I should remark that these are translations of the native names for different parts of its course; but there is one, namely, the first, and most important, because it is taken to be the translation of "Yang-tsze," of the validity of which there seems to be some doubt. Huc, who is a good authority—I am a believer in Huc—calls it the "Child of the Ocean;" though possibly knowing better, the Abbé did not like to interfere with an accepted poetical idea. It has also been interpreted the "Son that spreads," but I am informed that this interpretation is erroneous. The whole matter depends on the Chinese character "Yang," and it is difficult to say what it signifies in this instance. By the Rev. Mr. Wylie the literal translation is considered to be "the river of, or belonging to, Yang," Yang being the name of a former eastern division of the empire, of which Yang-chow on the Grand Canal to the north of Chin-kiang was one of the principal towns. With all this, however, judging from so many other names in China being expressive of poetical ideas, I am inclined still to believe that the first is the right translation, and shall continue, and I hope others will do likewise, to use this appropriate synonym for this greatest of rivers in the Old World. If we once begin to inquire too closely into our geographical names, and endeavour to substitute others for those which were first bestowed, although sometimes in ignorance, there will be no end to the task, and great confusion must be the result; we should have no "Father of Waters" for the Mississippi, and the names of places famous in British India and in the colonies would suffer severe mutilation.

Soon after starting on the 15th, the 'Bouncer,' which was leading, ran into shoal water, and the 'Coromandel,' being instantly stopped and backed, caused our junk to come into collision with her. No more damage, however, was done than giving the old craft a good shaking, and carrying away what is called in nautical language some of the "gingerbread" upper works. We were hailed from the flag vessel to "cast off the hawser," but casting off was no easy matter, for the old skipper had so twined and twisted ropes round the bumpkin to which the hawser was made fast, that it was not until short work had been made of the Chinese grass ropes with a hatchet that we managed to get it clear. For my part I must confess that I was not very energetic in my endeavours to let go, because I thought it very likely, if we once did so, we should never get hold of the steamer again. Sir James Hope, however, was too well inclined to render us every assistance as far as he went, and to give us a good start on our long journey, to think of leaving us in the lurch; so after the channel had been found, and all was in a fair way for going ahead again, we were once more taken in tow.

The weather was a decided improvement on the two previous days; and we sat most of the time on the roof of the deck-house, looking at the different objects of interest which met our gaze in the numerous craft which dotted the water, the inhabitants on shore, &c. Both our military mandarin and the old skipper took great delight in viewing the passing scenes through our field-glasses, the mode of using which they were not long in comprehending. What we always found amuse the Chinamen very much was to reverse a telescope after they had been looking through it the right way, and let them see the same objects thrown to a great distance. The skipper, who was a piratical-looking old fellow, informed us that he had been once a merchant at Canton, but that he now belonged to Tung-an (hien) in the province of Hoo-nan. He stated himself to be sixty-three, but from the habitual use of opium he looked much older. He had the remains of a pigtail of a grizzly nature, a few hairs on his chin, and a thin moustache; his countenance was very peculiar, and, with his small eyes, gave one the idea of a droll dog, but an accomplished scoundrel. We called him the "Aulo Piecy." In the descriptions of his former life, which he favoured us with occasionally, he amused us exceedingly; and we had many a good laugh when he got on the subject of the navigation of the river, and commented on the doings of the gun-boats when searching ahead for the channel. On some occasions he would get quite irate at the stupidity, as he thought it, of the commander in losing the lead of the channel, and would go through all kinds of antics in describing to us the proper way. He evidently knew all this part of the river very well, and I would strongly recommend him as a pilot to any vessel intending to navigate these waters. He rejoices in the name of Ou-hung Foo.

After passing great numbers of junks bound both up and down, on the forenoon of the third day we came to the open town of Sing-ti, on the left bank, ninety-eight geographical miles from Hankow. Its appearance gave us the idea of its having a large population, and the number of junks and piles of timber along the shores manifested considerable mercantile prosperity. As the vessels of the squadron passed up, the inhabitants crowded in immense numbers on the roofs of the houses and high sterns of the junks, in wonder and amazement at the "barbarian devil ships," for the first time ploughing these virgin waters; and we might perhaps have formed too high an estimate of their numbers.

In this part of the river, when our party returned in June, the water had risen to such a height that the whole country to the north was submerged, showing in many places a clear horizon, the only signs of land being the tops of some embankments, clumps of trees, and housetops; while on the other side, the flooded valleys of the Kiun range and its extension had the appearance of arms of the sea. Yet all this, if we are to believe Chinese report, is of annual occurrence; goods and chattels are removed, and whole villages deserted. Where do the people go? It has been said of the lower portion of the river that "they flock to the higher grounds." But the higher grounds were fully peopled before. We suppose they live afloat and support themselves by fishing.

Towards the upper end of the long straight reach above Sing-ti are a couple of narrows; in the second of which, during low water, a rock, called "Mo-pan-shih," stands exposed nearly in mid-channel; and from near the first a pagoda is visible, which marks the site of the town of Ling-hiang (hien), situated between two and three miles inland from the right shore, but not visible from the river. Proceeding upwards, we got a nearer view of the "Kiun-shan," and were reminded very much of "Lieu-shan" behind Kiu-kiang; but we did not consider this to be above three thousand feet at the outside, whereas the other, as I have mentioned, was calculated by the naval surveyors at four thousand feet above Poyang Lake. It is noticeable that these two similar mountain masses occur just at the outlet of the two greatest lakes in the empire.

At four o'clock in the afternoon of the 15th of March the squadron arrived at the junction of the outlet of the Tung-

YO-CHOW.

ting Lake and the Yang-tsze Kiang, one hundred and twenty-three sea miles above Hankow; where, thinking that it was but a short distance up to the lake, and that we of the junk would do very well with the fair wind then blowing, the Admiral cast us adrift. But who can foretell the wind or the weather? We did not reach Yo-chow, only seven miles distant, till eight o'clock next day, night having overtaken us and forced us to anchor in a creek filled with wind-bound junks, the crackers and gongs of which "chin-chinning"— as we supposed for a fair wind—kept us awake half the night.

Yo-chow (hien) is well situated on high ground, on the eastern side at the outlet of Tung-ting Lake. It does not seem to be an important place of trade. The chief gate in the western wall, on the brink of a steep bank, is a picturesque structure, with a fine flight of steps leading down to the water, and afforded the subject of a sketch for our artist. The suburb lies along the water to the south of the city, in which is a fine pagoda, while another low one stands on the summit of a hill a little inland. Beyond a promontory, jutting into the lake from the Hoo-nan shore, is an island about eight miles distant. Inland to the east the country is mountainous, while the opposite shores are so low that they cannot be defined at any distance, and must during summer be overflowed. A shoal, dry in March, bears from the city south-west, and about west from the large pagoda; it is about a mile in length, with a north and south position. The Taipings were at Yo-chow in 1852 or 1853 for one year, but then passed on down the Yang-tsze on their way to Nanking.

With respect to the Tung-ting Lake, not much is known concerning it. To the south there are extensive black-tea districts, in which the most important place seems to be Siang-tan, some distance up a river of the same name, coming from

G

the southern part of the province of Hoo-nan, where teas are collected for manipulation and packing for foreign markets. It has hitherto been in communication with Canton, viâ the "Meling Pass;" but now that Hankow is open as a foreign depôt, this produce is taking the more easy water route to that place. Great Kinshan, a hill on which a small quantity of tea is grown for the Emperor's own use, is to the south of the lake. The price for this tea is said to be 6400 cash per catty (about 20s. a pound), but it is not to be had for money. Chang-teh, a short distance up a river on the west of the lake, and Chang-shah on the east, are subsidiary ports to Siang-tan. Sinte, on the left bank of the river, is also a place of activity and importance. Pao-king, in the same province, and approachable by water from the Tung-ting Lake, is the place whence, we were informed, the coal which supplies the Hankow market is brought. The Canton expedition, which passed subsequently to our visit, speaks of seeing immense numbers of boats on the Tung-ting Lake; and there can be little doubt that a very large portion of the trade which centres at Hankow is from the country around that magnificent sheet of water; and it is consequently hoped that before long some port may be opened on its shores to foreign enterprise.

From the uncertainty of the date at which the Gulf of Pecheli might become suitable for naval operations, Sir James Hope decided not to delay any longer on the Yang-tsze. He had with vessels built in England, and which had "rounded the Cape," pushed into the very heart of a country hitherto so pertinaciously closed against foreigners; he had ascended over eight hundred miles, and so broken the seal of the Yang-tsze; he had done well, and could return with all honour. But we had expected to be towed a little farther; at least we wished it, and were therefore rather disappointed at the sudden decision of the Admiral. Three

CHAP. V.   RETURN OF THE SQUADRON.   83

hours were allowed us for our letters, and then, steam being up in the vessels, we paid our last visits to our friends on board.

Hoisting a red ensign in the junk, we dipped to H. M. S. 'Coromandel' and 'Bouncer.' They returned the compliment three times three; the paddles moved, the screw revolved, a signal was run up which we read, "Success to the expedition," and we were left to our own resources.

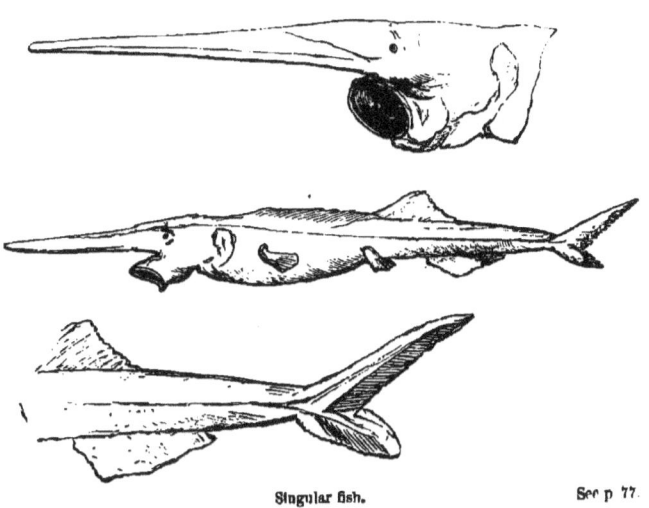

Singular fish.   See p 77.

CHAPTER VI.

JUNK-TRAVELLING IN HOO-PEH.

BEFORE proceeding to narrate the incidents of the next fifteen weeks that were consumed by our boat voyage in the interior of China, during which our own was the only European society we enjoyed, I ought to mention the composition of our party.

On leaving Shanghai we were four Europeans, four Seikhs, and four Chinese; but one of the latter falling sick was sent back with the naval squadron from Haukow. The three remaining were, a Chinese "writer," or as often called "teacher," to the missionary gentleman of the party; and two "boys," as servants are called in the Far East, Messrs. "Quei-quei" and "Bin-quei." The Seikhs were Sepoys of H. M. 11th Punjaub Infantry, Havildar Kumal Khan, and Privates Zuman Shah, Fuzil Deen, and Mahomed Buksh, with whom we had been allowed to augment our party by the Commander-in-Chief Sir Hope Grant, who showed in this and other ways his desire to conduce towards the success of our enterprise.

Our intention when the expedition was proposed was, by taking advantage of a clause in the Treaty of Tien-tsin, to have passed through China, thence into Tibet, and across the Himalayas into North-western India. The idea, I believe, originated with two of us simultaneously; and the third, throwing up, rather sooner than he would otherwise have done, a lucrative practice, jumped at once at the prospect of so novel and adventurous an undertaking. Our great difficulty at the outset was to engage the services of a competent

CHAP. VI. CHARACTER OF THE EXPEDITION. 85

interpreter, and this in the short space of time at our disposal for preparations we found impossible. At the eleventh hour, however, through the mediation of Bishop Boone, the head of an American mission, the Rev. Mr. Schereschewsky, being desirous of penetrating the country, agreed to form one of our party; and we thus, in place of a hireling, secured one who was himself interested in the success of the enterprise. The expedition was entirely private, the two military members being simply on leave of absence. Such was the expedition, which, although frustrated in its original object, has explored and surveyed over nine hundred miles of the Yang-tsze Kiang, where, if we except a few Roman Catholic missionaries disguised as natives, no European had ever penetrated, and reached a point eighteen hundred miles above its mouth, and beyond all trade, from whence it only returned on account of the disturbed state of the western country rendering farther progress impracticable.

I need enter into no more particulars connected with the organization of the Upper Yang-tsze Expedition, except that, during the few days which were at our command for making preparations, by the assistance of our friends and through the instrumentality of "taels," we managed to fit ourselves out pretty well in the way of arms, ammunition, tents, stores, and provisions. A portable boat was also made for one of the party, who, from his previous experience to the north of the Himalayas, judged that it would be a most useful auxiliary for sporting and exploring purposes. For the information of European readers I should mention that a "tael" of silver is the standard of value in all mercantile transactions at Shanghai. Its nominal value is, on the average, nearly one-third of a pound sterling; but experience proves that it really represents but one shilling, and in that respect is on a par with the dollar at Hong-kong and the rupee in India.

An eight-inch sextant and artificial horizon, prismatic compass, pocket compasses, and thermometers, together with a couple of aneroid barometers furnished by gentlemen in Shanghai, telescopes and binoculars, were our scientific instruments; but a good pocket chronometer was not obtainable, and we were forced to be contented with a very inferior article supplied at an exorbitant price. For our expenses by the way, we each took some couple of hundred Mexican dollars to commence with, but the rest of our money, amounting to eighteen hundred dollars or four hundred pounds, was in lumps of silver known as "sycee." In arms we were well supplied, having swords, shot-guns, rifles (breech and muzzle loaders), and revolvers. The tents were small ones made to our own patterns, and would no doubt have been most useful on the highlands of Tibet, but as it was they were never unrolled. What we took in the way of provisions was principally confined to some tins of soups, sauces, pepper, mustard, butter, a ham to begin with, chocolate, tea, salt, and preserved vegetable. This last we found remarkably useful, and I would strongly recommend it to the consideration of future travellers. For the main articles of animal food, as well as sugar, rice, flour, and such like, we trusted to the resources of the country. The heaviest portion of our baggage was the ammunition, preferring to start with a goodly supply of bullets and shot, even if we should be obliged to abandon some, rather than fall short of what might be of vital importance. We carried a few small things for presents, such as knives and scissors, and as we went along got rid of most of our superfluous articles of toilet in that way. We took a supply of brandy in two small kegs, which was intended to last us on the overland journey; besides which we laid in some beer and wine for the boat voyage, the premature exhaustion of which will account for the names of "No Beer Channel" and "Last

Bottle Reach," which appear on the chart much lower down than we had anticipated. A bag of ship biscuit was taken as a stay to fall back upon in the event of our flour at any time failing, or the cook falling sick; but such a capital boy was our *maitre de cuisine*, and so good a baker, that when we returned half of it still remained. Some missionary books in Chinese were amongst the cargo. Cooking utensils, tin plates, a couple of sheet-iron stoves, portable camp bedsteads, and our saddlery, served to swell the amount of "*impedimenta*" unfortunately necessary in such an expedition.

The last chapter closed on the receding forms of Sir James Hope's steamers, as the strong current accelerated their speed towards the ocean. We had sent letters informing our friends that we had fairly started for Tibet, and that everything looked propitious; they were dated "Yo-chow, entrance of Tung-ting Lake, 150 miles above Hankow, 16th March, 1861."

The skipper of our junk is ashore engaging extra hands, as he will now have no steam to help him along; two of our number are on a visit to the principal mandarin, to see about a flag and lanterns, as a pass for our junk; and the boatmen are all drunk in the nearest samshoo-shop: I have therefore time to describe our Celestial craft. She is a large flat-bottomed vessel, drawing between eighteen inches and two feet of water, eighty feet long by ten wide, with a rising bow and cocked-up stern. A guard or sponson runs along each side, which is used as a means of communication from one part to the other, and on which the crew walk when poling. She has only one mast erected, but another is on board to be used if required. On the mast, which is nearly amidships, is a large sail of very light cotton, a rather ragged-looking affair, with many bamboos crossing it horizontally. It is of the ordinary Chinese butterfly-wing form, and has a cord from each bamboo, which are collected and fastened to three sheets leading aft. With the exception of a small space forward, where there are three grapple-looking anchors lying over the bows, and a small capstan stands, the whole length of the junk is housed over, with doors and windows along the sides, the latter of oyster-shell and paper. The wheel-house, as we called it, is higher than the rest, to allow of the helmsman seeing clearly, and is occupied by a long unhandy tiller connecting with a large double-fanned rudder. She is varnished, and appears of a dark oak colour. The cabin accommodation is good, divided off by bulk-heads athwart-ship, moveable at pleasure, and affords room for, in the fore part, the crew, cook, and servants, then our mandarin and his attendants, two bedrooms and a dining-saloon for ourselves, and still another portion aft for the Seikhs. The hold is divided in compartments—a fashion, by the way, only lately adopted by our enlightened shipbuilders, but general in Chinese naval architecture ever since a former emperor, as the story goes, kicked off his shoe as a model for junks. Such was our junk. She lay to an anchor off the principal gate of Yo-chow, in the province of Hoo-nan, an English ensign waving proudly from a Chinese bamboo.

We begin to get tired of waiting so long; we have sketched in the headlands of the commencement of Tung-ting Lake, and so we rouse the skipper, and he raises a deafening noise on a brass gong. It is some time before our boatmen turn up, but they drop in gradually by ones and twos, and at last only the chief mate is wanting. We advise the captain to clear out without him, but he replies that he is a chip of the old block.

It was near six o'clock before we got under way that afternoon, when, rounding the point of Yo-chow, we lost sight of the Tung-ting Ho, skulled steadily down stream, and halted for the night at the mouth of "Seven-li Creek," only two and a half miles distant. The afternoon had been rainy, and evening set in for a wet night. As soon as the boat was secured, dinner was served in our cabin; and attended by one of the Chinese boys and two Seikhs, one of whom proved a very handy servant, we discussed the tin of soup, couple of roast fowls, and bread and butter, with the feeling of men who, now clearly launched on an enterprise which to prove successful required the exercise of perseverance and determination, could do no better than intrust themselves to the care of One ever watchful over the least of His creatures, but still keeping in mind that "God helps those who help themselves." An erroneous idea seems to have established itself that there existed a "chief" in our expedition; I therefore reiterate my former statement that it was strictly private, the expenses being defrayed by the three original members. H. M. Government had nothing to do directly or indirectly with the expedition, and no report has, to my knowledge, been made to any official quarter. My colleagues will, I know, be sorry that of themselves, now that difficulties and dangers are past, any one should be looked upon more than another, while in their far wanderings all had been by mutual consent equal.

After dinner the mandarin was invited into our apartment, and over a cup of tea he inhaled the fumes of tobacco and carried on a conversation with Mr. Schereschewsky, of which some portions were occasionally interpreted for the information of the rest of the company. Captain Mur-king-kow, for such was the rank and name of our gallant protector, was a large man for a Celestial, inheriting in this and his features a likeness to his ancestors the Manchoos, being a sprig of the ruling race, a Tartar. In common with large men in general, his intellectual powers, being distributed over a goodly frame, were not at first sight so apparent as they might have been in another; in fact, having been born and bred a soldier, his literary attainments were of narrow scope. But he had a good-natured countenance, and was of quiet disposition; too quiet, indeed, for us. As I have before mentioned, he had been appointed by the Viceroy at Hankow to accompany our party; and he had with him a servant-boy and a full private of the Celestial army. He was ever anxious to learn all he could about foreigners; and we being equally desirous of obtaining similar information from him, our usual conversations were confined to a series of questions and answers, in which, of true knowledge gained, he certainly had the advantage.

The next morning, St. Patrick's day, a day to be remembered by the members of the " Upper Yang-tsze Expedition," four miles and a half on a N.N.E. course, down the stream of the " Tung-ting outlet," brought us to its confluence with the upper waters of the Yang-tsze, called by the Chinese "Kin-ho-kow," *i.e.* Mouth of the Golden River, whence its united streams flow towards Hankow and the ocean. The place will not be easily forgotten by me, for it was where we had two days previously been cast off by the 'Coromandel,' since which we had been to Yo-chow and back again, and whence we were now to commence our voyage of discovery. A wooded knoll crowned by a temple is situated here; in the winter season this spot is connected with the eastern or Hoonan shore by some low land, but during the summer level of the water it is an island. It is called " Lui-ku," the drum-beating knoll. Looking towards Tung-ting Lake, the left-hand shore of the outlet is broken by some red clay cliffs, then a bluff close to " Seven-li Creek," beyond which " Yo-chow Point " projects, and the top of the seven-storied pagoda is seen above it. On the opposite side, which belongs to the province of Hoo-peh, the land is quite low, and the Upper Yang-tsze makes its *début* with no more adornment than crumbling alluvial banks. Kiun-shan and the mountains to the eastward look well from this point, and distant hills can be seen from W.N.W. to N.W.

Commander Ward, R.N., and his assistants, had surveyed the one hundred and fifty miles of river between Hankow and Yo-chow; but, being unfortunate in the weather, no celestial observations had been obtained during those three days, while that of our start was equally unpropitious, so that the position of the confluence or junction rested on dead reckoning. This is, I am happy to say, not now the case; for on our return I obtained an observation at the "Red Cliffs," giving the latitude 29° 27·9′, which, cutting a south-west line from Hankow, places the confluence in lat. 29° 28·9′ N., and long. 113° 15·5′ E., differing only two miles from its position by dead reckoning carried for so long a distance, which I am glad to record in proof of the accuracy of which naval surveying is capable in skilful hands. This error has been still farther reduced on the Admiralty charts, for, the weather being more propitious during the downward voyage of the naval squadron, observations were obtained at two or three places between Yo-chow and Hankow. And here I ought to mention that, through the kindness of Admiral Hope and Commander Ward, our party was supplied with lead-line, boat-compass, and patent log; besides which I am indebted to Messrs. Farmer and Bedwell for kindly rating our watches, and rendering every assistance to start us fairly on our way.

At 7·25 A.M. we rounded the sand-point; and some of the boatmen, jumping ashore, commenced to track against the muddy current of the Upper Yang-tsze. The difference in colour from that of the "outlet" was striking, the latter being comparatively clear and of a much lighter hue; while the mingled current below was a sort of compromise between the two. In the amount of water the two streams were of about equal magnitude, but the "outlet" was somewhat wider and of less velocity than the Upper river. At a short distance up the left bank* there is a scattered village among some trees, and thence we continued still tracking, and occasionally, when the direction of the river allowed, helped a little by the sail. The alluvial banks, which exhibited various strata, more or less mixed with sand, were about eighteen feet high, and always quite precipitous on the concave side of the river; while opposite, the shore sloped gradually down, or ran out into long sand-points and mud-flats. The adjoining country was one dead level, with scattered hamlets and clumps of trees occurring at intervals, which, with the rain which continued almost incessantly the whole day, and our comparatively slow rate of progression after steaming, rendered this first rather a tedious day's journey. We named the first reach of the river "Tibet Reach;" but when we descended in June, and looked over the names we had bestowed, we decided that, as we did not reach Tibet, it would be as well to abolish "Tibet Reach;" it was consequently rechristened after that celebrated missionary whose writings had in many weary hours interested us, and in whose footsteps we had in many parts trodden; nor could we have done better than call the first reach of the Upper Yang-tsze by the name of Huc.

After passing a large temple, somewhat distant from the right bank, for the purpose of gaining that side most favourable for tracking, we crossed the river, which averaged about nine hundred yards in width. One of the party amused himself heaving the lead, which showed from five to seven fathoms; and thus we obtained a section of the river's bed, which was

---

* Geographical readers will excuse my saying that, when "right" and "left" are applied to the banks of a river, they indicate their position in reference to a person facing *down* the stream *towards* the sea.

almost invariably done whenever we crossed the river afterwards. The soundings are shown in the published chart of the river. We had made a considerable curve during the day; but now we entered a very decided bend, and, as we anchored in it for the night of the 17th, we named it "St. Patrick's Bend." The distance travelled was but fifteen geographical miles, making us only eleven and a half up the river.

On the second day we continued round "St. Patrick's Bend," passing a tolerable village called Sze-pa-kow, situated on the left bank. An observation for latitude on our downward voyage places the northern limit of this bend in 29° 36·5′. Thence our course was south, until we were within less than two miles of where we had been the day before, whence a sharp curve to the westward took us to the lower end of a long north and south stretch, which, from the first good view of the Nan-tsuin Hills which is obtained from it, we called after a prominent point on them, "Camel's Reach," and we anchored—that is, made fast to the shore—about a third of the distance up it, opposite the lower end of a shoal.

I think it was on this day that one of the party who had undertaken the catering—under the most favourable circumstances a most thankless office—decided that it was high time we should have a change in our daily fare. It had hitherto, ever since leaving Hankow, been fowls and eggs, eggs and fowls, until we had begun to wish that Noah had forgotten all about the genus *Gallus*. Whenever we wanted meat, one of the China boys went ashore with a string or two of copper cash, and invariably returned with eggs and fowls; the necks of the latter were forthwith wrung, and that evening we regaled ourselves with fowl soup and boiled fowls, I believe those out of the soup. We used eggs in place of milk for tea, ate eggs and rice for breakfast next morning, and tiffined off bread and butter. We were glad, therefore, to see the prospect of a change. Sheep we would have got if we could, but we had seen none since leaving Yo-chow, nor did we ever afterwards; goat would have served as a substitute, and have done equally for our Mussulmans, but goats appeared to be scarce in this region. A pig—a happy idea— yes, a pig. For this purpose, that is to get one, after an ineffectual attempt to shoot the sun at noon, which just at that particular time thought fit to hide himself behind a large mass of cloud, we went to a small collection of houses near by, intent on pig. The prelude to any business or transaction in China appears to be a series of compliments, not so much of the season as personal, and so it commenced in this instance; but when the subject of pork was at length broached, the Celestial agriculturists seemed unwilling to comply with the demand, at least so we, the uninitiated in the vernacular, were informed. Unfortunately we had not brought our guns ashore, or we should, I feel sure, have made pork in no time; but espying one likely-looking animal, and thinking we could take first and pay after, a grab was made at the quadruped. He escaped and bolted, and we after him, round the houses, in and out of fences, until we were fairly blown, and were obliged to haul off and acknowledge an activity in Chinese pigs for which we had not before given them credit. Our boats had moved some distance on; and during our walk to catch them up, the Chinese language, people, and pigs, came in each for a share of abuse, ending always with the poetical termination, "I'll go ashore and *shoot* a pig;" with the reservation, however, that no chow-chow turned up in the mean time. I do not know anything which is more likely to excite one's ire than deficiency of food; touch a man in the pocket you make him feel, but touch his stomach and he's a savage.

On the third day we made fifteen miles in a northerly direction, passing the village of Hia (lower) Chay-wan, and anchoring at Shang (upper) Chay-wan. They were both prosperous-looking places, and at the first we saw a large quantity of spars suitable for junk-masts. Some hamlets were also passed; but as these occur so frequently along the banks, I cannot pretend to notice them separately. During the whole day we had a capital view of the Nan-tsuin Hills; they are a group lying to the westward of this portion, and to the southward of the river higher up. One remarkable hill, which approaches within four miles of the river, we named the "Camel's Hump;" it is an excellent mark, and can in clear weather be made out distinctly from the "Tung-ting Outlet." We estimated it at about nine hundred feet above the river. From it the range runs towards the south-west, the intervening country being undulating and partially wooded. An observation for latitude was obtained this day, which allowed of some points being well laid down.

I should mention that in June, when we descended the river, we found the whole country to the southward of the Nan-tsuin Hills, as far as the eye could reach, under water; so much so that the course of the river could only be known by the strength of the current. It appears that the waters of Tung-ting Lake were unusually high at that time, so we were informed by the people, and that its effect of backing up the river and extending its own shores was the cause of this tremendous overflow. I fancy that there was one uniform sheet of water from the Upper Yang-tsze, below these Nan-tsuin Hills, to the lake itself.

Leaving Shang-chay-wan at 6 A.M. on the 20th, the course of the river first of all doubled back to the southward and south-west, forming the "Chay-wan Tongue." Then we tracked along the bank to the N.N.W. until the afternoon, when we ran seven miles before a fresh nor'-easter under full sail, and halted at the next point at four o'clock, on account of the wind being too strong to allow us to proceed up the reach beyond. There was a village nearly opposite, but we did not learn the name of it. As we were running up this reach, with the "Ass's Ears"—a prominent and peculiar hill, so named from its resemblance to a well-known landmark made in approaching Hong-kong from the southward—right ahead, we came suddenly on a shoal in the middle of the river; a portion was bare at that stage of the water, but on our passage down it was totally covered. It occurs very awkwardly, where one would hardly expect it; but is well marked by a peculiar boulder, on the top of an outlier of the Nan-tsuin Hills, called the "Ming Hill," and a south bearing of the Camel's Hump through a gap. The proper channel is to the north of it, in which in March we had 5, 6, and 6½ fathoms, and in June up to 9.

Our fifth day was that of the vernal equinox. We ascended a reach nearly north, and coming round a long sand-point halted for a noon observation, and by evening passed the village or open town of Tiau-hien, where a creek of considerable size comes in from the southward, having made between twenty-one and twenty-two geographical miles. On the left bank a level plain, from twenty-five to thirty feet above the river, stretched as far as could be swept by the eye, the soil being of a sandy loam, and the country having the appearance of being occasionally flooded, perhaps periodically in several years. Wheat was the staple production; but carrots, and especially beans, were also largely cultivated. Hamlets and scattered farm dwellings lined the banks where they were steep; but on the opposite shore the houses were far removed from the river at that season, which showed that the sand and mud flats, and low points, must be overflowed always during high water. In fact, throughout this portion of the river, that is, from its confluence with the outlet of Tung-ting Lake up to Shi-show, which we shall soon come to, a direct distance of 44 geographical miles, the river is so exceedingly tortuous that its course measures 120 miles. At every point is an extensive flat; and, the whole plain being of an alluvial nature, the river seems to be continually gouging out the land on one side and forming these flat points on the other, so that embankments have frequently to be renewed and dwellings shifted. Much of the country is not dyked in, and there we observed buffalo carts,—roughly-made vehicles with solid wheels; a Chinaman was usually perched on the back of the animal in the shafts, which made its way at a pace very suitable to Celestial patience. Some four-wheeled conveyances, but only a few, were also seen.

The view which is obtained from the river before reaching Tiau-hien is very fine. The Nan-tsuin Hills are then to the southward and eastward, and the nearest portion—a range running about south-west from the "Ass's Ears"—seems to be the highest of the whole, reaching up to fifteen hundred feet. This range is very decided, and, failing in getting any satisfactory name for it, we called it "Tiau-hien Range." At its foot are three or four pyramidical-shaped knolls, and between them and the river an extensive lake, which may during summer be connected with a lagoon which we observed in June to the northward of the "Ass's Ears." Looking westward, a couple of pointed hills may be seen in the far distance; they are the temple hills of Shi-show, only fourteen miles distant, but it took us two whole days in following the winding course of the river before we reached that place.

When the sky was sufficiently clear we usually halted

H

at mid-day for a latitude observation, and at first I found very great difficulty in inducing the Chinamen, who of course immediately collected around, to keep quiet, so as not to ruffle the surface of the mercury. Generally two or three Seikhs, and sometimes my companions, used to come ashore and keep the people at a distance; but as this caused a good deal of trouble, I afterwards hit upon a plan which answered admirably. It was, to allow the people to come quite close and have a good look while I was preparing for the observation, and when I wanted to commence I made them all sit down on the ground, having one Seikh alongside me to call any unruly one to order. They, thinking, I believe, that I was engaged in some "joss pidgin," or "medicine work," as Indians call it, were generally very orderly, and any one who was inclined to be restive was hissed down by the crowd. I could easily detect a movement by the vibration of the mercury in the artificial horizon; and seeing that I knew if a man moved behind me just as well as if before my eyes, they seemed to think that I had some mysterious mode of detection, which was not without its effect upon them. Latterly, however, on account of the too great altitude of the sun at noon, my observations were carried on mostly at night, when I was seldom much troubled with spectators.

Since commencing our voyage on the Upper Yang-tsze the thermometer had ranged from 47° to 64° Fahrenheit, the prevailing wind being north-easterly, with such variable weather as was to be expected at the season. As we walked along the banks, which we frequently did when the junk was tracking, we could do so with comfort in thick clothing. Waterfowl were still common in these latitudes, and we often saw large flocks of geese on the sandy flats, where they were of course unapproachable. There were moreover

A MID-DAY HALT.

pelicans; and one morning, having wounded one, we had an exciting hunt after the fellow with the junk, but he drifted so fast down stream that we were forced to give up the chase. Carrying our guns when ashore, we served to vary our fare occasionally with a brace or two of teal and a pheasant. The country people, who were all agriculturists, were invariably civil and quiet; they examined our cloth clothes and buttons with much interest, but I think what most took their fancy were our boots, particularly the laced ones. The people seemed poor, but not wretched; though the brushwood, reed, and mud-plastered hovels in which they lived would have been almost rejected as cattle-housing in any civilised country. The old mistress of the house was usually engaged spinning out cotton wool, and very frequently we found an old man perched on the frame of a revolving millstone, keeping a water-buffalo in company at its monotonous work. A shot from our guns was sufficient to bring out a crowd of young hopefuls; the pigs looked suspicious, but the dogs bolted at first sight. Below Shi-show large quantities of oziers are grown, which were being cut and transported up the river; and reeds we saw in large quantities, which are mixed with mud in the manufacture of houses.

On the 23rd of March, at 4 P.M., we reached Shi-show (hien), a small walled town of little importance. It is situated on the right bank, just at a very sudden bend of the river. Its wall was in a very dilapidated condition, and it might almost be passed without notice, were it not for a group of small hills which attract the attention at a long distance, and are the only eminences for miles round. These hills were visited by some of our party, and were pronounced to be of granite, though I certainly thought I could discern with a glass strata running N.E. by E., and S.W. by W., inclined about eighty degrees to the northward. The two most pointed ones were crowned with temples, and each had a few trees on its summit. The highest is about four hundred feet above the river. This was the first place where hills had touched upon the river bank since our leaving the Tung-ting Lake. Some extensive swamps lie to the eastward of the place. There was no appearance of business, and but few junks along the shore of the small suburb which lies just above the walled town.

The point or tongue of land opposite Shi-show runs into the river with a sandy spit, and, as there was some wind blowing at the time, we had a little difficulty in rounding it. This afforded our skipper an excuse for wanting to cross over to the town side; but, as we foresaw that the inevitable consequence of such a proceeding would be a delay there until next morning, we advised the old gentleman to the contrary. Finding that direct appeal did not answer, he resorted to stratagem, and tried us on the humane side, stating that he required rice for the crew, and, notwithstanding we had made him an advance of half the passage-money when we engaged him, he wished money from us to purchase it with; but we discovered that there was a sufficiency on board. He then turned rusty, ordered the men to knock off work, and went into his cabin. The crew was at this time six or seven in number. It was evident that a lesson was required; so two of the party forthwith hauled the skipper out by his tail, the boatmen were ordered to "proceed," and one of us kept guard on the roof of the house with a rifle, on the look-out if any should attempt to escape, and stirred the unwilling ones up with a mop-handle. One of the crew stepped forward to interfere between our people and the skipper, when a push sent him spinning over the bows backwards into the river; but not letting go of the bamboo pole

CHAP. VI.   OUR SKIPPER REFRACTORY.   101

he had in his hand, he passed under the junk and came up inshore of her, and was got on board. This so frightened both skipper and crew, that they set to work with a will, and, having poled along the shallow until we got to a suitable place, they jumped ashore with the tracking-line, and thus we carried the point in more ways than one.

"Skipper Point" will be seen on the chart opposite Shi-show. It marks the upper end of the most tortuous portion of the river, and will long be remembered by the members of the first Expedition on the Upper Yang-tsze.

Our Skipper and Mandarin.   See pp. 79 and 89.

CHAPTER VII.

SHI-SHOW TO I-CHANG.

By the foregoing chapter the reader should have gained some notion of the tediousness of boat travelling, and he can well imagine the impatience with which we looked forward to meeting with a place on the river marked on the map, as if to assure ourselves that we had made some real progress on our western journey. The day of our passing Shi-show, already mentioned, was our seventh on the Upper Yang-tsze, and we halted that night about a mile and a half above the place. The good effect of the principal incident of that day was evident on the following one, by our making good twenty-six geographical miles; and, the river's course being now tolerably direct, the evening found us well advanced northward, and we anchored above the village of Ho-hia. The first island of any extent which we had yet met with, since parting with the naval squadron, was passed early in the day, from which circumstance we named it "Sunday Island."

It is almost needless for me in this place to offer suggestions concerning the navigation of the river, as our observations on that head appear in connection with the chart; but I would remark that from Shi-show upwards the nature of the river differs considerably from what it is below that place. As I have already stated, for the first hundred-and-twenty miles, the Upper Yang-tsze is exceedingly tortuous. We passed up it at that season when, the waters being at their winter level, we could discern the position of the shoals and flats, and the nature of its banks: we returned when the water being at its highest concealed those features, and the country was so overflowed that the course of the river was only discoverable by the strength of the current and colour of the water. Future navigators, however, need apprehend no difficulty in the first state, if they will keep in mind that the channel is generally—I might say invariably—close to the *concave* shore, that precipitous banks only occur where the strength of the current sweeps past them, and that the shelving ones should be avoided. A few shoals exist, but they are well marked by bearings of hills, and other objects. Above Shi-show the river's course is comparatively direct; its average width is half a mile, but in some parts it expands to double that width. Low islands occur, and in some reaches shoals are not unfrequent; and the nature of the banks being, excepting at the bends, no longer a guide, some caution will be required. But the continual use of the lead enables us to say that as far as I-chang, which, for reasons which will be hereafter adduced, must be considered for the present as the head of steam navigation on this magnificent river, three fathoms will invariably be found at low water in the channel, but usually much more. The navigation cannot be called difficult, and I see no reason why steamers of large size should not ascend to that point, although no doubt river steamers would be more suitable. The current is moderate at low water, and far from strong at other times.

Ho-hia is a considerable village situated on the left bank of the river, just below where it turns to the eastward. Two of us walked through the place without being armed, and, save the heterogeneous mob which followed and preceded us, bidding fair to block the narrow street, we suffered no annoyance. Above the village is a large joss-house, and considerable expense has been incurred in facing the high embankment with stone, a part of which was then in course of construction of cut blocks, to guard against the encroachment of the river, which, being contracted to less than 700 yards, had here a stronger current than we had yet experienced, with eddies and whirls. We crossed just at these "narrows," and found it very deep, getting sixteen fathoms; and eight and a half, at twenty yards from the right bank, was the least. A good many cattle and ponies were seen about this neighbourhood, and the following words from the expedition "log" describe the country sufficiently for the day:—"Country quite flat. A very great deal much below the summer level of the river and as low as the river at present. Immense and finely-made embankments prevent inundation. The whole country highly cultivated; the dwellings distributed in small hamlets, usually with a few trees around each. Tobacco, cotton, rice, and wheat grown."

One swallow was supposed to be seen four days before, but this day, the 24th of March, there was no doubt about it; the pleasant associations usually connected, however, with the advent of these harbingers of summer, were somewhat marred by the feeling that we were yet advanced but a small stage of the long route we had cut out for ourselves before the close of the season. Other birds were also gathering from southern climes; and though geese, ducks, teal, and cranes had not yet entirely left us, three days later we saw a hoo-poe, and daily observed the mina, blackbird, black-capped tit, lark, green woodpecker, rook, white-necked crow, magpie, sandpiper, snipe, pheasant, and dove. Vegetables and fish were easily procurable in exchange for the requisite "cash."

We were brought to a stand next day soon after noon by a strong north breeze, which, later in the day, increased to a gale with heavy rain, but our barometer showed only a slight fall. It was just at the lower end of another island where we were forced to anchor, nor could we move for the whole of the following day; from this circumstance we named it

"Storm Island." The temperature fell to 46°, but the wind remained the whole time steadily at the one point, and blowing a gale. The country was a dead level as before described, and the same embankment, in some places twenty-five yards across the top, existed on the left bank of the river; but just at this place there was an intervening space of about a mile, and it is interesting to observe that this part without the embankment is a higher level than on the land side, so much so that many hamlets are built on it and only raised a few feet on earthen mounds. This difference of level, which a few miles higher up was as much as fifteen and twenty feet, and on which wheat was growing on ordinary arable land, in place of paddy-fields, into which the other part was cut up, might be accounted for by supposing the embankment or dyke to be of great antiquity, and that successive deposits of alluvium from the annual overflows have raised the level of the part outside. This system of dyke-land is continuous for some distance farther up the river; but there does not seem to be the same attention paid to its security everywhere, for we observed several places where the embankment was broken through; and in June, when we passed down, there was a great rush of water into such places, and the country was flooded far and wide. One would have thought that such works as these, the stability of which must affect thousands of industrious people, would have been under the supervision of the government, and such they may have been; but if so, their condition only proves the rotten state of that power. No creeks or streams entered the river at this part.

Making a start on the 27th, our eleventh day from the Tung-ting Lake, we reached by evening the town of Sha-sze, 170 miles from Tung-ting junction. It is a long unwalled straggling place on the left bank, with a fine stone pagoda on a point which juts into the river, and which may be seen at a very considerable distance. We were rather surprised at coming suddenly on a place where such a number of junks were collected, while we had met with so very few on the river between this place and the Tung-ting Lake; but this was accounted for when we learned that the "Taiping Creek," or canal, which we had before heard of as connecting the Tung-ting Lake with the upper river, comes out only eight li above, and that we were now at Kin-chow, a place which may be seen marked in large letters on any map of China. It ranks of the first order as a provincial city—a "foo"—but is only a garrison or Tartar town. It is about a mile above Sha-sze, and equally as far inland to the north of the river. In form it seemed, from the view we got of it, to be nearly a square, enclosed with high walls in the usual manner.

Sha-sze seems to be of considerable importance in a mercantile way, and the immense number of junks which we observed closely packed along the river bank, for nearly two miles, indicated a large trade on the river. It appears, however, that its importance is chiefly due to the transit business, the junks from Sz'chuan for the most part making this the end of their voyage in an easterly direction, and the cargoes for Hoo-nan and the south, as well as for Hankow and the lower Yang-tsze, being transported onward in boats of a different description. True, one sees Sz'chuan junks with their rounded sterns in the crowded waters of the Han, but their contents are but a very small proportion of the exports from that fertile province. Some transshipment is also done at I-chang, but it is not of the same amount as at Sha-sze. The reason of it appears to be that, as the Sz'chuan boats are built very strong, and suited especially for the rough navigation of the rapid river above, where sailing is a matter of secondary importance, they are too heavy and unsuited for the lake and tranquil river waters below; besides, the boatmen of Sz'chuan being a peculiar class, and bred up to one kind of occupation, and it requiring a far larger number to work each boat on the upper river than below, the discharged extra hands would be thrown out of work; in fact, we judged that that law which regulates such affairs in other places besides China, caused this particular division of labour, as any other would not pay.

We saw cotton in bales loading in Sz'chuan junks for transport to the west, and were told that cotton stuffs were manufactured in the neighbourhood. We also learned from the masters of junks and others that the cargoes from Sz'-chuan are mostly composed of salt (monopolized by government), sugar, tobacco, hemp, pepper, spice, opium, medicinal and other drugs, some silk and wax, and a little gold. Tea goes up the river. But more information on this head will be given when I come to speak of the trade of Chung-king, the principal mercantile place in the province of Sz'chuan. Coal is brought to this place from Hoo-nan on Tung-ting Lake, viâ the Taiping Canal; but it seems astonishing that such is the case, for one would have imagined that it might more easily have been brought down from Kwei above I-chang. A Mexican dollar passed for one thousand cash, and the prices of provisions were—tea, 140 cash per catty, charcoal 1800 cash per picul of a hundred catties, and flour 29 cash per catty. Persons unconnected with China may not be aware that a "catty" equals $1\frac{1}{4}$ lb. avoirdupois, and a "picul" consequently $133\frac{1}{4}$ lbs.

Having lain one night among the crowd of junks off the town, the next morning we moved up about a mile above, where we waited for the boys to procure provisions, and to give our mandarin a chance to visit his family, who resided at Kin-chow. The Doctor and myself took advantage of the delay to visit the pagoda, from the summit of which we obtained an extensive view of the surrounding country, and the river for a considerable distance. A round of angles was taken, and we did not forget to include some distant mountains to the N.W. and N., as they were the first we had seen for a long time, and relieved the uniform plain which lay stretched out in every other direction. From this elevated position we looked down on Kin-chow, although from the river it is not visible, being built on ground lower than it, and completely hidden by the embankments; the wall appeared to be in good repair, and in the eastern face we saw a gate surmounted with the usual pagoda-like edifice. Cypress, or a kind of cedar-tree, was common in the vicinity of the city. Sha-sze, we could observe, was built partly on the embankment and partly behind it, and is no doubt a populous place. On descending from the pagoda, we found the yard crammed full of people, waiting to get a sight of the two curious specimens of humanity; and great numbers followed us to the boat, where we found by this time a very large crowd collected. Of course on these occasions we could not be expected to admit visitors gratis, and, as the expedition had been got up without any notion of making it a mercantile speculation, we could not think of demanding admittance fees; therefore, to save ourselves trouble and annoyance, the sepoys had strict orders to allow no one on board, and I must say that in general this restriction on their inquisitiveness was taken very kindly by the people. The Seikhs themselves rather enjoyed being looked at, and their peculiar dress and dark complexions were often the means of screening us a good deal from special scrutiny.

Some of the principal mandarins paid us a visit, as they had heard from the Viceroy of the province that Sir James Hope would come thus far, and were consequently in daily expectation of seeing him; they expressed their regret that the Admiral had not carried out his original intention, in which we, who were beginning to get heartily tired of boat-travelling, entirely concurred. Our own mandarin also brought his wife and family to see us. They were Tartars, or rather went under that name, and followed the Tartar fashions in dress, and in not cramping the feet of the women. The ladies of the party were really pretty—if an European may be allowed to call any females pretty out of Europe—and were tastefully dressed in loose jackets and fancy trowsers, the younger ones having bright-coloured flowers set in their elaborately-dressed hair. A Chinese would never have thought of introducing the females of his establishment, particularly on an occasion like this, when they would be brought face to face with "the devils of the Western Ocean;" for it is even considered bad manners to refer to females in ordinary conversation, and yet we never recollect to have heard that Chinese ladies were particularly noted for chastity. It is another of the incongruities of this favoured nation.

It was two o'clock in the afternoon before we got away; but being helped along by an easterly breeze, we made good way up " Kin-chow Reach," and put ashore after dark at a small hamlet round the first point. At two and a half miles above the pagoda of Sha-sze there is a creek about forty yards wide, coming in from the northward; and three miles further up, but on the south side or right bank, is the Tai-ping-kow, or mouth of the Taiping Canal or Creek. A small village stands on the east side of the entrance, which is about one hundred yards wide. The stream is out of the main river, and in summer is considerable. On Chinese maps, and European ones which have been copied from them, this creek or canal—for I do not know which to call it—is shown making a direct course to the Tung-ting Ho, before reaching which it is joined by other waters. The time occupied by the voyage, we learned, is five days; and we were informed that on the upward journey between Yo-chow and Kin-chow there would be a saving in time by taking this route rather than keeping on the tortuous and strong current of the Yang-tsze; in fact, our skipper, before we left the Tung-ting Lake, wished very much to go by that way, but we then considered that a knowledge of the river was the more important. The next people who travel on these waters should explore this line of communication; for it would be very interesting to know what amount of the water of the upper river is carried away by this channel, and whether it would be navigable for large craft. There is a small creek—dry in winter—the entrance to which is opposite the lower end of Sha-sze, which is said—by joining, during high water, with the Taiping Canal—to save junks going up to the regular mouth. Two miles above the latter, as we passed down at midsummer, the embankment was broken away for about a quarter of a mile, allowing a considerable flood of the river to make its way in, and junks were taking this passage into the canal.

I have omitted to mention that Kin-chow is easily approached by land from Hankow; the distance, as the crow flies, is about a hundred miles west; it is called only five days' travelling on horseback, so that, unless the Tung-ting Lake be an object of interest, I should recommend others to travel this portion overland, as by so doing, unless they should go the whole way by steam, they would save themselves a very tedious journey on an uninteresting portion of the Yang-tsze.

From Kin-chow (speaking of going upwards) the river has a general westerly direction for thirty-four miles, when, curving sharply round to N.N.W., it skirts the edge of a mountainous country lying to the west of it, whence it receives one considerable tributary, at the mouth of which stands the town of I-tu (hien); before reaching this town Chi-kiang (hien) has to be passed, also on the right bank. Then a straight course, continued in the same direction, carries you to I-chang, where this fine river, averaging half a mile in width, suddenly changing its nature as if by magic, narrows to less than one-fourth of that width, and disappears in a deep and precipitous gorge through a confused mass of rugged mountains. This point then, I-chang (foo), I will not pass beyond in the present chapter, but will leave for the next chapter the account of our voyage through the gorges and rapids which monopolise the Upper Yang-tsze for the next one hundred miles.

But I have passed too quickly over the seventy miles between Kin-chow and I-chang. I should have said that the country retained the same dead level until we reached Kiang-kow, a village situated on the left bank of the river, about which in itself we observed nothing very particular, beyond the usual amount of Celestial architecture and Celestial odours, but here the first sign of a shingly beach was seen. Thence westward the country on the north bank rose a little some two miles inland, and distant hills were observed from north-west to south-west. We anchored only a short distance above, and next day in the forenoon passed the village of Tung-tsze, noticeable from a couple of red and white temples prominently situated, and soon came to an undulating and partially-wooded country on the left, and at first to a hilly and then to a mountainous country on the right bank. The soil is different from the alluvial deposits below, being mostly of a clayey nature, but gravelly in part, and the bed of the river in places stony. The change was to us most welcome; we had travelled for so long through the great alluvial plain which seems to fill up the triangular space between the two directions, south-east and north-east, of the Yang-tsze, above and below its junction with the waters from the Tung-ting Lake, and which may be said to extend from Hankow to I-chang, that we were heartily sick of the monotonous muddy banks and uniform horizon which had bounded our view. We hailed with delight the appearance of a hillock, and were in ecstacies when we beheld fine ranges of mountains backing one another, until they became faint in the blue haze of distance. These are called "Shih-urh-pei," or the "Mountains of the Seven Gates," and rise to about 2500 feet. It was on this day, too, that we observed in the vegetation the first signs of spring, which will account for the name "Spring" that we bestowed on an island which occurs immediately above the last-named place; and I recollect that we carried a fine slashing wind past it, which served fair for us until we reached a notable point where the river suddenly changes from its S.S.E. course downward from I-chang, and proceeds thence eastward towards Kin-chow. The village of Yang-chi, where there are lime-quarries, is situated on the right bank at this elbow, but is imperfectly seen on account of a low island which intervenes between it and the point. We obtained observations at this spot on our downward voyage; and in acknowledgment of the interest taken in, and encouragement and help bestowed on our expedition, by the two leaders in the late China war, we took the opportunity of attaching the names of "Hope" and "Grant" respectively to the island and the point. Good red-burnt tiles are made here.

A few miles of tracking above "Point Grant" brought us up to the town of Chi-kiang (hien); but as we kept the left bank, and were undesirous of any delay at this period of our journey, we saw only its somewhat imposing river front. We were told—and we saw substantial evidence of it as we repassed in June—that an unusual rise in the water, in the summer of 1860, had caused considerable damage among the buildings and to the wall in the lower part of the town, besides having destroyed much live stock on this part of the river. This accounted for the water-marks which we observed on the cliff at a confined part before reaching I-chang, at a height of fifty feet above the mean level of the river, and which we found it difficult to believe could be due to the ordinary summer rise.

Above Chi-kiang a tall pagoda, with a bush growing from its side, is seen up the river, and the following day, after somewhat of a *détour*, we passed another place called I-tu, also a hien, situated at the mouth of the Chin Kiang, a river which, from its delineation on native maps, has a course of considerable length, but, judging from the nature of the adjoining country, is likely to be for the most part through a mountainous region; and as we heard and saw no signs of trade, it cannot be of much importance. Hence to I-chang is a matter of a day's travelling up stream, but only a few hours down with the current; and a nearly perfectly straight reach, which absorbs the last seventeen miles, tends to set off the beauties of this truly picturesque district. With us the weather was just such as one would wish for—a cloudless sky with clear and dry atmosphere—it was the first really warm weather of the year, and it seemed as if we had skipped the intervening season and jumped suddenly from winter into summer. The thermometer stood at 47° at sunrise, and rose twenty degrees by noon. I-chang, or rather its smoke, and the pagoda about a couple of miles below the place, are within sight a long way down, and I thought at the time that I had never beheld a more beautiful river scene. On either hand the banks had become high and precipitous, bold cliffs of rock—a mixture of conglomerate and sandstone—rose immediately from deep water, allowing our boatmen no chance either of tracking or poling, and we were fain to make our way along with the skulls, assisted by a slight breeze. To our left hand, as we ascended—that is, beyond the river's right bank—was entirely a mountainous country, and we could observe it extended to the northward beyond the town, that lay on the other side in the river valley, behind which the country rose gently into plateaux and ridges, broken occasionally by a narrow, rice-planted valley, through which a quick-running stream carried the surplus drainings of the

I

paddy-land to the river. The vegetation was a beautiful combination of temperate and semi-tropical forms, while the occasional palm occurring here and there served to remind us that in these inland regions one must expect the extreme temperature to reach a high degree. Wheat was now over a foot high, and peas, beans, and peaches were in blossom. The country everywhere, except on the steepest slopes or where rock was exposed, was highly cultivated.

We had not seen our mandarin since leaving Kin-chow, and, thinking that he was following us by water, and that if he was to be of use anywhere it would be at I-chang, where we should have to change our junk, we halted about five miles short of the place, crossed to the west side of the river, and anchored for the day—the 1st of April—being the first time that we had stopped on our own account anywhere on the route. The professed sportsmen of the party employed themselves climbing the rugged conglomerate hills in search of game; but though an inviting-looking country in that respect, and wild enough in all conscience, for it was everywhere split up into ravines and gorges, they were but poorly rewarded in the feathered way, without even catching sight of a single four-footed creature. The day's bag, besides one pheasant and a woodcock, contained a specimen of the Chinese magpie (*Urocissa sinensis*), and a white-collared crow, which were added to our ornithological collection. Another of our party made his way to a kind of monastery situated on a pinnacle of rock, detached from the precipitous side of a mountain, at some distance from the river; while the fine day was made good use of for obtaining astronomical observations and getting through arrears of work. The river was found by sextant measurement to be 940 yards wide, and the depth varied from three-and-a-half to seven fathoms, with a moderate current. In June the water was fifteen feet higher.

Next day our maudarin turned up, having come overland. We moved up within a mile of the town, and at once commenced negociations for another junk and crew, the junk which we had brought from Hankow being unsuited to the navigation higher up. This, however, was not to be done in a hurry, as it appeared that nearly all the junks had been pressed into the Imperial service for the purpose of transporting troops to the country infested by rebels. I have forgotten to mention that we met several days below a fleet of some 150 junks bound down, while others were being despatched for the province of Sz'chuan. By the way, we have been so often, since our return to civilized parts, questioned as to whether the Sz'chuan rebels are connected with the Taipings, and if we had heard of Shi-ta-kai, one of their leaders, in Sz'chuan, where his friends on the Lower Yang-tsze maintain that he has gone, that it will be well to state at once, that as far as we could learn—and we made much inquiry on the subject —there is *at present no connection* between the rebellion in Sz'chuan and that which has devastated such an extent of country nearer the coast; and of Shi-ta-kai we heard, when in Sz'chuan, that he was in the province of Kwei-chow, near the frontier of the former. Possibly he may be able to induce the Sz'chuan rebels to join with the Taipings; but from what little we have seen of them, and judging more from their effects, we do not think that they are likely to improve even the Taipings; and, rather than insurrectionists with any fixed object in view, we should be inclined to call them unconnected bands of robbers. They differ from the Taipings in one particular, that they cut off the pigtail; not a bad plan either, since a man once deprived of that appendage would be slow to return tail-less among his former comrades; besides which, they do not appear to carry on any special crusade against the temples and pagodas. We heard also of rebels in Kwei-chow province; and in Yu-nan they are said to be very powerful, but the movement there is confined to Mussulmans. But more of this anon.

I-chang (called Y-lin in some maps), in latitude 30° 42' north, and approximate longitude 111° 20' east, is by the river 363 geographical miles above Hankow, or 950 total distance from Shanghai. Situated at the head of the navigation of the Yang-tsze for any steamers now in China, it must become an important place. The city is a tolerably-sized foo, or provincial town of the first order, and contains no doubt a considerable population; but I should add nothing to the accurate knowledge of the population of the empire, were I to give the numbers we obtained from the natives of this or any other town we visited. "Some myriads," was the usual answer to our inquiries on this head. The trade of the place would seem to be small; but as at Sha-sze, already mentioned, part of the Sz'chuan produce is here transshipped, and we observed a great many junks laid up awaiting employment. Mexican dollars sold for one thousand cash. Some Celestial Mussulmans here recognised our attendant sepoys as fellow-followers of the Prophet, and soon became remarkably familiar, "chin-chinning" to a great extent, and bringing presents of sweet cakes and other "chow-chow." We here noticed some scarlet-painted boats used for the preservation of life from drowning, an institution quite contrary to the doctrine which is prevalent in South China of never saving a drowning man.

We took up our position at some distance from the town, which practice, or that of anchoring on the opposite bank, when possible, we invariably adopted, to save annoyance; as, when circumstances necessitated our lying alongside the shore at a town, we were most terribly mobbed. The people were not usually uncivil, but they wished to "makey look see," and stray lumps of earth and an occasional stone would fall much too close to the junk to be agreeable; but we hoped that these were not thrown at us, or at any rate, if they were, we charitably believed that it was only done to attract our attention, and cause us to show our faces out of the windows; and a little forbearance on our part prevented any unpleasant disturbance. On these occasions we had a fellow feeling for the latest addition to the gardens of the Zoological Society, and, while realizing that most uncomfortable sensation of being gazed at to the fullest extent, we felt equally for the hippopotamus in his bath and the black bear at the bottom of the pit. "The animals will feed at — o'clock!" We don't know that such a notice was actually posted up in Chinese characters on our junk, but we likewise don't know half the ways in which our Chinese servants made money out of us, although we do know a good many. I feel sure, however, that our meal-hours were in some way made known to the populace, for at such times the crowd was always greatest and most inquisitive. To future travellers in the Central Flowery Land I would recommend a good bull-dog as a companion; he would, I think, be found most useful.

During the transfer of our traps from the old junk into the Sz'chuan passenger-boat in which we were to travel henceforward, by some carelessness the bag containing the screws and nuts belonging to Major Sarel's portable boat, which were intended for joining the sections together, fell overboard. The four Seikhs thereupon stripped themselves, and went through a lengthened series of aquatic performances, much to the amusement of the bystanders, who, to the no small detriment of the crops of the farmer of the land, were collected in a great crowd on the bank. But all endeavours proved fruitless, and the screws were irrecoverably lost. This was rather annoying, as it could not be expected that we should be able to wait long enough, even if others could be made, at any town on the way: but at the same time it was some satisfaction to know that a most useless piece of furniture was thus rendered unserviceable, and that, when we should come to arrange our things for travelling overland, it would allow of our lightening our baggage very considerably.

I-chang stands on a blunt point of the Yang-tsze and on its left bank, a small branch of the river forming an island immediately above the walled part of the town. The water is shoal off the city, the main lead of the river being nearer the other shore. The country to the rear or east and south-east is broken into small hills and ridges, and the upland soil is of a red clayey nature. Much ground is appropriated to graves close to the city, but beyond it is cultivated by irrigation, except the hill-tops and steep sides, on which clumps of small pine are dotted about. To the north, west, and south-west, the whole country is mountainous; but it is impossible to select any decided ranges or peaks from the confused mass. There are many curiously-formed mountain-tops, usually with one or more sides precipitous; but they are all much about the same level, and so jumbled together that seldom any particular one can be distinguished from more than one point of view. The monastery previously mentioned is on one of the most commanding positions, and was estimated at about 1000 feet above the river. Just below the city, and on the opposite or right bank, is a very decided cliff surmounted by a sharp peak, which has been called "I-chang Peak;" it is not nearly as high as others more inland, being about 400 feet, but has an imposing appearance from the river. The geological formation of this rugged region is a very coarse conglomerate, with sometimes sandstone associated.

It was on our seventeenth day from the Tung-ting Lake that we arrived at I-chang, and we remained there three days.

CHAPTER VIII.

GORGES AND RAPIDS.

NOTWITHSTANDING that at I-chang we were a thousand miles from the sea, porpoises had kept us company the entire distance, and it was only here that these last relics of the "briny deep" bid us farewell, and, giving an extra roll or two over for our especial edification, seemed to say, as plain as Canton English could speak—"That top-side river no belong Mr. Neptune King, hab got too muchey rock and rapid, makey all same chow-chow water!"—meaning thereby to inform us that the river above was no longer suited to their constitutions, and that, not being imbued with any great ardour for exploration, they preferred to remain and disport themselves in the more placid waters below. But we are in a new boat! and some five-and-twenty naked and half-naked fellows are dragging us along at a smart rate by a long plaited bamboo line, while I-chang is fast fading behind us. See how they have to scramble along the precipitous rocky shore! Sometimes on their hands and knees, at others with foothold only for their toes, or on sloping smooth rock where their grass sandals only keep them from slipping into the foaming current below. Now we see them high above us, running along on the verge of a precipice, and shouting like a lot of madmen; then they are down again and clambering round a point of rock which projects out into the river, and where some little cautiousness, which they seem to have among them, causes the leaders to get past the impediment first without the line, and then, it being thrown to them, they run on again with it, and leave the others to get round as best they can; then again they all come up, except always two or three who keep behind for the purpose of clearing the line from projecting rocks, and, hitching on the cords of their breast-straps to the towing or tracking-line by an ingenious turn of the button round it, away they go again like a pack of hounds in full cry. When they come to a place where the rush of the water is unusually strong, and necessitates a harder tug, one fellow, a wag or actor, jumps out from the rest, and, running ahead of the crowd, turns summersaults on the ground, and goes through other grotesque antics for the amusement of his companions; then, by way of a change, beginning with the foremost, he belabours them all round with a stick he carries for that purpose; then he runs ahead again, and going down on his knees "chin-chins" them, after the manner in which praying before the altar is performed in Bhuddist temples, as if to induce them by his entreaties to exert their strength; again he gives them a sound licking, or appears to do so, all round, and so on. He is the fool of the gang, and for a long time we considered the first whom we saw act in this capacity to be really an idiot. The line is now paid out from on board the junk, and made fast nearly amidships on a level with the gunwale, but is sprung upwards by a supernumerary line coming from the mast-head, and we sheer out into the stream to clear an outstanding rock; then in again and the line is shortened, and off the trackers start with a shout, and lay to their work like thoroughbreds. These are the Sz'chuan boatmen; we may well call them *voyageurs*.

For three miles above the town of I-chang the river retains the same character as it has for some distance below, except that on the right shore the banks are high and rocky; and in width the river has lessened nothing since dividing from the waters of Tung-ting Lake, being a good half-mile across;

but suddenly, as if by magic, we lose the "Son of the Ocean," and in its stead an impetuous current comes rushing towards us out of a long deep cleft in the mountains to the westward. The mouth of this gorge is not above two hundred and fifty yards in width, and its sides mount up vertically to three and five hundred feet, broken into crevices and ledges, where ferns and creepers of the brightest green flourish on the scanty soil of the moss-covered rock by the sides of dripping waterfalls; other plants, nestling in holes and corners, live a sunless existence, and relieve the rocky aspect of much of its harshness; while the dark foliage of small pine-trees on the tops of the cliffs, and an occasional bunch of bamboo, flourishing in all the freshness of spring, with the rugged peaks and sides of the higher mountains in the background, make up a scene of wild grandeur which baffles description, and might test the skill of no mean artist. The deep dark appearance of the water shut in from much of the light of day by the stupendous side-walls of rock, and the distant part of the gorge tinged by the bright atmospheric blue, yet still without end, and only broken by a miniature-looking junk with her spread of white canvas—this view, as it burst so unexpectedly on us as we rounded "Mussulman Point," and shut out I-chang and the plain of Hoo-peh, is one that will never become dimmed in my recollection by the lapse of time. I shall always remember—and it will recall many pleasing associations too—the entrance of the first gorge on the Yangtsze.

Our first day from I-chang we made ten geographical miles, which carried us just above the upper end of "I-chang Gorge," the course through which is first west-by-north, and then northerly. After the novelty of the thing wore off, this kind of travelling, where the view is so confined, became tedious, and we were glad to see a little more daylight on emerging from the dark shadows. At a small recess, which occurs about half-way through, there is an excise establishment; we were not interfered with, however, by the officials, but they came across the river for the purpose of taking a look at the novel description of human cargo which our junk carried. We tried soundings with the lead, but could find no bottom with sixteen fathoms in the middle, and got five, and sometimes more, close in to the banks. The mode of progression was for the most part with oars, of which the crew pulled about eight on either side, standing up to their work facing the bows, and taking short and quick strokes, stamping and singing away merrily the whole time. Occasionally we came to a part of the river where the shore, not being quite precipitous, allowed of a short spell of tracking; and advantage was always taken of such a place, it being much easier than rowing in so strong a current. When the wind was fair, and it is always either right astern or ahead in these narrow passes, the sail, a large square cotton one, was used, which was a very great help. The geological nature of this gorge was the conglomerate and sandstone already mentioned, and a kind of hard limestone; but on this subject I shall have more to say by and by.

Three or four junks, containing military levies proceeding up country to take part against the rebels of Sz'chuan, halted for the night near where we had taken up our station; and these same boats, sometimes ahead and sometimes following, kept company with us for the next day or two, affording us plenty of opportunities for making acquaintance with the *braves*. They are usually what would be called, among most communities, "ugly-looking customers," and, if all I hear be true, they do not belie their appearance. A *brave* seems not very particular about his nether garments, except that the lower part of his legs and his ankles are bandaged with black or dark blue cotton—a practice by the way common among the male sex throughout Sz'chuan; but he invariably wears a loose tunic of scarlet, yellow, or other gaudy colour, on which his number and the name of the corps to which he belongs are marked on a white circular patch in front—possibly designed for the enemy to aim at—and again on his back, in the largest Chinese characters that can be inscribed on so small a soldier. His *queue*, which is interwoven with a great deal of false hair and black silk, is coiled about his head, and round it he has twisted a turban of large dimensions. The practice of wearing turbans seems to be confined to these fellows, although most of the people in the western country, especially the boatmen, wear a single piece of blue or white cotton tied round the head; but the head-piece of the *brave* is of "brobdingnagian" proportions. Occasionally you see one with a matchlock, but they are for the most part armed only with a short sword or knife worn in the girdle. These gentlemen of the profession of arms, or I had better perhaps say plunder—no offence to the heroes of Yuen-ming-yuen by the way—seemed inclined to be pretty familiar with us, and were in most cases not disrespectful; but still I have to record, even during the first few days of our acquaintance, an unpleasant occurrence with one of their cloth, who stood in the way of a member of our party while engaged in sketching an interesting scene on the river, and, in place of moving quietly away when asked in the most polite English to do so, clutched the handle of his large knife, for which piece of impertinence he was instantly knocked down, and no more was heard of the matter.

The junk in which we were now travelling, and which we had hired at I-chang to take us as far as Quai-chow for the matter of fifty-five thousand copper cash, was a Sz'chuan "travelling" or passenger junk. She was not nearly as commodious or convenient as our former craft, being wanting in the platform round the outside; besides, the roof of the housed portion was so taken up with coils of bamboo ropes and lines, which were constantly being required for use, or being recoiled, that it was difficult to find a place anywhere outside of our cabin where you were not in somebody's way. We found it, therefore, rather an unpleasant change, particularly as the warm weather was now coming on; but it could not be helped, for it was the only kind of passenger-junk used on this part of the river. The forward half of the boat was uncovered, and the cook had his fire and copper in a hole in the middle. At night, or when we halted on account of the rain, a framework was quickly set up over this portion, and, being covered with waterproof mats, made a shelter under which the crew slept. The regular cargo-junks are much larger, some being above a hundred feet in length, with only a comparatively small portion housed over. All these Sz'chuan junks are of much the same form, with flat bottoms, square bows, and turned-up sterns, and are strongly put together to resist the knocking about which they get in the rapid and rocky portions of the river.

Soon after starting the next morning, the 6th of April, we experienced a heavy thunderstorm; the vivid flashes of lightning among the crags and peaks of the mountain-tops, and the continued reverberations of thunder,—echoing and re-echoing from the nearer cliffs and slopes of their sides, and then taken up by the more distant heights on either side of the magnificent river,—were extremely impressive. "There is but one God," they seemed to say, "and these are His works, and this His voice." Then after a deluge of rain, as the weather cleared up, and the mists slowly rolled up the valleys, and clouds yet hung over the mountain-tops, the little rills, now increased to impetuous torrents, came tumbling down the dark hill-sides, and leapt from high precipices, till they reached the turbid current below, which was rushing with irresistible force past the rocky impediments that here impeded its onward course. The scene was one that would

FIRST RAPIDS ON THE YANG-TSZE.

seldom be witnessed elsewhere. Foreign residents on the seaboard, desirous of a relief from the confinement of business, would do well to take a trip into the interior, and, without going beyond the limits of the province in which Hankow stands, they might see some of the finest river scenery in the world. This might be easily done by going overland from Hankow to I-chang, or, better still, a large party might take a steamer from Shanghai the whole way up; and then from I-chang, a couple of days by boat would take them beyond some of the finest rapids and into the midst of the gorges; a few hours' run down with the rapid current putting them again on board their own craft; after which I am sure they would admit that they had been well repaid for the little inconveniences incident to travelling under any circumstances.

The first rapid on the Yang-tsze occurs at a bend of the river shortly above the west end of "I-chang Gorge," at a distance of fifteen miles from I-chang, where some islands of rock stand out towards the middle of the stream, and large boulders of granite line the shores, indicating an uneven bed in the river. Here, although in April it could hardly be called a rapid, the rush of water in June was very strong, and immediately below were strong eddies and whirls. A small village stands on the right bank, just above this rapid; and less than a mile distant to the south, some high rugged peaks mark the end of a mountain-range of about two thousand feet in height, which runs thence in a south-westerly direction, nearly parallel with a short reach of the river, all along which lie heaps of granite boulders, forming small islands and promontories, causing the river to narrow in some places to 150 yards. Then we come to the village of Shan-tow-pien, where the river, pursuing a straight course south-east, is obstructed by a couple of dangerous rapids, and runs the whole way with a very strong current, while the shores are still broken with boulders and solid rock. The scenery here is very fine, for the hills near the river are not of such a height as to impede the view beyond, fine mountains being in sight on every side, but particularly to the west, where a very decided and precipitous range, having an altitude of about 2500 feet above the river, runs northward, and, crossing the river, causes the next but only a short gorge, known as "Lu-kan," the entrance to which may be seen in the distance. However, a few miles farther, another, the "Mi-tan," hems in the river for a couple of miles, whence a portion of the stream, very full of rocks and reefs, carries you up to Kwei—a small walled town, with neither trade nor anything else to give it importance—standing on sloping ground on the left bank, thirty-nine miles from I-chang.

But we did not get up in such a hurry, for, what with the difficulty of the navigation and the badness of the weather combined, we did not reach much above Shan-tow-pien, and halted at the foot of the rapid of Kwa-dung on the 6th; and it was on the fourth day from I-chang that we passed Kwei, our men having had hard work to get the boat up some of the more difficult places.

A very necessary prelude to the ascent of a rapid is for the skipper to go ashore with some strings of cash, and beat up all the people he can find (there is usually a permanent or temporary village close at hand) to help in hauling the line. Then all hands being ashore, except two or three men to manage the long sweep-oar (which projects out from the bow of the boat, and is used to shoot her out into the current, so as to clear rocks, which the steersman unaided would be unable to avoid), and two more to attend to the paying out and hauling in the tracking-line and to pole off rocks, and all else being ready, the strongest bamboo line being in use, the word is given and off the trackers start, sometimes eighty or a hundred on the line at once, and the boat stems the troubled waters and steadily ascends. Frequently there is a hitch in the performance, caused by the line getting foul of a rock out in the water, and then one or two of the most daring venture to swim out and clear it; or the junk itself runs on a sunken rock, and then great is the thumping on a small drum by the one-eyed cook, and shouting to stop the trackers hauling, which, amid the noise of the rapid and the general hubbub, is no easy matter. Then there is great difficulty to get her off the rock, and the boatmen have often to go into the water in the middle of the rapid. When she starts again, perhaps she goes safely up; or it may be the line breaks, and then away go boat and cargo at the mercy of the current, and probably do not bring up till she is a mile or two below; and not then, if she should strike a rock and go down in the middle, as sometimes happens. It is an animated and enlivening sight to see half-a-dozen boats following one another up a rapid, to hear the cries and shouts of the *voyageurs* echoed back from the cliffs, the fellows scrambling over the rocks, the crews working away on board to keep the boats from impending danger; and yet it is a scene that one may see enacted any day, on any one of the rapids between Kwei and I-chang on the Yang-tsze Kiang.

Now let me say a word or two concerning these rapids as influencing the future navigation of this great artery of China. In the first place it must be known that the state of the river depends on the seasons. Our expedition passed up in April, when, although not at its lowest (for the water was very muddy), the great summer rise—caused by the melting of the snow on the mountains between China and Tibet, and the highlands of the latter region—had not commenced. We repassed this portion of the river in June, when it was probably nearly at its highest, and had in appearance totally changed, rapids existing where there were none before, while former ones, by the rise in the water, had become smoothed over.

We were told at I-chang (and this agreed with information we obtained at other places) that the river is highest in June, continues high till the ninth month, say October, and is at its lowest in December, when its waters are said to be clear. During the great flood of 1860 the water rose at I-chang up to the permanently-built houses on the top of the bank, which were twenty feet above the water-level in June, 1861. Such an additional rise, where the river is half a mile wide, must have been enormous in the gorges and confined portion above; and we noted, on our upward voyage, water-lines on the precipitous sides of the gorges up to seventy feet above the level at that time; and all houses in the narrow parts are at a very considerable height.

The velocity of the current we had no means of determining as we ascended, for, our mode of getting along being to keep in the back eddies and close along the rocks, the "Patent Log," which we had used on the lower river, was here of no use. However, by the time we took coming down stream, we measured the force of the current to *average*, between Quai-chow and I-chang, six knots (geographical miles) per hour; while, below I-chang, for thirty miles it was not over four, and below that still less. Some of the rapids ran at least ten knots.

With regard to the situations of the rapids, I have before stated that the first occurs at fifteen miles above the city of I-chang, in the province of Hoo-peh, though in winter there may possibly be no rapid there at all. Thence upwards the course of the Yang-tsze is interrupted by rapids, more or less, as far as Chung-king in Sz'chuan, and even beyond that; but the greater number are mere minor rapids caused by the lowness of the water, and during summer would certainly be no obstruction to steam navigation, and most probably not even in winter. In the section of river from I-chang to Quai-chow, a distance of 102 miles, in which are the principal gorges, the case is different. Here occur many rapids, some of which are bad both during high and low water; and though I cannot here particularise them, so as to give a separate description of each, they will all be found marked on the large chart; the worst are below Kwei, and near the village of Shan-tow-pien.

But the question is, Is the river suitable for steam navigation? The opinion that my colleagues and myself came to on this matter was, that for steamers of any kind to ascend the rapids without being towed would certainly be impossible during low water, and probably so when the water was high; and that the only steamers that could ascend the rapids, or navigate any portion of the river above I-chang with safety, would be short, flat-bottomed, and full-powered vessels, with unconnected wheels and separate engines, something similar to the boats on the Upper Mississippi. A forward rudder, or sweep on the principle of the Sz'chuan junks, might be requisite; and light draft of water would be a consideration on the score of not catching the current sideways, and sheering off in eddies and whirls. No anchoring-ground being obtainable in many parts, vessels would require means for securing them to the shore. The difficulty of want of water need not be apprehended at any of the rapids; and, as to hauling up a small steamer, there would not, I think, be more difficulty, when aided by the engines, than with the large junks which now ply on the river. With another clause inserted in the treaties between foreign Powers and His Celestial Majesty, in regard to foreign bottoms above the open ports—and perhaps without—we may look forward to the time when steam-vessels, constructed, or at any rate put together, at Shanghai, will be ploughing the upper waters of the great Yang-tsze Kiang, even beyond the highest point reached by its first explorers in 1861; and we may yet hear of ordinary travellers from

K

Calcutta, to save the time and inconvenience of the sea-voyage by way of Singapore, coming an overland route through Burmah to meet these steamers in Yu-nan.

On Sunday the 7th of April, having been hauled up the Kwa-dung rapid in the morning, where a small island of rock stands in mid-stream, we continued on for a few miles up a rocky portion of the river. The weather was dull and rainy, and lowering clouds hung in heavy masses below the mountain peaks, veiling much of the scenery in that uncertainty which leaves scope for the imagination to picture forms and features to suit its own taste, often more grand and beautiful than the original. But in this case the reality was quite equal to the phantasm, for, when returning through this part of the country in June, we remarked that as a combination of mountain and river scenery it equalled, if it did not excel, any portion of the Upper Yang-tsze which we had seen. Shortly before one o'clock, on rounding a point of the river, we suddenly opened to view a huge split in the mountain mass ahead of us. It was the second, or "Lu-kan" gorge, by which the river escapes, as through a funnel. As we entered, the gloom was very impressive; huge walls of rock rise vertically on either hand to a prodigious height, with great table-shaped slabs standing out from the face of the cliff, for all the world like the sounding-boards of pulpits, hanging from which are long pointed stalactites; and on the upper surfaces of some are trees, looking like diminutive bushes, whose roots droop in festoons from their edges. This is not a long gorge, but it is much more imposing than the first one, and it should be visited by any one who may go up specially to see the gorges of the Yang-tsze. As I now write, I think I see it before me in all its stern grandeur, and I can well say with Humboldt, that "such recollections, like the memory of the sublimest works of poetry and the arts, leave an impression which is never to be effaced."

Divine service was performed in the afternoon; and one could not but feel that we were in a situation, and under circumstances, where the word of our Maker had full force; and I have ever felt, when amid the wild solitude of Nature, that I have been more inclined to centre my thoughts on religion, and to give expression to supplications for mercy at the hands of the Great Author, than when cooped-up in closely crammed churches among the busy haunts of mammon. And I will even go so far as to say that divine service performed in camp by a plain chaplain, in the open air, surrounded by men whose profession is that of blood and strife, has more effect on me than the most impressive of our cathedral services.

Soon after four o'clock we reached the village and rapid of Tsing-tan; in fact, there is a village on either side the river at this place, but that on the left bank, or northern shore, was the principal one. Built at some height above the water, and, owing to the broken nature of the ground, having none of the monotonous sameness of the villages of the low country, with grand mountain-scenery all around, and the foaming but magnificent river below, these places gave us the idea of some of the villages in the higher valleys of the Alps. The rapid being one of considerable strength, the ordinary bamboo towing-line was changed for a much stouter one, and the junk was secured by a strong hawser to a rock while the preparations for the ascent were going forward. A number of the villagers, both old and young, turned out, and, for the payment of a few cash which the skipper arranged, they tackled on their breast-straps to the line. We counted, including our boatmen, 103 people, and, if so many were required to haul up our craft, many more must be requisite for the large Sz'chuan cargo-junks. At a signal given on board, the line is stretched, the hawser cast off, and the large bow-sweep sheers the junk out into the foaming water, and then is regulated so as to keep her at the required distance from the bank, and to avoid sunken rocks. In this ascent we managed to strike one rock, when in an eddy, pretty heavily, and, had it not been for the use of a spar of hard wood which is projected forward and eased in-board by a kind of stopper-rope made fast to the junk, and twisted three or four times round the spar, we should have suffered much more severely.

At 5·30 we reached the head of the rapid, and immediately entered the "Mi-tan," or "rice month" gorge. This was in no way inferior to its predecessor, the cliffs rising almost vertically eight and nine hundred feet, with the strata much inclined, dipping to the north-west; nor could we manage to obtain bottom with the lead except close in to the rocks, where we got twelve fathoms. We halted for the night just out of this gorge, and next day, the 8th of April, after passing a reach where several reefs and rocks showed above the water, which, in its present stage, caused the whole to be almost a rapid, we came to Kwei, where are a number more reefs caused by the inclination of the strata. There is also a pretty strong rapid, when the water is high, right opposite the place; and, to afford facilities for tracking up the boats along the steep bank, flights of steps and paths have been cut out in the solid rock, an arrangement which we observed not only here, but in many places on the river; and at other points chains have been fastened to the face of vertical cliffs to assist in getting junks along, where there is no foothold on shore for trackers. The country around is very mountainous, and it is interesting to see in what places Chinamen's huts are perched, to take advantage of some few yards of level ground for cultivation. Some of the hills, a thousand feet above the river, are thus cultivated in patches to their summits. Kwei is just on the line of 31° north latitude, as shown by an observation obtained on the downward voyage two miles west of it; it lies N.W. by W. from I-chang, from which it is distant by the windings of the river thirty-nine miles.

We had not proceeded more than a couple of miles above Kwei, when we came to a place where coal was being worked out of the hill-side, on the right or south shore of the river; and as this is the first place where it occurs on the Yang-tsze itself, I may mention that during the remainder of our voyage we saw a great deal of coal, and the regions are,— first, from Kwei to Wan; then again in the ranges of hills which cross the country in the neighbourhood of Chung-king; and lastly, near Sü-chow, and between that and Ping-shan. The last appeared to us the best, the specimens having proved it to be so, and it was worked much more extensively than lower down: I shall have occasion to speak of this subject at greater length hereafter. As to the mines, they are small galleries driven horizontally into the sides of the hills. Between Kwei and Quai-chow the coal does not seem to be of a very good quality, and no trouble is taken to get it out in large lumps; it is pounded up, mixed with water and loam, and then dried into bricks, in which form it has much the appearance of "Patent Fuel," and stows well. We brought away small specimens from each place, and they have been examined, among other mineralogical speci- mens, by the authorities at the Museum of Practical Geology in London, and by several competent judges, who agree that the formation of all this part of the Yang-tsze is that of the true coal-measures. Wherever we found coal, the rock was a kind of grey sandstone; and I observed that it was everywhere the same, whether in Hoo-peh or in Sz'chuan, although the localities were hundreds of miles apart, so that it must all be of much the same age. I remarked also that, wherever there was coal near this sandstone, such portions of the rock as were exposed to the action of water and the atmosphere along the shore were glossed on the surface, as if polished with a greasy substance like black-lead, although seldom quite black. This may perhaps throw some light on the nature of the rock; but I must leave the deductions to be drawn by geologists. So unvarying is this, that wherever you see this peculiar dark glaze on the sandstone on the Upper Yang-tsze, you may be sure there is coal.

From Kwei we stopped once before we came to Pa-tung, the last town in the province of Hoo-peh. It is a small place without a wall, situated on rather steep sloping ground on the right bank; and on the opposite side stands a josshouse, at a considerable height above the river. Above this, the hills bordering the river are for some few miles rather less steep, and two or three streams enter. We passed one rapid and then came to the mouth of a gorge where are situated the rapid and village of Kwan-du-kow. High precipitous mountains rise on either hand, which, where the rock is not bare, are covered with a growth of small brushwood, and woods of small pine and cedar occur in some places; but wherever the slopes are such as to admit of cultivation, they are occupied for that purpose by the industrious country people; while below, on the river, others are employed catching fish by various devices, among which the common scoop-net, used by one person standing on a point of rock in a rapid, or -anywhere that the current is swift, is so frequent that, in the visions of gorges and rapids which occasionally haunt my recollection, the stolid Chinaman, in his bamboo hat and reed palctôt, continually dipping his net automaton-like, and as constantly bringing out nothing, is ever in the foreground of the picture.

The gorge, commencing at the village of Kwan-du-kow, is continuous as far as the city of Wu-shan, a distance of over twenty miles, and is the longest on the river. About half-

PART OF WU-SHAN GORGE.

BOUNDARY BETWEEN HOO-PEH AND SZ'CHUAN.

Page 135.

way through is the boundary between the provinces of Hoopeh and Sz'chuan. The course of the river is nearly directly east, and one might, were it not pointed out, pass the place of boundary without notice; but the *voyageurs* drew our attention to the fact that we were entering their native country, and the old grey-bearded skipper went off into a long disquisition on the superiority of that favoured province over the rest of China; while our Chinese servants and Mr. Schereschewsky's teacher, who were Kiang-su men, and had been listening to the marvellous stories related by the boatmen, seemed to look upon it that in entering Sz'chuan they were commencing a pilgrimage in a foreign land; and from this I think commenced the growth of their disinclination towards the idea of going out of China, which, though it was never openly professed, yet, from their becoming sick one after another, and chiming in so readily when any objections were raised against our further progress, was sufficiently evident to some of us; and I believe that, notwithstanding due weight be given to mandarins, rebels, and boat-skippers, the failure of our enterprise was in a great measure caused by treachery in our own camp.

On the south side the boundary was marked by a narrow glen running into the mountains, on the Sz'chuan or western side of which were a few houses that, in this wild and desolate region, did duty for a village. On the northern bank the boundary is half a mile lower down, and is marked by a mountain stream or creek coming down a narrow ravine. We halted for the night a couple of miles or so above this point; and next morning, being favoured by a fresh breeze, we emerged from the regions of darkness and came to Wu-shan (hien). This was our first sight of a Sz'chuan town, and we looked eagerly to detect if possible some change in the appearance of a Chinese city; but no,—it was the same lead-coloured mass, overtopped by the curved roofs of one or two conspicuous temples, and kept together by four antiquated-looking walls, with the usual half pagoda and half house-like structures over the gates and at the angles. It was of the regular pattern, and might have been punched out of the same mould with half a thousand others. A tributary of small size enters the Yang-tsze at this point from the north. I ought to have mentioned that at the last place, Patung, we obtained supplies at the following prices: fowls, 240 cash each; flour, 34 cash per "king" or catty; and eggs, four cash apiece. This last was the same as we had paid all along from Hankow; but a shilling apiece for fowls, in a fowl country, seemed rather exorbitant.

A discovery was made by us this day, which, if it be a correct one, will account for a multitude of incongruities, namely, that a Chinese "li" is not an actual measure of distance, being longer or shorter according to the nature of the country; but that a day's journey is reckoned at one hundred li, either on a river or by land. When we hit upon this mode of reckoning, we seemed to have got the key to Chinese distances, and we were able to account for a place being thirty li (ten miles) distance when it was within half an hour's walk of us, or our having easily travelled a hundred and twenty li in one day, when we knew for certain that we had not gone over fifteen miles. Whether this agrees in theory with the Celestial mode of reckoning length, I leave to the learned in the language to determine; but as a practical hint I would caution future travellers against believing all they hear in China.

From Wu-shan to Quai-chow is about a day's travelling; we will say nothing about the li in this instance. The first reach above the former place obtained the name of "Poison Reach," from the fact of my having incautiously eaten several nuts having something of the appearance and taste of Brazil nuts, but which, as was afterwards discovered, are used for the manufacture of oil. I was seized with acute pains in the bowels, vomiting, purging, and cramps in the stomach and legs; and it was not until after much suffering, and by the aid of morphia and laudanum administered by the Doctor in sufficient quantity to have killed any man under ordinary circumstances, that I got over the effects. I would caution all future wanderers in these regions against this fruit. It grows on a tree not unlike a small walnut-tree; the flower is rather pretty, of white and pink. The tree is called "Tung-shu," and seems to be much cultivated in these parts; and the nut is known as the "Tung-tsze." It has been made out in England to be *Eloococca verrucosa*.

Before coming to Quai-chow there is yet another gorge to be passed. It is a short one, and known as "Fung-siang," or Wind-box. Although the last, it is by no means the least in grandeur. One pass at its upper end is not over 150 yards across; cliffs rise towering above to a prodigious height, and large caverns have been scooped out by the mighty current, allowing of fishing-boats lying in perfect security from the wind and weather. We went through aided by an easterly breeze, and our boatmen made the gorge resound with their wild shouts, which echoed to and fro between the vertical cliffs on either hand. They were calling for the wind; and it is curious that this whistling or shouting is, among so many different nations, the recognised method of propitiating Boreas. An isolated rock stands out nearly in mid-stream; as we emerge from the gorge, a tall white pagoda comes in view, and Quai-chow lies before us.

CHAPTER IX.

EASTERN SZ'CHUAN.

ARRIVED at Quai-chow (foo), our first business was to determine how we were to proceed onwards: the choice lay between the land and the water, the latter having the advantage of ease of travelling and the opportunity of surveying the river; but as we had progressed so slowly thus far, we were desirous, for the sake of saving time, to take to the land. Sending cards—pieces of red paper with our names inscribed on them in large Chinese characters with Indian, or rather China, ink—two of the party proceeded without delay to the "Yamun" of the Prefect, or Governor, to whom admittance was gained without difficulty. Official duty at Canton had worn off any novelty for me in Yamun visits and Chinese ceremonies, and, not having recovered from the effects of the dose of poison taken on the day previous, I kept the Doctor company on board the junk. Meanwhile, in plain English, translated of course into Chinese, the Prefect was informed who we were and our object, and his assistance was requested in forwarding our views, in the course of which the "Treaty of Tien-tsin" was referred to, but he seemed to be ignorant of anything concerning it, except the bare fact of its existence, and therefore, as we had a number of copies of that peculiar document, he was presented with one. And I should here mention that, notwithstanding it expressly stipulates that the convention was to be published throughout the empire, at no single place on our route after we parted with Admiral Hope's squadron did we find it posted, or that the inhabitants had any knowledge of it; and farther, at many places the mandarins themselves admitted that it had never reached them at all. Let us hope that the Prince of Kung, from whom so much more is expected than any Chinaman, I think, is capable of, will, when he reads this book—and I shall prevail on the publisher to send him a copy—have this error rectified.

The business with this Celestial Prefect was overlaid and interlaid with an immense amount of small-talk; but the upshot of the conversation was, that the Prefect, who was a very polite old man, gave us his advice that we had better not think of leaving the river, as it was by far the easiest way of travelling; in fact, that there existed only the most inferior road by land from Quai-chow westward; that the regular route left the river at a place called Wan some few days further up, whence we should find ready means of getting to Ching-tu, the capital of Sz'chuan, which was a principal point in our intended journey, as we had letters to the Viceroy, who is at the same time Governor of Tibet, and from whom we expected to obtain the requisite authority for travelling as government officials over the Yun-ling mountains to Lassa. Whether the Prefect told the truth or not, I cannot pretend to say,—the chances are against him; and I consider this to have been "shunt off" the first.

The Chinese have a notion that foreigners can see into the ground, and can tell whether it contains minerals or treasure. This is, I am told, a very general impression with them, and hence, perhaps, their antipathy to Europeans travelling by land. I fancy that a geologist must have at some time astonished their Celestial minds by indicating the existence of a valuable mineral substance in a certain locality, and thus have given rise to this belief.

Having carried out his instructions by accompanying the expedition into Sz'chuan, Captain Mur-king-köw,—the officer whom I have already mentioned as having been sent by the Viceroy of the "two Hoos,"—notwithstanding he had constantly expressed a wish to accompany us into Tibet, and had even thrown out hints of his desire to visit our "honourable native country," decided on returning home. He had, we supposed, "made his pile," as a Californian would say, by extracting from the petty mandarins along the route money to pay his way, although there can be no doubt that he lived on us the whole time. However, it is the custom of the country; and although, when this theoretically perfect system of government was worked without intrigue and abuse, it would not have been tolerated, alas! there is now nothing but a system of squeeze within squeeze from highest to lowest, and a mandarin is necessarily a rogue. I recollect, on our return to civilization, taking a walk with a friend after the heat of the day to the top of a hill at Hankow which overlooks the river. The Taipings were at the time reported to be near at hand, and the whole garrison of Wu-chang was in readiness for them. Over the top of the hill runs a part of the wall of Han-yang, and the little pagoda stands in an enclosed space. A number of three-cornered banners floated from the wall, being stuck into crevices or propped up with piles of bricks, and distributed equally along the line of defence. As we were contemplating the scene of inundation which presented itself on all sides, a Chinaman began to take down these banners and stow them away carefully in the pagoda, while another was in place of each substituting a paper lantern, until, as the shades of evening drew in, the illumination was complete. Across the river the walls of Wu-chang, which are of great extent, were similarly lighted up, and had a most animated appearance, not really so animated as they should have been, however, for my friend, as he descended the hill, said, "Each of those flags and lanterns represents a man—you know, every soldier carries a banner by day and a lantern at night;—and, believe me, the Imperial Government at this very time is paying some one, perhaps a mandarin high in office, a rich merchant, or some large proprietor, for the number of soldiers these things represent, while the two coolies you saw are the only men he finds. If it were known at the proper place, the individual would assuredly be decapitated; yet such corruption and villany exist throughout the public departments, that these frauds are overlooked, and the reason is—bribery. Is it likely that rebels will be put down in this way? and what can we expect to result from such a state of things?"

In place of our gallant protector, a Lieutenant of the Celestial army was appointed, along with six soldiers, as a guard; a boat being found them by the Prefect. We also here engaged a second junk for ourselves, finding that the increase of the heat caused close stowing to become disagreeable; and while the skippers were making preparations for our farther progress, we scribbled a few letters to our friends and relations, detailing how we had thus far prospered. These were made up into a sealed packet addressed to the representative of Messrs. Dent and Co. at Hankow, with an order for the payment of five dollars on delivery written on the outside in Chinese characters. The Tartar Captain, who was to start in a day or two, took charge of the packet, and we subsequently learned that he delivered it in safety. One of the letters was to the Editor of the 'North-China Herald' for the information of the foreign community at Shanghai; and as it gives a tolerable summary of the first part of our voyage, I give it with the editorial remarks upon it entire:—

"The interest which 'The Child of the Ocean,' 'The Great River,' and *par excellence* '*The* River'—as the Chinese call it —is now creating in the commercial world, receives additional prominence from every new feature or incident connected with it. Not the least so is the exploration of its upper waters beyond the treaty boundary, whether its object be scientific or mercantile ; we therefore have pleasure in giving below the copy of a letter we have received from one of the party who left Shanghai in February last to travel through Thibet to India. After taking leave of the steamer that conveyed them to the Tung-ting Lake they proceeded slowly, against the current, to I-chang. There, having to change their boats, they found difficulty in procuring any, as they were all engaged to convey troops to the eastward for the Imperialists. The mandarins and people everywhere treated them with respect and civility. Nothing appeared to be known respecting the treaty. They passed several rapids ; the strength of some was very great in the narrow passes between the mountains which impinge on the river. They had but little shooting, and few adventures worth relating. At Wan (hien), their next halting-place, they hoped to be able to leave the river, and proceed across country to Ching-tu, the capital of Sze-chuen, which is about half-way from Quai-chow, where they were, to the borders of Thibet. The military mandarin who had accompanied them thus far from Hankow would not proceed farther, having reached the border of the province to which he belonged—Hupeh. He left our friends in good health, and brought their letters to Hankow.

" ' Quai-chow, Yang-tsze River, Province of Sz'chuan,
12*th April*, 1861.

" ' MY DEAR SIR,—In taking a chance and unexpected opportunity—for I much doubt if this letter will ever reach you—I have but a few moments to tell you how our expedition, in which you manifested so much interest, has fared.

" ' Parting with the naval squadron at Yo-chow, at the outlet of Tung-ting Lake, a tedious voyage of eleven days— tedious from its comparative slowness after steaming—and through an uninteresting country—uninteresting on account of its flatness—we arrived on the 27th March at Kin-chow (foo), or rather Shasze, the port as it were of the former, which is about a mile distant from the river, and is more of a Tartar town than a mercantile place. This (Shasze) was the first place having anything of a business-like appearance, the number of up-country junks attesting a considerable trade with Sz'chuan, in the way of cotton up, and silk, sugar, tobacco, and such like, down.

"'The country we had previously passed through was purely agricultural, and one immense plain, which indeed may be said to extend the whole distance from Hankow on the north side of the Yang-tsze, and so low that inundation is only prevented by the existence of embankments (enormous works) apparently of great age.

"'About six miles above Kin-chow is the mouth of a river said to communicate with Tung-ting Lake, and to be a shorter route to Yo-chow than by the Yang-tsze, which is very tortuous; and this may account for the small number of junks which we observed below it. However, one ought to have expected a great difference in the amount of craft, for it would appear that the imports at Hankow — our uppermost open port—including coal, are derived rather from Hoo-nan, surrounding Tung-ting Lake, than from the Upper Yang-tsze. In fact, one would be inclined to call the Yang-tsze above the Tung-ting outlet by another name as rather a tributary of the other. In size it is wanting one-half above this point.

"'Above Kin-chow the country soon becomes hilly and even mountainous. The towns of Chi-kiang (hien) and Itu (hien) are passed, and proceeding up a most picturesque part of the river we arrive at I-chang (foo), 363 geographical miles above Hankow, and 951 up the Yang-tsze, or in round numbers 1100 English miles from Shanghai, a place which from its situation must ever be of considerable importance.

"'Below I-chang the Yang-tsze is navigable for steamers of considerable size, its width above the Tung-ting outlet being usually about half a mile, and the least water when we passed up, at which time it was probably near at its lowest, was, in mid-channel, three fathoms in one or two places, but generally much more.

"'Knowing full well how unthankful an office it is to have to undeceive persons on a point on which their previous notions have been agreeable to them, I necessarily feel somewhat disinclined to divulge our discovery—if discovery it can be called—that the Yang-tsze above I-chang, at any rate during this season of the year, is unsuited to steam-navigation. At a distance of three miles above the city the river suddenly changes its character altogether, and, narrowing to less than one-half its former width, rushes with a strong current through a long gorge, with stupendous cliffs rising on either hand. At fifteen miles above I-chang the first actual rapid exists at this season, and thence upwards as far as we now are, about one hundred miles above I-chang, its course is through a continuous mountain country, passing through several more gorges, and obstructed occasionally by rapids. But there is no want of water, for the river is very deep in these narrows.

"'I would not give as a decided opinion that these rapids will altogether prevent steamers from ascending to the upper waters of the Yang-tsze, because in time light river steamers of full power, and adapted to the peculiar navigation, may be constructed: besides which, the nature of the river may be very different under altered circumstances of high water; for it would appear that the rise during summer is very great, water-lines having been observed in the confined parts some sixty or seventy feet above the present level. But then the additional force of water might present another obstacle.

"'Coal exists in Hoo-nan, on Tung-ting Lake, that being the district whence Hankow is supplied. We have found it at Kwei (not Kwei-chow), about forty miles above I-chang, and for some distance above that in the mountainous country.

"'We are all in good case, and have as yet encountered no serious difficulties, finding both mandarins and people remarkably civil. We have travelled thus far entirely by river, and proceed to-morrow onward towards Wan (hien), where circumstances will decide whether we still continue on the river, or proceed overland to Ching-tu.

"'I would have sent you a chart of the river thus far, but I have no time to prepare a copy. I may yet have another chance before we are out of China. "'B.'"

The new mandarin brought with him a new flag; and, in place of the old yellow one, which was beginning to look the worse for wear, a bright red banner, bearing in Chinese characters "Lord High Ambassador," now graced the crooked mast of our leaky craft.

Quai-chow is prettily situated, and the surrounding amphitheatre of hills, covered with the bright vegetation of spring, was most lovely. A high rugged peak, which appears in one of Dr. Barton's sketches, rises above the mouth of the Fung-siang gorge just below the place, and the valley of a small tributary which falls into the Yang-tsze at the town trends away to the north-east. The clean white pagoda which we had observed on emerging from the last of the gorges overlooks the mouth of the creek, proclaiming to all travellers on this great highway that a city is near at hand, while one or two other smaller ones crown the hills to the rear of the town. And I may here observe that I do not remember a single instance of getting to a town without being made aware of its proximity by one or more of these picturesque structures presenting themselves to our view. Sometimes there are several perched on the summits of hills around the place, and you often are in sight of one many hours before you reach a city. At another there is perhaps one standing near the river a mile or so below, and often another above; and I fancy they are intended to impress the traveller with the dignity of the town, just as in a yamun or official residence you pass through a number of arches and gates before you arrive at the hall of audience. And I would here also remark that, of the hundreds of pagodas I have seen in Southern and Central China from three to thirteen stories in height, I never saw one with an even number.* The city is a *foo*, and is well situated, as will be seen by the map, on high ground on the left or northern side of the river, but portions of the southern wall have slipped down the bank. All walled cities in China have attached to their names the rank of the governmental districts of which they are the chief towns. They are of three grades, *foo*, *chow*, and *hien*, but the second has of late years ceased to be used. Quai-chow did not give us the idea of being a place of much business. We settled the balance of our boat-hire from I-chang, and allowed something in advance for the voyage to Wan. We had hitherto paid in Mexican dollars, but, having run out of our supply of those useful auxiliaries, we were forced to make an inroad on our stock of "sycee." Each of us carried 450 taels weight of silver in this form (*i.e.* in small lumps), equal to about six hundred dollars, and, for fear of loss from shipwreck or other mishap, we distributed the amount among our different packages. Mine was tied in old socks, and kept very various company: one lot was in the next

---

* This fact seems to have escaped the attention of the designer of the edifice in the Royal Pleasure Grounds at Kew.

compartment of a box to my sextant; another lay snugly between two dangerous bedfellows, a bag of No. 1 shot and a tin of "Curtis and Harvey;" while the remainder was distributed so as to equalise the weight of each box as nearly as possible, along with nautical almanacs, logarithm tables, flannel shirts, quinine, fish-hooks, and, writing-paper. A money-changer was sent for, and came on board with his balance-scales, and after some little time rendered us a statement to a fraction of a cash—ten cash go to a halfpenny—of the exchange, at the rate of 1720 per tael. The Sz'chuan tael was here in use, and is of greater weight than that on the lower river. The proportion is, 100 Sz'chuan taels equal 101·6 Shanghai, or 102·48 Hankow taels. Mexican dollars had been taken as far as I-chang, in the province of Hoo-peh, at 1000 to 1100 cash.

The country around Quai-chow afforded a great, and to me a most agreeable, contrast to the gorges, being under cultivation to a considerable extent; and we observed peas, beans, millet, "durra" (like large millet), barley, and bearded wheat, besides melons and other garden vegetables. There were also the castor-oil plant, peaches, apricots, water melons, hawthorn, honeysuckle, and poplars, while the "Tung-shu" tree, with the poisonous fruit called "Tung-tsze," before mentioned, was very common. We saw thick-shelled walnuts, but not growing. A kind of dye like indigo, if it is not it, is grown in this part, being used for colouring the blue cottons. The season was so far advanced, although it was not yet the middle of April, that wheat and barley were well in the ear, and peas and beans almost mature.

It was in this neighbourhood that we first observed the poppy cultivated, and hence onwards it was very common; and, from the amount which we saw along the banks of the river, it would appear that the quantity of opium raised in Sz'chuan must be very large. In the same patch one sees pink, lilac, and white flowers, and the appearance of the beds of poppies on the terraces of the hill-sides among the other crops is very beautiful. When the flower dies off, the seed-pod, or head, is scored with several cuts vertically, from which oozes a substance of the appearance of freshly warmed glue; this is collected by the farmers and their families, who scrape it off with a knife and deposit it in a little pot which each person carries for the purpose, and the operation is repeated every two or three days, according to the state of the weather, which influences the yield. The plants were considered by one of our party, who was competent to give an opinion, as equal to those of India. The price of opium at Quai-chow was 3000 cash per catty, and we paid subsequently at Chung-king 380 cash per tael weight for some which we brought down as sample, and which was pronounced very pure. It differed from the Indian drug in being of a darker colour; and the result of an analysis at the government establishment proves that it may well compete with the far-famed "Patna." A great deal of opium is exported from the province of Sz'chuan, finding its way to the southern and central parts of China, and this accounts for the impossibility of getting rid of a large supply which was sent up the Yang-tsze to Hankow *on spec.* on the opening of that port to foreign trade; and although British merchants have the credit of poisoning the whole Chinese nation, I think it will be found that their trade is not very much extended beyond the coast. A limited amount of the Indian opium no doubt always goes up country, because those who are able to pay for it will use it in preference to the native produce; "a caprice," as Huc says, "only to be accounted for from the vanity of the rich Chinese, who would think it beneath them to smoke opium of native production;" just as in our country the productions or manufactures of other lands are often preferred to those of home. Such is fashion, and such I suppose it will always be. This is doubtless an important question with the government of India, for at the present high price of the drug from that country it cannot possibly compete with that of Sz'chuan.

The poppy crop is over by the end of May, and is followed by sugar-cane, Indian corn, and in some districts cotton. Huc mentions that for several years before 1846 Indian opium was largely smuggled into Sz'chuan, through Yu-nan and Burmah, and that on his way his escort was increased for fear of meeting with the smugglers, who travelled in bands quite openly in defiance of the law. I have remarked furthermore that the worthy missionary does not mention a word about the growing of the poppy in Sz'chuan; but the reason of this may be that he traversed that province too late in the season to observe it under cultivation. Still one would think that, so thoroughly as he exhausts every subject on which he treats, he would have told us if the drug was grown at all in the province into which he says it was smuggled. May we infer from his silence that this species of agriculture has only grown up of late years? If so, it is most likely but in its infancy, and we may live to see a part of his prophecy carried out by " the English going to buy opium in the ports of China." Yet all this cultivation—for it is said to be also grown extensively in the south-western provinces—and consumption of opium, are in violation of the law, and furnish only another instance of the universal state of decay of the government of this wonderful country, where, to use the words of Huc again, "pipes, lamps, and all the apparatus for smoking opium, are sold publicly in every town, and the mandarins themselves are the first to violate the law and give this bad example to the people, even in the courts of justice."

The captain of our extra junk proving a smart active fellow, and the effect of the affair of " Skipper's Point " not having died off,—although our boatmen were now beginning not to consider us quite such savages as the former crew had given us the credit of being,—we were ready on the day after that of our arrival to start from Quai-chow. The forenoon of the 13th April found us again *en route*. The country immediately above is hilly, with distant mountains; the soil is mostly of a reddish clay, which is used extensively for making bricks. The hills are cultivated to their summits, and there are scattered trees, but no woods. Banks of sand and stones are thrown out at the mouths of the small creeks and mountain streams, which narrow and impede the river sometimes to such an extent as to form a minor rapid, or rather a rush of water, along the shore. Such places as these, although they would not be the least impediment to a craft which could ascend in mid-stream, offer some hindrance to junk navigation. We had not left Quai-chow above two miles and a half behind us, when we came to one of these places, in endeavouring to pass which, by means of sail and tracking together, through some mismanagement on the part of either the helmsman or those working the bow-sweep, the large junk took a sheer off, broke the bamboo line, and went twisting and twirling about in the eddies till she drifted into a regular whirlpool, where all command of her was lost, and she heeled over so much as to capsize tables and chairs and send every moveable article flying, the effect of which was a further diminution of our already reduced stock of crockery. The outer fan of her rudder broke, and it was a considerable time before we could manage by dint of pulling and sweeping her head round with the sweep-oar to get out of this precarious situation; we then drifted down, and made fast to the shore some distance below. This delayed us the remainder of the day, having to send back to Quai-chow for a carpenter; and as the weather, which had been rainy all the forenoon, did not clear up till evening, we were forced to amuse ourselves as best we could on board.

CHAP. IX. CHINESE IGNORANCE AS TO FOREIGNERS.   151

Our stock of reading matter was not large, being confined to a volume of Knight's *Half Hours*, a number or two of *All the Year Round*, a *Geographical Journal*, and Abbé Huc's works.

When two of our party were on a visit to the white pagoda at Quai-chow, they met with some students whom they asked what they took us for. Their reply was that we were from "the Western Sea," and that the only object we could have in coming so far up the river must be to trade, and that they supposed us to be merchants. Some Chinese merchants also made a call on us while we were at dinner, on the evening of our stay at Quai-chow, and left their cards. They had, no doubt, the same idea of us. But the prevailing notion among the uneducated was, that, as we spoke a different language from them, we must be from Canton or the neighbouring provinces, being perfectly ignorant, I fancy, of the existence of any people beyond the "Central Flowery Land." In fact, China to them is the world; and we may talk as we like of the influence of Western nations on the Chinese generally, but I am inclined to agree with Huc in the opinion that "the people at large care little enough about what is thought or done by Europeans, whose very existence is all but unknown to them." As an instance of the general ignorance of the outer world, as late as last year only, a model was found at Tien-tsin accurately representing the flag-vessel of Admiral Hope in the unsuccessful attack on the Peiho forts in 1859, which was, I am told, exact in all particulars, even to the blue-jackets leaning over the gunwale smoking their pipes; but the vessel's name, which was a rather long one and ran across the stern, had puzzled the modeller, so in place he had substituted the following inscription:—"BASS&COSPALEALE." No one for a long time could interpret this, till at last some officer, sharper-witted than his comrades, discovered in it a familiar title; and the explanation of this seemingly curious jumble of the alphabet turned out to be this: when the squadron retired after the attack referred to, the Chinese, anxious to discover what species of barbarians they were who had disturbed their tranquillity, had searched along the muddy shores, where the only relics they found were some *ci-devant* quart-bottles of the deepest jet, each of them bearing the label of the maker of the thoroughly English beverage they had contained, which was at once taken to be the designation of the barbarians. Thus do "ye Britishe" go half-way round the world to fight a battle, and the only mark indicating our nationality that we leave behind is "Bass & Co.'s Pale Ale." But our junk's rudder is repaired, and the old skipper says we shall be able to start again in the morning. So good night!

On the 14th we came to several rapids, which prevented our doing more than fifteen miles—geographical of course. The first occurred at the village of An-ping, and is called "Low-ma," which means "Old horse." Here, although the rapid is one of those which may be called minor ones, and, as I have before explained, is rather a rush of water close to the bank than a regular rapid, we managed in the ascent to smash our bow-sweep, which for some minutes placed us in an awkward predicament, and the old junk struck heavily two or three times on the rocks; but at last she was got up without more serious damage than the increase of the leak. The skipper's boy, or mate, as we called him, came to beg one or two Chinese tallow candles from us; and with these and some cotton he descended into the hold, and went to work caulking the offending seams. This boy was a source of great annoyance to us, for the fellow used to go down into the hold four or five times daily for the purpose of baling, and always required to get off the hatch at the most awkward times. It is certainly very unpleasant to be asked to move the table and two or three chairs, on which all your paraphernalia of gun-cleaning are methodically arranged, just as you are in the act of putting together the lock of a Whitworth rifle,

CHAP. IX.   FEATURES OF THE COUNTRY.   153

which you have taken to pieces for the purpose, if possible, of damaging some portion of the intricate machinery by your clumsy fingers; but the full annoyance of such things is only to be felt by those who have their whole heart and soul in guns, their affections centred in a sear-spring, and no two ideas beyond a greased bullet and a clean barrel. I own I am not true sportsman enough fully to sympathise.

The general course on which we were now travelling was west, the river being usually about four hundred yards wide, but from projecting rocks or heaps of boulders, it was sometimes contracted to half that width. We sounded, as we crossed the river, five different times this day, never getting less than five and a half fathoms, and on two occasions we crossed without getting any bottom at all with ten fathoms of line out. The country was hilly on both banks, with mountains to the north and east, which we occasionally caught sight of through gaps in the nearer hills, by which the inland waters find their way to the Great River. At one of these places we observed a peculiar mountain-ridge broken into a number of sharp-pointed peaks, which we called the "Nine Pins." The general rock was a grey sandstone in horizontal strata. Coal was being worked at An-ping on the south bank, and farther up. The mid-day halt was at another second-class rapid called Shih-cham; we passed the white-washed temple and village of Ku-lin-tu, or "Spiritual ferry," and soon after came to the rapid of Miou-ki; and two and a quarter miles more brought us to that of Tung-yan, at the foot of which we halted for the night. At these two last places celestial observations were taken for determining the latitude and absolute longitude; and now that the season was so far advanced that it was impossible to use the meridian altitude of the sun for the first purpose, such work had to be performed mostly at night, the only counterbalancing advantage to the many disadvantages of which was, that I was not so bothered with Chinamen; and I found that by the help of an oil lantern and a Seikh a good deal might be done by perseverance, even without an assistant observer. Tung-yan rapid is therefore one of our principal stations, a list of which is given in the Appendix. A mean of distances of the sun west and Jupiter east of the moon, gives the longitude 109° 25' east of Greenwich, and the latitude is 30° 56' 50" north, by double altitudes of Sirius and Spica, which method was used on account of the sky threatening to become overcast before the time the required star would come on the meridian.

There were a couple of pagodas at this part of the river, one on either side, in very commanding situations, the first overlooking the rapids, and the second about three miles above. They belonged, I fancy, to Yung-yan, because we came to that town, after three hours' work round a turn to the north-west, on the following morning; we here passed through a very narrow portion of the river. This place is a *hien*, situated on the left bank 130 miles above I-chang. We remained here an hour, on the excuse of stopping leaks. The suburbs, which lie above, that is to the westward of the town, seem more extensive than the town itself, in which are one or two fine temples. There is also a handsome "kung-kwan," or guildhall; and we observed a three-storied, green-roofed pagoda, supposed to be coppered. The country immediately around has not an inviting appearance, being hilly and rather sterile.

The night of our stay at the Tung-yan rapid we were in company with two other large passenger-junks, which, like our own, carried lanterns and inscribed flags, denoting them to be occupied by official persons. After dinner a polite message was received by the Doctor, requesting his attendance; and though at first he uttered an execration or two against all "fukies" (the usual name for Chinamen among the

Europeans in China) in general, and mandarins in particular, he afterwards went to visit them. The passengers were a high mandarin with his family, and they turned out to be Roman Catholics. The old gentleman's son had a sore leg, which the Doctor dressed for him; but as the wound was of but little consequence, the application for medical aid was made no doubt with a view of getting a sight of some of us, rather than from any need of assistance.

We reached fifteen miles above Yung-yan on the 15th of April. Hills of much the same character as those we had passed the day before bordered the river, but no mountains were visible until we got to the village of Siau-kiang, where we stopped for the night, and in which neighbourhood we observed the first of a number of small towers on the tops of the hills, a feature in the scenery which after this continued general for some distance above. Most of the hills have these towers or houses on their summits, or, when these are wanting, are frequently surmounted by a single group or tope of trees. The strata of the rocks were still mostly horizontal, causing the hills often to have flat tops, and giving the country a peculiar appearance. We passed several rapids, but none of any great moment; also a good many reefs and rocks which would be covered during high water. At one south bend the river has scooped out a remarkable bay, in which lies a pretty village closed in by partially-wooded hills; while, on the point opposite, some large "josses" or gods stand in excavations in the solid rock; and from the neat and clean appearance of these idols and everything around, we concluded that more than ordinary attention must be paid to religion by the people in these parts, and surmised that the edifices on the hill-tops might have some connexion with their religion. In fact, we were now getting into the prosperous part of Sz'chuan, while all we had hitherto seen of it had been comparatively poor. We had entered it among rocks and crags, and had gone on through gorges, only occasionally treated to a view of anything approaching an open and properly cultivated country. Now we had got out of that confused mass of mountains which lies between it and Hoo-peh, and encroaches so much on both provinces; and leaving gorges and rapids behind, could better compare Sz'chuan proper with the plain of Hoo-peh.

I walked for a considerable distance along the bank of the widened reach of the river below Siau-kiang, and arrived at that place some time before the boats. Ascending a small hill overlooking the village, a fine view opened before me. To the left hand, and with a south-east direction, the Yang-tsze rolled away on its downward course, until, rounding a bend about three miles distant, it disappeared; while above, to the west, it was visible for a like distance till lost in a broken country. The sides of the hills on the north were dotted with houses looking like white specks, and were crowned by more of the towers or clumps of trees already mentioned. Looking north-east, a small river, about forty yards in width, was seen coming down a highly-cultivated but narrow valley for a long distance inland. Immediately round me were fields, or, from their size, perhaps I should say gardens, of the poppy, beautifully variegated with pink, white, and lilac; others, more advanced towards maturity, had lost their flowers, and were attended by men, women, and children, in their universal blue cotton dresses and bamboo hats, scoring the pods and collecting the first of the juice. The late warm weather had brought on the wheat so that some of it was partly turned; and the industrious farming people were nursing up the little irrigating streams, and carrying them along all sorts of places, leading them round corners and through banks, so that they might pour out their fertilizing waters in the paddy-fields preparing for rice. Altogether it was such a scene of beauty and quiet domestic life, that I felt how great a sin would be on the head of any ruler in a country like this, who should by any act disturb, or by incapacity cause others to disturb, such harmony. I looked back on the scenes at Nanking and the region of the Taipings, and it made me shudder to think that such should ever become the state of this beautiful and peaceful region. Far distant be the time when the "long-haired men" shall disturb these quiet people, and lay waste this scene of productiveness! Let the "Son of the Ocean" reject from its bosom the lawless intruders, should they endeavour to ascend by his help; let gulfs and caverns open and swallow up the host, should it attempt to march into the beautiful Sz'chuan. But while I indulge in these reveries a crowd of inquiring children are gathering around me; and some of the peace-loving husbandmen have dropped their spades and are hurrying—if a Chinaman can be said to hurry—to gaze at the queer-looking specimen of humanity who stands by himself; while the women keep aloof, and peep round from behind corners:—It is a "foreign devil"—a "*Yang-quatz.*" Granted, but the animal wears clothes; he has on a pair of old serge trousers, a grey flannel shirt, and a Pekin felt cap, with a large woollen turban around it to protect his uncelestial skull from celestial rays or celestial brickbats; his hair has evidently not been cut for months, and he is already terribly sunburnt. An urchin, more precocious than the rest, approaches and feels the stuff of his trousers, but evidently does not know it, for it is the fleece of the sheep; he then looks at the thick boots, which reach half way to the knees, and would be all the better for a pair of new soles, and utters the exclamation of astonishment, "eh-yah!" at which the bystanders giggle; he says something in the best Chinese he can muster, on which the barbarian nods, as much as to say, "All right, I don't understand you," and the crowd laughs; however, as the animal does not look displeased, they approach him nearer and nearer until they close in and examine every article of his apparel minutely, appearing much satisfied with the inspection. But there is something on their minds; they make motions with their hands to their heads; what do they want? to see his cap?—no; they have examined it minutely, and had explained to them, by "bah-bah," that the turban is of wool. Ah! I have it. I take off my cap and make the most polite bow to the assembly. "Chang-mow! Chang-mow!" ("the long hair! the long hair!") echoes from all sides; the babies instinctively squall; one old fellow, in his eagerness to look, stumbles over a stone and falls down, which causes the whole crowd to laugh and jeer at him, and in the confusion I retire from the scene. I again reach the bank of the river, where a boatman readily offers to take me across to the junk, which is on the other side; and when I get there I give him a few "cash" for his trouble. Soon we halt for the night, which is the signal for dinner; I tell my companions what I have observed, but they say they have seen all that and much more, and so I "shut up."

For a couple of miles or so above Siau-kiang the river continues of considerable breadth; then, in a north-east reach, it narrows to about one hundred and fifty yards, where the banks are bare sandstone, and for some distance a flat of rock borders the river on either side. The lay of the strata is horizontal, causing it to have a general uniform level; and not being over eighteen feet above the water, this flat must at times be entirely covered. In some places there are inscribed tablets cut out in the solid stone, and "josses" stand beside the water, before which the boatmen stop and pray. Fishermen, with their scoop-nets, were common here, being perched in all sorts of queer places, the overhanging slabs of sandstone forming capital shelter and protection for them from the weather. The Doctor and myself walked along a great part of this peculiar formation before breakfast, and bathed in one of the quiet lagoons formed by a basin-like excavation. A specimen of the rock was preserved, and turns out to be the same sandstone which occurs in the coal districts throughout this portion of the Yang-tsze. We observed the houses to be of much better construction than heretofore, some being two-storied, whitewashed, and with shelving roofs; sometimes there was attached a square white tower, some forty feet in height, with shelving roof, and with a balcony around the top story under the overhanging eaves. It took us three hours to get past this narrow and rocky portion, after which the river widens out, and sand and shingle flats occur, which we hailed as a new feature in the landscape.

In the forenoon we came to one of these shingle-beds, where a number of people were at work turning up the sand and stones, and washing it in rockers. They were gold-washing; and from this point upwards, for a considerable distance above Wan, we often came on large parties of people similarly occupied. Five men are employed at each rocker; the labour of digging and carrying the gravel being divided between two, another carries water to a trough alongside of the one who rocks and washes, and the remaining man collects the washed sand and removes the shingle. The cradle or rocker is simply a shallow wicker basket resting on a frame which has a joint, and allows of an oscillating motion to and from the washer, who, as each coolie arrives from the digging—which is usually but four or five yards distant—and deposits his load in the cradle, pours water on it, then rocks away, pours more water, and rocks again, until all the sandy particles are washed from the shingle, which is thrown away. The sand and the gold it contains, which by the way is in extremely small particles, run down a wooden inclined plane. The gold, we were informed, is subsequently smelted out; but the yield is so small that only the very lowest coolies care to work at this laborious employment. When there is a large accumulation of washed shingle, so as to get in the way of the workers, and the diggings get too far from the cradle, the whole apparatus is shifted to another spot. We observed just below Wan that a large shingle flat was marked out in sections, the angles of which were indicated by whitened stones, and white lines were drawn across the "bar." Thus there seems to be some method in the business, and most probably the Government claims a royalty, or requires a licence or ground-rent to be taken out by the workers. Every flat which was being worked for gold was, when we passed up, but a little above the level of the river; and on our return nearly all the workings were submerged. The number of people employed during the low-water season at this work must be very considerable. The Chinese believe that the "dust" is washed from the mountains of Tibet; and the Yang-tsze above is known as the Kin-cha Kiang, or "River of Gold Sand," while at its junction with the waters from Tung-ting Lake, much lower down, it is called the Kin-ho, or "Gold River." Some of this sand which we brought to England has been examined by competent persons; and although it contains a large quantity of scales of yellow mica, the amount of gold is so small as hardly to be detected. Probably we were unlucky in the selection of our specimens.

We continued to travel on the 16th on a south-westerly course, passing only one place that could be called a rapid, at about four o'clock in the afternoon; subsequently we sighted a fine nine-storied pagoda, and, having made a distance of nineteen or twenty miles from Siau-kiang, we got up to the town of Wan (hien) at half-past seven in the evening; and this being rather too late for the news of our arrival to spread far, we enjoyed a tolerably quiet night. We however sent to inform the mandarins of our arrival, and

CHAP. IX. MESSAGE FROM THE TARTAR GENERAL. 161

received a very polite message in answer, that the Tartar General, whom we had missed seeing at Quai-chow, would do his "insignificant self the great honour of calling on our Excellencies" on the following morning at six o'clock. This was most unexpected condescension on the part of so high an official; for we were afterwards told that he was the Commander-in-Chief of Eastern Sz'chuan; and we could account for it only by the bold face we had put on hitherto, and the fame of our red flag which had preceded us.

Natural Arch near I-chang.   See p. 114.

CHAPTER X.

VISITS AND CEREMONIES.

THE scene is Wan, the head-quarters of a prefecture of the second provincial grade—a *hien*—in the far interior of China, removed from its eastern seaboard some thirteen degrees of longitude, and at a distance of 1100 sea-miles up the Great Yang-tsze Kiang. Surrounded by a hilly and broken country, with a fine range of mountains standing as a barrier against the north-west breezes, Wan has many features of situation and scenery which differ much from our preconceived notions of China, as derived from geographies; where it is represented as one immense fertile plain, intersected in every direction by canals and rivers, wooded with mulberry and tea *trees*, in which golden-pheasants innumerable nestle, and under the shade of which fishing cormorants industriously pursue their avocations; where porcelain pagodas and high-arched bridges meet the eye at every turn, and water-wheels revolve through an old habit which they cannot shake off, though the river has long since been diverted from its course to aid in supplying some enormous canal at the other extremity of the empire; where the people are a nation of astronomers and star-gazers, living in such crowds that they require to construct floating islands and hanging gardens in order to supply the demands of the commissariat. These notions must certainly give way before China in 1861, as seen on the Yang-tsze; these phantoms of China must fade, if we would learn how this thoroughly utilitarian and not in the least degree star-gazing nation exists in a country the size of half of Europe, and holds sway over a region almost rivalling the southern continent of the New World. We must believe in mountains, in inland seas, and all the usual physical features of other parts of the world, and cast from us the "fertile valley" notion, and the "willow pattern," before we can even begin to realize China.

The town of Wan is one of some size, and foreshadowed that mercantile prosperity which was afterwards to surprise us in this western province. It covers some undulating ground close to the left, which is there the western bank of the river; and a tolerably sized creek, coming from a deep valley in the highlands at the back of the place, divides the city into two portions. An amount of suburb all along the river-face prevents the wall from being easily distinguished when on the water, while the curved roofs of numerous temples and yamuns denote it to be a place of some importance. Two junks are lying a little removed from a crowd of others which line the shore, on the larger one of which is flying a well-known red bunting, indicating that these boats contain four of those people whom the Chinese believe are born in ships, live in ships, and die in ships, except when they land on Celestial shores to sell opium, purchase tea and silk, batter down forts, or burn palaces. It is a foggy morning, so that the beautifully cultivated hills on the opposite shore are but dimly visible, and a thick haze hangs over the rippling waters.

All is bustle on board our junks, for the leading men of the procession have arrived at the river bank. Blankets are rolled up and stowed away; the China servants and Seikhs are arranging tables and chairs under direction of the " writer," whose knowledge of the customs of official etiquette has been derived from a residence at a yamun in some official situation, possibly that of shoe-black. He is very particular that this chair should be towards the west, that to the east, and others to the north or south; but I don't think he is very particular which, for his notion of the points of the compass are anything but clear. He has donned a silk dress and mandarin hat with gilt button, in virtue of an examination which he bribed the examiners to pass him through, and which entitles him to the rank of literary mandarin of some class or other. We get ourselves up each in the costume of his profession; the reverend gentleman appears in the cloth of his calling, and the two military members turn out in their war paint, one of whom wears the uniform of a lancer in Her Majesty's service, and is so bedaubed with gold lace and braid, that, as it is likely he will create a great impression on our visitors, it is unanimously voted that he shall "do the swell," and act as chief man among the party for the day; because it would be incompatible with Celestial ideas that we could be all on an equality; besides, at the official visit at Quai-chow the other day, this military costume had the effect of our being presented with the flag of "Lord High Ambassador," and we could not do better than keep up the silent delusion. The Doctor managed to get up a capital rig, by taking an old frock coat, sewing on it a pair of shoulder-straps of gold-lace, taken from some part of a naval officer's uniform, and distributing "Peninsular and Oriental" buttons over the remainder, in positions where they could be of no possible use in their proper capacities, in such a way as to relieve the monotony of the blue, and complete a tunic, which, had he not destroyed it afterwards in a fit of frenzy at our having to turn back after we had got half-way through our intended journey, might have been brought forward as a pattern at the next change of dress which the British Army undergoes, for it well fulfilled some of those conditions which enter into the composition of our military equipment. Then he extemporized knickerbockers, so that he might not be behind the age, and crowned all by an old gold-banded staff cap, which we had purloined from the kit of the author of the 'Narrative of the China War of 1860,' in expectation of its coming in useful. The Seikhs were dressed out in the uniform of their corps; and being stuck all over with pistols, swords, bayonets, telescopes, and ammunition pouches, they were instructed to present themselves at every possible point where they might meet the eyes of our visitors; and it was left to the havildar (sergeant) to dispose of his three privates and himself, and go through such manœuvres with them as he thought most likely to impress the Chinese with the high state of discipline, and might lead them to form as exaggerated an estimate as possible of the strength of our army. He acquitted himself admirably, for during the visit he was constantly engaged in relieving guard; the "old guard"—excuse me, my unmilitary readers, for this digression into professional matters—the "old guard" marching off to the "present arms" of a supposed "new," and then by a clever manœuvre, executed with admirable skill, in which they made the circuit of the junk's deck, the same three men came round again, and took up their former position, except that the situation of each with respect to his neighbour was changed, and the delusion was thereby made perfect. Whichever way the old Chinese general looked, there was sure to be a revolver pointing directly down his throat, or a fixed bayonet bristling within a few inches of his breast; the military air and voice in which the havildar issued his commands seemed to gain the old fellow's admiration, and I several times saw him making side remarks to his aide-de-camp on the admirable appearance of our troops.

Arrangements were scarcely complete when the main part of the procession moved up to the tune "the old cow died of," played on Chinese bagpipes, which should not be called bagpipes at all, being a kind of flagelet; but they utter certainly quite as detestable sounds as those instruments which so delight the ears of our northern brethren. The soldiers, of whom there were some two or three hundred dressed in scarlet tunics, ranged themselves along the river bank, and a red umbrella or two, which are always part and parcel of a procession, formed upon their flank; some spearmen came next, and then the sedan-chair of His Excellency the Commander-in-Chief of Eastern Sz'chuan, borne by a dozen coolies in holiday caps with blood-red tassels. This was followed by several other chairs, but, not containing men of very high rank, they had a paucity of coolies. Numbers of attendants followed and walked on either side of the chairs, most of whom were armed with respectable rattan-canes, with which they laid about smartly around them whenever the crowd of townspeople became too pressing. His Excellency and staff alighted, and, being invited on board our junk by the officious "writer"—for it would have been beneath our dignity to have gone out to meet him ourselves—they passed our guard of Seikhs, who were drawn up with open ranks, and "presented" rifles and shot guns, and were ushered into our presence. We rose to receive them; they all bowed in the regular Chinese manner, with their two fists together before them, and we raised our caps. The general was invited to take the uppermost seat, which, in perfect accordance with Chinese etiquette, he refused to do, saying at least half a dozen times that he was unworthy; we knew that, but forced him at last to bring himself to an anchor; and the others followed suit according to their rank.

A conversation was commenced in the orthodox manner by our demanding, through Mr. Schereschewsky and his secretary, what was his "honourable age"? and this was followed by a series of questions and answers on both sides, which bore upon no particular point. Some brandy was then served out, and our visitors were asked to partake of "our execrable sam-shoo." The old fellow seemed half afraid; but some of his staff took at once to it so kindly, that we thought they must at some time or another have seen the inside of the factories at Canton; and before the visit was over the quartermaster-general was certainly in a state that would only have been allowable in the very highest grades of our service. But the old general still held off; and it was not until he had been pressed repeatedly, and had seen us drink some of the liquor ourselves, that he got over his scruples. Unluckily, just at the moment that he was raising the cup—we had no glasses—with both hands, as is the custom in their polite society, to his lips, our officious commandant, the havildar, in a loud voice gave the word of command, "Port arms," and the sentry obeyed by bringing his rifle smartly into the position ordered. Poor general!—the cup dropped from his hands, the contents went over his blue-silk dress, and one out of our three remaining tea-cups went to pieces on the floor. "D—n the general," I was going to say, but a recollection of the contents of a military publication, entitled 'Rules and Articles for the better Government of Her Majesty's Forces, &c.,' restrained my mutinous spirit, and I only said, "the brute!" consoling myself by the thought that the proverb must be right, and that it was only an instance of the "many slips between cups and lips." I turned to "Quei-quei," one of our Chinese boys, and made signs to him to bring another cup in as authoritative a way as possible, though I knew it was quite impossible for him to obey me; but in China there is nothing so important as keeping up appearances. However, the general, being composed again after this shock to his nerves, proved not to be proud, and "took a drain" out of his aide-de-camp's cup. After this he seemed to freshen up a little—some men do—told us a good deal about himself, and put to us several searching questions. He had come into this part of the province to arrange the plan of a campaign against the "Tu-feh," or local rebels, and, having made part of his arrangements, was now leaving the army to carry out the rest, and going down the river to Quai-chow, where, being at a respectful distance, he judiciously fancied that intelligence concerning the operations would be more unbiassed, and he would not be so apt to be led into giving rash orders on the spur of the moment, or encourage the troops by his example to perform an operation often known under that ambiguous term "a retrograde movement." He expressed his regret at being able to pay us only so short a visit—respect is denoted by the length of the visit in China—but a junk was now ready for his reception, and he had only called on us *en passant*. We bowed him and his colleagues out with every mark of respect, and the havildar again gave him the "general salute," in which manœuvre he narrowly escaped poking out the eye of the adjutant-general, but luckily there was no harm done, and the visit concluded most satisfactorily.

The general now passed along the line of troops drawn up on the bank, who stowed away their fans and pipes which they had been using while the cat was away, and tried to look as military as possible. He then embarked with his staff and sedan-chairs on board his junk, the soldiers fired three volleys as a salute with their matchlocks, at each discharge of which they turned their heads quite away from the direction in which they fired, and did not raise their pieces above their hips; after which they went down on their knees and knocked their heads on the ground. Then the "dismiss" was sounded, and each one filed off on his own hook; but I observed that many entered the nearest sam-shoo shop, to recruit their animal spirits after the arduous work of the morning. The general's boat was quickly out in the stream, floating down the broad current of the Yang-tsze, while he himself was doubtless soon beyond the reach of all rebels, or other earthly annoyances, in the oblivious regions of opium-smoke.

The next thing to be done was to inquire concerning the best means of getting forward on our journey; and as the Prefect of the place had sent us a very polite message that he was willing to render us any assistance in his power, we decided on paying him a visit forthwith. Our mandarin was despatched at once to procure sedan-chairs; and before the middle of the day we were making our way through the crowded streets of the city towards the official residence, or "yamun," of the Governor. Passing through a series of folding-doors, painted with immense dragons and other fabulous animals, we were set down, and the Prefect, meeting us as we stepped out of our chairs, welcomed us to his " humble abode." Then there was an immense amount of bowing and scraping, and a discussion as to who should occupy the highest seats, which ended in the Prefect himself taking one of the lowest, and perching us up on a raised ottoman. Tea was served round, and the conversation commenced as usual with a series of complimentary questions and answers. We produced cigars, and the Prefect condescended to take one, and out of politeness attempted to smoke it, but commenced by putting the wrong end in his mouth, and then, being shown the right one, he persistently endeavoured to light the one he had wetted in his mouth; and ultimately gave up the attempt in despair and took to his miniature "hubble-bubble." He was a very prepossessing-looking mandarin, and, not being a Mantchou, was devoid of the coarse licentious appearance of most of his brethren in office. We heard afterwards that he was very much liked by the people; and when we descended the river in June, we found the inhabitants of Wan bewailing the loss of so temperate a governor; for his three years' term of office having expired, he had been removed to another prefecture.

This system of frequent removals, instituted by the present dynasty with a view to hinder influential Chinese from taking root anywhere and creating themselves partisans, has been productive of many evils, and "in making," as Huc observes, "into a law of the empire what ought to have been a mere transitory expedient, the imprudent conquerors of China have deposited in the very root of their power a poisonous germ, that has developed itself gradually and borne fatal fruits. The magistrates and public functionaries," he continues, "having only a few years to pass at the same post, live in it like strangers, without troubling themselves at all about the wants of the people under their care; no tie attaches them to the population; all their care is to accumulate as much money as possible wherever they go, and to continually repeat the operation, till they can return to their native province to enjoy a fortune gained by extortion in all the rest. It is in vain to cry out against their injustice and their depredations; it matters little to them what is thought of them, they are only birds of passage; the next day they may be at the other extremity of the empire, and will hear no more of the cries of the victims they have despoiled. The mandarins have thus become utterly selfish, and indifferent to the public good. The fundamental principle of the Chinese monarchy has been destroyed; for the magistrate is no longer a father living in the midst of his children; he is a marauder who comes one knows not whence, and who is going one knows not whither. Thus since the accession of the Mantchou-Tartar dynasty everything in the empire has fallen into a languishing and expiring condition. You see no more of those great enterprises, those gigantic works, which are indicative of a powerful and energetic life in the nation that executes them. You find in the provinces monuments that must have required incredible efforts and perseverance: numerous canals, lofty towers, superb bridges, grand roads over mountains, strong dikes along rivers, &c. But now, not only is nothing of the kind undertaken, but even what has been done under former dynasties is suffered to go to ruin." And again the Abbé observes, "There are, we doubt not, governors of provinces, and prefects of towns, capable of effecting useful reforms, of creating beneficial institutions, and executing works often much wanted; but, considering that they are only there for a day, they have not courage to put their hand to the work; egotism and private interest easily gain the upper place in their thoughts; they occupy themselves exclusively with their private affairs, leaving the interests of the public to be looked after by their successors, who in their turn leave it to those who may come after them. This system, supposed to be established with the object of withdrawing the mandarins from private and family influence, and rendering their administration more free and independent, has had the very opposite effect."

I should like to draw much more from the writings of M. Huc on the Chinese system of government and its effects, but the foregoing must suffice for the present; any of my readers, however, who have never perused the works of that worthy missionary, I should recommend to do so rather than continue reading this dull narrative. In his 'Journey through the Chinese Empire,' which may be had either in English or French, the character of the Chinese, their customs, government, and institutions, will be found described in a most instructive and pleasant manner; the book once taken up will, I know, not readily be cast aside till his amusing narrative is finished, and the reader will close the volume with a better idea of China as it really is, than had he laboriously studied half the other works on the "Central Flowery Land."

But I have digressed from our visit to the Prefect of Wan; and, had I confined myself to my proper subject, should have mentioned how very civil he was to us, how ready he was to afford us information concerning the country between that place and Ching-tu, which he declared to be infested with rebels in every direction, through whom it would be impossible for us to make our way, and how he pressed upon us not to think of attempting it, but advised us, if we would persist in going on, to continue to travel by water as far as Chungking, where we should be able to hear more with respect to the rebels in the immediate neighbourhood of the capital, and perhaps—but he judged it very unlikely—be able to reach that place. We thanked him very much; and after finishing up with almost as many compliments as we had commenced with, we were bowed out of his yamun, and, our chair-coolies pushing their way through an enormous crowd of people at the gate, proceeded down a long flight of steps to the river, where we got on board our junks again, and held a consultation on the aspect of affairs, which looked anything but propitious. In the afternoon the Prefect paid us a return visit, and we entertained him much after the manner of the Tartar general in the morning. He again tendered his assistance in anything we required, and even offered to procure us suitable junks for our passage to Chung-king, and pay half the expense from his prefecture, the remainder to be defrayed from the revenue of the place. He was under the impression that we were travelling under the immediate authority of the emperor, and wished to treat us with proper respect. In fact, government officials who are on a journey are forwarded from place to place in this way, the districts through which they pass being obliged to provide for their transport.

In the evening we received some presents of fresh meat— I believe to this day that it was dog—and some of the better kind of "sam-shoo," as all spirit is called, and in return we sent to our friend the Prefect a bottle of choice brandy and two or three articles of European manufacture, with elegant excuses of our inability to offer him anything better. But our stock of beer and wine had long since run out, and we were reduced to living almost entirely on the resources of the country. I have before noticed the exorbitant price which we paid for fowls in another part of the country, but we found it no exception to the general rule, and it is only to be accounted for in this country of fowls by supposing that in a general way fowls are more kept for the sake of their eggs than for eating. No doubt we paid far more than we ought to have done, but where do Englishmen not do so? in China, with Chinese servants, one must expect to be fleeced; the only way, unless you wish to keep yourself in a continual state of fever, is to submit quietly to the imposition. If any one can give me a prescription by which to remedy this evil, which is incidental to most modes of travelling in most countries, I shall be delighted in my next cruise to try it; but let it be one which will allow me to have a quiet life.

Having endeavoured without success to find a junk the captain of which would agree to take us forward at a lower price than was asked for those we were in, we were at last compelled to come to an arrangement with our old skipper, by which he agreed to take us in our two present boats to Chung-king for a matter of 46,000 cash, and promised to be ready to start on the following morning. The evening turned out cloudy, and precluded the possibility of any astronomical observations which I had wished to get, so as to complete the series commenced on the previous night. We therefore amused ourselves in the evening by a conversation with our mandarin and some few respectable people whom we allowed to come on board; but we obtained little more information to be relied upon about Wan than about any other place we passed on the route. "Some myriads," was again the answer we received with respect to the population, and everything else was alike indefinite and uncertain; the only way of gaining a knowledge of the Chinese either in their domestic or government relations is by living among them at the place about which you require to be informed. Reports and accounts through their hands are apt to receive such an amount of colouring and transformation that they can never be relied on, and hence most of the compilers of works on the Celestial Empire should have confined themselves to what they actually saw with their own eyes, by pursuing which course they would have given to the world quite as much true information, and would not have been liable to have many of their statements afterwards disproved, and thus their whole narrative doubted.

Then again it has been too much the fashion to generalise on China, and I don't know any one who has brought forward this fallacy better than M. Huc; he says,—"Let us suppose that a citizen of the Celestial Empire, wishing to become acquainted with that mysterious Europe whose products he has so often admired, makes up his mind to visit the extraordinary people of whom he has no knowledge beyond a vague notion of their geographical position. He embarks, and, after traversing the ocean till he is sick of seeing nothing but sea and sky, he reaches the port of Havre. Unfortunately he does not know a word of French, and is obliged to call to his assistance some porter who has picked up, somehow or other, a little Chinese; he adorns him with the title of interpreter, or *toun-sse*, and gets on with him as best he can, eking out his words with abundance of pantomimic gestures. Furnished with this guide, he traverses the streets of Havre from morning to night, disposed to make an astonishing discovery at every step, in order that he may have the pleasure of regaling his fellow-countrymen with his wonderful adventures on his return home. He enters every shop, is enraptured with all he sees, and buys the most extraordinary things, paying, of course, two or three times what they are worth, because there is an understanding between his interpreter and the shopman to get as much as possible out of the barbarian. Of course our Chinese is a philosopher and a moralist, and therefore takes a great many notes; he devotes the evening to this important labour, to which he calls in the aid of his guide. He always has a long series of questions ready for him, but is a little embarrassed because he can neither make his own questions quite intelligible, nor understand very clearly the answers returned. Nevertheless, after making the effort of coming to the West, it is absolutely necessary to acquire a mass of information, and to enlighten China on the condition of Europe. What would people say if he had nothing to tell them after his long journey? He writes, therefore, sometimes according to the information of a porter whom he does not understand, sometimes at the dictation of his own suggestive imagination. After a few months spent thus at Havre, our traveller returns to his native country, well disposed to yield to the entreaties of his friends not to deprive the public of the useful and precious information he has collected concerning an unknown country. No doubt this Chinese will have seen many things he did not expect; and, if he be at all well informed, might prepare a very interesting article on Havre for the 'Pekin Gazette.' But if, not content with that, he takes up his too ready pen to compose a dissertation on France, the form of its government, the character of its senate and legislature, its magistracy and army, science, arts, industry, and commerce, not to speak of the various kingdoms of Europe, which he will liken to France, we much suspect that his narrative, however picturesque and well written, will contain a mass of errors. His 'Travels in Europe,' as he will no doubt call his book, cannot fail to convey to his countrymen very false ideas regarding the nations of the West." In another place Huc says,— "Even a missionary, who has resided many years in the bosom of a Christian community, will no doubt be perfectly acquainted with the district which has been the theatre of his zealous labours; but if he undertakes to extend his observations, and believes that the ways of the converts around him are those of the whole empire, he deceives himself, and misleads the public opinion of Europe."

We remarked that the inhabitants of the country as well as the townspeople of Wan were in a much better condition than those who dwelt among the gorges and in the mountainous region which we had lately passed. Everything looked thriving; and during a walk which we took a little way into the country on the opposite shore of the river, we were all struck with the carefulness displayed in the cultivation of every inch of ground which it was possible to irrigate. A number of the townspeople had come down to the boats to get a sight of us, and, not finding us on board, many of them followed us across the river, and we gave such as chose to keep up with us a walk across the paddy-fields and gardens which, in their thick-soled clumsy shoes, they were hardly prepared for. We found them very civil and polite, and I will say once for all that the only people of all those we met who caused us the least annoyance were the soldiers, or "braves," at some of the towns. Such was, however, the exception, and I very much doubt if a party of grotesque-looking strangers in travelling through some of those countries of Europe which boast so much of their civilization and refinement would have met with equal civility.

At or near Wan coal exists, and is extensively used. In the town we observed exposed for sale sulphur, ginger, sulphate of copper (?), spices, and cotton prints. Tobacco, peas, beans, wheat, barley, and poppy were growing, and the rice was beginning to spring. We saw plenty of sugar-cane, but none in the ground. The "Tung-shu" tree was still very common. The weather was now becoming oppressive, although the thermometer seldom stood over 71° at noon, and ranged from 56° to 62° at sunrise; but by the 21st of April we had the temperature in the shade above 80°. There was usually little or no wind, and the atmosphere was thick and hazy, which caused us to feel the heat more than we otherwise should have done. All meteorological details will be found in the Appendix, where it will be observed that readings of the thermometer were made four times daily; the barometer, which was an aneroid, was recorded thrice, and the wind and weather were always noted five times during the day; but the latter have been condensed so as to bring them within a limited space. Specimen pages of the Expedition 'Log' and 'Field Book' have also been appended, to give an idea of the mode in which we kept our records, and to enable those who are particularly interested in the subject to judge of the degree of dependence to be placed on our observations, and as a hint to future travellers. I may mention that every part of the river navigated by us was sketched in the manner shown on the page of 'Field Book;' in pencil on the spot, but inked in always within twenty-four hours; and no additions or embellishments have been since added. The 'Log' contains information picked up by all the members of the expedition, besides which each kept his own private note-book. Nothing was left to memory, and the little difficulty I now find in collecting facts is a proof of the fulness of those records. I should, however, have missed many of the minor incidents of our journey, if Dr. Barton had not kindly placed at my disposal all his private notes, and being now in this country he has afforded me the most valuable assistance in many ways. I am moreover indebted to Lieut.-Colonel Sarel for several valuable observations which he has forwarded to me from India, where he is now serving, besides a pamphlet, entitled 'Notes on the Yang-tsze Kiang from Hankow to Ping-shan,' which he published at Hong-kong for distribution among his friends, and which has been read before the Royal Geographical Society. This, though it contains nothing more than is recorded in the 'Log,' a copy of which Lieut.-Colonel Sarel made each day, has been of some assistance to me in arranging my own notes. Mr. Schereschewsky, the missionary gentleman who accompanied our party, moreover placed at my disposal some of his observations on the people with whom we came in contact, and my best thanks are due to him on that score. My readers will I hope excuse me for these few remarks, which I have placed here, where they are applicable, rather than lengthen out a preface which few would read, and no one recollect.

The breadth of the river at Wan was, at the time we passed up, within a few feet of 550 yards; but just opposite the place there then existed an extensive shingle-bed, which being covered at high water, the width of the river would be increased very considerably. Just above, however, the stream is contracted very much by rocks which jut out from either bank. We carried a line of soundings across in a north-east direction from our anchorage off the middle of the town, and found the depth to increase from three and a quarter to nine fathoms, and then gradually decrease again to the other shore. On the chart, which is on the point of publication by Mr. Arrowsmith from our survey, all the soundings will be found inserted, and the nature of the banks, the shoals, rocks, and country adjoining the river, laid down as accurately as was possible under the circumstances. The reduced scale of the map of the river attached to this work of course precludes the possibility of showing anything more than the general features.

Some Christian Chinese discovered themselves to us at

Wan, and, taking Mr. Schereschewsky for a padre, they prostrated themselves before him, but he raised them up and quickly gave them to understand that such was not the fashion in our religion. They appeared much affected at meeting with Christians of another nation, and really seemed to have some sparks of religion in them. There is little doubt that the Roman Catholics have done much more in China than the world gives them credit for, and from this place upwards we observed numerous Christians among the Chinese. They used to make themselves known to us by the sign of the Cross, and seemed always to look upon us in the light of superior beings. The number of Christians in the province of Sz'chuan is said to be about one hundred thousand. There are two bishops, and we had subsequently the pleasure of meeting one of them as well as two of his priests, and my remembrance of them will ever be associated with the idea of missionaries indeed. To such men as these, who leave their country and friends with the sole object of carrying salvation to a heathen people, whose dress and habits they adopt, and among whom they live, often in a manner which would not be coveted by the very lowest among an European population, to say nothing of the risk of their lives, and the tortures of which they must ever stand in danger—cut off from all intercourse with the outer world, with none of the luxuries and few even of the necessaries of European civilization—is due a meed of praise which I am unworthy to proclaim, and will therefore only refer to the contrast between them and the Protestant missionaries. Located among the European and American communities at the open ports on the coast, the latter live in all the ease and comfort of civilized society, surrounded by their wives and families, with dwellings equal, and often much superior, to what they have been accustomed to in their own country; they are in constant communication with all civilized parts of the world, by a regular mail service; and I believe I shall not be wrong when I say there is not a single Protestant missionary a hundred miles distant from an European settlement. I am informed, however, that some Protestant German missionaries are adopting the Roman Catholic plan, and intend to penetrate into the interior disguised as natives; but I have not had the pleasure of meeting any of them. What is the reason of this? It may be said that to disguise oneself in native clothes and travel through the country would be a species of deceit incompatible with the sacred office. I have always thought that Huc was a little severe on Protestant missionaries when he referred to "the Bibles prudently deposited by the Methodists on the sea-shore." The Abbé doubtless held that the end justifies the means; but on the other hand, Protestants urge that if their heads were in danger they would be forced to deny their calling and nationality without the advantage of "mental reservation;" while Huc himself allows that for a "long pilgrimage" to "terminate in some ditch behind the ramparts of a Chinese town," is not "the martyrdom that missionaries sigh after."

But what with mandarins, missionaries, and mistakes, I have run on so far that I must leave our voyage above Wan to be commenced in another chapter.

CHAPTER XI.

THE GOLD-SAND RIVER.

Two hundred miles lay between us and Chung-king on the morning of the 18th April as we left Wan. It was our thirty-third day on the Upper Yang-tsze, and over two months since we had left Shanghai. The first few miles our course was a little east of south, after which we entered a long reach of the river in a south-westerly direction, in which we passed a short rapid called Hu-tan. The Chinese affixes which we found most common were "tan" or "chi," each of which signifies "rapid;" "hia" meaning "gorge," and "shun" "village." The river was nearly half a mile in width in many places, with extensive sand and shingle flats, intermixed with reefs of rock, where were numerous gold-diggings; and the hills being less confused, and assuming more the form of ranges, gave a more open and pleasing appearance to the scenery. Some high hills were observed away to the south-east. The rock was a grey sandstone, which was occasionally scattered in blocks along the banks in great confusion. Near the tops of some of the hills were temples hollowed out in the cliffs, and approached by flights of steps. The door of one could only be reached by a ladder hanging vertically some sixty or seventy feet. We anchored for the night about fourteen miles above Wan, at the small village of Ta-chi-kow, where the latitude was determined.

The next day was one of great interest. The river varied considerably in width, but with no rapids, and only a few strong places. The general direction was S.S.W., and parallel to a range of mountains some twelve hundred feet high, distant about six miles to the eastward, which were partially wooded, and between which and the river was a beautiful hilly country, wooded in a few patches, and highly cultivated. We passed the villages of Hu-lin and Si-kiai-tow, the former on the left and the latter on the right bank. Si-kiai-tow is not built close to the water, but runs back from the river up a steep incline. The houses had the black and white appearance of the old-fashioned farm-buildings of Cheshire, although a closer inspection would no doubt dispel the resemblance. On rounding the point opposite this village, the rock, temple, and pagoda of Shi-pow-chai came in view, the interpretation of which name is "the House of the Precious Stone." The rock is a detached mass, with the appearance of a block or stump; its sides are perfectly vertical and about two hundred feet high, while the base is about an equal height above the river. We took it to be about fifty by thirty yards across the top. A nine-storied pagoda, said to be fifteen hundred years old, is built against the eastern face, and the rock is crowned by temple-buildings. It is a most singular place, and I can best do justice to it by referring to Dr. Barton's illustration. We took frequent soundings this day when crossing the river, and on three occasions got no bottom with ten fathoms. We halted for the night two and a quarter miles above Shi-pow-chai, at a sand-flat.

Hu-lin, which we had passed during the forenoon, seems to be almost entirely a Roman Catholic village; and when the inhabitants saw our junks approaching, they came out in great numbers to welcome us, having heard who we were from boats which had preceded us from Wan. The small junk (we still travelled in two) was ahead, and the delighted villagers seized upon the Doctor and Mr. Schereschewsky, brought sedan-chairs for them, and hurried them off to see a place of worship which they had lately finished. Here they

SHI-POW-CHAI.

laid out sweetmeats, tea, and sam-shoo for them, and requested that our party should stay a day among them; but of course this was impossible, as we had a long journey before us, and, considering how far the season was advanced, we were jealous of any delay. We remained, however, about half an hour; and during the whole time there was nothing but one continual *feu-de-joie*—crackers and guns going off every instant, and in all directions. The following I take from Dr. Barton's journal:—

"The larger junk, containing the rest of the party, being far behind, we gratified them by visiting their chapel. Sedan-chairs were in waiting, and we landed under an imperial salute of three guns, while crackers and fireworks were let off without number. No common coolies carried our chairs, but the gentlemen of the place, who disputed among themselves for this honour; and as we passed through the narrow crowded streets, fireworks and bombs were exploded by a procession in front, almost suffocating us with the smoke. We found their chapel to be a miserable building containing the usual Romish decorations; but they told us that the mandarins had recently destroyed their little church, and that they had not yet the heart to rebuild it. In spite of our remonstrances, these proselytes prostrated themselves before us, bumping their foreheads three times on the ground, considering it a great privilege, and repeatedly asking our blessing. Mr. Schereschewsky tried to explain to them the difference between Roman Catholics and Protestants, but they could not understand it, saying that we all worshipped the same Jesus Christ and his Mother. On returning to our boats they loaded us with presents of sweet cakes and other Chinese dainties, and begged us to report to the Bishop of Chung-king the shameful treatment they had received from the mandarins." Dr. Barton farther remarks:—"This was only one of the many instances we witnessed of the good the Catholic priests have done in China, while throughout our journey we did not meet with a single Protestant.

On the 20th the same range of mountains as on the day previous stretched on our left hand, to the east and south-east, between which and the river the country was hilly, partially wooded and cultivated as before described. The river was tortuous, and in parts very wide, with many reefs of rock, extensive shingle and sand points, and islands. At one place there is a tract of high land about a mile and a half in length, which is cut off by a loop in the river-bed; water was seen at both ends of the loop, but from there being no current we supposed that at that time of the year the communication was not complete; sand and rock flats extended over a mile above the upper entrance. When we descended in June this was a *bonâ fide* island; and a large volume of water passed by the north-western channel. We hauled up the rapid of Tow-to-hiu soon after the middle of the day, where we had some difficulty on account of the water shoaling out a long way from the right bank on which the trackers were, requiring a very long towing-line; we got on one or two rocks, and once broke the line. The reefs, which are numerous in this part of the river, often form rapids, but not always entirely across the river; these are frequently difficult for boats, which have to tow up along the shore, but there is no rapid in which there is not deep water in one part; and I fancy that a well-powered steamer would make nothing of them. These reefs were not usually more than two to four feet out of water, and would consequently be dangerous when the river is higher. Nearly all the gravel-flats and "bars" were being worked for gold.

We had seen and obtained a bearing of a tall nine-storied pagoda on a hill at noon, but from the crooked nature of the river it was evening before we arrived at Chung (chow). Mountains lie to the west and west-north-west, and a hilly country to the south-west of this place, which is itself situated in a very picturesque region, much wood existing close to the town and about the temples. We passed a little above the town, which is but a small place, notable I think for its temples and pagodas more than anything else, and made fast to the opposite shore. The forenoon had been oppressively hot, with but little breeze; at noon it was calm, cloudy, and hazy; and at three in the afternoon we had a thunder-storm, with heavy rain and wind from the westward; it calmed down by evening, and the thermometer stood at 69° at 8 P.M. Some more Roman Catholic Chinese visited us here, continuing to come over in boats from the town till a late hour. They were extremely desirous that we should provide them with a written order such as the mandarins would respect, as they had heard (perhaps from the Christians at Hu-lin) that the late foreign treaties stipulated for religious freedom throughout the empire; but we informed them that we were only private individuals travelling through the country, and that we had no authority or power to grant their request. They stated that the mandarins had persecuted them and burnt their church, and they begged that we would mention the fact to the Bishop, if we should meet him.

In the evening the black cuckoo enlivened the groves with his sonorous notes, while the frogs in the neighbouring terraced paddy-fields kept up a chorus that we might well have dispensed with. With these latter it is one uninterrupted chirrup, perfectly regular and monotonous, except when the hoarse croak of the bull-frog comes in, for all the world like the bark of a dog; this fellow only drops in his note occasionally, for there are usually not more than one or two to a pond, while the chirping of the others is continuous.

They are very curious creatures, and I have rather an affection for them, excepting always in curry; and I sometimes would go and have a talk to them on the side of a pond. When they are all in full cry, I suddenly bawl out at the top of my voice, "Stop!" There is a dead silence immediately; then, after a little while, one by one they commence "chirrup," "chirrup," until they are again all off "chirruping" away as hard as they can go. Again I shout, and they stop again; but they do not heed my command long, and so I bid them "good night;" and as I stroll towards the boat I fancy how many of them will be strung on a string to-morrow, and sold to delight the Chinaman's appetite. Even now I fancy I see a sunburnt fellow, with his drawers rolled up on his thighs, a little net, for all the world like a miniature landing-net, in his hand, and a sort of creel at his back, prowling along the edge of the pool: suddenly he makes a dart; and one of my friends of the previous evening is soon struggling away in the wicker basket. It was the father of a fine young family of frogs. In a minute or two one of his children is consigned to the same cage, and the mother and the others hop and swim away out of reach of the net. How cruel! Separate the father from his loving children!—for there is love among frogs—or, being all caught, sell them separately, to be boiled in different kettles! Shocking! Why, it's as bad as the negro auction. The catcher of frogs must be a hard-hearted man.

From Chung it took us two days' travelling, at the rate of eighteen geographical miles a day, to reach Fung-tu, during which we passed four villages and two islands. The first day the river was somewhat tortuous, and very irregular in width, being three-quarters of a mile in one or two places, with extensive sand, shingle, and rock flats, with numerous rocks and reefs; nearer Fung-tu, however, its course is more direct, but still in some parts it contains many rocks. A line of soundings between Binquei Island and the left bank gave only four fathoms as most water; and I particularly note this, as it was the least we had obtained anywhere above I-chang. Three miles above the village of Yang-tu-chi (all the places here referred to will be found on the map), a mass of rock, projecting from the left bank, forms a narrow pass, not over two hundred and fifty yards across; and immediately above Fung-tu the river is similarly obstructed. The rock which causes this was, at the time we passed up, ten to twelve feet above the water, and with a generally level surface; but on passing this place again in June, when on our downward voyage, the river had risen so as to cover nearly the whole of it, and the impetuous stream rushed past with irresistible force, the dark, earth-laden, chocolate-coloured water boiling up in the deep parts, and foaming over the shoals. We ran down, however, without accident, the only precaution required being to keep the boats in mid-channel.

We continued to travel among ranges of mountains; and below the village of Wu-yang a peak, some 1500 to 1700 feet high, is seen, distant about eight or nine miles to the south-east. It is probably the termination of the south-south-west range mentioned as running nearly parallel with our course on the 19th and 20th. Another range commences near Chung, and, running in a south-westerly direction, is, at the village of Yang-tu-chi, about five miles distant to the north-west, and is observable thence as a continuous and well-marked range as far as W.S.W., with a hilly country intervening between it and the river. These mountains were not under 1500 feet, and were more wooded than any we had before observed. Below Fung-tu the country in the immediate vicinity of the right or east bank is merely slightly broken by low hills; while, on the other bank, heights border the river almost without intermission. Around the place there are hills to the north, while across the river to the south and east the country is also hilly, backed by mountains, some of which take the form of decided peaks, but the mass appear to have no regular arrangement.

Fung-tu (hien) is, I think, one of the prettiest places on the river; the town itself is not of a very imposing appearance, but the scenery around it is most beautiful. Situated in a picturesque neighbourhood, where either river or mountain meets the view on every hand, the lower heights close to the place are thickly wooded, and half-hidden temples, with their curved roofs and curious windows, peep out from among the groves, bringing out by their patches of red the fine dark green of the foliage. Near the embouchure of a tolerably-sized tributary falling into the Yang-tsze opposite the town, stands a seven-storied pagoda, which is visible for some distance before approaching the place; another marks the north end of the town; a third is situated on an island between the city and the mouth of the Kow-kia-wan; and a fourth stands on a hill away to the south-south-east. On the opposite bank there are several of the peculiar black and white Sz'chuan farm-houses, amongst groves of bamboo and larger trees, and a few bananas and palms are intermingled with cedars, poplars, and other extra-tropical forms, while the land around is cultivated with that garden-like minuteness for which China is so famed.

It was evening as we passed Fung-tu, an evening after heavy rain in the afternoon—a Chinese April shower; vegetation was in its most lovely stage, the light and dark greens alternating in the most beautiful manner; birds were singing their farewell chorus to the departing sun; and we could well believe Huc when he pronounces Sz'chuan to be the finest province of the empire. "Its temperature," says the

SZ'CHUAN HOUSES.

Page 188.

Abbé, "is moderate, both in winter and summer; neither the long and terrible frosts of the northern, nor the stifling heats of the southern provinces, are ever felt in it. Its soil is, from the abundance of rain by which it is watered, extremely fertile, and it is also pleasantly varied. Vast plains, covered by rich harvests of wheat and other kinds of corn, alternate with mountains crowned with forests, magnificently fertile valleys, lakes abounding in fish, and navigable rivers. The Yang-tsze Kiang, one of the finest rivers in the world, traverses this province from south-west to north-east. Its fertility is such that it is said the produce of a single harvest could not be consumed in it in ten years. Great numbers of textile plants are cultivated in it; among others, the herbaceous indigo, which gives a fine blue colour, and a kind of hemp or thistle, from which extremely fine and delicate fibres are produced. On the hills are fine plantations of tea, of which all the most exquisite kinds are kept for the epicures of the province. The coarsest are sent off to the people of Tibet and Turkistan. It is to Sz'chuan that the pharmacists from all the provinces of the empire send their travellers to lay in their stocks of medicinal plants; for, besides that immense quantities are collected in the mountains, they have the reputation of possessing more efficacious virtues than those found in other countries. A considerable trade is also carried on here with the rhubarb and musk brought from Tibet. It would seem as if the richness and beauty of Sse-tchouen had exercised a great influence on its inhabitants; for their manners are much superior to those of the Chinese of the other provinces. The great towns are, at least relatively, clean and neat. The aspect of the villages, and even of the farms, bears witness to the comfortable circumstances of their inhabitants; and throughout Sse-tchouen you hear nothing of the unintelligible *patois* so common in the other provinces; the language is nearly as pure as that spoken in Pekin."

We can bear testimony to much of the above, but not all; for we did not, like Huc, traverse the length and breadth of the province, nor had we the means of obtaining the reliable information which he had from his fellow-missionaries. For instance, on the banks of the Yang-tsze we found no tea; nor did we see the "vast plains" he speaks of, because we were not in the vicinity of Ching-tu. But we did observe the general well-to-do state of the people, the contrast presented by the towns, villages, temples, and homesteads to those of other provinces we passed through; and we noticed, moreover, the difference in the people. The effeminate face of the southerner was here seldom to be met with, whilst at the same time the heavy and harsh physiognomy of the northerns was wanting in the more spirited and independent features of the men of Sz'chuan. The only characteristic of the women that particularly struck us was a peculiar mode of dressing the hair above their usually very ugly faces; but I think that it would be hardly fair for us barbarians to pronounce on the beauty of the women in any part of China—save always some of the fair sex about Canton and Hong-kong—for it is quite exceptional to get a good look at them, and it was seldom during our five months on the Yang-tsze that we could induce the people to believe that there was not something about us that they ought to be afraid of. When we landed for a walk on shore—and there were usually some of us walking ahead of the boats as they were being slowly tracked along—and showed any of our bearded faces in the vicinity of a farm-house, or collection of cottages, the female portion of the population instantly "whiloed," as the term is in Canton parlance, that is, bolted off as hard as their little goat-like feet could carry them, and hid themselves in the inmost rooms of their dwellings. Sometimes I used to try and cut them off by a flank movement across the paddy-fields, but seldom succeeded, on account of the innumerable small ditches, and the narrow and winding nature of the paths between the little fields; and I on one occasion was so near going head foremost into one of the numerous cisterns of liquid manure which are common around the farm-dwellings, and take away so much from the pleasure one has in inspecting the other agricultural arrangements, that my ardour in this species of hunting was rather damped; afterwards I adopted stratagem, as being safer than open pursuit, and more adapted to the hot weather which we experienced in the latter part of our journey. Sometimes I crawled stealthily round behind out-houses and pigsties, until I knew that I was within a few yards of an interesting group of Celestial females, when a brute of a cur which lay near would jump up and bark, and the whole assembly dispersed in no time; just like a disappointment that many of my readers have no doubt experienced in their younger days, when in the act of pulling the trigger for a good plumping shot among a lot of fieldfares from behind a hedge, an officious magpie commences chattering in a neighbouring tree and gives the alarm. On other occasions I have been baulked by some dirty, tail-less children being in places where they had no right to be, running away at the sight of me, bawling out "Chang-mow! chang-mow!" But it must not be supposed that my ethnological researches were always so unsuccessful, for I have in more than one instance hemmed a fair one in a corner, where, like a hunted pelican, she has stuck her head against a brick wall, and cried in the most bewitching manner; but after much entreaty, and a little force, I have managed to get a view of her countenance; the sight of that face, when in supplicating mercy it should have been angelic, was—oh, don't ask me! But they are not all quite so bad, and I have seen some very pretty faces in China; but China is a large country.

The Major—I beg his pardon, he is now Lieut.-Colonel—and I were on board our junk as she crossed the river to get to a suitable place for making fast for the night, when we observed a couple of swimmers in the water; they were the "doctor sahib" and the "padre sahib," as the Seikhs called them, and, notwithstanding the swift current, they were making a traverse of the river while enjoying their evening bath. They arrived safely at the opposite bank, and we halted for the night. It was our usual custom to take a bath in the river after the sun became low in the evening, which we found most refreshing after the heat of the day, for the weather was now, although in April, uncomfortably hot. Some of us preferred the morning bath, and usually took advantage of the halt for the men's breakfast, about seven o'clock, to perform our ablutions in the cool though muddy water of the Blue River. Notwithstanding this, we frequently went in for another dip in the evening before sitting down to dinner.

On the 23rd, leaving Fung-tu at 5·20 A.M., we passed during the day the villages of Sou-mun-tze, Lan-tu, and Sun-chi, the two first on the right, and the last on the left bank; at 5 P.M. we arrived at the tail, and at 6·30 anchored at the upper end of the long shingle beach of St. George's Island, so called, in default of any Chinese name for it, in honour of the day. The river had been quite narrow for a few miles after leaving Fung-tu, but after that it widened out; and at a very considerable bend below the island the bed contained large flats of sand, shingle, and rock, and there existed some small rapids below. Gold was being collected from the sand and shingle in the crevices of the exposed rock flats; the mineral, no doubt from its specific gravity, taking up its position at the bottoms of such cracks, and being consequently more easily collected than in the wide-spread shingle-beds.

A fine range of mountains is seen from St. George's Island to the north and north-west, having, like the previous ranges we had observed, a general lay of north-east and south-west. Satisfactory observations were obtained this night, for the latitude by "Spica," the time by "Procyon," and lunar distances east and west of "Jupiter" and "Antares;" and it was midnight, long after everybody had gone to bed, before I completed the observations. This island is another of our crucial "stations," and I wish that I could have found a native name for the place, but the boatmen were totally ignorant of any.

Future travellers on this route must not expect to find the Upper Yang-tsze mapped for them in the most approved nautical manner. My chart professes to be no more than it is,—a route sketch. As such, should it be of use to anybody, I shall feel satisfied; but where it fails in accuracy or want of detail, my excuses must be, the uncertain rate of travelling, the indifferent accommodation in a Chinese junk, and the weather. This last has much effect on travellers in different ways, and is nowhere more prejudicial than in the matter of surveying.

The cultivable portion of St. George's Island is a mile and a quarter in length, and about six hundred yards wide. At the time we first saw it it was covered with poppy, which is grown throughout this part of Sz'chuan very largely; and it is deplorable to think that such an amount of fertile land is devoted to this poisonous drug, so much valuable labour and time being bestowed in this way which might otherwise be devoted to enriching the inhabitants of this favoured land. Tobacco is also very much grown, which, as it is a crop that requires the whole season to bring it to maturity, perhaps takes more soil away from the necessaries of life than its rival luxury, opium. The channel to the east side of the island appeared to have no current in it in April, so that I doubt if the connexion is complete at that season; but in June a very considerable portion of the river passed that way. Immediately above the island there is a pass, or "narrows," formed by a large reef of rock projecting into the river, and which, lying north-east and south-west, is probably caused by the upheaval of the strata, in the same way as the mountains which range through this district, only in a less degree. It gave us some little trouble to get through this pass on the following morning, as it was necessary to haul up one side, then to take to the oars and pull across to the other in the strong current, for the purpose of getting to good tracking ground; in doing which we were nearly drifted through the pass, and it was only by the men jumping out at some peril that we saved ourselves. The town of Fu (chow) is only nine and a half miles above this point, and we arrived there at eleven o'clock.

Fu is situated on the right bank of the Yang-tsze, and on the left of the Kung-tan Ho, which comes from the southward, and is the first large tributary met with above the Tung-ting Lake. On all maps that I have seen, this place has been called "Pei;" and even Williams, the author of the 'Middle Kingdom,' has it so marked on his map, which is somewhat surprising, because he has corrected the names of many other places; and from the method of orthography which he has adopted, his names are much more intelligible to the English reader than the old French translations which have been adopted in most maps. And I will here take the opportunity of stating that in general the copies of the maps by the old missionaries are, with regard to the Yang-tsze Kiang, very correct. On our journey we had not one of these on a large scale, that which we used being forty-two miles to the inch. Mr. Arrowsmith's 'China' also agrees very well with it, except in a few cases where, with his usual sagacity, he has slightly corrected the longitude with advantage. These maps, Arrowsmith's, Williams's, and a Chinese reduced copy of the Jesuits', were the only ones which we possessed of the interior of China; and now that the "Great River" has been surveyed for nearly sixteen hundred geographical miles from the ocean, and with instruments and appliances such as were unknown in the days of those energetic and persevering men, no small praise is due to the first Christian explorers for the extraordinary correctness of their maps and records.

The orthography adopted by us is that used on the charts of the Lower Yang-tsze, the vowels being pronounced as in the following English words: *a*, as in father; *e*, as in there; *i*, as in ravine; *o*, as in go; and *u*, as in flute. This method may be open to some objection, but, take it for all in all, I think it is good and simple. There are certain sounds in the Chinese language which it is impossible to express by English letters, and therefore our attempts are only approximations: "kow," in Hankow and such words, is not strictly correct; and "Sü" is the nearest we can come to in Sü-chow. However, there is nothing like uniformity in such matters, and therefore the system pursued in the naval charts has been carried on in our own.

To the east and south of Fu the whole country is mountainous, ranges running still north-east and south-west, and rising about 1000 to 1300 feet. To the north-west, up the river, there are some sharp-pointed peaks ranged N.N.E. and S.S.W., several of which are crowned with masonry redoubts, said to have been lately constructed by the people of the district. The hills are partially wooded, and near their summits some are quite thickly covered with a growth of small wood. The river in this part contains many rocks, and some dangerous reefs are caused by the upheaval of the strata of grey sandstone. Immediately above the town is a very awkward reef of this kind running parallel with the banks and nearly half way across the river; in April it showed two and three feet out of water, but in June was completely submerged; the strata ran W.N.W., dipping about 30° N.N.E. A piece was broken off the reef, and proved to be sandstone of the carboniferous era identical with what we found for a long distance on the river below this point.

The colour of the Kung-tan when contrasted with the muddy current of the main river seemed clear; and its width at the mouth was from 250 to 300 yards. It is said to be much used by boats for commercial purposes, for by following its course into the province of Kwei-chow there is a connection overland with the waters of Canton. A young priest whom we met when we got to Chung-king had only just come from Macao by that route, and he stated that during the whole journey he had only travelled a very few days overland. I believe, however, that in saying there was a connection with the Canton waters, the people meant that you could get to the waters leading towards Canton; and the route followed by this missionary, as well as we could make out, was from Canton by the "North River" to the "Meling Pass," thence to the Tung-ting Lake, and up what is called on maps the Yuen Kiang, and from it to the Kung-tan Ho, which falls into the Yang-tsze at Fu. I won't say, however, that between the provinces of Kwei-chow and Quang-si there is not a connection over the watershed between the valleys of the Yang-tsze and Canton Rivers, because on maps the waters are made to approach very near one another; but I think it must be a mountainous country.

Fu (chow) is a walled town, but has some fine temples on the summit of a hill outside, and boasts of a large suburb near the water. It has a very business-like appearance, and we noticed a number of junks building and repairing. In the way of vegetable productions we observed a large quantity of poppy under cultivation, the opium-crop at that time being gathered; wheat, barley, peas, beans, and tobacco as before; sugar-cane in small quantities, a few bananas, the castor-oil plant, and some young Indian corn.

Sha-sze. See p. 105.

CHAPTER XII.

CROSS RANGES.

AFTER being pestered by the mob for about two hours and a half we got away from Fu at 1·25 P.M. on the same day that we arrived, the 24th of April; we were forced, however, to stop again before we had gone more than a mile and a quarter, to allow of some of our hands coming up who had gone ashore at the town, and there was a good deal of hammering of brass gongs before they all made their appearance. Our crew was a very mixed lot, with some curious characters among them. There were about five-and-twenty to the large boat, but at different places where we stopped a good many of them changed; so that by the time we gave up these Sz'chuan boats there were very few of the original hands remaining. Among those who kept by us was an inveterate opium-smoker; indeed many of them, from the cheapness of the drug, used opium more or less. He was a tall, well-built, but rather slender fellow, and had evidently been good-looking; but the continued sucking at the opium-pipe had given his mouth a screwed-up and parched appearance, and his eyes were constantly bloodshot, and of that yellowish fishy appearance consequent on a life of debauchery. He was still a young man, and not a bad worker when he was at it, and I often thought of his case, and reflected how sad a thing it was to see a young fellow in the prime of life destroying himself day by day through this vile infatuation. Immediately his work was over in the evening he took to his opium-pipe, and often when kept up late with night observations I stumbled over him stretched on the deck beneath a small grass mat with his little lamp still burning. Then again at mid-day he frequently indulged in a few whiffs in place of the bowl of rice which he should have eaten for his dinner, and I wondered how the man stood the severe work of voyaging when he thus encroached so much on his rest, and deprived himself of his necessary subsistence. There must in this drug be some power which by inducing nervous excitement keeps the frame fit for laborious occupation, under which it would otherwise succumb, without the usual subsistence and rest. Then there was a man who from continually going without clothes had got a skin on him almost rivalling that of the hippopotamus, and was as dark as many a nigger; he was a hard-working fellow, and the swelled and knotted veins on his legs attested a long continuance of severe labour. He was a great singer, and when they all came on board for the purpose of crossing the river, or getting past some precipitous portion of the bank where tracking was not possible, he was usually the one to strike up a song, in which all the others chimed in at each stroke of the oar, and at intervals joined in a general chorus. We could never make out exactly what their songs were, but fancied they were a mixture of voyaging work and licentious ditties, something akin no doubt to the Canadian canoe songs.

There were several others whom I now recollect as well as possible from some peculiarity of habit or physiognomy. The bowsman was a tall well-made handsome man, a fine specimen of the natives of Sz'chuan, with a noble countenance and handsome black moustache; his particular duty was to direct the men who worked the large bow-sweep, which has been mentioned as used in rapids and strong places for keeping the boat's head in the right direction; but when this was not in use he was generally standing at the forepart of the boat with a long iron-shod bamboo pole in hand, directing by his motions the man at the helm, who was guided by him as to the depth of water, which he frequently sounded with the pole, and how to steer so as to avoid projecting rocks and large stones, which he could discover by the eddies of the stream. A good bowsman is of primary importance. His son was among the crew, and assisted his father when extra strength was required in poling the boat's head clear of some obstruction, and the governor often set the boy to take his place at the bow when the navigation was comparatively easy; then lighting his long pipe he squatted himself down, and set to work in the most systematic manner to hunt for vermin in his cotton clothes.

The cook was a curious specimen of humanity, but I fancy quite an enthusiast in his profession, for he seldom got out of the hole in the middle of the deck where his fire and large open cooking-pan were situated; he used to amuse us by the methodical way in which he went to work in washing rice before boiling it, cutting up vegetables, and occasionally frying live eels, whose wriggling motions when scalding against the hot iron of the pan he seemed to regard with intense satisfaction. He was a little bit of a fellow, and owned an old straw hat, which, although it had no crown to it, he used always to take particular care to tie under his chin, for fear of losing so valuable an article. He was minus one eye, which increased the oddity of his appearance. When he came out of his hole at a rapid where every man's assistance was required, his particular department was the drum for signalling to the trackers, on which he used to beat away most vehemently, shouting all the time, like everybody else, as if the lives of all on board were in imminent danger.

Of plain food these men ate voraciously, and by reference to the "log," in which the exact times of starting and halting are invariably noted, I am enabled to give the average time for a meal at seventeen minutes and a half. During the latter part of our voyage, when the weather was very hot, they would eat no less than five times daily, stopping four times during the day for the purpose, and taking their last meal after halting in the evening. They were supplied with food by the skippers, receiving in money only 100 cash, equal to about 5*d*., per diem. But I cannot devote more space to my friends the voyagers, and only hope that others who may follow in our steps on the Upper Yang-tsze will be equally interested in these hard-working and poorly paid boatmen.

Three miles above Fu the course of the river brought us near the fortified hills mentioned in the last chapter, and after this we saw many more of such places. The whole summit of a hill was frequently enclosed by walls of masonry, on others were merely square redoubts sufficient to resist a *coup de main*. We were told that they were of recent construction, built by people of the district as places of refuge to which they might flee in case of rebel invasion, of which they live in great dread. After this we passed through a very picturesque region, and anchored at night about four miles above the small town of Li-tu, where there were some temples perched on the tops of some very pretty wooded hills. About this part of the country we observed a great deal of tobacco under cultivation, wheat, and some very fine four-ranked barley (*Hordeum tehastichum*); also the nettle hemp-plant (*Bœhmeria nivea*), so extensively used throughout China for the manufacture of what is called "grass-cloth." We had no difficulty in procuring vegetables, among which were French beans, peas, a purplish-coloured spinach (*amaranthus*), and cucumbers. Besides Colonel Sarel's ferns, which are given in the Appendix, Dr. Barton collected a few seeds in Sz'chuan; among them were the "Tung-tsze" (*Eloococca verrucosa*), already mentioned; a large creeper (species of *dolichos*); a *melilot*, probably undescribed; a strawberry (*Fragraria indica?*); a vetch, not known; a species of *Xanthoxylon*; an oak (*Quercus chinensis*); and some tubers of a species of *curcuma*.

On the 25th of April, which completed forty days of our pilgrimage on the Upper Yang-tsze, we started at five in the morning and halted at seven in the evening, having made eighteen miles, and reached Chang-show. During the day we passed the villages of Lin-shih, Shi-kia-tu, two other smaller villages, and the rapid of Hwang-pin-ma. The country was hilly, particularly around the village of Lin-shih, and near the rapid, at which latter place the range through which the river breaks was to a great extent clothed with a small growth of trees, and here we saw coal and limestone being worked within a few yards of each other. This was the first of a series of ranges of hills through which the river from the course it pursues is obliged to force its way. By reference to the map it will be seen that we passed through several of them. They are ranged generally within a point or two of N.N.E. and S.S.W., and spread over a large tract of this part of Sz'chuan. I examined them in several places, including the range opposite Chung-king, and always found that the principal rock was the same grey limestone which occurs on such a large portion of the upper valley of this river, but that the upheaval caused limestone to crop out, in the vicinity of which coal was always to be found. I have called these ranges of hills the "Cross Ranges;" and as they are a great feature in one of the geographical districts into which I have divided the country, I shall have to speak of them hereafter. We saw some more fortified camps or redoubts, also of late construction, before we came to Chang-show, which is, by observation made on the opposite side of the river, in latitude 29° 50', and is 677 geographical miles from Hankow, and 1265 from Shanghai. It is but a small place, and hardly worth mention but for a fine stone bridge which crosses a stream that divides it into two portions. At two different parts of the river we found no bottom with eighteen fathoms this day; Colonel Sarel was the leadsman, and I must say that he was most assiduous at that laborious work.

It was a usual thing to see numbers of women at work in the fields during our whole route, and it is right that I should here correct an error into which people in England have been led by taking the accounts of persons who have only visited Canton as descriptive of China. It is very generally supposed,—and I have been sometimes doubted when I have mentioned the contrary,—that the abominable practice of cramping the feet is confined to the ladies of the higher classes, because a visitor to Canton or Hong-kong, when he gets into a sampan from the mail steamer, is rowed on shore by large-footed girls. But we passed through the breadth of China on the Yang-tsze Kiang, and, with the exception of the women (not captives) among the Taipings, we observed that, both among rich and poor, ladies and farming people, cramping the feet was a universal custom. Moreover, the visitor to Canton has only to ride outside the walls of that city into the country and he will find the same thing. The females of the Tartar population do not follow the same custom, but use very high-heeled boots, so as to give the foot something of the same appearance.

It was on the morning of this day that the Doctor, having taken his gun on shore after bathing, struck a little way back from the river, and coming upon a place which had been flooded, but was now left with numerous small lakes and lagoons, got among some snipe. Here he commenced blazing away, intending to make a good bag for breakfast. Meanwhile the boats moved on and soon after crossed to the other side of the river; but the Doctor was so absorbed in sport that he did not observe them, and his partner on board neglected to make the boatmen wait for him; the consequence was that there was no halt called till after half-past eight, when we found our friend was not among the party. There was a village somewhat higher up on the side on which the Doctor was ashore; and, when he found that the boat had gone on, he was forced to walk all round the bend of the river and through this village, where, after much trouble in bringing the people to comprehend his desires, he at last crossed over in a small boat, and arrived on board. He was terribly hot and angry, vowed vengeance against the skipper, and threw his breakfast at the cook when he brought it in cold for him. He had certainly much cause for a good growl, for it was a most oppressive morning, and walking through crowds of stinking Chinamen is not a pleasant thing even in cool weather.

The hot weather was not without its effect on myself also, for I began to feel the continual work of sketching the river all day, and the late hours which I was so frequently obliged to keep for the purpose of obtaining the requisite astronomical observations. I used to awake frequently in the night with the idea that the boat had started, and could not satisfy myself to the contrary till I had got up and found every one fast asleep, and not a sign of morning in the eastern sky. Then I would lie down again, and dream a nightmare that the boat was moving on, while I was in some mysterious way tied down so that I could not get out to take the times and bearings as we rounded the points, or that I had lost my field-book in which I was tracing the river's course, or had met with a hundred other similar annoyances. Again, I would dream that I had arrived at some place where it was very important that I should obtain celestial observations, and the same mysterious force which had held me back before would not allow of my going on shore to do so. This

THE CLIMATE OF SZ'CHUAN.

anxiety of mind was such, that at one time I was almost going to give up endeavouring to survey the river any farther; but I was rather obstinate, and I thought that, having gone so far, it would be a pity not to carry it as far as we might go; we should not, I fancied, be much longer on the river, and once on land I might be more a free man; so, buoyed up with this hope, I continued. I had hundreds of miles, however, yet to go before my labours finished; and I do not know how many half-sleepless nights I endured afterwards; but this I know, that, had I been living luxuriously, instead of in the hand-to-mouth way in which we did, I should have been prostrated by fever long before the work could have been accomplished; and to this cause I attribute the almost uniform good health enjoyed by the members of our party during our five months' cruise on the Yang-tsze.

The next day we followed the river's upward course in a south-westerly direction, between two ranges of hills, from six hundred to a thousand feet in height, running nearly north and south, and distant from two to five miles. One reach of the river was long, wide, and clear of obstructions, and another narrower, and obstructed by numerous islands of rock. Making a westerly course, the following day carried us to the westernmost of these two ranges, when we observed again another still more to the westward, the intervening country being broken only by low hills. The river was very variable in width, with rocks and shoals. The thermometer stood at $88\frac{1}{2}°$ in the shade at noon; the barometer had fallen slightly since the day before, and in the afternoon a storm came over which forced us to halt with only eleven miles on the log for the day. The wind came from the north-east and east, with heavy rain and thunder; but it was a great blessing in one way, for it cooled the air very considerably, the thermometer standing at 8 P.M. at 71°, whereas at the same time on the previous evening it had been $87\frac{1}{2}°$.

By reference to the meteorological register which is appended to this volume it will be seen that the month of April in Sz'chuan is of a temperature that would hardly be expected in such a latitude; this hot spring was followed, in the year 1861, by a continuation of rainy weather. We inquired concerning this season of rains, and were told (but we never believed half we heard) that such was not exceptional, and that it would be followed by a very hot summer. Observing the times at which the crops are got in, it will be seen that wheat, barley, and opium ripen during the early part of the hot spring I have mentioned, and are housed before the May rains set in; and that these rains are most favourable for forwarding the young plants of the crops which take their place, and are grown in the same ground—the second crop. Must it not strike every one that this is one of those wise provisions of nature, whereby, when the climate is rightly understood, the greatest amount of produce may be got out of the fertile soil? And I challenge any philosopher, in the conceit of his imagination, to have invented a more harmonious arrangement. The only thing I know of for which these rains are not good is boat-travelling, but every one does not go about voyaging in junks.

On our voyage down the river, when the rice was growing in the paddy-fields, we frequently saw immense bands of domestic ducks being driven about by Chinamen; and it is very interesting to observe the perfect manner in which a duck-keeper manages his troop. He will turn them into a paddy-field with the growing rice, where they can feed at leisure on the smaller aquatic animals, and you see nothing but the quivering of the stalks of the paddy; but immediately he makes a peculiar call, or rattles a split bamboo, out come some hundreds of these intelligent creatures on the banks, and file off at his command to some other feeding-ground, with military precision. Notwithstanding one hears so much of fishing cormorants, and sees a good many in some parts, I do not recollect noticing a single one during our cruise on the Yang-tsze. Many preconceived notions regarding this wonderful country are derived from reports of the embassies which travelled through the length of China on the Grand Canal, or on a highway through most populous districts, where every kind of means has to be resorted to to keep the supply of food up to the demand; and hence, perhaps, many of our exaggerated notions respecting Chinese agriculture and population.

Continuing our voyage on the 28th, we passed a gorge somewhat over a mile in length, by which the river makes its way through another of those ranges of hills already mentioned, after which (without any more high hills, except the continuation of that range in a direction of south by west) we followed a bend to the north, then round to the west, and a southerly reach brought us within sight of Chung-king. At about two miles below the place is a temple situated in a walled garden, and surrounded by some fine trees; inside are statues (one of a joss riding on an elephant), and outside, near the gate, there are two more immense gods made of plaster and painted red, in front of which pieces of "joss-stick" were burning; and some of the more superstitious of our boatmen ran off to knock their heads on the ground before these worthies. It was a very pretty little spot; the temple seemed in good repair, and its bright tiled roof quite perfect, indicating a prosperous state of the country. We observed that one of the high roads to Chung-king ran along the opposite or left bank of the river, being carried across a watercourse by a large and substantial stone bridge of three arches. It must not be expected, when I speak of fine roads in China, that anything is meant more than a paved pathway, for probably the only approach towards anything which we of the West designate as a road is to be found in the north of the empire, about the neighbourhood of Pekin, which district differs in so many ways from other parts of the empire that it can hardly be called China. My experience, which is limited to the country around Canton, Shanghai, and touching the Yang-tsze Kiang, has never shown me anything (if I except the interior of Nanking, which is also exceptional on account of having been once the capital of China) more than a causeway carried through the paddy-fields, seldom as much as, and never exceeding, six feet in width; and such roads, well paved as they are near the large cities, often dwindle into indifferent pathways when you get into the rural districts. There are no doubt some parts of China where good works of this kind have been carried for long distances, but they are of a former age, and under a more vigorous dynasty; you now see only the ruins of such beneficial provisions, and the dynasty of "Sing" seems to be one of beggary and corruption; everywhere its rule appears one of decay; and say what you will of Prince Kung and the regeneration of China, the latter days of the Manchoos have begun,—ay, are well-nigh accomplished. Then the question arises, What is to become of China? Who shall take the reins of government? —the Taipings? I think not; and my conviction is founded on the want of organization among them, the absence in their religion of the first principles of Christianity, and the total disregard they appear to have for the comforts of the population, the encouragement of agriculture, or other settled pursuits.

The Chinese are a people easily governed, for the simple reason that every one has a desire to mind his own business; and if they are not too severely "squeezed" or taxed, they are content to be ruled by any one. Huc mentions that, when he was speaking of the succession to the throne, which one would imagine should have awakened some interest among his listeners, to all his suggestions "they replied only by shaking their heads, puffing out whiffs of smoke, and taking great gulps of tea." At last one spoke to him in the following words:—"Listen to me, my friend. Why should you trouble your heart and fatigue your head by all these vain surmises? The mandarins have to attend to affairs of state; they are paid for it. Let them earn their money, then; but don't let us torment ourselves about what does not concern us. We should be great fools to want to do political business for nothing." Just as I have heard a tradesman at Canton say,— "That no belong my pidgin; my pidgin belong tailor pidgin."* And in another part of his interesting 'Journey through the Chinese Empire,' the Abbé puts the following sentence in the mouth of a Chinaman,—"We do not meddle much in public affairs, because we are persuaded that the empire would not be well governed if three hundred millions of individuals attempted each to make it go his own way." Such is Celestial political philosophy; but still there can be no doubt that there is some antipathy to the Manchoo-Tartar rule; and I am one who believes that, setting religion aside, were an influential *Chinese* party to start a rebellion to-morrow, with the express aim of overthrowing the present dynasty, it would carry the whole country with it. But will this be done, or will China split up into two or more kingdoms, ruled by different sects, and kept from internal strife by foreign bayonets? Are we to see the tricolor, the union jack, and the Russian eagle floating over the capitals of Canton, Nanking, and Pekin? Or are we to take to some other beverage instead of tea, and leave China to fight out this revolution as she has others in former times? Rebellion is no new thing in that country, for the establishment of the Tartars at Pekin was only the end of a period of twelve hundred and twenty-four

---

* "Pidgin" is best translated *business*.

years, during which "China underwent fifteen changes of dynasty, all accompanied by frightful civil wars."

On approaching Chung-king one sees a sharp-pointed pagoda perched on the summit of one of the peaks of the range of hills on the opposite side of the Yang-tsze, to the eastward of the place, and we took it to be a very high one; but a visit to it on our downward voyage proved it to be not above eighty feet in height, its imposing appearance being due to its situation. As we could find no name for it, we called it the "Pinnacle Pagoda," and as such it is laid down on the chart. The mouth of the Ho-tow river, which separates the two towns of which Chung-king is composed, and falls in on the left bank of the Yang-tsze, was reached by us at 2·15 P.M.; but the immense crowd of junks which lined the shore caused us to take a very long time in moving another mile and a quarter up, and it was near half-past four before we came to an anchor off the Taiping Gate, or "Gate of Peace;" but there was no peace for us.

CHUNG-KING.
As seen from the River above. Expedition Junks in the foreground.

CHAPTER XIII.

CHUNG-KING.

SECOND only to Ching-tu in a political way, Chung-king is the most important place in the province of Sz'chuan, while as a trading mart it stands on an equality with the largest cities of the empire; and situated as it is in the centre of the most populous and thriving part of that fertile province, and at a point on the greatest highway of China whence radiate rivers and other means of communication towards all parts of the country, it enjoys an enormous amount of mercantile business. Hence converge all the products of Sz'chuan, to be distributed in various directions; and through it must pass all the imports to supply the demands of this populous province. It is in the west of China what Hankow is of the centre, Shanghai of the coast, and Canton of the south; within its walls northern and southern productions, as well as eastern and western, interchange.

Chung-king is composed of two walled cities, each of the first order, Chung-king (foo) and Li-min (foo); the former on the left, and the latter on the right, bank of the river Ho-tow, at its junction with the Yang-tsze. The present population, from reports of the Roman Catholic missionaries, is about 200,000, of whom between two and three thousand are Christians, besides 500 Mussulman families; but I find it stated in a French translation of a Chinese geographical account of Sz'chuan, that the number of inhabitants at the commencement of the present dynasty was not quite thirty-six thousand. Within the limits of the jurisdiction of the two *foos* are eleven prefectures of the second order, *hiens*.

Both Chung-king proper, and Li-min, are situated on high ground, which still rises as it recedes from the banks of the Yang-tsze; and their walls enclose large areas, which, as is the case with so many other cities, are not entirely occupied by houses. In Li-min there is a large pagoda, and an "outlook" is built on the highest point within its walls, while others are perched on commanding situations outside, for use during the disturbed state of the country.

The Yang-tsze at this place is about 800 yards wide, which is the width of the Thames at London Bridge, and very deep; above, it is narrowed to 300 yards by the existence of large shingle flats and beds of rock near the south wall of Chung-king (foo), but during high water these are covered, and a width of two-thirds of a mile of water must exist, and will in part account for Abbé Huc's exaggerated description of the river at this point. The Ho-tow is at its mouth about 130 yards wide, and enters the main stream with a strong current, which, when we were first there at the end of May, was clear water, contrasting greatly with the chocolate-coloured Yang-tsze; and could be traced for a considerable distance down, before it became altogether lost in the latter. This river receives two tributaries not far above, and thereby drains a very large extent of country, bringing some of its waters even from the province of Kan-su, and the mountain region of Tibet. It is one way by which you may approach within an easy distance of Ching-tu, and is much used for commercial purposes, being said to be navigable for the large-sized inland junks up to Shun-king, even when the water is low.

The country to the west of Chung-king, as far as can be seen from the river, is a good deal broken, though without any high hills; but to the eastward, that is, on the opposite side of the river, there is a continuous line of hills ranged north-by-east, and south-by-west, with numerous small peaks and ridges, varying from 500 to 700 feet above the river, and at their nearest part about a mile and a half from the town. The principal rock of which this range is composed is a grey sandstone, which is general throughout the coal districts; but owing to the upheaval of the strata, limestone crops out and both coal and lime are obtained from these hills. The strata, wherever observed, ran directly in the line of the range, and dipped about 75° or 80° to the west. Specimens of each—the coal, the lime, and the rock—were collected. The great eastern road from Chung-king ascends these hills by a succession of stone steps. There is a collection of temples on the summit of one point, and there are a number of other joss-houses scattered about, as well as some pretty dwellings on the slopes facing Chung-king and the river.

On descending the river at the beginning of June, when we were delayed here some days without occupation, the Doctor and myself ascended these hills, and made a visit to the "Pinnacle pagoda." We mounted the steep slope by means of the flights of steps, and on the road passed a number of eating-shops, such as are usual near any large town, where the coolies, or porters, halt and refresh themselves after a long and weary journey, and where, before they set out on another, they loiter about and spend their cash in liquor until, from necessity, they are forced to leave. At one house the road passes through an archway, and is sheltered by a roof; here we found a large bucket of hot tea, with a bamboo ladle floating in it, ready for the use of any passing traveller who might desire to refresh himself with a draught; and by the number of inscriptions we were led to believe that this was a place of gratuitous refreshment, erected and kept up by some philanthropic individual. Such things are not uncommon in China, and a rich person thinks a public donation of this kind a very honourable act; in the same way that drinking-fountains have become all the rage in England of late years; but we are behind the Chinese in this respect, for our fountains do not spout forth tea. We found some places on the river where public ferries are kept up in like manner.

On the road we met numbers of coolies loaded with coal, grain, and other produce, and others were passing both ways with human freights—fat Chinamen in sedan-chairs. Sometimes the chairs were followed by long strings of ponies carrying baggage, being the travelling party of some mandarin or rich gentleman; and a number of boats were kept constantly employed in carrying these passengers over the river to and from the town opposite the Taiping Gate. The cattle wore straw shoes to prevent their slipping on the wet ground, in the same way as is customary in Northern Japan. We continued our walk to the pagoda, which being situated on one of the highest points near Chung-king, a good view of the surrounding country is obtained from it. To the eastward are more ranges of hills, of a similar nature to that on which the pagoda stands, while the space intervening was occupied by a fertile valley, terraced out in the most symmetrical manner, and the crops, now in their best spring colours, spread an uniform green over the whole landscape. Dotted about were the cottages of the labourers, with usually a clump of graceful bamboo and one or two larger trees alongside each quiet homestead. A couple of hawks soared above our heads, seeming to look upon us as intruders, while a crow sat perched at a respectful distance, awaiting the scraps of food that we might leave behind us, having perhaps in his head the idea that, like the people of the country, we had come to make offerings at the shrines of our ancestors. A little boy ran out from a solitary house hard by, and showed us up to the top of the pagoda, whence we took some bearings, and noted the features of the surrounding country. When we descended we found an old shaven-headed priest in his grey cloak awaiting us, and by invitation we followed him to his house. It was one of the usual form, built round a square, enclosing a covered court, and with a doorway of some pretensions. The old gentleman was surrounded by a fine troop of fowls of a choice breed; a hang-dog looking cur snarled at us as we entered; and a couple of pigs seemed to be as contented, and as well cared for, as the inmates of an Irish cabin. Besides the priest two other men made their appearance, one coming out from a little side room rubbing his eyes, as if he had been taking an unusually late nap; but we saw no women, so we inferred that the old shaven-pated gentleman was a monk; who, while guarding the pagoda and sacred ground in its vicinity, devoted his spare time to farming, and had borrowed the little boy from some family to keep him company in his lonely habitation. We were presented with some very nasty hot water intended to represent tea; pipes and tobacco were handed to us, and we sat down to rest ourselves in the shade of the portico, and enjoy the refreshing coolness of the air of this elevated region. The Doctor's dog, "Bill"—and I must beg his pardon for not introducing him before—attracted a good deal of attention. He was a setter, and his hanging ears were always a great curiosity to the Chinamen, only accustomed to the cocked-up forms of those of their own dogs; and being of quiet disposition, he never got himself into trouble, but allowed the children to play with him and maul him about to their hearts' content. Sometimes, however, we made use of him to keep the people off, by pretending that he was a very savage brute; and by opening his jaws and displaying a fine array of white teeth, we kept alive the notion of his ferocity. Poor "Bill!" he still remains in a distant land, roaming about the settlement at Shanghai with a fine brass collar, on which is inscribed, "'Bill,' the faithful companion of Alfred Barton, and one of the first explorers of the Upper Yang-tsze." When we bade adieu to the old monk, the little boy followed us some distance along the hill-side, and pointed out the best path for us to take to gain the lower country, and then ran skipping back to his adopted father, who came out to watch our progress, fearing, perhaps, that we might deprive him of his child.

The civility which we experienced on our visit to the pagoda was nothing unusual; it was only such as we were in the habit of receiving from the country people all along the route, who always appeared only too glad to welcome us into their houses, and to invite us to partake of the best which their establishments afforded; invariably asking us if we would "eat rice," as the term is in Chinese. Often have I gone into a temple and drank tea with the priest, and then, being presented with an Indian-ink stand and a brush,—for pens are unknown in China,—I have whiled away the time in sketching European ships and steamers, churches, houses, and men and women, which always seemed to delight the bystanders exceedingly. Then I often had fans given me on which to draw and write, and some design which I made in the middle I used to surround with mottos and epigraphs, with the name of the place and date, and sometimes the names of our party; and I should not wonder if the next expedition which may penetrate into the western regions of China may find some of these records. The Chinese are very fond of mottos, every house having numbers of them inscribed in their symmetrical characters on the door-posts and other parts of the establishment; and rich people delight in having long pieces of board or slips of paper hung about on the columns and walls of the interior of their dwellings, on which are inscribed in letters of gold, blue, or vermilion, some of the sayings of their sages, little bits of poetry, sentences of moral advice, or precepts of "filial piety;" and thus they always have before them something to look at and reflect upon in their idle moments. The plan is not a bad one; and were our English characters as picturesque, if I may so draw the comparison, as the hieroglyphics of the Chinese, we might well adopt the fashion.

But there devolves on me a more unpleasant duty than that of acknowledging the civility shown us by the people of the rural districts, for I have now to record the hostility of those of the town, and from this point I may date the commencement of our troubles. As has been already mentioned, the day of our arrival at Chung-king was Sunday, the 28th of April, and the only thing done by us that day was to send our cards to the Governor or "Tau-tai," and a message by the mandarin of our escort to inform him that we should wish to do ourselves the honour of calling upon his Excellency on the following morning. In the evening we received a note by the hands of a Chinese Christian from M. Vinçot, the resident Roman Catholic priest in Chung-king, who had heard of our arrival, containing a polite message from the Bishop of Eastern Sz'chuan, requesting our company to dinner on the following day, with a postscript stating that, if we were not accustomed to use chop-sticks, we had better bring our own forks and spoons. We accepted the invitation, informing him that we should make our way to his house after we had visited the mandarins.

During the evening there was an immense crowd of people collected on shore, and on the junks which we were alongside of, and they had every opportunity of inspecting us as much as they chose at a distance. The *braves*, or militia soldiers, are always the most troublesome; and on this occasion some of them managed to escape the vigilance of the Seikhs and our native guard, and walked into the cabin of one of the boats, no doubt thinking that they could carry matters with us with as high a hand as with their own people, for they are a terrible set of ruffians, and always go about armed, keeping the inhabitants in great dread of them. The Doctor was engaged in writing his notes, or something of the kind, in which he did not wish to be disturbed; and as these fellows began to make themselves rather too much at home in pulling about and examining everything they could lay their hands on, and none of us having a great opinion of the honesty of any Chinese, particularly of these gentlemen, he showed them the door and requested them to walk out, which, after some demur, they did; but when farther motioned to pass along the gang-board ashore, one of them strongly objected, and seemed to argue that, China being a free country, and *braves* being used to roam about and do pretty much as they choose, he did not exactly see why he should not remain on board. The Doctor, however, did not view it in the same light, and so he pushed him towards the board; upon this the fellow resisted, and commenced gesticulating in a most ferocious manner, and attempted to get back into the cabin, having probably seen a good knife there which had taken his fancy. But he was prevented; and when forcibly taken hold of, threw himself down and struggled violently; it was, however, of no avail, and, as he had refused the polite invitation to "pass over the side" in a proper manner, the Doctor quietly took him up and dropped him into the river, to the no small amusement of the bystanders, who, as he mounted the bank wet and dripping, reviled him with all sorts of choice epithets and slang, and he seemed to gain not the least sympathy except from a few of his own cloth,—*braves* of equal plundering propensities.

On Monday morning our mandarin was despatched at an early hour to procure sedan-chairs from the authorities for the purpose of our visit, but he returned with a message from the "Chi-hien," or Prefect, to the effect that it would not be safe for our party to enter the city, as the people were intent on attacking us, should we attempt to do so. Our Chinese servants also told us that they had heard a report of a similar nature the evening before; and just as we were sitting down to breakfast a note was brought, addressed to Major Sarel, of which the following is a free translation. It was dated the previous evening; and a copy of the original, as well as of one that followed it, will be found in the Appendix. " I have heard from my Christians that the Chinese soldiers intend to murder you to-morrow morning when you go to see the mandarins. Take precautions. I have advised the mandarins of the town to look to your safety. I pray you to take your best uniform (with epaulettes), otherwise the Chinese will mock your dress. I expect you and your travelling companions to dinner. I think that the rumours of assassination are serious, and that you should take necessary precautions for your personal safety. I have the honour to be, Sir, your most humble and obedient servant, (signed) J. P. VINÇOT, Mis. Ap." This looked rather serious, but still, knowing how easily Chinese reports are magnified, we sent off the mandarin again to the Prefect to demand chairs, and in case of refusal a letter was given him in which was enclosed a copy of the "Treaty of Tien-tsin," which he was to deliver himself to the Governor; moreover we demanded an audience with him, and that the usual means of transport and escort might be provided immediately. But before we had time to receive a reply, another note came from M. Vinçot. It ran as follows:—"I hear that the Chinese soldiers will certainly murder you and pillage your boats. They have determined to commence the attack during dinner; they intend to destroy my house. I think it, therefore, prudent to defer the invitation till to-morrow, until the mandarins have taken measures for your safety. If you come to-day there will be murder. I pray you, then, excuse me. My dinner is already prepared; but it is impossible for you to come. In greatest haste."

This was altogether beyond a joke, and what made it look worse was, that, in the excited state of the one who read it out, he represented it to mean that the attack was to be made on our boat at dinner-time; whereas the real meaning was that they intended to attack the missionary's house while we were there at dinner, and plunder the boats during our absence. What looked also rather suspicious was, that during the whole morning there had been hardly a soul near the boats, and the only people to be seen were those crowded on the city wall, which was but a little distance from the river, and within easy gingall-shot. Expecting that at any time a large body of men might come sweeping round from behind the houses and fall suddenly upon us, it was debated whether it would not be prudent to move the boats to the other side of the river; but we decided to remain where we were, as any demonstration of fear on our part might be to our disadvantage, and there was always the chance of being able to push off quickly into the stream, should matters come to extremities. But I must say that I did not look up at the battlements above us with much pleasure, when I considered what a confounded slating a lot of gingalls and bows and arrows would give us at that distance.

Immediate measures were taken for defence; the two junks were lashed alongside one another, and the gang-boards taken in. Guns, rifles, pistols, and swords were laid out handy, and we loaded the smooth-bores with revolver slugs in place of bullets, as more adapted for use against large numbers at close quarters. The Seikhs were supplied with the spare arms, told off to different stations, and we all prepared to give soldiers, braves, townspeople, or whoever might be our enemies—for we had heard different rumours—a warm reception. A red ensign was flying in each boat.

The forenoon, however, passed off quietly; and later in the day we sent again to demand chairs, in order to make our intended visit to the governor. It must be remembered that, putting out of the question the impossibility of passing through narrow streets crammed with Chinamen, it would have been beneath our dignity to have thought of walking when on a visit to the officials; and although I am one of those who hold the opinion that, whenever you can break through the customs of a country of which the civilization is considered inferior to your own, you should invariably do so; yet, in a case of this sort, when four Europeans in the heart of an immense empire, cut off from all connection with their own countrymen, and far beyond the sound of the cannons of their gunboats, were endeavouring to pass off as men of high rank, and where anything which might tend to lower them in the estimation of the people or officials, who must be totally unacquainted with the customs of their country, would have been fatal to their enterprise;—under such circumstances I consider that we were right in demanding the utmost respect to be shown to us. If we could even have reached the residence of the governor, it would have been an awkward thing to have found the gates closed against us; to have met officials and servants, particularly civil, and yet protesting that they knew nothing of us, and could not without authority admit us to the presence of his Excellency. Such might very possibly, and would in all probability, have happened; and if so we should never have been called the "Upper Yang-tsze Expedition," but have been forced to return disappointed and irate, and have proclaimed to all the world that we were prevented from continuing our journey by the mandarins. Whereas, as will be seen, by conforming to a custom of the country, which was quite the reverse of derogatory to us as Englishmen, we succeeded in carrying our point and created a precedent—and precedent goes a long way in China—for the benefit of future Europeans travelling in the interior.

The answer of the governor was still the same, that, great as his desire was to meet the "ocean men," it would be impossible for us to pass through the city while the populace continued in such a disturbed state; and he farther mentioned that, with a view to put down the feeling that had manifested itself, he had already issued proclamations, which were posted on the city gates and other public places, showing who we were, that the object which had brought us to Chung-king was peaceful, and forbidding any one to cause us annoyance; and in concluding his letter he said, "I await the result of these measures, and look forward to that bright hour when I shall have the extreme felicity of an interview with their foreign Excellencies." We did not relax our state of "readiness for immediate service," but kept sentries on the junks all night.

Whether the mandarins themselves were at the bottom of the whole affair or not, it was difficult to say. Having no good opinion of Chinese mandarins in general, we were at the time inclined to that opinion; but from subsequent events, and from what we picked up from the Chinese themselves, and were told by the missionaries, I am doubtful if the officials had anything to do with it. At the time of our arrival at Chung-king a large number of people were collected from the neighbouring districts for the public examinations; and the real result of the late war against the Allies, and that a "squeeze," or tax, was to be instituted for the purpose of helping to pay off their demands, had only been known a few days; besides, the treaty had not been promulgated; and all this, together with a report that was current, representing us as the advanced party of a large army of Europeans who were coming up the river to enforce the payment of the ransom money, was, I think, sufficient cause for the excitement. Some may imagine that the forcible ejection of the soldier from the junk, which has been mentioned, might have had something to do with it, but my opinion is quite the contrary. Chinamen understand what comfort is as well as any people, and they were quite able to realize the annoyance which persons pressing on board our junks caused us. In a case of that sort it is not usual for those not directly interested to meddle, and they are only too glad to see an offender punished. Possibly the colleagues of the gentleman who got the ducking might have taken offence at the affair; but M. Vinçot heard of the rumoured intention to murder us so early in the evening as to preclude the possibility of its being concerted on that account. If there was anything in it at all, I think the reasons which I have adduced above were quite sufficient; but apart from those, an attack on our boats may have been meditated for the sake of plunder, for it had somehow got abroad that we carried an immense amount of valuables about with us; though what gave foundation to the report I cannot say. I can answer for myself that I was not at the time worth 500 dollars, and I am sure my wardrobe put up to auction anywhere would not have fetched thirty shillings, and in China probably nothing at all.

On the 30th we sent another letter to the Tau-tai reminding him of his obligation by treaty to afford protection to Englishmen. After some time the necessary sedan-chairs, and a large escort of soldiers provided with stout rattan-canes, were sent down to our boats, and, arranging our plans, three of us, armed, and accompanied by one Seikh also armed, proceeded to visit the mandarins. The number of people in the streets was immense, and during the whole course of our progress we passed through one continuous sea of heads. Cramped up in a sedan-chair, one is not in the best possible position for self-defence, and it struck me as I went along that, if a ruffian made a stab through the side or back of the conveyance, or even came to attack me openly in front, I should be entirely at his mercy. However, thank God! all passed over peaceably, and we entered the yamun of the Governor under a salute of three guns, and the national anthem played on most excruciating bagpipes. During the audience with his Excellency, who looked a thorough scoundrel, he explained, or endeavoured to do so, why we had not been able to pay him our intended visit before, and in many words offered to afford us all assistance in his power in prosecuting our journey; which, however, he said, overland to Ching-tu, was quite impossible, on account of the number of rebels in those districts. But he thought we might be able to proceed by water, going as far as Sü-chow on the Yang-tsze, and thence ascending the Min; and he promised to give us letters to all the prefects on the route, add to our escort, and aid us in every way in his power—fine expressions in English, but, rendered into Chinese, *nil*.

We spoke about other matters, and, like all these men, he seemed anxious to know everything about our "honourable country." After this we proceeded to the yamun of another mandarin,—I think he was a general or something of the kind; and thence, under the guidance of a Christian whom M. Vinçot had sent us, we went to quite another part of the city, where he lived, passing among houses and shops the whole time, built very closely. The place gave us the idea of being a very populous one, and many of the shops and stores were of fine appearance. Altogether I can say without hesitation that the two cities comprising Chung-king more than rival the three which make up the celebrated Hankow.

The house of the missionaries was in no way different from any of the other Chinese houses of the better class. We were met at the door by Monseigneur Desflèches and M. Vinçot, and escorted by them into the inner part of the establishment; for all Chinese houses are made up of two or more kinds of courts, from one to the other of which you pass behind screens thrown across the centre and overlapping each other. Here we were introduced to a younger Frenchman, the one whom I have already alluded to as having just come from Canton by the inland waters. They were all three dressed as Chinese, with shaven heads and queues, but wearing beards, as people in China do who can manage to grow them. Even their manners were Chinese, and, I suppose from the habit they had got into, they used very much the same forms of politeness as Celestials. After relating all the news we could scrape together, we sat down to a repast which had been prepared in Chinese fashion. We commenced as is usual by nibbling away at melon-seeds and other unsubstantial viands, the fish, ducks, pork, frogs, slugs, bird's nests, and many other kinds of Chinese eatables followed in quick succession, and we drank some samshoo of the first quality in a warm state out of beautiful little China cups, carrying on meanwhile a lively conversation in French. But I shall not attempt to describe the dinner, for all dinners are much alike in China, and I need only refer to that stereotyped one which has been copied from one book on China to another ever since the time of Lord Macartney's Embassy to Pekin.

From these missionaries we derived much information concerning the progress of Christianity and the disposition of the officials towards the Christians, which in some places they spoke of as being still hostile, but stated that as a general rule the mandarins cared little what the people thought upon religious matters. They also informed us (and this was of more immediate importance to us) that the whole country between Chung-king and the capital of the province was in such a disturbed state from the presence of rebels, that it would be impossible to get any Chinese to accompany us on a journey overland, and that our only course to pursue would be to travel by water to a place called Sü-chow, whence, if the rebels were not in the vicinity, we might possibly be able to proceed to Ching-tu. They, however, considered it very doubtful if we should be able to make our way, and looked upon travelling through China in European costume as a very bold undertaking. They said that European influence was not yet sufficiently felt in the interior to allow of their adopting the dress of European priests, or avowing themselves openly as Christians; but they looked forward hopefully to the time when, proclaiming their faith openly, the thousands of Christian Chinese would exercise some influence in the affairs of the empire.

In taking leave of these worthy people we received from them many protestations of the pleasure it had afforded them to meet with men whom they might almost call fellow-countrymen, with hearty expressions of their hope that we might be able to accomplish our undertaking. When men exile themselves thus in the midst of a heathen people, whose habits, customs, and sympathies are as contrary to their own as black is to white, and live in continual danger of being brought to trial by barbarous rulers, and suffering at their hands torture, and perhaps death, I ask if we ought not to call them missionaries indeed?

I must not fail to mention that during all the time that the rest of our party were visiting the mandarins, and dining with Monseigneur Desflèches, Dr. Barton was fulfilling an arduous duty—that of guarding the boats. He had three Seikhs left with him, as we only took one, just for show. Barricading the doors and windows of the junks, he stationed his men at their posts so as to resist an attack; and I feel sure that, had any hostile demonstration been made, many a Chinaman would have bitten the dust on that day. As it was, it was with difficulty that the Doctor could restrain the Seikhs from opening fire on some Chinese soldiers who showed themselves at a distance, but without any warlike intentions.

Happily this day, which might have been most eventful, passed over quietly; and neither in the city nor at the boats was there the least annoyance caused us.

After what we had heard, there was no question as to how we should proceed; on the 1st of May we came to an arrangement with our old skipper with regard to boat-hire, he agreeing to take us up in the two junks in which we had travelled to this place, to Ching-tu, for 225,000 copper cash; and the refitting commenced without delay. On the 2nd we moved about a mile farther up the river, to the south side of Chung-king, where we should be more out of the way of the mob, and in a place where we could enjoy our morning's bath without annoyance; and from this position Dr. Barton's sketch of the city was taken. The water of the river had risen very much during the days we had been lying here, commencing very suddenly with muddy water on the 30th of April, rising between five and six feet by noon on the following day, thereby forcing the removal of a number of temporary abodes used for eating-shops and such purposes along the river-bank during the low water season. It is wonderful to see how quickly Chinamen will run up or pull down one of these structures, which are composed of only bamboo poles, bamboo matting, and sometimes palm-leaves; and the enormous works of this kind which are put over any building in course of construction are among the things which appear most marvellous to an European landing for the first time at Hong-kong. Of the same nature are their temporary theatres, which are edifices of a great height. There is at present in the International Exhibition a model of one of these, which will give an idea of the mode of construction, although a few figures, and a house in course of erection, should have been introduced for the purpose of comparison in size. The water of the river began to fall on the 2nd of May, and fell so rapidly that by the day following it had regained its ordinary level for the time of year, leaving a considerable deposit of mud behind it.

Concerning the trade of Chung-king we obtained most information when we visited it the second time. It appears that of late years the trade in European articles has been from Canton, the goods passing by way of the Tung-ting Lake; but previous to the occupation of the lower Yang-tsze by the Taipings this commerce was with Soo-chow, in the province of Kiang-su, and it was by no means inconsiderable. The Appendix will show the description of goods, their prices, and the average demand, as furnished to us by a native merchant at Chung-king, and the list of imports and exports in that paper was obtained from the same source; but I need not here refer to it more than to observe that much of the iron and coal is obtained in the immediate neighbourhood; the copper, lead, and "seih" come from the province of Yu-nan. Hemp, tobacco, sugar, and opium, being generally grown in the province, are from various parts. The silk (which is of coarse quality) and white wax are mostly from the districts near Kia-ding on the Min; but as these districts are now infested by rebels, the quantity of these articles is much less than formerly. Salt, as in many other countries, is a Government monopoly; and we observed none of the works on the Yang-tsze which are mentioned by writers on Sz'chuan. The principal imports, besides paper, spices, and foreign manufactures, are tea and cotton, the former from Hoo-nan, there being only an inferior quality grown in Sz'chuan. The duty on silk, before it arrives at I-chang, is about three taels per picul. Freight from Chung-king to I-chang is, for silk, drugs, &c., one tael per picul, and for less valuable articles thirty cents of a tael. The upward freights are a little less. The average time of transit to Hankow is called twenty days. Embroidery in silk is carried on at Chung-king, and a coarse kind of silk is manufactured. A very fine quality of calcined lime is made from the limestone which crops out from under the sandstone and coal in the neighbouring hills, a little of which was preserved among the geological specimens. The immense number of junks, the greater part of very large size, which we observed collected at Chung-king, and those which we saw *en route*, convinced us that the mercantile importance of this place had not been overrated by our informants.

Before leaving Chung-king we received presents of a superior quality of spirits, sweetmeats and other eatables, from our friends the Roman Catholic missionaries, as well as a peace-offering from the Tau-tai; but owing to our stock of luxuries being very nearly exhausted, we were not able to make them as suitable returns as we could have wished. I shall now take leave of Chung-king, concluding with an extract from a letter sent at the same time that our own letters were forwarded by the kindness of Monseigneur Desflèches, and communicated to the Royal Geographical Society by Sir Hercules Robinson, the Governor of Hong-kong. It reached Canton about the 15th of June:—

" The English caravan (travelling party) arrived at Chung-king the 28th of April. Monseigneur Desflèches was absent in the country. M. Vinçot received them. On Tuesday, 30th April, Monseigneur Desflèches returned, and invited them to dinner. The city was in such commotion, and its people (who had never seen Europeans in their costume before) were so threatening, that Dr. Barton and the other gentleman remained on board to guard their property, with the four sepoys; and Major Sarel and Captain Blakiston accepted the Bishop's invitation. These gentlemen also saw the mandarins of the place, who at first refused, but afterwards granted them chairs (*des palanquins*). They carried on their boat the flag of an ambassador, being so directed by the authorities at Hankow. They left for Ching-tu, the capital of the province, on the 4th or 5th of May, expecting to reach the Himalayas about September or October. They were to travel by water to the capital, the land-route swarming with rebels; and Monseigneur Desflèches had doubts of their making their way. M. Vinçot gives a deplorable account of the state of Sz'chuan, and calculates the number of the rebels in those parts at over 300,000. The Government troops, he says, are as great ruffians as the rebels, and invariably finish the work of plunder that the latter have begun."

CHAPTER XIV.

THE FOUR VALLEYS.*

AFTER having determined the Taiping Gate to be in latitude 29° 33′ 50″ N., and longitude 107° 2′ E. of Greenwich, ascertained the variation of the compass to be 2° 26′ E., and gained all the information possible about the city, the neighbouring country, and on that all-absorbing topic the rebels, we left Chung-king on the afternoon of the 3rd day of May. The son of the Mussulman high priest, whose acquaintance our Seikhs had made, accompanied us the short distance we went before halting for the night; and he departed much delighted with some devices which we had put on a new fan he had brought to us for the purpose; the names of our whole party, Mussulmans included, were upon it. The fitting of our junk had been somewhat altered; both the large bow-sweep and the sail had been done away with, and the mast was now only used for tracking, the line running through a ring which traversed up and down, so that it might be accommodated to any height. The skipper had also hired a small boat or sampan to accompany us, which was found very useful in putting ashore and bringing on board the trackers, when the depth of the water did not allow of the junk approaching the land; it was manned by three men, one of whom steered by a large sweep-oar at the stern—a method which we observed very general in this upper portion of the river. Some of the boatmen of the junk were fresh hands,

---

* This is the meaning of the word "Sz'chuan."

and it was some days before they got over their inquisitiveness respecting our appearance and habits. One of the things which always interested the Chinese very much was our mode of eating; they were besides very curious to see us write; and I often had half a dozen round me when I was taking bearings, and sketching in the course of the river and adjacent country; but our regularly washing in the cold water of the river, and persisting daily in bathing in it, seemed marvellous to them. Not that they never washed themselves, for they frequently, when we halted during the day, got into the river to cool themselves, but they could not understand why we, who were travelling as men of rank and education, should do so; for as a rule the Chinese wash, or rather sponge themselves, with warm water, which after hard work is, I believe, very refreshing. Then our walking on shore seemed to puzzle them, for they could not comprehend why people should walk when they paid for being carried. No doubt they thought us droll beings; and, if they ever reflected upon the subject, must have considered England a very curious place.

During the 4th and 5th we made thirty miles, reaching Kiang-tsze (hien), the first place of any size above Chung-king, on the evening of the latter; having passed in the forenoon of that day the mouth of the Chi Kiang, a tributary which joins the Yang-tsze from the southward, and is delineated on the maps of the country as coming from the province of Kwei-chow. It is only one among the numerous tributary rivers in this province, which, bringing their waters from the mountainous regions lying both to the north and south, tend to swell the flood of the Great River, and add to those vast deposits of sand and alluvium which cause such difficulty to navigation at its mouth; and it seems wonderful, when we think of it, that shoals, islands, and even large tracts of country in the province of Kiang-su, now inhabited, and adding their quota of grain to feed the teeming population,

KIN-TIN-TSZE ISLAND.

have been made up of the soil of the mountains of Tibet and Western China. The range of hills which has been already mentioned as lying to the eastward, and on the opposite side of the river to Chung-king, approaches the river near a village and creek, of which we failed to get the name, some thirteen miles above; while another range lies parallel, at a distance of about six miles to the west, and through this the river breaks by what has been called the "Limestone Pass," after which the country is more open. At this pass there is a village on either hand, the one on the right bank containing a pagoda. The names of the two places (Lo-whan-chi and Pa-sha-do) indicate the existence of coal and lime— "black earth" and "white earth"—both of which we observed worked on the hill-sides, the former being carried by bullocks, here used as pack-animals, and on the backs of men and women porters. After this range is crossed, the same sandstone of which I have spoken resumes its position at the surface. These hills are for a great part uncultivated, and covered with stunted scrub.

Just before coming to this place we passed an island in the river called Kin-tin-tsze. It is nearest to the left bank, and, partaking of its rocky nature, seems as if it had been cut off by the wearing force of the current; and now stands alone, prettily wooded and crowned by a temple and small pagoda. It was early morning when we passed it; and as the trackers made their way along the rocky shore, below a large group of cypress-trees, Dr. Barton took a sketch of the place. A large Sz'chuan junk was floating down at the time; two or three specimens of a beautiful species of tern or sea-swallow, with black crown and red legs and bill, skimmed about near the surface of the water; and the whole scene was one most characteristic of the upper waters of the Yang-tsze Kiang.

Coke was seen exposed for sale a few miles below Kiang-tsze, and on the same day the first mosquitoes were observed.

They were not, however, at all troublesome; and I think it must have been more the recollection of the associations connected with these tormentors than from feeling their effects at the time, that caused the Doctor to rail so unmercifully against them. And it is as well here to remark, that during our voyage of five months (in all the latter part of which we experienced warm, and occasionally most oppressive weather) we were very little troubled with mosquitoes; even at Hankow, at the very end of June, there were none to speak of, it being only when we got among the low lands near the mouth of the river, and most of all on arrival at Shanghai, that we experienced any real annoyance from them. I think it speaks well for the civility of the Celestial mosquitoes, that they did not add their torments to the many other annoyances which a party travelling as we did must necessarily be exposed to.

The weather had now become intolerably hot, the thermometer during the warmest part of the day, which is usually from two to two hours and a half after noon, ranging above 90° Fahrenheit, and at sunrise, which ought to be the coolest part of the twenty-four hours, sometimes up to $77\frac{1}{2}°$: in this, however, there was very considerable variation, as it frequently was as much as ten degrees below that point, while the midday heat depended altogether on the state of the sky. We experienced moreover, at this season, frequent thunderstorms; but these were hailed with delight, as having always the effect of ameliorating our roasting condition; while, during the continuous rainy weather which followed the hot spring, the range of the thermometer, during the night and day, was sometimes not over a degree.

Kiang-tsze is notable for its pagodas, there being two of thirteen stories each, the greatest number of stories I have seen anywhere in China. One is on the right bank, on the same side as the city, which stands on an abrupt point, and is enclosed by a wall in good preservation; the other is on a hill rising suddenly on the left bank. They are of nearly uniform thickness for about half-way up, and then taper rapidly; so that, although of many stories, they are not of extraordinary height.

The country is hilly to the north and west of Kiang-tsze; and we observed many of the hill-sides dotted with orange-trees planted in regular rows, and giving a very pleasing aspect to the country. In this part, where shingle-beds are so common, there is a good deal of semi-formed conglomerate. A range of hills, about three and a half miles west of Kiang-tsze, runs in a southerly direction, striking the river just below the village of Yo-chi, which appears to be its termination, where coal and lime are both worked; in other places the ground is only undulating, with occasional low hills for some distance up. However, about the villages of Chung-pa-sha and Shi-mun there are cliffs; and some of the slopes which rise from the river are almost entirely bare rock, and appear as if the heavy rains of this region prevented the earth from obtaining a permanent footing on them; but the land, with the exception of such places, is entirely cultivated, some of the hills being almost covered with orange-groves. Near the village of Shi-mun, and at the foot of a cliff, is a fine seven-storied pagoda temple; and in several places about this part we observed numerous devices cut in the rocks.

Since leaving Chung-king we had noticed many places where the shingle-beds, which are numerous in this part of the river, had been washed for gold; and I may here mention that a friend of mine has discovered, amongst some old records which he has hunted up in the British Museum, that M. Fage, a missionary, when travelling along the Kin-cha Kiang, or "River of Gold-Sand," by which name the Yang-tsze is known farther up, mentions that three short days after leaving that river he came on the "Lou-tsze" Kiang, which discharges itself into the sea to the south-west, on the banks of which he found "numerous gold-washings, and an abundant mine of silver." My friend then argues:—"The nature of the strata could not be much changed in the distance of three days' travel. This, and the name of the upper portion of the Yang-tsze, amply corroborate your *mica* grains." He laid stress on *mica*, because the specimens of sand which we brought from the gold-washings were at first pronounced by "the authorities" as containing nothing more valuable than mica. Is it likely that Chinamen, of all the people in the world, would wash for gold, and, what is more, get it, where there is none? The explorer is an unfortunate man who finds gold, or discovers any peculiarity in the physical nature of a country, not predicted by some eminent man of science.

All the way above Chung-king we had noticed numerous wooden stages occupying the commanding heights along the course of the river, more especially in the vicinity of the villages; and they came in very useful as points for bearings in laying down the river. We were informed that they are used as "outlooks" by the people, and by the detachments of troops which are scattered about during the present disturbed state of the country. Such structures are not peculiar to this part of China, for I have seen them used in other parts for a similar purpose. We also observed, on this portion of the river, numerous rafts composed of planks and small deals, also others entirely of bamboo. They are mostly steered by means of sweeps at either end, after the Upper Mississippi fashion; but some with "rakes," by which the men on them draw them in the required direction by raking the water. This latter mode was something quite new to all of us. There are small shanties on them for the accommodation of the crew.

In the way of farming operations I find noted on the 7th of May that a good deal of the wheat and barley was then cut. It is threshed out in the field by hand, namely by beating the ears against a basket, into which the grain falls, in the same way as the Chinese about Canton thresh out the rice. In other parts, however, we observed flails used, and they are to my mind superior to those of England, the portion which strikes the grain being made up of two or more pieces joined together, so that the striking surface is larger. If it were not that threshing machines have now superseded the old method, we might well take a lesson from the Chinese in this. Of the poppy we did not notice so much about Chung-king as we had lower down the river, and, although the remains of that crop were seen in some places, I think that the plant is not very extensively cultivated above that place. Both rice and maize were being planted out, but there did not appear to be very much of either, the most extensive crop at that season being tobacco. "Dhal," an Indian seed, is grown, and cucumbers were very common; of which latter we consumed a great many, but not in the Chinese fashion, by munching them whole, rind and all. The ordinary lead-coloured water buffalo was common throughout the country, being used for farming purposes; but in the region above Chung-king we saw a few pink or flesh-coloured ones, a variety I never noticed elsewhere.

We observed that the boats plying on the river higher up than Chung-king were, like our own, without sails, and that most of them were of a different description from those common below that place. There was not, it is true, very much difference in them, but they all rejoiced in high masts, usually topped by a long slender bamboo dressed with some miniature pendants, mostly of the favourite colour, red. We saw few of the shear masts, so common with the Chung-king trading junks, which are formed of two spars stepped on either side of the boat and meeting overhead, being steadied by guys fore and aft, and braced across by horizontal spars, and are convenient for lowering. The sail, a large square one without any transverse bamboos, is hoisted on a yard to the crossing of the spars, and being only used for fair wind sailing is allowed to belly out very considerably. A junk of this description is represented under sail in one of the illustrations. The larger kinds are often attended by smaller ones, on which most of the trackers take passage when getting past any difficult place, when it goes ahead with the line until a place is reached where the men can obtain footing; then they jump ashore and haul the large junk up by main force, which it would be impossible to do with the oars. The small attendant junk has generally the same kind of white cotton square sail as the large one, and these sails roll up very snugly with the yard a-cockbill. The Chinese seem to practise this river navigation to perfection, and it is amusing to observe the remarks about the "clumsy and awkward native boats," and the "primitive mode of navigation," which one sees so often in print in England. I have seen something of boat voyaging in North America, where it is carried to great perfection, but I am free to confess that the inland navigation of China beats it, to use a trans-Atlantic expression, "all to pieces." The only way in which we can hope to overreach the Chinese on their inland waters is by the powerful agency of steam, and that no doubt is destined soon to work a revolution on the Yang-tsze Kiang. It will be by our steamers and mercantile enterprise rather than by our arms and missionaries that we shall humanize Celestials.

For several days, commencing with the 8th of May, we made very short distances, owing to a continuance of rainy weather; and the tortuous course of the river still more reduced the direct distance. But on the 10th we reached the town of Ho-kiang (hien), where a good-sized tributary, the Chi-shui, comes in from the southward. The main river varies much in this region, being in some parts almost sluggish, and at others obstructed by sand islands and reefs of rock, causing in some places small rapids. The country is also very diversified in appearance, but without being what can be called mountainous. At Ho-kiang it was hilly to the south-east and east. When we passed upwards, the weather was too thick to allow any thing to be seen at a distance, but on descending we observed a beautiful country on the south side of the river, to the south-west of the city, with distant mountains.

Some of the cottage scenes on this part of the river are very lovely. The day before arriving at Ho-kiang I recollect very well going ashore in the evening after we anchored and walking along the bank, which was there formed by the steep side of a hill, when I came suddenly on a delightful retired little nook. A small neat cottage stood under the lee of a rocky cliff, and was entirely secluded from public view by a profusion of foliage. The ordinary bamboo formed of course the mass, the orange added a deep green, while the banana and a solitary palm gave a tropical touch, and the whole was softened down by the graceful curves of the top shoots of the feathery bamboo. Blocks of rock split off in ages past from the adjoining cliff, left entombed where they had fallen, gave a romantic appearance to this little place, and I thought I had never seen profound repose so beautifully represented before. A couple of long-legged "Shanghais," a small pig, and a dog, shared with a family of Celestials the pleasures of this retreat.

A pagoda stands on the point opposite the mouth of the Chi-shui, which is about two hundred yards wide. The walled part of Ho-kiang is small, but there are some suburbs which have something of a business-like appearance; we saw a good many junks lying along the shore, and there is probably some traffic up the Chi-shui.

The day after leaving Ho-kiang we came to the village of Tow-pung-shih, where there is a rather strong rapid under the left bank, while on the other side the water is shoal. After this, with highlands bordering the river all day, we passed Mi-tu-nieu, then an island, past which there are two or three channels, and Liang-tiow-nieu, where the river takes a sudden bend to the northward; and we halted at the commencement of another of the semicircular curves so common on this part of the river. The next day being again rainy, we made hardly twelve miles, and halted at a sand-bar for the night. The river winds about between highlands, only approaching them at the extremities of its bends, as if the valley had once been of much greater extent. It contains numerous sand islands and low shelving points, and some portions of the banks are deep beds of gravel; one was seen quite thirty feet thick. We also noticed old gold-workings. The country was entirely cultivated, there being at least two kinds of tobacco, distinguishable by the colour of the flowers, one being yellow and another pinkish; but very little is seen in flower, because the top shoots are nipped off to add more vigour to the lower and larger leaves. "Khusumbah," an orange-flowered plant, cultivated in the Punjaub for a yellow dye, was also found growing; it was then in bloom, and not ripe for picking. Our Seikhs hailed with much gratification this plant of their native country. We also observed a plant of the hemp family, which was considered to be the same as that used in North-Western India in the manufacture of rope; it was in full leaf, and has much the appearance of a gigantic nettle, with the lower parts of the leaves whitish. It has been pronounced to be *Bœhmeria nivea*, and is that from which "grass-cloth" is made. Maize, sugar-cane, and rice were seen in abundance; but the wheat and poppy crops were over. Colonel Sarel collected some shells on this portion of the river.*

The country having retained the same character as for the last two days, we arrived on the 13th at Lu (chow), situated on the left or west bank of the Yang-tsze, where the Fu-sung river enters it. It is a populous place, and its importance is manifested to the traveller by a seven-storied pagoda, which he sees long before reaching it; then there is another low one on the side of the river opposite to the town, and a fine old structure of a similar kind stands in the centre of the town itself. A large quantity of pine timber in spars of 1½ to 2 feet diameter and 45 feet long was seen. Lu appeared to be of some mercantile importance, but there was no wall enclosing any portion of it that we could see. We arrived at eight in the morning, and halted on the opposite shore till after twelve o'clock, the delay being for the purpose of obtaining reliable information concerning the rebels, as our boatmen, in consequence of the reports which they heard by the boats we met making their way down, were beginning to fight a little shy of going on. Mr. Schereschewsky's "writer" was sent into the city with a letter to the officials, but it was with the greatest difficulty that he could persuade them that the members of the expedition were not rebels in disguise, which idea was no doubt heightened by the appearance of the blood-red ensign which floated at the mast-head of

---

* British Museum, Tuesday morning, 29th April, 1862.

DEAR SIR,—The shells sent by Colonel Sarel were few in number, consisting of only seven species. Amongst these are two or three which I think are most probably undescribed. They consist of—

1. A species of Nanina (sub-genus *Ariophanta*), probably new.
2. A Nanina closely approximating to *N. vitrinoides*.

3. A species of Helex, most probably undescribed.
4. A species of Bulimulas, ditto.
5. Lymnæa plicatula.
6. Bithinia largicornis; and
7. Bithinia striatula.

Believe me,

Yours very truly,

W. BAIRD.

Capt. Blakiston.

one of the junks. The information with which the "writer" returned after a long absence,—a good part of which I have an idea he spent in an opium-shop,—was by no means definite. He had learned that there were large bodies of rebels not far off, that they had captured some towns and destroyed a great number of boats on the river above; but the chief mandarin said that he should receive fresh intelligence by courier that evening, and he would then inform us. However, we could not think of delaying all day, so after some trouble we persuaded the skipper to leave, and continued our upward voyage.

On rounding the point above the town we entered a long westerly reach, where the river being of considerable width, and the country open on both sides, we noticed a great contrast to the scenery of late. The river seemed now to be much above its winter level, how much it was impossible to ascertain; but it was evident that it had risen considerably lately, as grass and weeds were inundated to a depth of five feet, and in some places the tobacco was under water, indicating an unusual height for the time of year. Possibly the late rains might have caused this, for it had rained during the last seven consecutive days. Cloudy and rainy weather continued for the rest of May; and, one or two days excepted, no clear weather was experienced during the month, so that May and the early part of June in Sz'chuan may well be called the season of rains. This accounts for the paucity of astronomical observations on this part of the river, where from its winding nature I should have been glad of a large number.

Our mandarin and his escort, whose indulgence I must crave for having said so little about them, always travelled in a separate boat of their own; and at a place where there was a partial rapid formed by the current running over a shingle bank, but which on account of the height of the water we were forced to pass, their small craft unluckily struck upon a projecting stone, and, not being in particularly good condition, settled quietly down, to the no small discomfiture of the mandarin and his gang, who swarmed out like a lot of rats and perched themselves on the roof, where they howled and bewailed their fate until a small boat was procured, and they were rescued from their awkward if not dangerous situation, with no hurt except that a few of their things got wetted ; as they carried most of their worldly possessions on their backs, the harm done could not have amounted to anything very serious. For our own part, we should not have felt much embarrassed if the whole party had gone to the bottom of the Yang-tsze, as the only way in which we made use of the mandarin was in sending him on errands at the towns, which the "writer" could have done equally well; and as to the soldiers, they were of little use in keeping the crowd off, for the people cared nothing for their threats unless one of our Seikhs was present.

Above Lu the river, from the number of places on its banks, becomes very interesting, and in the seventy miles which separate that place and Sü-chow there are three walled *hiens* and a proportionate number of villages. The first town is Na-chi, where we arrived on the 14th, and where another river, the Yun-lin, enters, which separates the walled city from the open commercial town. The breadth of the Yang-tsze by sextant measurement is 660 yards, but a little way below this place it is obstructed by a number of shoals and reefs, caused by the out-cropping of the rocky strata running east and west, which makes the ascent for boats which have not the power to keep in the deep channel somewhat difficult. In this neighbourhood we noticed a falling off in the appearance of the farm-houses, while the dwellings of the humbler classes were often only mud-huts thatched with straw, indicating a less productive country; and as far as our wanderings led us above this we never observed that general appearance of comfort and prosperity that we had seen lower down. The soil on the higher ground was often stony, but nearer the river generally of a sandy nature. The cedar was now a common tree, and a few small pines appeared on some of the hill-sides, with bamboo, ash, and other trees as before. We were forced to wait a few hours at Na-chi for the mandarin to come up after his shipwreck, as he had to press another boat into his service.

The next day took us generally on a west course, with ranges of hills to the southward, rising to six hundred feet, and running parallel with the river: in the afternoon we rounded a sharp point, near which there were some extensive beds of shingle; this we named "Gingall Point." The Doctor and myself were ashore, walking ahead of the boats, and as we came up to the point we observed, on the top of the bank, a flag flying; and we immediately ascended to see what it meant. We found that we had come on an Imperialist outpost, or outlying picket of soldiers, stationed there for the purpose of giving the alarm by running off as soon as any body of rebels might heave in sight. They were housed in a little hut, their arms being one sword, one chopper, two old matchlocks, a spear, one banner, and a gingall. This last was evidently what they prided themselves on, for, after they recovered from their first fright on taking us for "tu-feh" (rebels), they seemed only too glad to exhibit this curious piece of ordnance for our edification. It was an iron barrel about six or seven feet in length, the butt-end fitting into a sort of gun-stock, and pivoted on a tripod stand. The whole picket was there, consisting of three men, very shabbily dressed; and I could not discern who was the officer, sergeant or corporal, for the only difference among them was that one wore some European-made brass buttons on his jacket, on which was the device of a lion rampant, and a death's head or star, with the names of the manufacturers on the back, "W. and T. Smith, treble gilt." Each seemed to be in command; possibly they were all Brigadier-Generals, Brigade-Majors, or something of the sort, but they didn't look like it. We explained to them that we should like to see some practice with their artillery, on which the bombardier, as he seemed to be, went to the powder-magazine, which was an old sack carefully tied up and lying under a bed in the hut, and brought forth the charge in a teacup. Then he mounted on a stool and poured the powder in at the muzzle; the gingall was thumped on the ground, and, with a long bamboo, which served as a ramrod, they rammed the powder home. A little of the already soft powder was then mealed, and the touch-hole filled with it. One man then held on tight to the butt, while another coming out with a hot poker discharged the weapon, the effect of which in noise and smoke was marvellous; but the poor fellow who had been doing the marksman was knocked heels over head backwards. He seemed, however, quite accustomed to that sort of thing, for, picking himself up in a minute, he performed what I certainly took for the *coup d'état* of the whole proceeding; suddenly swinging round the gingall on its swivel, he applied his mouth to the muzzle and blew violently down it, which sent the remaining sparks flying out of the vent, and then swung it back into its former position, by which manœuvre he nearly knocked my companion off his legs. The piece was then left with its muzzle inclined well upwards, so that any rain which might fall would trickle nicely down the barrel, and accumulate at the breech. The picket seemed to be without any shot for their gingall, for we tried to get them to put one in, so that we might fire across the bows of our junks, in order to test the courage of the boat coolies; probably shot are not used in the warfare of the interior: our after experience was favourable to this supposition.

On the 16th we passed Kiang-an (hien), near which one of

the party went ashore with his gun and bagged some fowls, as we were hard up for food, and the boys could not succeed in getting any. This summary proceeding may appear to some unwarrantable, but under the circumstances it was absolutely necessary, and the people being well paid for what were taken could not but be satisfied. It was the only time that we were obliged to resort to such means of obtaining subsistence, and the principal reason was, I believe, that the gentleman who spoke the language did not care to trouble himself in interpreting for the commissariat department, although I do not recollect his ever refusing his dinner. Kiang-an is a small place, and, as we passed on as quickly as possible, I had no opportunity of ascertaining whether the river laid down on Chinese maps as falling into the Yang-tsze at this place existed or not. There was an arm of the main river close to the town, which, during high water, is probably connected with the river above and forms an island; but as there was no perceptible current in it, I was led to doubt the existence of a tributary. The native maps are, however, most likely right, and there may be a small one. In the afternoon we arrived near Nan-ki: before rounding the point there is a rapid between the main shore and an island, which we named "Barton Island." A fine old pagoda stands on a bluff overlooking the rapid, and another at about a mile distant inland. It was a beautiful spot. Nan-ki is a walled town situated on the north side of the river, on one of those remarkable bends which are so conspicuous in this part. It is an ordinary-looking place, and we remained there only for the night.

After leaving Nan-ki we only anchored once, and that was at the open town of Li-chuang-pa, before we reached Sü-chow, at the mouth of the "Min," on the 18th of May, our sixty-third day from the confluence of the stream from the Tung-ting Lake with the Yang-tsze Kiang.

CHAPTER XV.

SÜ-CHOW AND THE WESTERN REBELS.

WISHING to defer the subject until I should bring the reader well into the districts infested by them, I have omitted all reference to the Sz'chuan rebels in the chapter which has just closed; but it must not, therefore, be supposed that on our voyage we heard nothing of them, for the whole way above Chung-king there was one continual flow of reports of the depredations and atrocities committed by these lawless bands. Day after day we heard the same story, that they had possession of the river just above, and that it would be impossible for us to proceed much farther; but at the end of each succeeding twenty-four hours of our journey we found ourselves no nearer to them; the remains of the plundered boats and the murdered crews were nowhere to be seen, and the visions of rebels, which had been aroused in our brains each day grew dimmer and dimmer, till at last we ceased altogether to believe in the phantom "Tu-feh." The people of the districts through which we passed were in great consternation at all these reports, and we found that on account of the weakness of the Imperial power they had formed associations for their own protection. These combinations were to protect themselves against the Imperialist *braves* as much as against the rebels; for, as the levies of the Imperial government arc entitled to but very little pay,—and that little, by the time it has passed through the hands of those in authority, dwindles down to nothing,—they are forced for their own support to live on the people of the districts in which they may be quartered; and, being in general a set of the greatest vagabonds in the country, they are not content with simply subsisting on the people, but plunder, pillage, and destroy everything that lies in their way, so that their track is marked by murder and rapine; they leave behind them the stain of blood, and sounds of lamentation and woe follow their retiring footsteps. The words of Scripture come forcibly to the mind when contemplating the devastations of these locust-like hordes—"And the locusts went up over all the land of Egypt . . . very grievous were they." Persons may talk as much as they choose about Chinese rebels in general, of whom they know nothing, and Taipings in particular, of whom they know very little, and against whom it is now the fashion to be very much prejudiced; but in my experience I have not found that, after the war has begun in any section of the country, they do a whit more harm than the Imperialists; and the consequence is, that, wherever the Imperialist troops are in the field against the insurgents, the people are worse off than when left to protect themselves, being plundered by both parties: hence the combinations for mutual protection referred to.

In the narrative of our progress I have mentioned both the frequency of redoubts and walled enclosures, and the numerous "outlooks" along the river; and I might have mentioned that the picket at "Gingall Point" was not the only armed force which we saw; for at the towns, some of which had their gates closed in anticipation of attack, there were numbers of soldiers, and at different places along the river we found small out-stations, at one or two of which we were questioned; and the authorities seemed rather suspicious of us. Such places were always marked by a number of spears stuck in the ground, having three-cornered flags with scolloped or jagged edges flying from them, and occasionally a gingall or two; but these camp colours usually far exceeded the number of men in the detachment. On several occasions I observed women manufacturing paper cartridges, or rather chargers, in which the powder is carried ready for use, and a sort of cartouche-box for holding them: these are also made of bamboo. When we see the people forming these "vigilance committees" for the safety of their homes, one would suppose that, "if the Chinese Government had the least energy, rebels would have no chance of establishing themselves in a country where the popular feeling is so strong in favour of law and order;" but, as my friend Colonel Sarel has farther observed, "should the present state of affairs continue much longer, the feeling of the population will probably undergo a change, and, finding the Government powerless to protect them, they will lose their respect for it, and the habit of carrying arms will make them less likely than formerly to submit to the exactions of the authorities."

The majority of people in England are under the impression that in China there is at present but one rebellion,—that the Taipings are the only rebels. I would they were; but such is the state of decay into which the Government has been forced by the peculation and corruption of the mandarins under the ruling dynasty, that there are now no less than four distinct kinds of rebels; and revolt is rife in every province of that once prosperous empire. Besides the Taipings on the Lower Yang-tsze, who have been alluded to in the earlier chapters of this work, there is a formidable band of revolutionists in the north-eastern province of Shan-tung; then there are the Sz'chuan rebels, or "Tu-feh," who seem restricted to that western province; and, as if it would not do to confine rebellion within narrow limits, there is an important insurrection of Chinese Mussulmans in Yu-nan. Of these last we heard a good deal from various sources, but more particularly from Mussulmans whom we met in Sz'chuan.

The leader of the rebellion is a Hadji, by name "Yussuf Ma;" his head-quarters are at Ta-li (foo), in the west, and on the high road from the Burmese frontier to Yu-nan, the capital of the province, and Ching-tu, the capital of Sz'chuan. The followers of the Prophet form a numerous body in China; at one town alone—Ching-tu—we were informed there were at least a thousand Mussulman families; if this insurrection should therefore spread, it might attain very formidable dimensions. Who knows but we may yet see a Christian rebellion?

With respect to the Sz'chuan rebels, they appear to have been in existence for some considerable time; in fact, the province has always been noted for being infested by bands of robbers, but they did not become formidable before the ninth year of the reign of the late Emperor Hien-fung; and, as far as we could learn, they have never reached the eastern part of the province. We were desirous of obtaining all the information we could on the subject; and the following names of places, which the mandarin of our escort furnished us with, are on three different lines of route towards the capital, and were then *said* to be in possession of the rebels. First, between Wan(hien) and Ching-tu—Ping-chi, She-kung, Chung-kiang, and Shün-king; between Chung-king and Ching-tu—Ho(chow), Ting-yuen, Mien(chow), Nan-ching, and Si-chung; between Lu(chow) and Ching-tu—Niu-fu-tu, King-yen, and Hoei-yuen; between Sü-chow and Ching-tu—Kia-ding, Kien-hoei, Yow-ku-tu, Kioh-kih, Manien-chang, and Utung-kiow; while the son of the Moolvie, or Mussulman high-priest, gave us the following as the places he knew to be in the possession of the rebels in the same province:—Mé(chow), Sin-tu, Mien-(chow), Kin-shu(hien), Pun-shan(hien), Kien(chow), Kwan (hien), Ho(chow), Ting-yuen, and Sü-ling(hien). The information may be taken for what it is considered to be worth, hence my reason for giving up my authorities; for my own part, I will be frank and admit that I never believe half I hear in Europe, and nothing I heard in China.

If we are to credit the statement given above, these rebels must be in possession of a large portion of the province, and the report when we were there was, that they had burned the suburbs of the capital, and were then besieging Ching-tu. All that we can testify—and I will step a little ahead of my narrative now that I am on the subject—is, that everywhere in the western part of Sz'chuan we found the people in great dread of the "Tu-feh;" that large levies of troops were proceeding up the river at the time we passed up; that at Sü-chow numbers of headless bodies were floating down the Min, which comes from the direction of Ching-tu; and that a night-attack was made by them on Ping-shan, a small place farther west, while we were there. Whether they will ever gain sufficient strength to wrest the province of Sz'chuan from the Imperial mandarins; whether they will form a coalition with the Taipings, one section of whom I have elsewhere stated is supposed to be as far west as the province of Kwei-chow; whether both together will overthrow the dynasty of the Manchoo-Tartars; or whether Prince Kung will regenerate China,—I shall leave events to prove, as I rather pride myself in not following the popular fashion of setting up for a prophet.

Having reached Sü-chow on the 18th May, the first thing that struck us was the number of boats collected at the mouth of the Min, the cause of which we soon discovered to be the presence of rebels on that river, and there were certainly unmistakable signs of savage work somewhere, for at all hours of the day headless bodies floated down, swollen and distended by the heat of the sun into revolting-looking masses. It had been our intention to take this route for Chung-tu, and, in fact, our boats were engaged to go there, but these signs were enough to deter Celestials; and the next five days were consumed in fruitless endeavours to persuade our skippers or boatmen to undertake the voyage.

Sü-chow is on the verge of a mountainous country lying to the westward. The immediate neighbourhood is of a rather hilly and rugged nature, but a few miles down the river takes you into a more open and hospitable region. From a hill just at the junction of the Min with the Yang-tsze, above a pagoda opposite the town, an extensive view of the surrounding country is obtained; and the following notes made on the spot may assist the reader in comprehending the map. The general direction of most of the ranges is N.E. and S.W., being nearly all parallel to one another. To the northward is one about 500 to 600 feet in height, which crosses the Min just above Sü-chow, and is continued, but lower in elevation, parallel with the course of the Yang-tsze, some five miles above. A range of hills, some 900 to 1000 feet in height, lies to the westward about six miles, and beyond can be seen other N.N.W. and S.S.E. parallel ranges, stretching away in the distance. To the southward is a range which strikes the river a little distance below the place, and has a pagoda on it; but it becomes mixed with others to the south-west. No distant hills are visible to the N.W. by W., and there is supposed to be the valley of the Min, which river can be seen coming from that direction for about three miles, at which distance we distinctly made out a pagoda on its left bank. The whole country to the eastward is broken by hills and ridges, which, being near the river, have been laid down on the chart.

The city of Sü-chow is situated just at the angle formed by the Min coming from the north-west, and striking the previous north-east course of the Yang-tsze, whence, taking a resultant, as it were, the "Great River" flows on a little to the northward of east. On the old Jesuit maps, or, rather, the Chinese copies of them, it is given on the wrong side of the river, the reason for which it is difficult to account for, as, from the nature of the ground, it never could have been there. Mistakes of this kind, which one sees in those maps, I am inclined to attribute to error in copying; for now that this river has been laid down on a large scale, it is wonderful to observe the concurrence in the bends and windings of its course. When we ascended I had no idea that there was any accessible map of the river on so large a scale as I have seen since I returned to this country, or I might have thought much less of the importance of surveying it. It would appear, however, that there was a want of astronomical observations in the work of the ancient Jesuits, for the positions now obtained for many important places differ some miles in latitude. If the discrepancies had been in longitude only, one would have thought nothing of them, and I should not have been inclined to back my observations, taken as they usually were under rather adverse circumstances; but a difference of several miles in latitude is, I think, a proof of the absence of absolute determinations by celestial observation altogether. The Chinese themselves make very fair relative maps or route sketches, and I should not be surprised if the geographical productions of the early missionaries were merely compilations from native surveys.

The town is regularly built and enclosed by four walls parallel to the river banks, with suburbs on both its north and south sides. The walls must be about two miles round. A fine temple stands outside the east angle, just at the point formed by the two rivers. At the back and to the eastward of the place the hills are used as cemeteries. The Min, where it joins the Yang-tsze, is about of equal width; but a shoal is uncovered at low water just at its mouth. There is a reef or rock also opposite the south-east face of the city, but near the other shore, which seems to contract the Yang-tsze in width. Deep water exists along both faces of the city, and I look on Sü-chow as a good port, while its situation is, I think, most favourable as a commercial place. But Sü-chow did not give us such an idea of its mercantile prosperity as one would have been led to expect; probably the disturbed state of this region may have had its effect upon the place.

We obtained such information concerning the trade of Sü-chow as we were able, but found that it was mostly a transit trade, the boats which ship the produce from the upper waters of the Min and the districts of Kia-ding and Ching-tu passing on with their freights to the great mercantile focus Chung-king; while the trade on the main river above is but small. The productions of the neighbourhood of Sü-chow, we were given to understand, were silk (yellow and white), insect-wax, bees'-wax, tobacco, honey, green tea, iron, and coal; but the silk is said to be of a coarse quality, and the tea is not raised in large quantities. Coal exists in abundance; and we considered that what we saw taken from the mines of Pa-ko-shan, about five and a half miles below, and again in the "Coal Gorge" which commences at twenty miles above, was of better quality than any other on the river. Small specimens of it have been examined in England, and are considered to be well adapted for steam purposes. However, the locality is so distant from any present place of demand, that I should very much doubt its paying the expenses of working and transport; besides, the mines spoken of lower down might produce quite as valuable a quality, if worked in a scientific manner. If, in place of the exports of Sz'chuan exceeding her imports, the case were reversed, there would always be plenty of carriage to be had at a moderate rate; but as it is, the freight on downward cargo is, as has been noticed, much higher than upwards; and the only way to manage the transport would be, if timber was not extravagantly dear, to build boats specially for carrying coal and nothing else, sufficiently strong to last for a single trip, just in the way that those which now bring coal to Hankow from the Tung-ting Lake make only the passage down, and are then broken up and sold for the timber they are made of. But Sü-chow is 923 geographical miles, or, in round numbers, above 1000 statute miles, from Hankow, our highest open port; and this is a long distance. The voyage would occupy about eight or nine days from I-chang, to which, on account of the more sluggish nature of the stream, and the chances of delay from wind in this wide part of the river, at least ten days more would have to be added, making the time of transit three weeks from Sü-chow to Hankow. Some of the coal, however, would be taken at I-chang by steamers which will run to that point; but until regular river steamboats, such as I have elsewhere advocated for the up-river navigation, have been constructed in China, I very much doubt if the coal on the upper waters of the Yang-tsze will be much farther developed than it is at present by the Chinese. Then, when a revolution is brought about in the navigation of these inland waters, and small steamers are seen towing strings of junks against the rapid current of the Upper Yang-tsze, or carrying up the crews that have manned the coal-boats which have been broken up and sold at the European ports; then we may expect not only coal, but copper, iron, tin, and many other of the hidden treasures of the earth, coming from the far interior, to produce an effect on the markets of the coast. Such days, I firmly believe, are in the future.

But I wander into the region of speculation, and am verging on the domain of the prophet: let us proceed with what is, not what may be. The Min Kiang, we are told, is navigable at all seasons for junks of large size as far up as Kiading, a town about a hundred miles from its mouth, where it divides into two branches. Thence, during the season of high water, the same-sized junks can reach Ching-tu by a canal between the river and the capital; but when the water is low, the communication is kept up by means of smaller craft. The navigation of the Yang-tsze, from Chung-king to Sü-chow, would not be difficult for steamers such as I have spoken of, there being rocks and minor rapids, but probably always plenty of water; but concerning the Min I cannot speak. Above Sü-chow the Yang-tsze is called, in Chinese geographical works, the Kiň-cha Kiang, or "River of Gold Sand;" but the boatmen seemed only to know it as the Yunan river. We could learn very little about it much above this, and there seemed to be little or no trade on it. Those whom we questioned told us of falls, and spoke of the country as a barbarous one inhabited by wild tribes, not being a part of the "Flowery Land," according to their ideas.

During our stay at Sü-chow there was considerable variation in the height of the Min river. When we arrived it was quite a clear stream in comparison to the Yang-tsze; but during the night of the 20th it changed to a deep red clay colour, and on the 21st rose upwards of three feet, falling again a little at night; on the day following it continued steadily falling, and cleared very much in colour; the shoal at its mouth, which had become submerged, was exposed again on the 23rd. On the 31st, however, when we descended, this shoal was under water again, and the main river itself had risen a good deal. These sudden alterations in depth may be accounted for by the mountainous nature of the countries through which these rivers run.

Finding our boatmen could not be induced by all our entreaties, threats, or offers of money, to continue the voyage to Ching-tu, we sent a letter to the prefect of Sü-chow, requesting an audience with him; but he returned an answer that we could only hope to enter the city by being hauled up the wall by a rope, as the gates were kept constantly closed

CHAP. XV. CORRESPONDENCE WITH THE PREFECT. 257

for fear of the *braves*, of whom there were several hundreds then quartered outside in order to protect the place against the rebels, and who, if the gates were opened, would enter and pillage the city. We therefore wrote to him again, requesting his assistance in procuring ponies or coolies for the transport of our baggage on our intended journey to Ching-tu; but he politely excused himself by saying that in the present disturbed state of the country it was utterly impossible to get any one to venture on such a trip, and advised us to give up all idea of carrying out the intention. He farther stated that according to the last reports the rebels, or robbers as he called them, were but a few "tens of li" distant from Sü-chow, and that he fully expected that they might come and attack the place any day. We did not give it up yet, however, but sent him a copy of the treaty, underlining those parts to which we particularly desired to draw his attention, namely, that the mandarins are bound to afford protection to Englishmen in difficulties, and assist in procuring them means of transport when they are unable to do so themselves; thinking that perhaps he was only putting us off with these excuses to save himself trouble; but his answer was as civil as before, yet he stated his utter inability to help us in any way. Such is the state to which bad government has brought many portions of this country, which one has always been accustomed to consider as a despotic empire. Levies of soldiers are hired by the Imperial Government to protect certain places against rebels which its exactions and incapacity have fostered, and allowed to gain head; and when these are quartered at a city for its protection, the people are as afraid of them as of the revolutionists, and the mandarins are powerless in authority. It will be difficult to bring persons in Europe to realise such a state of things, I know; but that it does exist, Sü-chow, in May, 1861, was an example, and Sü-chow was no solitary instance.

s

We were a good deal bothered by these *braves*; and every day we lay at anchor alongside the bank just opposite the city, numbers came over, in boats which they pressed into their service, to look at us. I have before mentioned that they are the most troublesome part of the population; for, being accustomed to do just as they like, they could not comprehend our refusing them admittance on board our junks, and frequently became saucy, and so far impertinent as to throw stones at the boats. What they bothered us most for were firearms, and some of them made us considerable offers to induce us to part with some of our pistols or guns; but we did not feel at all sure of their bills being honoured, and, besides, we did not know how soon we might have to use our weapons even against themselves. We were once or twice nearly opening fire on them, when they became more than ordinarily obnoxious; however, by keeping our tempers, and occasionally making a sally, stick in hand, we managed to avoid any effusion of blood. As a whole, they were, I do not hesitate to say, the ugliest set of ruffians I ever set eyes upon. Dressed in gaudy but dirty uniforms, they all wore enormous turbans, and cummerbunds or sashes; and, thrust through the latter, each one carried large knives, and some few had matchlocks. Their turbans were of various colours, according to the bands to which they belonged—for there were *braves* from Yu-nan as well as from Sz'chuan—but yellow, dark-blue, and scarlet predominated. One or two who were represented as leaders we admitted on board, and showed them some of our rifles and pistols, thinking that the display of our power would more than compensate for exciting their cupidity by the exhibition of valuables. When these men were present, there seemed to be some show of order among the others; and we warned them that, if we suffered more annoyance than we could bear, we should assuredly reduce the number of their troops by piercing the bodies of some of them with pieces of cold lead. They however did not appear very anxious for the safety of their followers, and seemed rather to think that it would be a waste of a valuable mineral. The Prefect was, I am sure, quite favourable to any project of the kind for reducing the number of the gallant defenders of Sü-chow, just as the Viceroy of the two Hoos, when warned by the United States Commodore that the vessels would open fire on the Chinese soldiers at Hankow if they did not desist from trying to crowd on board, returned an answer that he would be very much obliged to the Commodore if he would do so.

Now the question arose, if we wanted to get to Tibet, how were we to do it? It was very evident that Sü-chow was the sticking-point; if we were to get on, we must pass Sü-chow, and, what was more, we must get to Ching-tu, the capital of the province of Sz'chuan, for there resided the Viceroy of Sz'chuan and Tibet, without whose aid it was hardly possible to get through the country, it being to him that letters of credit, if I may so call them, had been sent concerning us by the Viceroy at Hankow. If we could not get any one to accompany us overland, then we must continue our progress by water. But how could we proceed by water if the boatmen refused to go? To force them was impossible. What was to be done? No one could answer the question. At last a happy idea struck one of the party, namely, that if we selected a small-sized junk, just sufficient to hold the necessary part of our baggage, we might manage to get such a boat up ourselves; and, putting things in the worst light, there were but two hundred miles intervening between us and the capital, and at most it could not take us over three weeks. Three weeks, then, of coolie work would carry us through the difficulty; but probably, when we once got amongst the rebels (if we ever saw them at all, which I very much doubted), they would be equally anxious to do day-labour for a certain amount of cash as any other Chinamen, and we might really have very little manual labour ourselves. With regard to danger from the rebels, it was urged that if they proved hostile, which was most unlikely, except with the view of plunder, we could always push off into the stream, and find our own way down again. The proposition was made one evening, and the vote was to be taken next morning at breakfast.

Perhaps the less I say on this subject the better; I might be led away to say more than I wish. It will suffice to state that the heat of the weather, incapacity for hard work, the impossibility of the scheme, and, what seems only just then to have dawned on some minds, the loss of valuable time during a winter which would certainly have had to be spent to the north of the Himalayas, were urged against the proposition; the black ball was cast.

* * * * * * * *

I feel that, if the reader has hitherto taken any interest in our progress, I here lose his confidence. He has journeyed with us bound for Tibet, he has had his visions of the Himalayas as we had ours, and now they are gone; but I will ask him to bear with me,—although as I now write I have half a mind to throw my pen out of the window and my papers into the fire—whilst in the next chapter I relate how we made another attempt to get on our way to Tibet, and then in the way of narrative it will only remain to describe our downward voyage. With regard to affairs at Sü-chow, I need only say that in order to get farther up the Yang-tsze we agreed with our old skipper to take us for an exorbitant sum to Ping-shan, the highest point to which he was willing to go, and he signified his readiness to start on the 23rd.

Before leaving Sü-chow, however, I must not omit to say that, on a visit to the pagoda which I have before mentioned as opposite to the city at the mouth of the Min, we found a great number of refugees,—poor country people who had deserted their homes and fled before the advance of the rebels. They were mostly from the districts up the Min; and though a panic is sufficient to drive people from their homes, the small amount of anything in the shape of baggage which these unfortunates had about them attested a very rapid retreat. A great many were taking shelter in the buildings of the temple just below the pagoda, men, women, and children, some of the last still at their mothers' breasts; young girls of delicate form and appearance, as if used to polite society, and looking as if the tattered clothes they then wore ill befitted them; also there were old grey-bearded men and infirm old women, who must have had their physical powers well tested to have been able to reach this place of refuge. But amidst this scene the young men were playing at cards; and so infatuated are the Chinese in this practice of gambling, that I believe any number would be found willing to sit around a barrel of gunpowder with a slow match attached, if they knew that, for the period of time which must elapse before the match would ignite the powder, they could not play anywhere else, although the moment after they would be hurled into eternity.

As we recrossed the river in a sampan after our visit to the temple, headless bodies were still constantly brought down by the current of the Min. Though the rebels made no attack on Sü-chow while we were there, we did not leave the place without seeing a battle. On the forenoon of the 22nd we observed a commotion outside the city; this was followed by a number of the boats which lay alongside the bank pushing off and coming over to our side of the river for protection. After a little while firing commenced, and the city walls became crowded with people looking on at a fight which was taking place between two parties of *braves*. The cause of the quarrel we were informed was that the soldiers from Yu-nan wanted to enter the city, which as I have already mentioned was closed against its gallant defenders, and being foiled in an attempt to get in, and being in pretty strong force, they fell upon the Sz'chuan braves who were quartered outside with them, and a regular battle à la Chinois was the consequence. I shall long remember this peculiar engagement, for we were capitally situated at about 500 yards' distance, and could view the whole performance with the advantage of having a deep river between us and the combatants. The fellows were dressed in red, yellow, and blue, so that we could always distinguish the different sides. There were many hard struggles for important strategical positions, as, for instance, corner houses—for there were a good many buildings outside the wall—and such places would be assailed most valiantly by a party, of which each man carried a banner, approaching by stealth behind broken walls until within easy range, when a couple of matchlocks would be fired off; this alarming the garrison, they would reply with a volley of stones and brickbats, and a fierce engagement of this sort would continue for some time, until getting tired in the arms they commenced to shout and bawl, reviling one another, and, like schoolboys, telling one another to "come on." Occasionally we heard the explosion of a gingall among the houses, followed by tremendous cheering. Sometimes we saw a party retreat bodily out of a house, and the captors enter; but much as we witnessed of this fighting, we did not once see two men meet hand to hand, for one always ran away long before the other got near him, and the pursuit was not very eagerly pressed. One bone of contention during the whole struggle was a large temple just at the nearest angle of the city: this was held by the Yu-nan men, and repeated assaults were made on it without success; and as we sat on the roofs of our junks, binoculars in hand, we viewed with much interest the successive attacks on the position. At last, when a portion of the garrison were away on some other duty, the place was carried by a bold assault, and the banners of Sz'chuan floated from its walls. I never witnessed anything more ridiculous than this battle in my life ; it seemed more like a stage performance, and I should have been inclined to hiss it in anything but a pantomime ; a snowballing-match would have been far more warlike. The result of the engagement, which continued the greater part of the day, was, we were informed from different sources, that both parties were victorious. Three men were reported to have been killed, and we are certain one was, because we saw him stripped of his clothes and thrown into the river.

CHAPTER XVI.

PING-SHAN — OUR FARTHEST.

IT was but five o'clock when we left Sü-chow on the morning of the 23rd of May. Proceeding up the Yang-tsze in a south-westerly direction, we passed through a hilly country, the highlands first approaching the river on its right bank; at the large village of Pa-shui-chi they commenced also on the other side, and above this gradually rose in elevation, hemming in the river, which was sensibly narrower than below Sü-chow, in a continuous defile. By evening we reached the open town of An-pien, opposite which the Whan-kiang, coming from the southward, enters the Yang-tsze; here we halted for the night. Next morning, altering our course to the westward, we passed a very narrow portion of the river, and were soon enclosed on either hand by high cliffs, some of which were 500 feet in height; this was the commencement of a gorge where coal is extensively worked. At the rapid of Ta-tan-pa, which occurs just at the entrance, we were delayed some time by the larger junk being allowed to take a sheer into the current in the act of ascending, and all the endeavours of those on board were of no avail to get her head in the right direction again; the trackers on shore were forced to slip their collars, as the force of the current against her broadside overpowered them, and the old junk went gliding swiftly down the rapid, and very narrowly escaped striking on a couple of rocks, which if she had done she would most assuredly have broken up. At the lower end of the rapid she got into a whirlpool, and continued

COAL GORGE.

spinning round and round, and it was not until after very hard work with the oars that she was extricated, and ultimately brought alongside the shore lower down. Then the rapid had to be tried again. This rapid is of considerable strength, but not one of broken water, being simply the rush of the river through a confined channel; the depth is probably great.

In this gorge we noticed a method of working the coal which we had never observed before. Having to be got out at a great height up in the cliff, very thick hawsers, made of plaited bamboo, are tightly stretched from the mouth, or near the mouth, of the working gallery to a space near the water where the coal can be deposited. These ropes are in pairs, and large pannier-shaped baskets are made to traverse on them, a rope passing from one over a large wheel at the upper landing and down again to the other, so that the full basket going down pulls the empty one up, the velocity being regulated by a kind of break on the wheel at the top. At some places the height at which the coal is worked is so great that two or more of these contrivances are used, one taking it to a landing half-way down, and another from thence to the river. The hawsers are kept taut by a windlass for that purpose at the bottom. The quantity of coal worked in this gorge is very large, and numbers of boats are employed in transporting it to Sü-chow. I more than suspect that from that point some of it ascends the Min, perhaps to Ching-tu, because from the mines of Pa-ko-shan below Sü-chow it seems to be brought upwards, and I should not think it can be all consumed at Sü-chow. Certainly far more coal is used in Sz'chuan for domestic purposes than in those parts of China where charcoal is the common fuel, and we did not observe that in this western part of the province it was ever pounded up and made into bricks, as has been mentioned in Eastern Sz'chuan.

We continued in this gorge until noon, when between the villages of Lo-tu and Lo-tung-chan the river makes a considerable bend, and leaves a level space on its northern side. The inhabitants of these villages appeared mostly engaged in the coal business, and, judging from their tolerably well-to-do appearance, the occupation cannot be very unprofitable. Opposite the latter village there are some rocks very awkwardly situated right in the middle of the river, just where a vessel would naturally pass either in ascending or descending by steam-power. At the time we passed they were covered, but only a little below the surface.

Owing to a storm of wind we were forced to come to an anchor shortly above this point as early in the afternoon as a quarter past three, having made only twelve miles. We were hemmed in on all sides by mountains, of which the best idea can be formed by reference to the chart; some close to the river rose at least eleven hundred feet above it, and many distant ones reached over fifteen hundred; but cultivation was carried to the very summits of many of them. Others were wooded with forests of fir, while the sides of the nearer valleys were studded with various fruit-trees, including the orange, mulberry, and apricot, besides bamboo, chestnut, and other larger timber; whilst some of the gardens were enclosed with hedges of cactus. It rained and blew very heavily during the night.

Next morning on account of the weather we did not start till nearly eight. We commenced by ascending a long straight reach, where the last coal that we observed was worked. The hard sandstone along the banks is used for the manufacture of grindstones. The hills rise precipitously up to a thousand feet, and the village of Fo-yien-chi, the prominent feature of which is a high three-storied house, is reached just opposite a long point. Our course lay still among mountains, some of the distant ones we could observe

PING-SHAN.

being as high as 1800 and 2000 feet; we first turned south, then, passing a small village on the right bank, we pursued a westerly, and latterly a north-westerly course, past a steep cliff, a temple, and fine stone archway on the right hand, and came to the town of Ping-shan before four o'clock in the afternoon of the 25th of May, being our seventieth day on the Upper Yang-tsze, and seventeen weeks since leaving the coast.

Ping-shan is surrounded on all sides by a mountainous country, and from it to the westward we observed high ranges reaching 2000 feet, with general north and south directions. The opposite side of the river was the province of Yu-nan, the boundary between which and Sz'chuan we were told was but a short distance below. This to us was unexpected, as on no map of China is the limit of Yu-nan made to reach within a hundred miles so low down the Yang-tsze as Ping-shan, and in most not within two hundred. I have since been informed that among some documents on China in the British Museum there is a decree altering the boundary between Sz'chuan and Yu-nan, though I am not sure that it brings it so far down as Ping-shan. We did not discover the exact spot where it strikes the river. On many maps the town of Ping-shan does not appear at all, and on the better ones it has been marked in small letters a little above "Ma-hou." Now it is "Ma-hou" that should not exist, for it was the original name of Ping-shan when that place was the chief town of a "foo" district. An alteration was made in the governmental department, and now it is Ping-shan (hien). It is distant from Sü-chow 38 geographical miles by the windings of the river; and, as the events about to be detailed cut short our stay there, and we obtained no celestial observations, its position consequently rests on dead reckoning from Sü-chow. It is not my habit to insert the geographical co-ordinates of a place unless it is a "station".

where they have been determined absolutely by observation; but as Ping-shan is the most westerly point to which we penetrated, I will add it to the list of positions in Appendix VII. It is in latitude 28° 40' north, and longitude 104° 25' west of Greenwich, or about 12° 5' west of Pekin.

The principal productions of the neighbourhood of Ping-shan are silk,—of which we saw a good deal being brought in by the country people in the cocoons, both yellow and white, but the former in most abundance;—Indian corn, sugar, and rice; with cucumbers, a kind of vegetable marrow, French beans, garlic, and other vegetables of which we did not know the names; also turmeric. No cotton appears to be grown in this part; in fact, we were everywhere informed in Sz'chuan that most of the cotton comes from Hoo-peh in the raw state. We observed numbers of cacti, some as much as twelve inches through the stem. The only thing besides one boat-load of dried bamboo-shoots which we saw come down the river from above Ping-shan was coal, a few junks being loaded with this mineral, which we were informed was obtained at no great distance.

All we could learn respecting the Yang-tsze, or, as it is here called, the Kin-cha, above our farthest point was that there were what the people called falls about 100 li up, and that it was a difficult river for navigation. However, the best reason for its not being much used in the opinion of the Chinese was that there was no trade on it, and that above it passed through the country of the black barbarians, or "Miau-tze," who were not a commercial people. But it was impossible to get any very definite information on the subject.

On our arrival we informed the Prefect of the fact by letter, and he returned an answer by the messenger that he would call on us on the following morning, which he accordingly did. The interview took place on board the larger of our two junks, which had now their masts struck, indicative of an intention on the part of the skippers to proceed no farther; we informed the Prefect that we were on our way to visit the Viceroy at Ching-tu, and that we had come thus far out of the direct route to escape the districts infested by rebels; and requested his advice and assistance in getting forward. He assured us that he was perfectly willing to assist us in every way in his power, and sent for a map of the country lying to the north, which I am very sorry I allowed to slip out of my hands, as on it were marked the places in possession of the insurgents. He explained that the only way in which he considered it likely that we could get through the country was by proceeding overland from Ping-shan to a place called Ma-pien, and thence to strike towards the high-road between Ching-tu and Ta-tsien-lu, as by following any more eastern route we should certainly fall in with the insurgents. He considered that he should be able to supply us with ponies and coolies for our journey, and left us in high spirits as to our future prospects.

Unfortunately our party was partly composed of Chinamen, that is to say we had a "writer" and two servants of our own, and in our train was a mandarin with his attendants. The latter lived on us, and it would have been the most impolitic thing on their parts to assist us at all in getting off the river, because they would have had to return on short allowance whence they came. Besides this, the air of the western country had not agreed with our own Chinese, for they had successively been taken ill one after another, until they were of very little use to us, and our Seikhs had to do pretty nearly all the work. These things, put together, were to my mind quite sufficient to account for a letter we received from the Prefect the same afternoon, to the effect that he found it impossible to obtain ponies or coolies, which, always a difficult matter, was especially so now, as one-third of the population had left the place from fear of the rebels. He also mentioned that there was no way of getting beyond Ma-pien, the first place we intended to make for; and that, on account of the dangerous state of the country from rebels and the independent tribes, he would dissuade us from proceeding at all. On this we forwarded him a copy of the treaty, of which he seemed to be in total ignorance. The evening was consumed in discussing plans of action; and we came to the decision of giving up the boat here, and taking up our quarters at Ping-shan until we could obtain the necessary means of transport to enable us to prosecute our journey.

On the same day, also, we first made acquaintance with some people belonging to the independent tribes of the West. The Doctor and I had been on shore to bathe at a waterfall which was near at hand, and were returning on our way to the boats when we found a large number of Chinamen collected together, and in the midst of them was a tall and very dark-complexioned man, dressed in a long dark-grey coat, with his head tied up in a blue cotton cloth, which was so put on as to form a kind of horn at the top of his forehead. They made way for us, and formed a lane up to this queer-looking fellow. He immediately addressed us in some language which was beyond our comprehension, and seemed, as well as the bystanders, to be very much astonished that we did not understand him. We returned the salute, however, telling him that we were delighted to meet him, and by signs made him understand that we were astonished at his being so much taller and larger in every way than the other people, and invited him on board the junk, where, after Mr. Schereschewsky had discovered who he was from the Chinamen, we gave him a glass of brandy; and he made signs that he would come again and pay us a visit with some others. During the day he returned, with two other men of the same race and a half-bred Chinese, in clean holiday costume; and as the latter spoke both languages, Mr. Schereschewsky was able to carry on a conversation. I may here mention that the language of Sz'chuan is very nearly what is called the pure mandarin dialect; and as this was the dialect which Mr. Schereschewsky had studied at Shanghai, in preference to the Canton, Fokien, Nanking, or any of the others, he found that, the farther we got from the coast, the more at home he was in the language.

These "Miau-tze" were very different people from the Chinese in appearance. In the first place, their features were very much removed from the Celestial slanting-eyed type, the face being longer and the nose more nearly straight, and more prominent. The colour of their skin was very much darker, and not at all yellow. They were larger proportioned and more robust, and appeared as if they were less accustomed to a civilized life. I failed, however, to detect, what seems to have struck one of my companions, any great amount of honesty depicted in their countenances. One of them was a kind of chief; and he informed us that he had come from his country, which was at a long distance to the westward, to help in defending Ping-shan against the rebels. We got them to take off their turbans, in order that we might see their heads: one had his clean shaven, and the others partly, but the only one who wore a tail was the half-breed. They were very curious to see different articles which we had in the cabin, and were much astonished with the telescopes—things which we always found went a long way in the entertainment of any visitors, and by which they believed we could see through city walls; we showed them also our guns and pistols. They behaved themselves very well, brought us some choice wine as a peace-offering, and we supplied them with a butcher's knife and four empty beer-bottles, with which they were much delighted. They admitted that they could neither read nor write, and called themselves "Huh-i" or "I-jin," black barbarians, or rather foreigners or outsiders—barbarian being, I believe, a misinterpretation of a Chinese word which has become an accepted translation. They stated that in their country they had plenty of horses, cattle, sheep, and goats; and if we once got there, we should have no difficulty in travelling in any direction, but that, unless under the protection of a chief, travellers would be liable to be robbed. The chief gave the name of the place from which he came as "Ta-lia-shan," about twelve days distant in a westerly direction, but we could not find it on any of our maps; he intended returning in about five months' time. These fellows were much inclined to fraternise with us, believing that being foreigners we must belong to their nation; and the Chinese on their parts knew us as "White Miau-tze."

On the 27th a visit was made by some of our party to the Prefect; and as he could not offer us any immediate hope of being able to proceed, a house was demanded within the city where the members of the expedition might take up their quarters. We stipulated for a place inside the city, because our object was to get on; and we thought with Abbé Huc, that to gain this end the surest way was to make ourselves as disagreeable as possible to our entertainers. The Prefect was willing, and in the afternoon two of the party went again into the city and inspected a temple which was placed at our disposal; and we thought of getting into it the day following. We had many pleasant walks in the neighbourhood, and invariably found the people civil, so much so that it was remarked by all of us. Neither were we very much bothered by the crowd, as Ping-shan was but a small place, and there were but few soldiers quartered there.

On the morrow we were waited on by a large deputation of the townspeople; Mr. Schereschewsky received them. They came with a request that we would alter our intention of living in the city, because, said they, "the rebels are near at hand; and if they hear of your being in Ping-shan with all your valuables, they will be certain to come down and attack the place." Mr. Schereschewsky told them that we were well armed, and could assist in defending the town; and that they ought rather to be glad to have among them some of the warriors from the Western Sea, whom the rebels would be in dread of. Then they gave a number of other reasons why it would be better that we should not take up our residence in the city; until at last they were informed point-blank that it was our intention to do so, notwithstanding their objections. On this they went off in a huff, and uttered a good deal of abusive language to Mr. Schereschewsky, stating openly that we were rebels in disguise; fortunately the rest of us did not understand a word of all this abuse. Then they returned into the city and closed the gates, so that not even our China boys could get in to procure us provisions, of which none were to be obtained outside. It is very evident to me now that we were taken to be in connexion with the rebels, but at the time we did not think so, because, although we were constantly told that the rebels were within a few *li* of Ping-shan, we did not believe it. I am inclined to the opinion that the idea, if it was not originated, was certainly kept up, by some of the Chinese belonging to our party. This evening, after we had divided one fowl among four, another council of war was held; and it was decided that, if we could not get into the city, we would occupy some place outside; but, as the main road to the north left the city on the western side, it would be most advantageous for us to take up our quarters there; and a *reconnaissance en force* was planned for the following morning. Thus closed the 28th, darkly; the 29th was darker.

Before half-past 5 A.M. Dr. Barton and myself, accompanied by two sepoys, all well armed, started to reconnoitre. We proceeded by the north side of the city, from which the

T

hills rise abruptly, so that at a short distance from the wall one sees over the whole interior of the town—defilade, to use a military expression, having, in the laying out of Ping-shan, only been thought of apparently so far as it could be of any possible advantage to a besieging army. At first, although the easiest walking was close under the wall, we took particular care to keep at a respectful distance, as we observed, what is common in Chinese fortresses, that heaps of stones lay in the embrasures ready for use in case of an attack, and we did not care to have any of them dropped on our pates. But our vigilance relaxed after we had proceeded some distance, for the only person we saw was a full private of the Ping-shan volunteers, sauntering leisurely homewards with a bundle on his back, which we took to be the bed on which he had comfortably snoozed the entire night, and with a bamboo spear over his shoulder. Poor soldier! after the fatigue entailed by a night of such assiduous watching, he was returning homewards—having relieved *himself* off night picket—to the bosom of his family, where a little bowl of plain boiled rice, with a few scraps of fish and vegetable, awaited his arrival. He did not even turn his head to look at us, and I doubt if he saw us at all. We therefore approached the wall—a formidable structure—and found that almost in any part on the north side one man might climb up from the shoulders of a comrade, and that at one or two points a single individual, without being gifted with any great amount of Jack Sheppard's skill, could scale the battlements.

Gaining the west side of the city, we found all the temples of a suburb (which may have been, before the last siege, in a flourishing condition, but was now mostly in ruins) so filled with men, women, children, and lice—refugees from the present disturbed districts—that we pushed on at once farther up the river. On our way we passed a number of tea and "chow-chow" or eating-houses, mere temporary shanties, where we observed a good deal of silk, some in the cocoons, and some being wound off, which is done by the cocoon being placed in hot water and the end of the thread passed over a wheel which is set revolving. There are a few houses used as shops in pretty good repair, but most were in ruins. It came on to rain very heavily, but still we kept on, inspecting, by the way, one or two pretty-good-looking temples, but hardly suitable for us. At last, when we reached the mouth of a stream, coming down a valley from the north, about a mile above the town, we espied, on the far side, a good-looking temple on a small hill, so, getting ourselves ferried over, we proceeded to inspect it. We found the place to be in tolerable repair; and its situation was excellent, both when personal comfort was considered, and also, in a military point of view, for defence, which was not to be overlooked in the present state of affairs. We decided at once, and, having ferreted out the high priest, explained to him our views on the subject, namely, that eight people such as ourselves would come and reside there on the morrow, and that in the mean time we requested him to turn out the few refugees who were then there, and to have the place well swept and washed out; but we did not say anything about white-washing, thinking that, being only partially acquainted with the customs of our country, he might consider it an insult. Having expressed ourselves in the choicest English, we retired with the full conviction that the priest had not understood one word of what we said; but that from our gesticulation and manner he would have a dim comprehension of our wishes, and feel convinced that he had better accede to the demands. It was enough; the object of the reconnaissance was accomplished, but we were thoroughly wet through, for it rained heavily all the time.

Our party returned to camp, that is to the boats, by the south side of the city, the wall of which leaves from fifty to a hundred yards intervening between it and the river. No gingalls were seen, and only a few people; but many standards or banners were stuck up along the wall. These spears with flags on them appear to be so far of use in the Chinese army that each soldier carries at least one, which always denotes the place where he *should be* on the walls of a besieged city, the chances being that he is smoking his opium-pipe in the nearest shop, or sitting quietly at home attending to his household affairs, when he ought to be engaged in matters closely connected with the interests of the state and his own military character.

We arrived at our boats, had breakfast and smoked our pipes, and, a scheme having been concocted for getting the boatmen to move the junks above the city, it was tried. We stationed ourselves and our Seikhs so as to cut off retreat, and then proposed to the skippers that they should immediately cast off from the shore and get under way. Commencing with a polite invitation, we at last came to threats; but they were immovable. The men also refused; they would be fired on from the town, they were afraid; they could not go. We threatened that we would not pay for the boats, some passage-money being still due; but it was of no use; they would not move. We therefore formally gave up the blockade (several had been turned back who wanted to escape from the boats), and told them we intended to remain on board as long as we thought proper, and that they might leave if they liked.

The skippers had been previously threatened by the towns-people, that unless they took us away they would lose their heads. The south-east angle of the city was within easy rifle-range of our boats—about three hundred and fifty yards; and we had observed soldiers gradually collecting at that point all the morning. We now received a polite message from the city, that the gallant defenders—defenders against no attack—would forthwith open fire on our junks. Our boatmen, and those of the surrounding boats, were warned to get out of the way, which they accordingly did, our crew carrying away their beds and other property, and making off as fast as their legs would carry them. We received one or two more of these messages, but still the only sign of hostilities was the number of people and banners collected on the wall.

After waiting a long time the first gun was fired, and then commenced a regular cannonade from gingalls and matchlocks in our direction. We turned out to see the effect and be ready to reply, and found that our red ensign had been hauled down by some one. Going aft to hoist it again on the bamboo flagstaff, I found the old skipper, his chief mate, and our China boys, huddled together in the captain's cabin, in great alarm. The skipper begged and prayed that we would leave the boat, as his property would be destroyed, and he himself killed. We however said that it was not at present convenient to us to do so. We were ourselves all ready to reply to the fire, and had told off skirmishers who were to advance under cover of some old houses and pick a few fellows off the wall, which would no doubt have decided the battle in our favour immediately; but we waited, before doing so, to allow of a shot or two striking the boats. This, however, did not take place; and although the firing, and an immense deal of shouting, were kept up on the city wall for about an hour and a half, still during the whole time not a shot was observed to strike anywhere near us, and we did not hear the whiz of a single bullet. When the firing ceased, we were left under the impression that during the whole time there had been nothing more dangerous than powder expended; but, as our ensign was flying, it was any way a gross insult to the British flag.

After the termination of the battle of Ping-shan, as I suppose we are entitled to call it, people began to collect again on the bank, to see if any of the barbarians were left alive;

and the boatmen returned on board again one by one. When they had all arrived, they made a second and more serious attempt (for they had made a slight one before in the morning) to get us out, and, having opened two of the hatches, were commencing to land our stores. The Seikhs interfered; but they being few in number, we were forced to join in the affair, and were putting a stop to it by making the fellows walk off the boats, when one more garrulous than the rest,—though they were all kicking up a tremendous hubbub,—who had mounted on the deck-house of the junk, was ordered by us to come down and go ashore; but as he seemed either not to understand or to be obstinate, one of our party mounted the ladder after him; then giving him the chance to go down quietly, which he would not, he was caught up bodily and hurled into the air. He alighted on a cross-beam in the fore part of the junk, smashed through it, and came down between a Seikh and another of our party, by whom he was passed on into the river. A second was kicked into the water, and the effect of these decided measures was an unconditional surrender of the boatmen.

Notwithstanding that a large collection of people remained on the wall during the day in a menacing attitude, nothing else of consequence occurred. A sharp letter was sent to the Prefect in the afternoon, to which an answer was received in his own handwriting, in which he falsely stated that the guns fired from the wall had not been fired against us or the British flag; that the people of the city threatened his life for allowing us to remain there; and therefore he politely requested that we would return to Sü-chow, and take the water-route thence to Ching-tu, which he had just received intelligence (another lie) was now free. This again divided our party as to the course to be taken: those who believed that it was possible for Chinamen to tell the truth, except by mistake, and who were not over keen for going on, leaning to one side;

and the others, who felt that to move one step backwards was to render fruitless any after attempts, being anxious to get to the temple which has been mentioned, at all hazards, even if it were necessary, as a means of persuasion, to thrash the boatmen all round within an inch of their lives; and I believe so determined were some of the party that this course would have been adopted on the following morning. The night, however, brought fresh events which had not been foreseen.

During the day—the momentous 29th of May, 1861—a couple of disguised rebels had been captured in the city of Ping-shan; and after being tortured, as Chinese only know how to torture, to extract from them information concerning their associates, they were beheaded. In the afternoon we had observed a few people lounging about on the ridge of the hill which rises at the back of the town, who, although by the aid of our telescopes we made them out to have only hoes and spades in their hands, looked rather suspicious; but we had thought little about it, being all absorbed at the time in matters of our own concern. We had but just finished dinner at about 8 P.M. (it was quite dark), and were enjoying some of the last of our Manila cheroots, when we were suddenly startled by a most infernal yell, as if all the demons of the lower regions had collected in one moment at Ping-shan. Every one sprang to his arms, which were always kept in readiness, and, rushing out of the cabin, we found firearms going off in all directions, amid tremendous noise. Our first impression was that the whole population of the city were sallying out *en masse* on our boats; and our boatmen, not slow at comprehending the meaning, were clearing the roof from their usual sleeping quarters, and getting the boats shoved off. The Doctor, who was on board the large junk (for we always dined all together), rushed on shore to reach his own vessel, but he found that, the hawsers having been cut, it was already clear of the bank, and he only just managed to get on board by springing off the stern of the large one; which Mr. Schereschewsky, who was not quite so active in his movements, was unable to do; this was the more unfortunate as there was only one of the Seikhs in it, who had been on guard during dinner.

Now was a scene of confusion on board our junk. Boatmen were clearing away the temporary shed to allow them to use the oars; we all rushed to the gangway rifles in hand, and one of our party was on the point of shooting the fellows that were helping to get the gang-board in, taking them for some of the attacking party; Chinese servants ran wildly about; sepoys met one at every point with fixed bayonets, or with their fingers on both triggers of double guns; our "writer," white as a sheet, was rushing distractedly about with his hands over his head, blowing out lights, and upsetting everything in his way, until he was finally upset himself by a cuff on the head from one of us, and retired into a dark corner to ruminate on the chance of losing his head or his tail. Poor fellow! he had some reason to be frightened, for gingalls and matchlocks were now exploding in rapid succession, while shouts of triumph and intimidation rent the air. On board the junk hubbub and confusion, such as it would be useless to endeavour to describe, reigned supreme, from the old skipper to the one-eyed cook.

As soon as it was possible we scrambled on to the roof or upper deck, whence we could now discern that we were not the particular objects of attack; for, scattered in groups or singly about the hills overlooking the town, were numbers of lights, while the whole line of the city wall was illuminated by lanterns; and the firing towards and from the city informed us that it was a night attack of rebels on Ping-shan. None of the combatants were very near our boats, but the gingalls from the city appeared to be pointed in our direction just as much as any other. The boatmen were dreadfully afraid, and got the junk out into the river as quickly as possible; but a strong eddy, which sets up the stream just below the town, kept us for a long time under fire as it were, and we had a good opportunity of witnessing a night-battle according to the Chinese system. The smaller junk was making better way than our own, so I hailed Dr. Barton; and on saying that we would rendezvous on the opposite shore, or Yunan side of the river, was glad in return to hear, during one of the intervals of the deafening noise, "All right!" and then we saw or heard no more of our companion and his attendant Seikh.

We were all prepared with revolvers, swords, and rifles, on the top of the junk; but, none of the party being wounded, we did not think proper to fire. In fact, had we done so, it would probably have only added to the general noise without doing any injury; for, as has been already mentioned with respect to banners by day, it is in like manner customary for each Chinese combatant to carry a lantern by night, and, as in the former case, one could not tell how far the individual might be from his indicator: possibly, as in the Alabama duel, he might cunningly place his lantern on the top of a grave-mound, and sit himself quietly at a distance under cover, contemplating the enemy's gunnery practice; and we had no howitzer and shell to find them out with.

By the time we got well out into the stream we found that firing was going on at the place we had appointed for a rendezvous; and thinking that the other junk could not be there, we drifted down the river. We observed firing also at some other places as we passed, and therefore kept on. But the question was, where was the other junk? No one could tell; but the boatmen, being in fear of their lives, insisted that they saw it go on ahead. Every now and then we shouted as loud and in as un-Chinese a tone as we could, so that the Doctor might if possible hear us; but there was no answer. At last we ordered the boatmen to put in towards the bank, about two miles and a half below the place; but this order was not obeyed until a pistol had been pointed at the steersman's head; and then, much to the terror of the boatmen, we insisted on remaining there for the night. Many were the conjectures respecting the Doctor and his boat; nearly all said he must be ahead of us, because they wanted to get away. That night we lay on our arms; some slept a little, and others not at all; and the firing in the city could be heard far into the night.

I awoke in the morning and found that the boatmen had loosed from the shore, and were going down the river; but I immediately made them turn the boat's head in-shore, and we halted. The flag was hoisted on a tall bamboo, some shots fired, and then Colonel Sarel went off to a hill above to reconnoitre; but he soon returned without any tidings of the missing junk and our companion. The boat-people were questioned as to whether they had seen anything of her, and all took their oaths that she had passed on in the night. I was in this matter, however, rather a responsible party; for the last words I had called out to the Doctor were, "Make for the Yunan side;" and I could not believe that he would have passed down without being obliged to do so. However, determined that our boat should not move down till I had seen every part of the river between where we were and Ping-shan, I took one of the Seikhs armed with a pistol and rifle, and having myself a revolver, sword, and field-glass, started to reconnoitre. To get a better view of the upper part of the river, I struck back into the country; and had a long walk before getting a satisfactory survey. The country people, no doubt taking us for rebels, fled at our approach as we went along, and we came in contact with no one. Satisfying myself thoroughly that the Doctor's boat was nowhere in the first reach below Ping-shan, I returned along the river's bank to see if it had stopped lower down, and was nearing the place where our own boat was, with rather gloomy forebodings as to what had become of our companion, when just over the point I saw two red ensigns flying in place of one; the small junk was alongside our own. She had come down by the river while I went up inland, and thus I had missed her. Dr. Barton shall tell his own story:—

"Our boats were now away from the shore, and getting into the stream. Blakiston hails me to get over to the Yunan shore, soon after which, getting separated, I see no more of them. The crew were so frightened that they pulled down stream; but with threats and gesticulations I at last got them to pull quietly under the bank on the opposite side, where we groped about till we found a place and got the boat secured; but we were soon discovered by the guard stationed there, and a volley from gingalls frightened our boatmen off again. We therefore descended about half a mile, and made fast again to the shore on the same side. Here, however, we were not allowed to rest; for a crowd of men rushed down towards us with their gingalls, fuzes, and lanterns, and before we could get away they were within fifteen yards of us, uttering the most horrible cries. They were quite at our mercy; and twice did Zuman-shah (the Seikh) cover his man, but I threw his gun up. I distinctly saw the fuzes placed to the vents, and so close that I covered one as he was about to fire on us, but resisted pulling the trigger of my rifle, so sure was I of him, and the contents passed over our heads unpleasantly near. We now crossed the river to a perpendicular bluff, under the deep shade of which we found a resting-place for the night. From the opposite bank a fire was kept up for an hour, but without doing us any injury. We kept watch all night, not only for safety, but to look out for the other junk, that it might not pass us in the darkness. The night passed without farther adventure, but the fight was kept up at the city till 3 A.M. As soon as it was daylight the crew wanted to move on down the river, but I stopped them; and, leaving the Seikh in charge, I landed on the left bank, and walked along as far as the temple close to the town, where I had a good view of the river, but nowhere could I see anything of the other junk. The battle recommenced at 5·50, the city not then being taken. I returned to the boat; and then, descending for half a mile, I found my friends in a little bay on the right bank."

Miau-tze.   See p 271.

CHAPTER XVII.

THE UPPER YANG-TSZE.

THIS chapter, being specially devoted to what may prove dull and uninteresting to the general reader, I am sorry that it is not in my power to make it more scientific in character; but it must be recollected that the "Upper Yang-tsze Expedition" was not composed of *savans*, but simply of persons travelling together for the sake of amusement and adventure, at the same time that they kept in view the opportunity afforded them of adding to the geographical knowledge of their countrymen. Neither the botany nor zoology of the country is treated of, because the only specimens brought back in those departments were,—the ferns collected by Colonel Sarel, of which a list appears in the Appendix; a few seeds; and some birds collected during idle moments: these last have but just arrived in England. It is accordingly hoped that those who peruse this chapter will bear with its imperfections.

PHYSICAL FEATURES OF THE RIVER.

Glancing at a map of Eastern Asia, it will be seen that, rising by several sources in the elevated region of Tibet, and among the mountains separating that country from China proper, the Yang-tsze Kiang first takes a southerly direction into the province of Yu-nan, where, recurving northwards, it enters Sz'chuan, through which province its course is a general one of east-north-east, and in which it receives several important tributaries. Passing into Hoo-peh, it dips to the south-east to the edge of Hoo-nan, where its volume is swelled by the waters of the Tung-ting Lake, which serves as a reservoir for the drainage of that province, as well as of the mountainous confines of Kwei-chow and Quang-si. Immediately altering its course, it proceeds north-east till it is joined by the Han, a considerable river coming from Shen-si and Ho-nan; after which it again dips to the southward to another of the great lakes, the Poyang, in the province of Kiang-si, where it is augmented by the drainage of the whole of that province. Thence its course through An-hoei is north-east till it reaches Nanking, 200 miles from the sea, where the influence of the tide begins to be felt, and beyond which it gradually widens into the great estuary by which it is connected with the ocean.

Lower portions of this magnificent stream have been described geographically, if not geologically, by former travellers; and as the few specimens of rocks obtained (see Appendix) do not allow of any geological description by myself, the following remarks are confined to its course above Hankow, at present the uppermost foreign mercantile port, 600 miles above its mouth.

The Hoo-peh Plain.—The valley of the Yang-tsze, in the province of Hoo-peh, is one immense plain for about 200 miles, being only bordered by mountains to the southward at that part where it touches on Hoo-nan and the Tung-ting Lake; with this exception, from Hankow to near I-chang, 366 geographical miles by its windings, its banks are alluvial, and the great triangular space included by its course between those two places is so low, that an extensive system of embanking is requisite to keep its waters within bounds. This country is sufficiently described in the narrative,* so that no

---

* See Chapters V., VI., VII., and XIX., describing the constant action of the water on the banks, continually exposing fresh sections of the alluvial soil, and the effects of the annual overflows in adding year by year fresh deposit, and thereby steadily raising the level of the land between the river and the embankments.

special notice is here required, and I shall therefore at once pass on to consider the two remaining districts, viz.: the confused mountain mass between I-chang and Wan, on the confines of the provinces of Hoo-peh and Sz'chuan; and its course through the latter province.

The Hoo-peh and Sz'chuan Mountain District.—The direct distance from I-chang to Wan is 140 geographical miles, throughout which the general direction of the Yang-tsze is east and west. In this section of the river the great gorges and strongest rapids occur; and, as will be seen by reference to the chart, it is the narrowest portion during nearly eighteen hundred miles of its course.

In our tedious and monotonous junk voyage through Hoo-peh, the first place at which we observed any change in the one prevailing feature of alluvial plain was at Kiang-kow, a small town which will be found marked on the map attached to this volume, about twenty miles above Kin-chow (foo). Here we found a shingly beach, and the land on the left bank commenced to rise. Above this point the bed of the river was in places stony; the soil of the adjacent country was of a clayey or gravelly nature; near the village of Yang-chi lime was being quarried; and opposite Chi-kiang, just above, a pinkish limestone was exposed on the east side of the river, in low cliffs. (See Specimen No. 4, Appendix V.)

From this point to I-chang the Yang-tsze skirts the eastern edge of a mountainous country, and before reaching that place you have to pass between vertical cliffs of conglomerate of a very coarse nature. The adjoining country to the westward is mostly of the same formation, split in every direction by gorges and chasms, and of a very broken and rugged nature. Specimen No. 5 of this conglomerate contains pebbles of quartz, jasper, and limestone. On the side of the river opposite to the city of I-chang, sandstone is associated with this conglomerate; it is of a soft porous nature. (See Specimen No. 6.)

For the eighty miles between I-chang and Quai-chow, the Yang-tsze cuts through a very mountainous country by a succession of deep gorges. The cliffs often rise several hundred feet in sheer vertical walls, affording excellent opportunities for the examination of its geological structure; but, as I have no pretension to the character of a geologist, I fear my notes on the subject will be rather confused and undefined.

In the first portion of "I-chang Gorge" we still found conglomerate and sandstone, but at six miles above the city were limestone and chert. (See Specimen No. 7.)

The rapids commence fifteen miles above I-chang, and the bed of the river is full of granite boulders, many of very large size, which run out into points or form islands, much to the hindrance of the navigation. No. 8 is a specimen from one of these boulders, and gneiss (No. 9) was obtained before entering the second or "Lu-kan" gorge. In this and the "Mi-tan" or third gorge the cliffs rise nearly vertically from the river to eight and nine hundred feet, and the strata dip considerably to the north-west. The hills through which the river breaks and forms these gorges seem to have a general lay of north and south, though they vary considerably. At Kwei (see map) the strata run N.N.W. and S.S.E., dipping about 75° E.N.E.; and in this neighbourhood we met with the first signs of coal. Specimen No. 10 of sandstone is from two miles below, while 11, 12, and 13 are the coal and sandstone associated with it, only a few miles above. No. 12 can hardly be called coal, being no more than carbonaceous shale with traces of plants; but it was the material the native Chinese were working out of the hill-sides by galleries driven horizontally, the seams being from three to four feet thick. When got out it was pounded up and mixed with water and loam, being sent to market in the form of bricks, as already described. Above this we observed coal worked in numerous places, and these workings have been inserted in the larger charts published by Mr. Arrowsmith from our survey.

The village and rapid of Kwan-du-kow are at the mouth of the fourth or Wu-shan gorge, so named from its terminating near that town. This gorge monopolises twenty miles of the river without interruption. At its lower end is a fine-grained mouse-coloured limestone (Specimen No. 14); and at the boundary between the provinces of Hoo-peh and Sz'chuan, which occurs in the middle of this gorge, the general rock is a blackish limestone, of which No. 15 is a specimen.

In this portion of the river the disturbance of the strata is very great; and, the stream being hemmed in by high cliffs, it is impossible to get much idea of the general form of the mountains when boat-travelling. Above Wu-shan the hills recede from the river slightly, and are less steep for a few miles, until a fifth, the Fung-siang or "Wind-Box" gorge, is entered, which is in no way inferior to the most magnificent parts of the others; and after a course of three miles, one emerges once more through a pass not over a hundred and fifty yards wide, into the open light of day at Quai-chow, where specimen No. 16, a dark-grey limestone, was obtained, and where there is found a red clay suitable for making tiles. So much for the gorges. The general features can be best gained by a glance at the large chart published by Mr. Arrowsmith, where the hills, originally sketched in on a scale of half an inch to the mile, have been reduced one-half.

From Quai-chow to near Wan, a direct distance of forty-five miles, the country is much of one character, the general rock being sandstone of a rough calcareous nature (Specimen No. 20), usually horizontal. Coal is worked for in places, and the specimen (No. 17) obtained by us here is considered to be anthracite. We also found, a few miles below Wan, a very fine white lime in powder (No. 21), which is used as cement, but whether it is procured in the immediate locality or not I cannot say. With regard to the sandstone which is so very general throughout the upper Yang-tsze coal-fields,

U

I would remark that No. 13 is a weathered specimen, the surface of which is glossed over much as if it had been polished with black lead; and I observed that wherever the sandstone was glossed in this way, from exposure to the water or weather, in that locality there were coal-mines. I am told that this effect is probably due to the iron contained in the rock itself.

Sz'chuan and its Cross Ranges.—At Wan the character of the Yang-tsze changes. It widens considerably, and the hills (see narrative and chart), receding from its immediate banks, give to the country a more open appearance. Extensive shingle-flats exist, and these are worked for gold.* On examination in England a very small quantity of gold has been found in the sand gathered by us, which perfectly agrees with the information we obtained on the spot, that the yield is so small as to make the labour hardly remunerative. This sand is silicious; and Mr. Tennant, when examining it, drew forth a great many particles of iron with a magnet.

Continuing up the river, in a south-westerly direction, fine long and open reaches are passed, on the shingle-flats of which are numerous gold-washings. The same grey sandstone (Specimen No. 22) occurs *in situ* all along, frequently in reefs, and sometimes scattered on the banks in blocks. At the village of Shih-pow-chai there is a very remarkable geological feature, in the shape of a large isolated mass of rock.† I did not visit it myself, and no specimen of it was obtained. I take it, however, to be of the same sandstone.

Before reaching Fu, which will be found on the map at the mouth of the tributary Kung-tan Ho, the course of the river is between mountains ranging N.E. and S.W., which cause a disturbance in the level of the strata; and just above that place, specimen No. 23 of a grey sandstone was broken

---

* A description of the operation will be found in Chap. IX.
† For a notice and sketch of this rock see Chap. XI.

off a reef where the strata, running W.N.W., dipped about 30° to the N.N.E.; and here we entered a district which, from its peculiar conformation, I have called the "Cross Ranges."

By reference to Chapter XII. and the map it will be seen that, from the course the river takes, it is forced to break through these parallel ranges of hills; and at such places we almost invariably found limestone and coal cropping out from under the sandstone, and at some of them iron is worked. Specimens 24, 25, and 26 will speak for themselves of the country near Chung-king, where one of these ranges occurs, running N. by W. and S. by E., out of which coal, lime, and iron are worked.* Above Chung-king the country is still traversed by cross ranges, which can be traced as far even as Sü-chow; and almost invariably, when the river led us through one of them, we saw coal and lime being worked within a few yards of each other. As you get westward, however, their direction changes a little, being sometimes N. and S.† I have already observed that the nature of the river is very much influenced by the way in which it runs with respect to the axes of these hills—the course, when parallel to them, being usually long and straight, and when transverse very variable.

A few miles above Chung-king we obtained both hard silicious and soft micaceous and silicious grit, as well as a fine red calcareous sandstone (see Specimens 27, 28, and 29); and thence the general rock was sandstone, sometimes micaceous (Specimens 30 and 31), as far as Na-chi, except where, as before noticed, any of the cross ranges were passed through. Gold-washings were not uncommon on this portion of the river, and there was a good deal of half-solidified conglomerate in different stages of hardness. Moreover, in the tortuous portion of the river in the vicinity of Lu, Ho-kiang, and Kiang-an,

---

* See Chap. XIII. † See Chap. XVIII.

there were some deep beds of gravel exposed on the riverbanks, sometimes as much as thirty feet in thickness; and from the general appearance of the river-valley, I came to the conclusion that the bed of the river had in former times been of much greater width, and the water very much higher—the stream now meandering about from side to side of its former bed—just as if some obstruction to its course below had been removed, allowing of its draining off.

At Nan-ki there were both limestone and red and grey sandstone (Specimen No. 32) in horizontal strata, or with a very slight dip to the S.E.; and as we approached Sü-chow the N.E. and S.W. ranges became again well marked.

Six miles below Sü-chow are the coal-mines of Pa-ko-shan, where specimens of true bituminous coal, carbonaceous shale, and grey shale (No. 33) were obtained; and examination has proved the correctness of our surmises at the time, that at these mines the coal was superior to that found on any other part of the Upper Yang-tsze. Under the influence of heat, the specimens from this place exhibit far more combustibility than any collected lower down; and I have the authority of Professor Morris for stating that the coal of this district is of the above-mentioned description. It was being extensively mined, still by the same horizontal or slightly-inclined galleries elsewhere described, but it was got out in far larger lumps than we had previously seen, and at Sü-chow is used for burning in the pure state. From Sü-chow we brought away a piece of the general rock, which is a purple micaceous sandstone (Specimen No. 34); and we were informed that some iron is obtained in the neighbourhood.

Above Sü-chow the country commences to rise rapidly towards a high mountainous region lying to the westward, of which, as far as our wanderings led us—thirty-eight miles farther up—we saw no end. The hills, however, seem to lose any distinct lay, and beyond Ping-shan the view in every direction was nothing but a succession of mountains rising one beyond the other until their outlines were lost in the far distance. Between these two places, Sü-chow and Ping-shan, we passed through a rocky gorge of considerable length, where coal was being worked very extensively, and in a peculiar manner.* Specimens of coal, but not so good as at Pa-ko-shan, and sandstone (No. 35) were preserved.

Fall, Discharge, and Course.—On a voyage such as was made by our expedition, the results deduced from barometrical measurements cannot be expected to be anything more than approximations to the truth; but by massing the observations near certain selected stations, I arrive at the following result:—That the Yang-tsze Kiang at Ping-shan, 1550 geographical miles above its mouth, is about 1500 feet above the level of the sea, giving an average fall of 12 inches per geographical mile for its whole course, which may be divided into 10½ inches below I-chang, and 14 above that place; and in one part of its upper course as much as 19 inches in the mile.

In comparison with other rivers of which I can obtain reliable statistics, this fall is nearly double that of the Nile and Amazon, and almost three times that of the Ganges; while it is but one-third of the Rhone, even below Lyons; little over one-half of that given for the *whole* length of the Mississippi; and considerably under that of the lower course of the Thames.

The force of the current is very variable; but it is seldom sluggish. I find on the Admiralty charts two knots marked as the current for the portion between Hankow and the Tung-ting Lake in March. In June it was about four knots (geographical miles) per hour for thirty miles below I-chang; but below that much less. Between I-chang and Quai-chow

---

* For a description of this, see Chap. XVI. and Dr. Barton's sketch.

we found it to average six knots in June, while many of the rapids ran at least ten. At Chung-king in May it was about four. During June, between that place and Sü-chow, it averaged 5·8 knots; above Sü-chow the current carried us down at the rate of six and a half geographical miles per hour; and between Chung-king and Quai-chow it gave an average of 6·4.

This river is subject to extraordinary floods; but, as I have noticed these facts in the narrative, I need only here put together the observed differences between the winter and summer levels for 1861. Nanking, 12 feet; Kiu-kiang, 21 feet; Hankow, 33 feet: while, between the 17th of March and the 25th of June, the water at the outlet of the Tung-ting Lake had risen 20 feet; and at I-chang, between the 1st of April and the middle of June, 15 feet; but I do not believe the Upper Yang-tsze at that time to have been at its highest. The year previous, when there was an unusual flood, it was about 20 feet higher. Much, of course, depends on the width of the river and nature of the banks; and therefore the height at which we observed water-lines in the gorges need not be considered extraordinary, when in a broad part, as at Hankow, this river can rise 33 feet.

With regard to the volume of water discharged by the Yang-tsze Kiang, I have no *data* from which to deduce the total amount; but for the "Upper Yang-tsze," that is, above Tung-ting Lake, I have pretty sure *data*. From a careful line of soundings across the river, and its breadth by sextant measurement a few miles below I-chang, a section of the river was obtained, the measurements of which give, for the 1st of April, 2700 × 33 = 89,100 sq. feet; and for June, 2700 × 48 = 129,600 sq. feet; this, taking an average current of three knots, which I believe is quite below the mark, gives a discharge of 466,000 cubic feet in one second of time in the first case, and 675,800 in the other. Thus, I think we should be safe in putting down the average at 500,000 cubic feet in a second; and when we consider that this is at a distance of a thousand miles from the sea, and above some of the most important tributaries, it gives us a grand idea of the magnitude of this river. By comparison, however, it becomes even more striking; for, according to the best statistics I can find, it appears that even the Ganges when in flood does not equal this; the Nile is not above half; the Irrawadi is only seven-tenths; and the Bramapootra nowhere. Yet this is probably not more than one-half the water discharged by the whole river. The Yang-tsze Kiang must henceforth take its place as one of the greatest rivers in the world.

The basin area of the Yang-tsze is taken at 548,000 square miles; and its total length has been put down at 2900 miles.

With regard to the depth of water in the gorges and confined portions of the river, I was myself inclined at one time to doubt the depths we sounded without getting bottom; but since I have made the above calculations, I see that in such places, even taking the sides to be quite precipitous, we ought not to have expected to find bottom under twenty fathoms. The soundings are marked on the chart; but on the small map attached to this book they could not be inserted.

The course of this river is very varied, being in some parts extremely tortuous, while in others it is sometimes direct for considerable distances. The following measurements will show this variation:—From the outlet of the Tung-ting Lake to I-chang, the length of the general course, as it would appear on a small-scaled map, is 140 miles, but by following all the windings this is increased to 240, being in the proportion of 7 to 12; while the first 120 miles, namely, to Shi-show, when measured by a direct line, is but 44, making a proportion of 11 to 30, or nearly three times: this is, however, the most tortuous portion of the whole river. Above I-chang, the first section to Kwei is 31 and 39; from Kwei to Quai-chow, 58 and 63; from Quai-chow to Wan, 53 and 57; from Wan to Chung-king, 133 and 199; and from Chung-king to Ping-shan, 139 and 240. Taking the mean of all these, we get a proportion of about 9 to 14; or the course, as measured on a small map, would have to be multiplied by 1·3 to obtain the length of the river by its windings. This calculation may be some guide in estimating the lengths of other imperfectly known rivers.

I close this unconnected account with the hope that it may be of some little assistance to men of science who may at a future time wish more thoroughly to explore the same region; but with the full conviction that it can otherwise be of little value, I have only to urge as an excuse for not having prepared a more elaborate paper, that, our object being to make a rapid journey through an unknown country, we encumbered ourselves with as little as possible that would add to the weight of our baggage, and were prepared at any time to throw away our extra clothes, books, and instruments, if they should stand in the way of our progress: so that we confined our records to such as would be portable; and hence the paucity and smallness of our mineralogical specimens. I hope, therefore, that our expedition may not be compared to one fitted out with the sole intention of exploring a river, and returning from the farthest point accessible by water; but that the results of our labours may be looked upon as the passing observations of a party of private individuals travelling at their own expense with a farther object in view than the exploration of the Upper Yang-tsze.

REMARKS ON THE NAVIGATION.

The portion of river between Hankow and the Tung-ting Lake surveyed by the staff under Commander John Ward,

CHAP. XVII.   THE NAVIGATION.   297

R.N., is now published as an Admiralty chart, and is so complete in its details, that I think no one with any knowledge of river navigation would experience any difficulty in ascending by its aid. My route-sketch and observations commence where that survey terminates, at the junction of the waters flowing from the Tung-ting Lake with the Yang-tsze Kiang; but Mr. Arrowsmith, who has published the chart constructed from these materials, thought it advisable, with the permission of the Hydrographer to the Admiralty, to carry it down to Hankow, as being a well-known point to start from.

The course of the river was laid down mostly during low water,—for the first part, perhaps, nearly the lowest; shoals are consequently apparent which would be entirely covered in summer, at which season, in fact, it would be almost impossible to make a useful survey of the river. During our voyage on the upper portion, the changes of the height of the water were frequent and sudden, while the alterations in the banks and bed in the lower part, where its course is through an alluvial country, are so rapid, that a few years may make great differences; and hence future navigators may find some incongruities: but it is hoped that for ordinary purposes it may be sufficiently distinct and accurate. I must solicit indulgence from future surveyors, as many parts of the river were passed in foggy and rainy weather; and travelling with all speed with but one object in view, namely, the accomplishment of the overland journey, we made no especial halts for geographical purposes, and therefore some omissions will doubtless be detected. Besides, the towns— the most important points—were the very places where I found the greatest difficulty in obtaining observations; and altogether the chart is, as no one knows better than myself, far from perfect.

Remarks requiring the special attention of the navigator

have been engraved on the chart; while, in the narrative, reference is also made to some of the difficulties, so that here I need only confine myself to more general observations. We will therefore take a rapid run up the river.

Leaving the fine wide stream of the Yang-tsze Kiang six miles short of the Tung-ting Lake, the Upper Yang-tsze turns off at an abrupt angle to the westward, with a width of about half a mile. For the first 120 miles (geographical, of course) its course is extremely tortuous as far as a small hien called Shi-show. In this section there are some shoals, but they are well marked; and as the points or convex shores of the river are flat and shelving, while the opposite or concave banks are steep, these features are a sufficient guide for the deep channel which is almost invariably close under the precipitous banks. In summer, however, when the whole adjoining country is flooded, the strength of the current will be the best indication of deep water. The soundings shown for this part are for March, and are almost always on a line *across* the river; which plan was incumbent upon us, as in junk-tracking we usually kept close to the shore, except when crossing; however, they give sufficient indication of the lead of the channel where they are frequent. As in the lower portion of the Yang-tsze Kiang, the season of highest water is not the easiest for navigation, for the proper banks of the river become lost in the inundation; and care must be taken that the embankments which show above water during the flood, but which are often some distance inland, are not mistaken for the true banks. The Nan-tsuin hills, which have been laid down, will be found useful as points for bearings in this part.

Above Shi-show the river's course is more direct; and as the banks are no longer, except at the bends, any indication of the channel, I must refer to the chart as a guide against shoals and spits. I have marked any channel when considered to be better than the one we followed, but have been careful not to name those we did not pass through. They will be at once known by the banks being inserted only in broken lines; and I may here state, for the information of those who may take an interest in my work, that nothing is inserted in *continued lines* except it has been laid down from *actual observation;* a practice sometimes not so strictly attended to as it should be. This will account for the hills at any considerable distance from the river being shown as they are on the chart, because their exact position and form must be somewhat doubtful. I considered that it was of primary importance to attend more particularly to the features of the river and its immediate vicinity, which I sketched in the field-books on the spot. Notes and bearings were consequently all the records kept of the distant features of the country.

The least maximum sounding which we anywhere obtained, while crossing the river below I-chang, was three fathoms, that being in the northernmost channel at the upper end of Spring Island; and I do not fancy that any more water could be carried through by the other side of the island. I believe that sea-going steamers could reach I-chang, 950 geographical or nautical miles (nearly 1100 statute) from Shanghai or the mouth of the Yang-tsze, without difficulty.*

Leaving I-chang and proceeding upwards, the character of the river will be found very different from what it is below. Confined in narrow gorges, the force of the stream is great; and at fifteen miles, rapids are reached which would certainly impede the progress of anything but high-power, light-draft steamers, with double engines and disconnected paddle-wheels, specially constructed for river navigation. That such steamers will, before long, navigate these waters, I have no

---

* See Chap. VII.

doubt; and the conviction induces me to continue these remarks for the upper river. For about one hundred miles, as far as Quai-chow, the character of the river is the same, a succession of gorges with occasional rapids, but no want of water. The force of the current, estimated in June, was for this portion an average of six knots per hour, and in some of the rapids as much as ten.* The chart and native pilots will be the guide against rocks and reefs; but the commanders of the first steamers on these waters must not expect to find the river quite accurately laid down, for some few rocks and other obstructions may have escaped notice, and of course the scale to which the chart has been reduced renders many of the smaller features hardly perceptible.

Above Quai-chow, although the mountains are not so high, and the hill-sides are less steep, still the river continues for some distance in a narrow and rocky bed, and frequent rapids are met with, but they are neither so strong nor so awkward as those among the gorges; and what is a considerable rapid for junks might often be altogether escaped by a steamer keeping in the deep mid-channel. As Wan is approached, the river's bed enlarges, sand and shingle flats are met with, and one general remark may apply to almost the whole river above this, except in a few reaches where the upheaval of the rocky strata forms ugly reefs sometimes in mid-channel; and I consider that with a good pilot or junk-skipper, of which there are thousands in Sz'-chuan, a small handy steamer would find no difficulty in ascending the Yang-tsze to Chungking. So far as water is concerned, I think there never can be a want of it; for our soundings always showed a sufficiency, the most shoal crossing we made the whole time having two and a half fathoms in one part of it. This, however, was in April and May, and is no criterion of what it may be in

---

* See Chap. VIII.

winter, when the water is at its lowest; besides, we may have missed some shoal places. But the general appearance of the stream, and the volume of water which passes down it, give the idea that want of depth is not a fault of the Upper Yang-tsze.

Above Chung-king, the great mercantile centre of Sz'chuan, the Yang-tsze is somewhat narrower than between Chung-king and Wan; and when the different tributaries which fall in are deducted, of course the size of the main stream is considerably reduced by the time we reach Sü-chow, over fifteen hundred geographical miles from Shanghai. Up to this point no extraordinary difficulties in the navigation need be looked for, any more than below Chung-king; and I think it will be found quite suitable for such steamboats as I have advocated.

The Min, falling in at Sü-chow, is a large tributary, and the Yang-tsze is sensibly smaller above; while before reaching Ping-shan, thirty-eight miles above, there is a strong rapid or two, and the banks are very rocky. There are said to be falls about thirty miles above Ping-shan, but the truth of their existence depends on native report, not always to be relied on, but possibly correct.

COMMUNICATION BETWEEN INDIA AND CHINA.

Since the ratification of the last treaty with the Emperor of China, a good deal has been thought in some quarters of the establishment of a commercial route by land to connect that country with our Indian empire, and for the development of the resources of its more western provinces; it being urged that the present communication by sea, viâ the Strait of Malacca, is long and indirect. Several schemes have been proposed with this view, all proposing to take more or less advantage of the rivers of Burmah, or of those which find their way into the Bay of Bengal. The object of these schemes seems to be to get into the province of Yu-nan, from an erroneous notion—which originated in the mistake of a name — that the best teas of China are grown in that province.

That any one of these schemes is at all likely to be carried out seems to me most improbable, now that we know of a river suitable for steam navigation running through the whole breadth of middle China, and of the pitch of perfection to which sea-going steamers are now brought. It is too much the fashion to underrate the difficulties of land-transport now-a-days; still, for the sake of geography, I would say nothing that might discourage exploratory enterprise in the little-known region through which such routes would pass; but it appears to me that beyond the establishment of the fact of an overland communication between India and China, and its use by baggageless travellers, little practical good is likely to result from the expenditure of any amount of life and capital on such an enterprise.

It has been very generally supposed that the Upper Yang-tsze Expedition—our private enterprise—besides being a Government undertaking, with some deep political anti-Russian object, was made with a view of discovering a practicable route between India and China; but we might well have been looked upon as maniacs when we left Shanghai in February, 1861, if, in our intention to pass out of Western China into the mountainous regions of Tibet, and so along the north of the Himalayas, to the passes into North-Western India, we had the slightest idea that by so doing we should be advancing such a project. I would therefore correct this misapprehension by stating that no such idea entered our heads; but that our object was simply the exploration of the country and the pursuit of sporting.

As to a line of communication for travellers between India and Eastern and Central China, the most feasible route, judging from the map, seems to me to be up the Bramapootra by steam to Sudya, or near it, and thence to the Yang-tsze Kiang, which, in a direct line, would necessitate only about two hundred and twenty geographical miles overland. But then we know little or nothing of that interval, and, from its general geographical features, may fairly put it down as a mountainous region; while of that part of the Yang-tsze which such a route would strike, we are in ignorance as to its capability for navigation, and are led to infer, from native report, that it would be unsuited, at any rate for steam-vessels, much above Ping-shan.

However, that this route should receive the attention of Government is certainly advisable, for it is probable that by it a line of electric telegraph will be ultimately carried; and I would therefore hope to persuade the Government of India not to defer its exploration. Once on the Yang-tsze, an expedition would probably find little difficulty in descending that river by native craft to Ping-shan; and then it would be on known waters, whence the current of the great river would quickly carry it to our uppermost trading ports. Such an expedition, while costing little expense, would be of the greatest geographical value, if of no other importance.

(304)

CHAPTER XVIII.

DOWN THE KIN-CHA KIANG.

WE will now resume our narrative, in which the reader was left near Ping-shan, a place in round numbers eighteen hundred statute miles up the Yang-tsze Kiang, and eleven hundred distant from any place of residence of Europeans, excepting always the Roman Catholic missionaries in disguise. Having accompanied us so far, it would be unfair to leave him there in the lurch; and I shall therefore devote these last two chapters to relating our return journey to the coast. As no description of the country will be required after what has been said of it on the upward voyage, I shall confine myself to tracing our route, noting the halting-places, and giving the distances actually travelled;—which, by the help of the map attached to this volume, but still better by the chart of the river published on a large scale by my friend Mr. Arrowsmith, will be easily followed by any one: adding only a few observations which have been omitted in previous chapters.

Finding no inducement sufficient to prevail on our skipper or the boatmen to take us again near enough to Ping-shan to have another look at it, we left our halting-ground three miles below that place at 7 A.M. on the 30th May. Numbers of boats were continually descending with living freights of affrighted citizens, who gave us the most alarming accounts concerning the siege; but whether Ping-shan was ultimately captured or not we never learned. Twenty-five minutes down stream brought us to the village of Fo-yien-chi, where we halted for most of the day, on account of the junk skippers being unwilling to leave to our liberality the price we should pay for boat-hire when we should arrive at Sü-chow, but wanting to be settled with at once. But now that the tables were turned, and we had the advantage of not being in any particular hurry, while with the rebels behind them they were most anxious to get on, we carried the high hand, and were inclined to pay them off a little in their own coin for the squeezing they had previously subjected us to, and we dictated our terms accordingly. Hence we did not leave Fo-yien-chi, where the Doctor and myself went off for a stroll over the hills with our guns, until half-past four in the afternoon, but, aided by the strong current, by six, when we put ashore for the night, we were only two miles above the rapid of Ta-tan-pa.

After a rainy night, by no means an unusual occurrence at this season in Western Sz'chuan, we started the following morning at 5·40. At half-past six we passed the town of An-pien, mentioned on going up, the swift current of the river brought us to Sü-chow at ten minutes past nine; making altogether from near Ping-shan a distance of thirty-five geographical miles in five and a half hours, being at the rate of six and a half knots per hour; and as our boatmen did not over-exert themselves, but allowed the junk simply to drift a great part of the time, and at others only used the oars to keep her in the centre of the channel, this pace is certainly not above the force of the current. When we threw anything overboard, such as a half-filled bottle, or something that only just floated, we found that it usually kept about even with the junk. The times when we went slower than the current were when a strong foul wind prevailed, but in my estimate I have allowed a little for such places. Moreover, I have not given the times of starting and halting on our downward voyage as those when we pushed off from the shore or had made fast again, but the times are reckoned from the moment we got into the strength of the current until we again left it, because we were often some time in the eddies which occur in many places along the banks. The velocity of the current which I have estimated must be taken as that of the surface water in mid-stream, but not as of the whole body of water, the velocity of which would perhaps be less. I have confined myself to this, as it is the current which vessels must meet in ascending, and its bearings are more practical than any uncertain conclusion which might be arrived at in the other case.

At Sü-chow we found, as we had expected, that the story of the Prefect of Ping-shan with regard to the water route thence to the capital being open was altogether a fabrication; however, we had never built on it, at least I had not. There were now far more boats collected than before waiting to get up the Min; the gates of the city were still closed, and matters seemed pretty much as when we had left it the previous week. We had a letter written to the Prefect, and his answer was that the city was in as disturbed a state as before. We therefore halted only one day for the purpose of procuring supplies, and making some alteration in the boats' gear, and arranged with the head skipper to take us to Chung-king in the same two boats for thirty-two and a half taels of silver. We also changed our quarters, Mr. Schereschewsky coming into the large junk, while I shifted into the smaller one with Dr. Barton. We were troubled a little by the "braves," but not very much, as most of these gallant troops had been removed; the authorities feeling more at ease when their defenders were at a distance.

We saw some very fine grass mats at Sü-chow, and some of the boatmen laid in considerable stocks of them. The large flexible straw hats were also of very neat manufacture, and in the western country they seem to be more generally used than the ordinary stiff bamboo ones; but they are not waterproof, and therefore require to be protected by an oiled cotton cover in bad weather.

Before going any farther down I ought to notice that, besides the difference in the general appearance of the people of Sz'chuan, which I have before mentioned, we often observed, particularly in the west, some with very un-Chinese features, and on two or three occasions saw a few with brown hair; and I think I could have picked out a few specimens of the *homo celestialis* from among the coal-workers above Sü-chow, whose nationality would have puzzled the Europeans resident on the coast of China. But as we never found any of them public-spirited enough to be willing to part with their skins or skulls for the benefit of science, this interesting variety of the human family cannot at present be exhibited at the British Museum alongside of the gorilla. None however were ever seen with light-coloured eyes.

I forgot to mention that on our upward voyage Dr. Barton shot some quail at Sü-chow, which seemed to me to be of that species which is common at Canton and Shanghai; but the annoyance which we there suffered, and the want of stock for our larder, prevented my skinning any of them. And as I have been frequently asked since I returned to England what sport we obtained with our guns in the Yang-tsze, I may satisfy the curiosity of sportsmen and naturalists by saying that, being always under the idea that we should have sporting enough to satisfy us when we got to the highlands of Tibet, we did not lay ourselves out for it in ascending the river; besides, being always anxious to push on, our only delays were at the towns. We heard of wild pigs and goats, as they were called, in the mountainous districts; but besides a few pheasants—one of which was of a species which I cannot now determine from recollection,—a woodcock or two, some pigeons and waterfowl in the cold weather, we got no good shooting after we left the naval squadron. On the return voyage, when we might have had plenty of time for that sort of thing, the weather was too hot to allow of our taking exercise during the day. My ornithological collection on the Yang-tsze also numbers but a very few specimens, and those nearly all from the lower part of the river; for what with the constant occupation of sketching in the river's course and the adjoining country, added to the determination of geographical positions by night as well as by day, and the work of recording these so as to bring back as faithful accounts of the country as possible, I had no time to devote to the pursuit of natural history. In the botanical way, however, Colonel Sarel made a pretty fair collection of ferns in Sz'chuan, and Dr. Barton procured some seeds, of which I have appended lists.

It rained steadily during the first part of the day of the 2nd of June when we left Sü-chow, and was overcast all the afternoon and evening, but there was little or no wind, and for the next few days this kind of weather continued with more or less rain. The only advantage of it was that the constant humidity kept the air tolerably cool, as the record of the thermometer showed. The temperature on this day ranged only from $70\frac{1}{2}°$ to $72\frac{1}{2}°$; on the 3rd, $67°$ to $69\frac{1}{2}°$; on the 4th, $67°$ to $68\frac{1}{2}°$; it was not until the 7th that it rose above $80°$ Fahrenheit, and was never below the limit of the foregoing numbers.

Starting at 6·10 A.M., we reached the town of Li-chuang-pa in two hours, and passed Nan-ki (hien) at 10·30. The rapid at "Barton Island" below this place, in consequence of a rise in the water of about three feet since we passed it before, was only slightly broken close in to the right bank, and cannot be considered as any impediment to steam-vessels. On returning to Shanghai after a three months' absence in Japan, I heard wonderful stories of this island. Every one knows how reports increase in magnitude by passing through various mediums, and I was positively assured that at this magnificent island, which was described as growing all the delicious fruits and abounding in the most valuable productions of the tropics, gold was found but a little distance below the surface in bars; that ivory in the form of elephants' tusks and teeth lay scattered about, and only required to be picked up; and that this valuable property was now the freehold of Alfred Barton, Esq., having been bequeathed to him by the late Emperor Hien-Fung, by will. I am sorry to be obliged to dispel this illusion, or throw a shadow over the prospects of my friend's relatives, but all is not gold that glitters; elephants have not to my knowledge roamed of late years in Sz'chuan; and "Barton Island" contains at most a few square acres. It is a very pretty place however, situated in a beautiful part of the country, and I should be glad to hear of my friend having such a fine property bequeathed to him, where he might settle down with half a dozen Chinese wives, and ruminate over his past adventurous life. But I think he would find that at seventeen hundred miles up the Yang-tsze he could not have a clean copy of the *Times* lying on his breakfast table every morning, and he might possibly become tired of the only one tune which Celestial ladies play on the Chinese guitar.

It was astonishing to us to find how swiftly we glided down in a few hours where we had taken days to get up on our tedious voyage. Three-quarters of an hour took us to Kiang-an (hien); we left it again in two hours; and at 6·20 P.M. anchored a short distance below Na-chi (hien) on the left bank; having during the day made sixty geographical miles in ten hours.

The beneficial effects of change of air and scene on invalids is an admitted fact; but I never saw it more strikingly exemplified than during our voyage on the Yang-tsze. Already our Chinese servants were picking up; and though we had made hardly two days' progress on our downward voyage, it was wonderful to observe the difference in them. In these cases I think it was the scene more than the air. The "writer," who had been suffering much of late, began to get quite lively, and was as active now in his interpreting as he had before been indolent. The cook, too, who had been down with fever—that name under which all diseases which cannot be included in any other category are placed in China —did his work like a man; and even poor "Quei-quei," who really had something the matter with him, looked brighter. Circumstances were now very much altered. Hitherto we had been approaching a *terra incognita* with everything in the future seen through the haze of uncertainty; but now, thanks in some measure to their own intriguing, our Chinese were returning rapidly towards the land of their fathers.

On the 3rd of June it rained most of the day, still we travelled for twelve and a half hours, passing Lu (chow), the rapid of Tow-pung-shih, Ho-kiang (hien), and anchored near the village of Ur-chi, having made sixty-seven miles, and passed through some beautiful scenery. The next day we started again in the rain at 4·40 A.M., rested two hours at Kiang-tsze, passed the mouth of the Chi Kiang, and at 6·40 P.M., having done seventy-four miles in twelve hours, we halted one mile above Chung-king; at which distance we distinguished, or fancied we could distinguish, the stench from the city. In like manner as the olfactory nerves are assailed in entering a bath in Constantinople with a strong perfume of "boiled Turk," so in visiting a Chinese city does the peculiar odour of live Chinamen at once manifest itself to that sense which in most Englishmen is so particularly acute. Huc called it a "strong smell of musk," but I confess I have always failed in detecting anything half so sweet as that. I pity the traveller in the "Flowery Land" whose sense of smell is very nice; if he does not die of fever the first week, which would perhaps be a happy release for him, he must be content to exist in a continual state of disgust, occasioned by his over-sensitive faculty, and heightened very often by his fertile imagination. Those who suppose themselves more than ordinarily endowed with any of the senses except the common article, should refrain from travelling "strange countries for to see." Goat-flesh and rice will not taste like well-hung Southdown and green peas, even under the influence of "Worcestershire;" neither can a person during his short residence in a Chinese city induce the inhabitants,—so wedded to the customs of their ancestors, —to give up the delectable practice of using garlic in the preparation of their food; therefore he that cannot endure such petty annoyances had better "stay at home at ease."

On Wednesday, the 5th of June, we moved the boats down opposite to the Taiping Gate, just where the ferry spoken of in our upward voyage crosses; and as we remained in the same position for the three following days, and our flags were flying, we became the objects of great attraction. Crowds of Chinese used to cross the river for no other purpose than to see us; and, as we had now little or nothing to do, we frequently allowed the more respectable of the natives to come on board and look at our curiosities. We moreover made the acquaintance of some merchants, from whom we obtained samples of many products of the country, and from them collected a good deal of information concerning the trade of Chung-king, which has been detailed in Chapter XIII.: a list of the imports and exports, and their market prices, is given in the Appendix. Our visitors were always anxious that we should draw or write something for them; some came specially a second time with new clean fans, on which they got us to sketch figures and write mottoes; and I frequently amused myself during the heat of the day in turning over all my stock of proverbs, &c., in order to select the most appropriate or ridiculous for inscribing on their fans.

We usually strolled out in the morning for exercise, and again in the evening after or near sunset; but in the latter case, although of course we escaped the direct rays of the sun, which are so dangerous in most parts of China, we found it usually very close and warm. The country looked beautiful; the paddy-fields being a rich green from the rice, which was now growing apace. Indian corn was in flower, although the heads of grain were still hid in the envelope of leaves. Mandarin oranges and peaches were numerous; the former being about the size of marbles, but the latter nearly ripe. There is a curious kind of tree in this part of China, which grows to a large size and branches out, spreading over a large extent of ground. When the branches are broken or the bark cut, it bleeds a white liquid, like milk. Earlier in the season it used to be covered with a peculiar kind of black and orange beetle.

I recollect coming one morning on a Chinese angler, and he interested me very much by the neat minuteness of his tackle, and the methodical way in which he went to work. He was at one of those ponds partly covered with lotus and other water-plants, and overhung by the ever present but graceful bamboo, so common in some places, particularly about old temples or the gardens of the rich. His rods—for he had two—were single sticks of thin bamboo, got up with little rings and a reel, exactly like an English rod in miniature. I suppose we got the idea from the Chinese. The lines were of fine silk, and the floats simple pieces of wood fastened by one end only; the hooks being very small and without barbs. When he commenced to fish, he first separated the weeds with the point of the rod just sufficiently to allow him to drop the line through, and then, forcing a hollow piece of bamboo into the bank in a slanting direction, he inserted the butt-end of the rod in it. After he had done the same thing with the other, he quietly seated himself on a little bamboo stool which he had brought with him, put on his broad bamboo hat, and lit a long pipe. As he caught any small dace—for his aim was no higher, happy man!—he dropped them into a prettily formed bamboo basket which he kept in the water under the bank close at hand, where they remained alive; fish being usually kept in this way in the warm parts of China. He seemed to have a good share of patience, judging from the length of time he sat stoically waiting for a bite, and he required it; but probably he was a lover of nature as well as of sport, and while sitting for hours alongside that pond he could contemplate the beauties of the trees, the waterplants, the insects—of which he might study those both of water and land—and was diverted occasionally by the dip of the swallow into the water as she skimmed over its surface, or, enlivened by some of the winged songsters, he might have passed his time most pleasantly. I imagined, also, that he studied the frogs who came up and poked their noses out to croak. I dare say he was a naturalist.

The water was much higher than when we were at Chungking five weeks previously, and during our stay this time altered its level considerably, in the first three days rising about 6 feet, and falling again on the night of the 7th and following day 3½ feet. During our whole voyage the water of the river was extremely muddy, and it was impossible to use it for the purpose of cooking or drinking, unless cleared by alum being dissolved in it. This method is very generally adopted in China. The alum is either put in as powder, or the water is stirred round and round with a stick having a lump in a little cage at its end.

We had great difficulty in engaging boats to take us down;

and we now found out for the first time that travelling up is cheaper than going down river. At last we came to an arrangement with the same old skipper to take us on in the large junk, and another good-sized one which he hired in place of the former small one. He agreed to land us at I-chang for 200,000 cash, equivalent to about 200 dollars,— a very long price for a voyage of such short duration; but we could get no one to do it for less. We sent a letter to inform the missionaries of our return; but none of them were in Chung-king at the time.

While we remained here the festival of the Dragon Boats took place; and for a couple of days there was continual firing of guns and explosions of crackers, while naked Chinamen, in long snake-like boats, with prows like the head of the sea-serpent, and accompanied by music, rowed about the river, and raced against one another. They use paddles in place of oars, and manage to propel their craft at a smart pace. It is very ridiculous to see a fellow standing up in the bows waving two flags, by which he is supposed to split the wind, while one or two others hammer away on large drums, and as many more beat gongs; all keeping exact time with the rowers, who give a shout at each stroke. When two boats are racing, there is very great excitement. This festival does not seem to be kept throughout the country on the same fixed days, because we saw it going on at several places we passed some time afterwards. Chinamen are great holiday people, and go in for any amount of amusement— drinking, firing off guns and crackers, and such like, when they do begin—notwithstanding they are such hard-working and industrious people at other times: a Chinaman is no Jew.

The weather continued damp, although it was getting sensibly warmer; and Sz'chuan must, I think, in the middle of summer be very hot. The missionaries informed us that

Chung-king was hotter than Canton; perhaps it is at a certain time, but I should not think for a continuance. One week after this, when we were at I-chang, the thermometer was frequently above 90°, and after that we had much less rainy weather; I believe, as I have said before, that on the Upper Yang-tsze there is a very hot spring, then a season of rains during May and a part of June, and after that a roasting summer; and I have referred in another place to the adaptation of the agricultural operations in Sz'chuan to suit this peculiarity.

Many Christians came to visit us while we remained at Chung-king, and our Seikhs made friends with a number of Mussulmans. The havildar having a part of the Koran in his possession, they used to set to work together to decipher its meaning; but as they were not very well up in "their common language," they must have required a large amount of faith to give them any idea of the contents. However, I suppose Chinese Mussulmans are not much more strict in their religion than Chinese anything elses.

The following is an exact copy of a letter which we received from an old native Roman Catholic at this place on our way up the river:—

"REVERENDISSIME DOMINE,—Cuum ad hanc civitatim prosperè perveutum heri aud procul aspeixi; statim gaudio exsultavi, nam paucos antè aliquot annos ego ivi porpinnang ad studendum linguam latinam, sed linguam Vestram non multum didici, ideo non audeo caracteribus vestris Scribo Vobis—; antea inter Vos, multos cognovi et amiciciam cum eis habui; quapropter paucis verbis Vos saluto sicut meos olim amicos. Si est aliquis latine loquiendi peritus, statim mecum loquatur. VALETE."

This was addressed on the outside, " Ad Reverendissimum Legatum."

Of course we inquired at Chung-king whether there was any chance of getting to Ching-tu, but were informed that the rebels were making great havoc in the country, and were all round the capital and had burned its suburbs. It was currently reported also that our whole party had been massacred at Lu, a place on the river above. This was said to have been accomplished by the native militia or volunteers, who were turned out for the protection of the country against rebel invasion, and it was added that they had beheaded our skippers.

We bid adieu to Chung-king at 7 A.M. on the 9th of June, and the rapid current of the "Son of the Ocean" soon carried us far away from the great mercantile mart of the west. We passed the large village of Hu-tung an hour before noon, and soon afterwards halted for two hours and forty minutes on account of a strong head wind. The long reach which commences at the bend below Hu-tung, nearly opposite which place there is a peculiar high rock standing out in the stream, has a N.N.E. direction for some miles, this being the direction of the ranges of hills in this part of the country. It is quite straight; and the strata being upheaved, or rather the soil being worn away by the action of the water, the river is full of reefs, some quite in mid-channel. They are so numerous that I have called this "Reef Reach" *par excellence*. The same afternoon we passed Chang-show (hien), in which neighbourhood, the river's course being across the geological axis (if I may so call it) of the country, it becomes again tortuous, and of very varying width. A remark applies generally to all this portion of the river, where the "cross ranges," as I have named them, occur, both above and below Chung-king,— that, whenever the river's course is parallel to the range of the hills, the reaches are long and straight, while a contrary description will apply to them when the direction is transverse. This is so marked that it cannot fail to strike any one on looking at the map.

In this reach we saw pigs of iron of flattened form on the banks, apparently recently taken from the smelting-furnace; and as we passed along many small boats pushed off to us and offered thick, pliable, twisted rope of bamboo, such as is used for hawsers and cables on the up-river junks. The thin plaited kind, used for tracking or towing lines, was obtained at many places on the river, being made up in large coils and sold by weight to the skippers or owners of passing junks. One great advantage of this rope, when used for towing, is its extraordinary resistance to the sharp edges of the rocks, which would sever any hempen line.

We anchored this day above the village of Shih-kia-tu, as early as 5 P.M., because we came to a place where there are two immensely large josses or gods standing in "niches" in a high vertical cliff. I well recollect the circumstance, for it was a very close evening, which was rendered more unbearable by our situation; the great mass of rock, which had been heated by the powerful rays of the sun during the day, radiated it out again at night, besides keeping off any little breeze that might be stirring. However, we would not interfere with the boatmen, as they had politely asked us if we had any objection to halt, and moreover it was a religious ceremony that they wished to perform—a bit of "chin-chinning"—and it would have ill become us as strangers in the land to interfere with the customs of the country. It was either a thanksgiving to the deity of the Yang-tsze for having carried them through all the dangers and difficulties of the navigation without accident, or, what is more probable, an offering or bribe for him to send them good luck for the remainder of their voyage. The principal part of the performance consisted in killing a cock for each boat, the blood and feathers of which were sprinkled on the bows, accompanied by the burning of some quires of paper, and letting off a great many crackers. A pig's head also had been prepared, being seared over with a hot iron; but I saw nothing of it after it left the cook's hands, and suppose it must have gone the way of all such offerings, namely, that when it was found the joss could not actually eat it, it was eaten by the offerers.

We may be inclined to laugh at and condemn this idolatrous worship, but after all there is something *real* about this style of religion. Where in Protestant countries do we find people going to such an expense as is entailed by the number of candles, incense-sticks, and paper consumed every evening? and in fact how seldom do we even find simple forms attended to so regularly as in China! We may well boast of Christianity, and we cannot brighten its effulgence; but I think many of us have an example of earnestness set us by the heathen Chinese, as we call them. Among all the Chinese I have come in contact with, there is a want of two very precious qualities—veracity and gratitude; and it is to be hoped that, when our missionaries shall have completed their work on the coast, they will enter the country, and endeavour by Christianity to humanize these already civilized people. The work of the missionary in China is very different from that among savages, and consequently should be carried on on other principles. The fact is generally overlooked that in the South Sea Islands, or among the deserts of Africa, the poor heathens require to be in part civilized before any impression can be made on them by Christianity; and zealous ministers are throwing away their lives and labours in endeavouring to disseminate the "light of Christianity" where there is no atmosphere of civilization, or, in other words, in sowing the seed without the ground being previously prepared for its reception. But in China the obstacles to the progress of Christianity are of a very different kind. On landing, the missionary finds himself in the midst of a highly-educated people, thorough utilitarians, but professing a religion, if we can call that a religion, which advocates only the worship of ancestors, and relies on the turn of a die for the future. The soil is already cultivated, and the sower goes forth to distribute his seed on land overgrown with tares, where a skilful husbandman should be employed eradicating the weeds. It will not do to send school-teachers, boot-makers, and masons—men without education or manners—among a people of this sort. Let such as these go among American Indians and other savages; but men of education and talent are required as missionaries in the far East. How would any mercantile firm get on, were it to send out to China, to deal with the cunning Celestials, men of the stamp of many, and I might say the greater part, of the Protestant missionaries in China? Are not clever, sharp-witted, and industrious youths picked out from the best colleges in this country to go out as clerks? Why then should we not send in the missionary cause men of the same stamp? —young men, who, arriving comparatively quickly at a knowledge of the language, would be able to reason with the greatest sages of the empire. One such would be worth half a dozen of the present class. Far be it from me to put every missionary in China on a par with his fellow-labourers, for I know a few bright exceptions; but in speaking of a subject of this kind, we cannot individualize. When Christianity shall trample under foot the present *religion of veneration* of the Chinese, then we may hope to see China *progress*.

On the morning of the 10th we started again, our boatmen's carouse not having caused them to sleep heavily, for we were away by a quarter before five, and we did not anchor till ten minutes after seven in the evening, opposite Chung (hien), making ninety-three miles, and having travelled at the rate of nearly seven and a half knots all day. Our only halt was a couple of hours at Fu (chow) for the purpose of getting provisions. I am particular in specifying the times and distances for each day on our downward voyage, as they may be of use to future travellers, as well as a guide to persons calculating on the arrival of cargoes from the interior. We passed some fine scenery this day, and the country around Fung-tu looked exceedingly beautiful. All the land which, as we ascended in the latter part of April, was growing poppy and wheat, was now occupied by maize from four to five feet in height. We met numbers of junks towing up slowly against the strong current, but none seemed deeply loaded. They all had their masts erect, some of the "sheer" description and some single spars, and the sails were bent on for the chance of a favourable breeze, which is a different practice from what we observed above Chung-king, where sails seem not to be used at all. Ours of course, like all the downward junks, had their masts struck.

We went through the St. George's Pass at 11·30 A.M. The reefs on either side were submerged, except a point or two, and there was a strong rapid over them. The water seemed about ten feet higher at this place than when we passed it in April, and, from signs of watermark, it had lately been about as much above its present level. There would be no difficulty in a steamer passing these "narrows," with some one on board who knew the passage, either up or down. The connection of water around St. George's Island was complete, and junks passed up by the northern channel.

At Fung-tu the extensive flat of rock which I mentioned on going up, and which was then about ten feet out of water, was now covered, with the exception of one small piece at the upper end, and had a strong rush of water about two feet deep over it. Also about seventeen miles below, where a similar formation exists, a strong rapid was formed, and the rock covered.

Near Chung, where we anchored, the river was much changed, and here, as before, it was evident that it had fallen about ten feet in the last few days. The change in the height of the water of a river depends, however, altogether on its breadth and form; and therefore, when I speak of the rise or fall, I always specify the place where it was observed, otherwise most inconsistent notions of this river would be disseminated. For instance, in the confined and narrow gorges we saw signs of water sixty and seventy feet above the level of the river when we passed up, and yet, if the same flood had raised the river twenty-five feet in some parts of the low country, it would have overflowed the embankments, and carried destitution, and perhaps death, to thousands of families.

Starting at 4·20 A.M. on the 11th, we passed "Soldier Island," the village, rock, and pagoda of Shih-pow-chai, Hu-lin, Ta-chi-kow, and the rapid of Hu; and arrived at Wan by noon. No more time was spent here than sufficed to inquire concerning the road towards Ching-tu, which was reported impassable for any party with baggage, as, besides the rebels, there was a large Imperialist army in the district, who in the way of plundering were as bad as the "Tu-feh." Peaches were very plentiful at Wan, and we obtained some very fine ones of a bright rose colour for one cash* apiece. We started again at 1·40 P.M., but in two hours' time were obliged to halt on account of a storm of thunder and lightning; and before we could get to the shore a heavy squall from the south-west came very near capsizing the junk on board which the Doctor and myself were. We landed and walked about among some farm-houses, which were situated in pretty retired places. Here we first found cotton under cultivation. At and about Wan we had observed that most of the fields not under irrigation were not growing Indian corn as those above had been but had evidently a different crop; and people were seen working in line, hoeing, just like the negroes in the Southern States. It turned out to be cotton, and was then about six

* The twentieth part of a penny.

inches high. The country of the middle latitude of China has a very different appearance from the south, about Canton; the reason being that at that place the uplands which cannot be reached by irrigation are not cultivated, while on the Yang-tsze, the summer not being of such long and extreme heat, such land is farmed without irrigation.

In an hour's time we moved on again, but were forced to halt at 4·50 on account of the heavy rain, which continued without intermission during the evening. Next morning we started at 5, and immediately afterwards passed the village of Siau-kiang; but as it rained very heavily, we came to a halt at 7·30 at Yung-yan (hien), a place mentioned in our upward voyage. We remained there till 11·30; but when we came to start we found it to be blowing so very hard from the E.S.E., that our men were not sufficient to keep the junks in the middle of the river, and the wind, catching the high houses on them, made them heel over to a degree that became dangerous for such fresh-water craft. The large junk put ashore first, and we halted only 2¾ miles below Yung-yan, on the left bank, the "South Pagoda" bearing S.E. ½ S. about a mile. This was only 2¼ miles W. ½ S. from the position where lunar observations were made on the night of the 14th of April, and the sky clearing at night allowed of a latitude being obtained, which served to check that of the station "Tung-yan Rapid," which depended previously on a double altitude observation: an ill wind blew us some good in this case.

The next day, the 13th, was little better, for we only travelled from 4·35 A.M. to 9·50, when we came to Quai-chow (foo), where, as there was a great native festival, we remained for the rest of the day. In the evening we moved half a mile below the town, and made fast to the bank near the white pagoda. We had met with several wrecked junks on our downward voyage, and, as they had invariably more or

MOUTH OF THE FUNG-SIANG GORGE BELOW QUAI-CHOW.

Pages 137, 323.

less cotton among their cargoes, the rocks all around the site of the wreck were covered with this material spread out to dry in the hot sun.

Casting off at five o'clock on the morning of the 14th, we immediately entered the "Fung-siang," or Wind Gorge, and the rapid current hurried us onward until we were soon at a distance from Quai-chow. During our ascent I was too unwell from the effect of the "Tung-tsze" nut to be able to map this part of the river, and so I embraced this opportunity of getting a correct field-sketch of it. After passing through the gorge, one part of which is not more than 150 yards across, with immense cliffs rising vertically on both sides, and equal in grandeur to any on the river, the country continues mountainous, the general direction of the ranges being E.N.E. and W.S.W., with a height of 1000 to 1200 feet; and from a north-east reach of the river about nine miles below Quai-chow, which we reached in an hour and a half, there is seen a very fine gap in a steep mountain range on the right bank, which has a most romantic appearance. At 8 A.M. we passed Wu-shan (hien), but did not stop; then entering the long gorge of the same name, we crossed the boundary a few minutes before ten o'clock, and, leaving Sz'chuan, were once more in the province of Hoo-peh. We continued on; emerged from this gorge at the village of Kwan-du-kow at 11·30; passed Pa-tung (hien) at 12·10; and halted to rest the boatmen from 1 to 3·30, between the village of Niu-kow and the lower one of the two rapids near that place. These were the first strong rapids which we had met with coming down; many other places, which had been rapids when we ascended, were quite smoothed over by the rise of the water. Later in the afternoon we halted again for half an hour on account of the wind, which was very strong from the eastward, and anchored on the left bank, two miles above Kwei (chow), at 5·20 P.M., having come this day sixty-two miles in a little over nine hours, being at the rate of over six and a half knots. The range of the thermometer during the day had been from 71° to over 86° in the shade, while in the sun's rays half an hour after noon it was 116°. The water of the river preserved the same uniform temperature as had been observed of late, namely, 73°. The continual moving through the air and the occasional strong breezes served to tone down the heat a good deal, which otherwise in these gorges would have been almost unbearable. In the evening a fine male specimen of a beautiful species of fly-catcher was added to my small collection, and I am indebted to Dr. Barton for discovering it.

The 15th of June was the seventeenth day of our downward voyage, although, from delays at Sü-chow, Chung-king, and other places, we had hardly done ten days' travelling. We started at 4·35 A.M., passed through the Mi-tan and Lu-kan gorges, and halted for three hours and forty minutes in the heat of the day among the rapids. In the reach above Shan-tow-pien, as well as at that below, the appearance of the river had totally changed from what it was when we passed up two months before: for, the water having risen considerably, all the low boulder rocks and reefs were submerged, causing the rapids to alter their position; but as I have spoken of them before,* I need not recapitulate. The scenery in this part, that is, between the "I-chang" and "Lu-kan" gorges, is, I think, as beautiful as any on the river. There is not that terrible sternness of the gorges, nor the monotony of an ordinary hilly country; but distant peaks and beautifully-wooded hill-sides are mingled with a varied and interesting foreground, while the river, with its broken current, boats, and voyagers, adds a charm of motion and life to the scene. I would advise any one whose

---

* Chap. VIII.

business or pleasure may take him to I-chang to run up as far as the first rapids, and I am sure he will think himself well repaid.

It took us three hours to drift through I-chang gorge, which, however, looked tame after those we had passed in the morning and on the day previous. We were detained a short time at the Customs establishment in the middle of the gorge, but, on rounding " Mussulman Point " at four o'clock, I-chang and the plain of Hoo-peh were before us. The change was as great as it was sudden. What we had thought hilly before now appeared nearly flat; and the long stretch of broad river below I-chang seemed like a sea.

CHAPTER XIX.

RETURN FROM THE INTERIOR.

THE "Upper Yang-tsze Expedition," at the close of the last chapter, had just arrived in two Sz'chuan boats at I-chang; and while they are arranging for their farther conveyance in a junk, larger and more suitable to the placid waters of the lower portion of the "Great River," I will say a word or two on I-chang.

Eleven hundred statute miles up the Yang-tsze Kiang, at a point where, after coursing the fertile province of Sz'chuan, and breaking through a rugged mountainous region, that river emerges into the great plain of Hoo-peh, the situation of I-chang is one of the most important on the great highway of Middle China. Easily accessible to large steamers at all seasons of the year, and at the portal, as it were, of the more unmanageable upper waters, I-chang, when European traders push their commerce more into the western country, will probably become a great place of business as a port of transshipment. A slight alteration in "Article X." of the "Treaty of Tien-tsin," with regard to the distance to which British vessels may trade on the Yang-tsze, would encourage the building of steamers for the navigation of its upper waters, and cause another European settlement to spring up at this point, which, to say nothing of the advantages of trade, and its being the limit to which ordinary steamers can ascend, would, as a healthy and agreeable location, stand unrivalled. Thither might invalids, and those worn out by sedentary occupations, fly from the low lands of the coast. A pleasant voyage from Shanghai, of a week or ten days' duration, would place them in a mountainous country, where they might select any scene and climate suited to their tastes and constitutions; where, amid the temperate breezes of the mountains, they might enjoy field-sports and pedestrian exercise, and still be among a European community, and within easy and frequent communication with the coast; or they might select retreats in the mountain fastnesses, where they would be shut out from the hum of business, and secure from Celestial mobs. I know of no greater change for one accustomed to life at most of our ports in China, than a residence among the mountains at I-chang.

Commercially speaking, I-chang would present the advantage I have already alluded to, of commanding the uninterrupted navigation of the river for large vessels from the coast. It is also a place past which all the valuable produce of Sz'chuan, intended for the lower provinces and the coast, must pass; and, while near the frontiers of that extensive province, is within quick communication by land with Hankow. Another great advantage of I-chang is that it would be a coaling station, boats being able to run down from the pits' mouths in a few hours with any amount of this material; and if the present coal which is brought there from about Kwei and above prove not to be of very good quality, the geological formation of the whole district of the Upper Yang-tsze gives me good authority for saying that good coal will be found by proper working. With these advantages, I-chang must become one of the most important places in the interior; and I would strongly advocate it as another port to be at once opened on the Yang-tsze Kiang. We might perhaps also propose Yo-chow, or some place on the Tung-ting Lake, nearer the tea districts of Hoonan, as equally deserving of being opened; but at any rate let us have I-chang. By the time any steamers could be built in China, or manufactured in England and sent out to be put together, a large trade might be established at I-chang, the produce of Sz'chuan coming down there by native boats; and I think I am not wrong in saying that to open the interior to European commerce will have more effect on the *people* of China, and conduce more towards friendly relations with whatever Government may be in existence, than all our petty wars and inconsistent treaties. And " what time is like the present?" Statesmen will say, " Wait a little." I say, " Do not wait a moment; push on; treaty or no treaty, Prince Kung or the Taipings, we must have trade."

When I-chang shall become such a port as I firmly believe it will, Europeans will, I think, find the side of the river opposite to the Chinese town the most agreeable situation for their residences, if not their places of business. The river is there about seven hundred yards wide, with its main lead nearest to that shore. Off the city itself the water is shoal for some distance out. To the rear or westward of this situation, the country is hilly and much broken; and many very picturesque spots might be chosen.

While we remained at I-chang this time (part of the 15th, the 16th, and 17th of June), the weather, with the exception of one thunderstorm, was fine but hot, the thermometer rising as high as 90°, and standing at 81° both at 8 A.M. and 8 P.M. The mornings and evenings were calm, but a light breeze usually sprang up before noon, which in the afternoon blew quite fresh up the river, from S.E. to S.S.E., and was very refreshing. This prevailing breeze is possibly originated in some way by the mass of mountains and the adjacent extent of plain to the eastward.

The water of the Yang-tsze seemed more muddy than at any time before; and although we did not observe any rise and fall at our anchorage opposite the town, there was an eddy close into the bank, running up stream during the day, while at night it altered to a downward course. The reason of this change I could not determine.

I was anxious to obtain a bushel or so of the coal used here for trial at Shanghai, but our boys, whom we sent ashore, were unable to procure any in its pure state. They brought, however, a few of the bricks or "argols," the composition of pounded coal and earth before mentioned; but these were left behind in transferring from our junk to the steamer at Hankow, so that the only coal we brought down with us consisted of a few small specimens collected at the mines. In the geographical way, I-chang, from observations on the upward voyage, and lunars taken during our second stay there, is pretty well fixed.

We observed a great number of birds of the falcon tribe in this neighbourhood, probably on account of there being a rugged mountain country favourable for the nesting of those which glean their subsistence from the plains.

Our Sz'chuan mandarin bid us farewell at I-chang, and we fired three shots,—the orthodox number for a Chinese salute, —from a revolver on his leaving. His place was taken by a Mussulman military mandarin, supplied by the Prefect of I-chang, to accompany us to Hankow. The Seikhs became at once very familiar with this fellow-disciple of the Prophet, and the first evening invited him to a feast which they prepared for the occasion. However, they soon found out that he was not a very strict Mussulman; and "Fuzzeler," the one of the four who had picked up the most English, if such it deserves to be called, confidentially informed me, "China Mussulman no number one, Sahib." We also came to an arrangement with the skipper of a junk of the same description as the one we had ascended this part of the river in, only it was rather larger, and accommodated the party with ample room. It was a great relief to get into a boat where one could move about freely, and the poling platform on the outside was a very great convenience for bathing. This man agreed to carry us to Hankow for the matter of 62,000 cash, and accordingly engaged a crew of six or seven men, besides himself and wife, who lived on board. We consequently paid off our old grey-bearded skipper, who of course made all sorts of fine speeches to us; and we gave away a few articles of little value now that we were returning to European civilization. We also made the boatmen the usual present of two or three dollars, "drink-money," as they call it; and future travellers must add a little to their estimation of junk-hire for this "squeeze," which is always expected at the termination of a voyage or engagement.

At half-past four on the 18th of June we left I-chang, and proceeded down stream, the boat being propelled by the force of the current, and a couple of large sculls, worked on outriggers at either side of the junk by three men at each. This carried us past "Tien-chow pagoda" in fifty minutes, below which we sounded, where we had previously done so on the 1st of April, and found the water to have risen two and a half fathoms. Our lead was now an extemporised affair, being a half bag of No. 1 shot tied up strongly in canvas; but it answered the purpose admirably. Our proper lead had been lost on the day of our reaching Sü-chow, it having caught on the rocky bottom and caused the line to carry away. Colonel Sarel, who was heaving at the time, was near being pulled overboard, but luckily only his gold-banded cap went into the river; this valuable article was fortunately rescued by a small boat, and restored to its rightful owner. At 8·45 we passed I-tu (hien), at 11·15 Chi-kiang (hien), but at half-past twelve were forced to halt opposite Yang-chi, on account of a strong S.S.E. breeze preventing our leewardly craft from getting round the point. In the evening we managed to move on about a mile and a half farther, and made fast to the bank exactly at the extremity of "Point Grant," the east end of

"Hope Island" bearing 173° magnetic. The latitude was obtained by meridian altitude of a star at night. Next day we left at five in the morning, passed Tung-tsze (East Market), —where the houses were not more than eight feet above the water,—and were forced to halt as early as half-past eight at the village of Kiang-kow, on account of a fresh southerly breeze, against which we could not make headway. During the day we experienced a gale from W.N.W., with rain and thunder, and in the evening it blew strong from N., was clouded over, and continued to rain; but with all the breeze (before the rain) the thermometer stood at 93° at a quarter past noon, while at eight the same evening it was only 68½°. Such sudden changes seem not uncommon in the interior at this season.

We put out in the face of the storm in the afternoon, but the junk made such bad weather of it that we were forced in again to the shore, having lost rather than gained anything after a good deal of trouble. The fresh-water sailors of the Upper Yang-tsze don't seem at all to admire bad weather; and you will find junks bound down anchored when it comes on to blow heavily, even should the direction of the wind be fair for them. Certainly their craft are not very seaworthy vessels, but the principal explanation is to be found in the fact of the value of time being little understood in China.

We experienced north and north-east winds on the 20th, and heavy rain in the morning. This delayed our start till nine o'clock; but when we did get away we made good running as far as the point below "Sanford Reach," whence we were forced to tack backwards and forwards down "Kinchow Reach." During this operation we passed the "Taiping Kow," or mouth of the creek or canal before mentioned as connecting the river with Tung-ting Lake. The stream was setting into it; and at a mile above it the embankment was broken away, and a considerable rush of water passed through out of the Yang-tsze, flooding the country as far as was visible. Junks were seen going this•way, and I inferred that the new channel was connected with the Taiping Creek. We took frequent soundings down Kin-chow Reach, as far as Sha-sze, near which, as will be seen by the chart, are a number of shoals, which as we passed up were uncovered, but now in June were submerged. We passed Sha-sze pagoda at 4·10 P.M., and arrived at the tail end of "Storm Island" before seven o'clock. On this occasion we again passed through the small or easternmost channel, and sounded it. At this season four fathoms can be carried through, but it is narrow, and the larger channel on the other side of the island would probably be found to be the better. From the soundings we judged that the river at this part had not risen over two fathoms at the outside, and probably not more than ten feet. As there was a fine moon, we did not halt at all this evening, the boatmen every now and then taking a spell at the sculls, and then letting the junk drift again. Thus we passed "Ho-hia narrows" at 9·40 P.M., and did not put ashore till about 1 A.M. At 4·20 we started again, but before we had proceeded more than an hour and a half we found that the skipper, mistaking the lead of the river, had allowed the junk to drift into another gap in the embankment, just below "Sunday Island;" and as there was a strong rush of water through the opening, it took a great deal of pulling before the junk was got out again into the river, and we did not get clear of the place till after nine. In an hour we passed Shi-show and "Skipper Point," and anchored at 7·20 in the evening at a small hamlet on the north side of "Attalante Bend."

We were now in that tortuous portion which marks the last 120 miles of the lower course of the Upper Yang-tsze; and from the rise which had taken place since we passed up, banks which were then twenty feet out of water were now only from four to six; sand-flats, and the low shelving points, were covered; and the whole of this level district was but a few feet raised above the river. The current, however, was not strong. The temperature of the water was taken nearly every day, and showed a steady heat of 74°.

The reader will, I feel sure, be glad if I skip the diary of the next few days on this uninteresting portion of the river; suffice it to say, that, owing to foul winds and unfavourable weather, we did not reach the junction of the outlet of the Tung-ting Lake till the 25th. Our occupation in coming down was confined to correcting or confirming the survey made in the upward voyage, sounding for shoals, in which the important "Boulder Shoal" was not forgotten, and noting the rise of the water and the extent of country inundated, as already mentioned.* But it astonished us to find the dyke country so much below the height of the river, when the only protection in many places were very poor patched-up embankments. In fact, no embankment can exist for many years in this part of the river, unless in the first instance it is built a long way back from the bank, because year by year the current eats away the alluvial soil on one side, while low mud and sand flats silt up on the other, causing considerable alteration in the river's course in a few years. The common crop in June on the dyke-land was rice, while there were large beds of reeds at some places outside the embankment. Much of the land which was growing young wheat in March was under water; but the wheat had been gathered before the summer floods. The rise of the water at the "Tung-ting outlet" was twenty feet at least over its March level; and the water from the lake

---

* See Chap. VI.

itself was whitish when compared with the muddy current of the "Kin-ho." The temperature of the water of the river a couple of miles above the junction was 77½°, while that of the outlet was 80°. A strong current set down the outlet, and we were informed that the Tung-ting Lake was unusually high this year; which it is to be hoped was the fact, for there was very little dry land to be found anywhere on the west side of the outlet; however, these annual floods must have a very fertilizing effect on the land.

On the afternoon of the 25th of June we got into a snug little harbour at the "Red Cliffs," on the eastern or left bank of the "Tung-ting Outlet," and opposite the Kin-ho-kow, or mouth of the "Gold River," which the Upper Yang-tsze is called. The presence of gulls and terns indicated our proximity to the largest sheet of fresh water in China, and we were just seven hundred and eleven geographical miles from Shanghai, or, in round numbers, over eight hundred statute miles from the mouth of the Yang-tsze Kiang. Here our voyage of exploration ended. After a sojourn of one hundred and eleven days on a river hitherto practically unknown to Europeans, we had returned to the point which had been reached by Admiral Hope. During our absence an United States naval expedition had also ascended thus far, but, instead of continuing up the Yang-tsze, it had followed on the Admiral's track to Yo-chow,* where, by way of being able to say that the Stars and Stripes had gone the farthest, one vessel was sent about fifteen miles into the Tung-ting Lake. Another party which I ought to mention had also been here; it was the expedition composed of Mr. Robert Thorburn, Dr. Dickson, and the Rev. Messrs. Bonney and Beach, who left Canton in April, and, crossing over the "Meling Pass," came down the Heng Kiang into

---

* See Chap. V.

this lake, and thence descended the Yang-tsze to Hankow;—a narrative of which interesting journey appeared in the columns of the 'North China Herald.' I have thought proper to mention these several expeditions, because this point was never before 1861 reached by any Europeans, excepting always the Jesuit missionaries, who have been, I suppose, all over the empire; while our party ascended the Yang-tsze more than nine hundred and sixty statute miles above, and were the first undisguised Europeans in the western province of Sz'chuan. But our labours were now finished; and we had only to retrace our steps down the known waters of the lower river to reach the limits of European civilization.

Large camps of troops were observed on the hills to the east of Yo-chow, and we were informed that a body of Taiping rebels was not more than 180 li distant in the province of Hoo-nan, where they were then fighting; and that the camps which we saw were those of a large Imperialist army which was collected at Yo-chow. The evening before we had heard a good deal of firing, and this was accounted for by the arrival of a general who had come to take the command. If Yo-chow should fall into the hands of the rebels, it would interfere very much with trade, because all the teas collected from around the Tung-ting Lake have to pass that place, and the Sz'chuan junks on their upward voyage also go by that route. The night of the 25th turning out clear, I was enabled to determine the latitude at the "Red Cliffs," from which the "Lui-ku" temple bore by compass 76°, Yo-chow seven-storied pagoda 203°, and the "Camel's Hump" 305°; which, with the longitude from the Admiralty charts, gives a good position of departure for the survey of the upper river.

We got under way and left the mouth of the "Upper Yang-tsze" at half-past four on the morning of the 26th. The breeze was right ahead all day, but, the junk being in light trim, we made pretty good way in tacking. The long straight reach carried us through the pass between the cliffs abreast of Ling-hiang (hien), and at half-past twelve we were off Sing-ti, where, hoisting our colours on a tall bamboo which had been fastened at the head of our junk's mast, we were allowed to pass the Custom-house without interference. A little before five we passed the village of Lo-gi-kow, and at 7·45 P.M. anchored about ten miles below, making fifty miles during the day. The appearance of the river was entirely different from what it was when we passed up in March. None of the low lands were now to be seen; and the only remaining signs of them were, portions of the embankment, half-submerged houses, and groups of trees dotted about like islands in one great sea. On the right bank, however, the Kiun mountains, and others which stretch farther down the river, formed a background to the waste of waters; but on the left bank a clear horizon was in some parts visible.

The river was, as in March, crowded with craft of many sizes and descriptions; and, as it was a fair wind for those going the contrary way to ourselves, we met very great numbers. In going up they keep in close to the banks out of the strength of the current, and in some places make cuts across country where it is sufficiently overflowed. There were also always a great number in sight beating down like ourselves; and it was very interesting to observe the different descriptions of craft, and their relative sailing qualities. There were the heavy, square-bowed Sz'chuan junks, now sailing under two masts, which they never do on the upper river; the clipper-like boats from the Tung-ting Lake; and the large trading junks from Hoo-nan. Beside these were a few rough-looking vessels, with matting sails in place of cotton: these last were coal-junks from Pao-king, which are only put together sufficiently strong to last one voyage, being

THE YANG-TSZE IN FLOOD.

broken up, when they have discharged their cargoes, at Hankow. Our own junk was by no means the smartest of the lot, for, although she used lee-boards, the great mass of upper work for cabin accommodation drove her very much to leeward.

On the 27th we started at half-past four, sculling, for it was quite calm, and made pretty good progress. We passed between islands, and along low shores covered with immense beds of reeds filled with innumerable birds, which kept up an incessant chirping, while, as we went noiselessly along, we could hear the distant hollow voice of the cuckoo. There were a good many ducks, more indeed than I should have expected from the climate at that season. Herons and white egrets were seen in numbers, while magpies, white-collared crows, and black crows were common enough. We passed a number of large mounds, which, from the height of the water, were in some parts the only landmarks for the river's course; they were old brick-kilns. All the low land, as on the day previous, was under water. At half-past nine we came to a place where the skipper said he could make a considerable cut off: it was the neck of the Great Bend, and we left the river where the flat-topped "Golden Hill" opposite King-kow bore N.N.E., having no bottom with twelve fathoms close to the right bank. Here we found a number of junks in light trim on their upward voyage, getting through by laying out kedges, and warping and poling up against the stream, for some of the water makes its way across with a rather strong current. The distance across is only half a mile, and our junk drawing two feet of water just scraped over. We came on to the river again just above a small village, with nine brick-kilns below it, and thereby saved ourselves thirty miles. The skipper told us that the water is usually of this height every year, and remains so during the summer. A very slight cutting would form a canal through, which would be of great advantage to heavily-laden junks that cannot now get over.

Having made such good way, we calculated on getting to Hankow in the afternoon about two or three o'clock, but by the time we reached "King-kow Pass" it was blowing fresh; and although it was a side wind for us, so leewardly was our junk, that we could not hold a course down the river; and at 1·40 were obliged to come to an anchor only ten miles above Hankow, and within sight of Han-yang pagoda. Later the wind hauled round from north-west to a gale at north, with rain and wild scudding clouds, and every appearance of a cyclone. The barometer had fallen since the day before, but commenced to rise in the evening. A shift of wind allowed us to run in for the shore; and we luckily secured a snug little harbour, instead of bumping about in the middle of the Yang-tsze for the night. It continued to blow heavily during the night; but the wind had so far moderated in the morning that we were enabled to start at 6 A.M., and proceed on our way to Hankow.

It happened to be the anniversary of Her Majesty's coronation; and while we were yet at a distance we could see the flags of the different merchant steamers overtopping the Chinese houses, and H.M.S. 'Snake,' gaily dressed, lying in the middle of the stream. Wishing to give our friends a surprise, we dropped down without showing our colours, keeping the red ensign in a ball at the mast-head. The crew of the 'Snake' were at quarters, every man being on deck and dressed out in their clean white frocks. Just as we were getting abreast of her we broke the flag, and all eyes and several telescopes were at once upon us; we dipped the ensign three times, and the compliment was returned. Immediately that the commander observed a junk showing British colours, he ordered his first lieutenant to board her and haul down the ensign, as at that time no native vessel, even if she belonged to an English firm, was allowed to sail under the flag, and the Admiral's orders on the point were very strict. But when he distinguished our party on board, who every one expected were then on the highlands of Tibet, his order was changed, and the lieutenant pulled off to us and gave us a hearty welcome, almost his first words being those of congratulation to Major Sarel on his promotion to the rank of Lieutenant-Colonel.

By ten o'clock we were safely at anchor in the Han, where we were surrounded by crowds of junks flying the flags of European and American firms; and near to us lay the 'Scotland,' a large ocean steamer, besides the 'Rajah,' 'Hellespont,' and one or two other steamers. The 'Fire Dart,' a fine American coasting steamer, and the 'Governor-General,' another vessel of like class, sent out specially for the navigation of this river, had left the day previous, laden with teas and other produce of the interior, which were now swelling the commerce of the port of Hankow, where four months previously there was not a single foreigner located; it now bids fair to rival, if not excel, some of the old ports on the coast.* Already English, American, and other merchants were building substantial houses and "go-downs" (stores), and there were not less than thirty foreigners engaged in a lucrative trade. Much of the tea previously sent to Canton over the "Me-ling Pass" was now finding its way from the districts in Hoo-nan to Hankow by water, being thence shipped in steamers and junks under their safe convoy, down past the rebel positions on the Lower Yang-tsze to Shanghai; for which distance, owing to the want of sufficient steamers,

---

* At a meeting of the Royal Geographical Society, on the 24th of March, Sir Harry Parkes mentioned, among other statistics, that during eight months of last year 152 foreign vessels and 170 junks in foreign employ passed up from Shanghai to Hankow, and it was estimated that trade to the amount of 10,000,000*l.* would be done during the present year.

freights were up to 20 and 22 taels, equal to 7*l*. per ton —more than that for the whole voyage from China to England.

Here we found several former acquaintances, representatives of large mercantile firms, or carrying on business on their own account; and among the latter, a St. George's jack flying from the top of a house in Han-yang denoted the residence of Mr. Craven Wilson, the pioneer merchant of Hankow. The remainder of the day was fully occupied in making calls, hearing the news, and relating our own adventures. We also engaged a passage in the steamer 'Hellespont' for our whole party, and transferred all our things from the junk the same evening. All the low grounds were now under water; and, although we did not care to visit it, we were informed that the piece of land on the left bank, at the lower end of the town of Hankow, which had been selected as the British concession, and where our Consul had hoisted his flag, was for a great part flooded. The rise of the river above its winter level, as registered on board the 'Snake,' had been 33 feet; and the current in the main river was so strong that the 'Snake' had dragged her moorings more than once, on one occasion the whole sand-bank shifting, and carrying her anchors some distance down the river. Merchant vessels therefore preferred taking up their berths in the Han, where the current was not so strong, though there was no less than eighteen fathoms of water. The Chinese said that this summer the river was about three feet higher than usual. This, if true, was probably due to the waters of the Tung-ting Lake, for we had heard that it was unusually high, but the Upper Yang-tsze was not higher than in ordinary summers. In fact, I doubt much if the latter was at its full flood when we left it, and probably the uniform height of the lower river, during the entire summer, is to be accounted for by the Tung-ting Lake supplying it in the fore part; and when its waters begin to fail, the produce from the snow comes down from the headwaters of the Yang-tsze, and keeps it up to the average.

Before we left the junk I missed a thermometer which it was my custom to keep suspended from a nail on the outside of the cabin, and it was evident that some Chinaman had appropriated it, but to what use he could possibly put it I am at a loss to imagine; and from the fact that I always had a thermometer in a similar position during the entire time of our seventeen weeks' boat voyage, and that it had never been molested until the first day of our arrival at a place frequented by foreigners, I am inclined to attribute this act of pilfering to the effects of European intercourse. On only one other occasion did any of us lose, to our knowledge, a single article during our sojourn in the interior, and that was a polished iron bottle used for holding the mercury belonging to an artificial horizon, which, while waiting between the times of the meridian passages of two stars, I left on the ground alongside the horizon while I went about something else, and without a Seikh to guard it. When I returned it was gone, but luckily the mercury was not in it. The thief had no doubt, in the uncertain light of the moon, taken it for some precious metal, but most likely, on farther examination, fully realised the old proverb, that all is not gold that glitters. This occurred during our last night but one on the Upper Yang-tsze, and so did not much matter; if it had happened before, it would have caused us some inconvenience.

Owing to all the cargo not being ready, the 'Hellespont' did not start as intended on the 29th, and it was Sunday morning the 30th of June before we got away from Hankow, and commenced our steam voyage to the coast. The 'Hellespont' did not make very good way, on account of having a couple of junks lashed on either side, and the coal which had been taken on board at Hankow proving unfit for her boilers. Besides this, we had a couple more junks under convoy, which the captain was instructed to keep company with, so as to protect them against attack by rebels, or the exactions of the imperial mandarins; and we were consequently forced to anchor early every evening to allow them to come up, and let them get a good way ahead before we started in the morning. Captain Lecaan did everything in his power to render us comfortable, and our friends at Hankow had vied with one another in enabling us to break the monotony of the voyage by supplying us with newspapers and periodicals.

We reached Kiu-kiang, the next open port, on the evening of the 1st of July; and, going ashore with the captain in his six-oared gig, we were pulled right into the lower floor of Her Majesty's Consulate, where we found the representative of British power living in his attic, with piles of bricks for stepping-stones, and the doors, off their hinges, used as bridges on the ground-floor. The only other Europeans at this dreary station were the representative of Messrs. Dent and Co., the Doctor, and Lieutenant Poole, R.N., commanding the gunboat 'Havoc.' From this last officer I learned that at Kiu-kiang the rise of the river since April had been twenty-one feet, and that the natives reported it higher than it had been for twelve years previous. It is to be hoped, for the sake of the Consul and others who may take up their residence on the concession ground, that this is true. The temperature of the water, of which Lieutenant Poole had kept a constant register, was usually ten degrees below that of the air at noon. Lieutenant Poole had also been employed, in the early part of the year, in exploring the Poyang Lake, which is in this vicinity. It was found to be generally very shallow, at that season there not being sufficient water to float a gunboat, except in some deep channels which ran through it.

Several places of interest were visited by the gunboat, and among others Nan-kang, situated at the base of the lofty "Liu-shan." Nan-kang is celebrated as a resort of literary men; and near it the renowned philosopher and interpreter of the Confucian doctrine, "Choo-tsze," resided about A.D. 1200. Woo-ching, at the mouth of the Kan Kiang, down which river the Canton trade comes, *viâ* the Me-ling Pass, is notable as a manufacturing place for "sam-shoo," or Chinese spirits. Coal of fair quality, used in the distilleries, is said to come from Yuen-chow, situated on a tributary of the Kan in the western part of the province of Kiang-si, and also from Lo-ping, in the first-class provincial district of Yao-chow (foo), on the eastern side of the lake. In this district also the once famous porcelain manufactory of Kiu-te-chin is situated. A writer in the 'Dublin University Magazine,' who mentions these facts, says that the coal was of two descriptions, one of which, called "red-fire coal," burned without smoke—this was possibly anthracite; while some which was procured for the use of the gunboat, "green-fire coal," at the rate of six dollars per ton, proved to be better than that obtainable at Hankow. The fact of coal existing on this lower part of the Yang-tsze is, I consider, very important; and I would direct the attention of British merchants in China to the fact. A good deal of tea comes out of the country by the Kan Kiang. The southern portion of the Poyang Lake, not seen on the ordinary route to Canton, is described as more open; and it is considered that during the season of high water nearly every part of the lake would prove "navigable for even large vessels." Kiu-kiang is the foreign port to which the produce of the district of the Poyang Lake is brought; and although its appearance, as already spoken of, was far from prepossessing when we passed it in June, 1861, it will probably become ere long a place of considerable trade.

On the following morning we continued our voyage, passing the outlet of the Poyang Lake, the water from which was comparatively clear when contrasted with the still muddy current of the Great River. But I need say little concerning the remainder of our journey; for the uncertain rate of progression, from circumstances before mentioned, would only give a false idea of the time and distance of a voyage from Hankow to Shanghai, which, at the time I left China, was usually performed by steamers in four days, and even less. The greatest obstacle to the navigation—though this may seem rather paradoxical—is too much water; the difficulty in the summer season being to know where the proper course of the river is, for in many parts nothing is seen but a great lake-like expanse, and the pilots are often only able to detect the channel by the roofs of submerged houses and tops of trees. The passage is not without danger, especially to large sea-going craft, two ocean steamers having already been lost, and almost every vessel which has made the voyage has been aground. Our captain had, up to the time we came down with him, been very lucky, never having touched ground once. He had three pilots on board, all Chinese: two of them acted between Hankow and Chin-kiang, relieving one another by watches; and the third was for the more uncertain portion of the river at its estuary. Here the captain and his officers were obliged to be more cautious, as the continual shifting of the sandbanks causes the lead of the river to alter its position in an extraordinarily short time. It was interesting to see how quickly the Chinamen had got into the way of handling steamers; and I was amused at the confident manner in which they gave their orders, "Port," "Starboard," or "Steady," as they required the ship's head to be altered. I have no doubt that the Chinese pilots will hold their own on the Yang-tsze, because European pilots have yet to learn the river, and they would be always expensive.

On nearing An-king the steamer waited for the junks to come up and pass ahead, and then we steamed quietly down. When they got opposite the place, some mandarin junks opened fire with a view of stopping them; and, finding they did not bring to, several war-vessels started in chace. However, the two junks were a good way ahead; and when the steamer was seen coming down the cruisers desisted, and contented themselves with firing two or three blank rounds as we passed, which we took no notice of, although the captain had got the carronades ready in case of their firing shot. The rebel garrison appeared in much the same state as when we passed up in the beginning of March, and the Imperialist lines did not seem to have closed in at all nearer the beleaguered city. Unable to take it by storm, they had determined to starve the garrison out, which end they succeeded in effecting during the summer, and then they had butchery enough to satiate even Chinamen.

We passed the rebel town of Wu-hoo on the 4th, which was also the first day we observed the great comet. Three or four "lorchas," as the half-European half-Chinese craft used on the coast are called, were lying off the place; they belonged to foreign Shanghai houses, agents being sent up in them for the purchase of tea, which is procured from the southern part of An-hoei, by the way of the river that empties itself at Wu-hoo. We did not bring up, but, seeing a small boat put off from one of the lorchas, the captain stopped the engines. A rough-looking customer pulled alongside, and handed a letter for Shanghai on board; and while he towed astern he was very anxious to learn anything concerning the movements of the Imperialists, for he said that at Wu-hoo the rebels were in expectation of an attack, and, as he expressed it, "Every night they do be firing off guns and beating gongs horrid." The same evening after dark we anchored off Nanking, where we found H.M.S. 'Centaur,' a small steamer the 'Bo-peep,' an American schooner, and one or two more lorchas; and to give our junks time to get along, we lay there all the day following.

My friend Mr. Forrest, who had travelled hither, *viâ* Soo-chow, from Shanghai, and who was now living on board the 'Centaur' and acting as diplomatic agent at the Taiping capital, went on shore with us, and we paid a visit to the chief of the Taiping customs, into whose reception-room we were carried on the backs of our boatmen, for the place was so flooded that there was no getting in without going up to our knees in water. The flood was said to be quite unusual, the water never having been known to be so high since the occupation of Nanking by the Taipings; and this we could quite understand, or the ingenuity of the "Heavenly Leader" would certainly have invented some better kind of craft for going about the streets than the washing-tubs in which we saw females making voyages from house to house, to learn the gossip of the morning, or the last edict of the "Son of Heaven." The rise, as registered by the 'Centaur,' was twelve feet above the winter level; and this is very considerable for a river the size of the Yang-tsze at Nanking. I found out what on account of the number of captives I had not observed before, that the ladies of Taipingdom do not make a practice of cramping their feet; and this is one of the few redeeming points in the character and customs of these people: let us hope that, when the present disturbing elements in society have subsided, they may increase.

The weather was now very hot, the thermometer showing 95° at mid-day. We took a boat ashore again in the evening, and had a walk in the country. I was pleased to see a small show of cultivation in some places, which seemed to indicate that a few of the people were settling down to fixed occupations under the Taiping rule. Mr. Forrest informed me that on his journey from Shanghai to Nanking he had not been interfered with by the Imperialists, neither had he any trouble with the rebels; but I am inclined to attribute this in a great measure to his good management, for he is one of those who will get on in spite of obstacles,—

he belongs in fact to the Parkes school. Since his stay he had been a great deal among the Taipings, being on friendly terms with the chiefs, to whom he occasionally paid visits.*

On leaving Nanking we met one or two steamers upward bound, and a few miles below the city passed a Dutch barque at anchor. She had been I don't know how many days from Shanghai, and had remained in the same place waiting for a fair wind for a long time. The skipper was certainly not in a hurry, having on board probably a good stock of sour-krout, cheese, and tobacco. We arrived at Chin-kiang in the middle of the same day that we left Nanking, and found that, owing to the place having been attacked during the spring by Taipings, Her Majesty's Consulate had been shifted from its former elevated position to Silver Island. Here we found one of our junks detained under the guns of His Celestial Majesty's Customs hulk, which Captain Lecaan was forced to go on board of to clear the junk's and the steamer's cargo for Shanghai—this being the only port on the river where the duties are collected, or rather assessed, on foreign vessels. The staff of employés were foreigners—English and Americans in the Chinese Imperial service. We heard also that one of the junks which had refused to stop here had been captured by the 'Pluto,' a small screw-steamer in the same service; but the gentleman in charge at Chin-kiang was kind enough to give Captain Lecaan an order for her release, after the manifests, &c., had been examined. We then proceeded in the gig to the Consulate on Silver Island, and our Chinese boatmen had a very long pull before we caught the steamer up again. The same evening we got down to the mouth of a

---

* His opinion of these people may be gathered from Chaps. II. and III., and I consider that it is entitled to more weight than anything else which has been written on the subject.

creek where His Celestial Majesty's steamer 'Pluto' was at anchor, with the missing junk alongside. It appears that the junk, which had only a Manila sailor on board as supercargo, had incautiously put into this creek to await the other one, and, having no pass, the skipper of the steamer seized her, expecting no doubt to make a good thing out of it. But when Captain Lecaan showed him the order for her release, the visions of prize-money vanished; and I have no doubt he looked on us as most unwelcome visitors. However, like a sensible man, he made no objection, and the junk was allowed to proceed on her voyage. By the by, this same steamer 'Pluto' had made one voyage to Nanking, but, finding that place a little too hot, she did not make any protracted stay. When she was approaching Nanking, the British ship of war there was at gunnery practice, there being some of the Taiping high officials on board; and as the captain of the 'Pluto' thought that the firing was at him, he substituted the British flag for that of the Imperial Customs, and came up. The commander of the ship of war, however, knowing what steamer it was, immediately sent orders for the British flag to be hauled down. On this the Taipings, smelling a rat, began to man their batteries with the intention of sinking her; whereupon the captain begged and prayed to be allowed to keep the flag flying for a few minutes until he could get away, which the naval commander, taking compassion on him, I believe allowed him to do; and he very soon cleared out, with the feeling of having seen quite sufficient of Nanking and the Taipings. This little fact, trivial as it may appear, exemplifies our position in China: ostensibly neutral, but encouraging, if not assisting, the Imperialists. We took down with us one of the crew of the 'Pluto' supposed to be sick. He was a poor Lascar; and his story, whether true or not, was that the crew, who were all Lascars and Manila-men, were but half-fed and seldom paid, and were treated in a brutal manner by the English skipper and his one or two European assistants. If such was the case, I would recommend it to the notice of the Commissioner of Imperial Customs at Shanghai.

On the 7th we remained for a great part of the day at anchor near Starling Island, as the pilot had run us into shoal water, and we were forced to wait the making of the tide to allow us to stem the current and get out of our false position. I think I never recollect to have felt the heat more. Not a breath of air was stirring; a blazing sun struck down almost vertically upon us; and it was impossible to get cool anywhere. The cabin was insupportable; and the only way we obtained any relief was by the canvas awnings and deck being flooded with water; but the heat dried the moisture up so rapidly that the dose had to be constantly repeated. But with all these measures it was only like the transition from a brick-kiln into the interior of a Turkish bath; and I shall long remember this hot day on the Yang-tsze. One of the mates, having been sent off in a boat to sound for the channel, could not get back again to the vessel on account of the strength of the current; he had a tremendous roasting, and only preserved himself from getting sun-struck by continually dipping his pith hat in the water, which, when he came on board, was little better than a mass of pulp. His Chinese boatmen kept themselves cool by standing up to their necks in water. At night we observed large fires on shore, supposed to be burning villages marking the progress of the Taipings. The following day carried us safely past the bugbear of Yang-tsze navigation, the "Langshan crossing;" we anchored just outside the mouth of the Shanghai river; and steamed up to Shanghai on the following morning, the 9th of July.

Thus ended our cruize of 'Five Months on the Yang-tsze.' We all felt sincerely how much cause we had to thank God, who of His merciful goodness had preserved us in our far wanderings, and had carried us through the difficulties and dangers which had beset our path. And if under His guidance our journey shall have been the means of adding to the knowledge possessed by Europeans of this portion of China, and of thereby advancing the future progress of Civilization and True Religion, I, for my part, shall feel that we have been well repaid for any little privations and difficulties, and that we have not laboured in vain.

APPENDIX.

CONTENTS.

	Page
I. Itinerary of Distances on the Upper Yang-tsze	353
II. Trade of Chung-king	355
III. Form of Passport	357
IV. Two Letters (in French) from the Roman Catholic Missionaries	358
V. Geological Specimens from the Yang-tsze Kiang	359
VI. List of Ferns collected by Lieut.-Colonel Sarel	361
VII. Geographical Positions	368
VIII. Meteorological Register	369
IX. Specimen Page of Log-book	379
X. „ „ of Field-book (Woodcut)	380

APPENDIX I.

Itinerary of Distances on the Upper Yang-tsze,

From the *confluence of the waters of the Tung-ting Lake* and the *Yang-tsze Kiang*, distant from Hankow 123, and Shanghai and the sea 711 geographical miles or 818 statute.

	Geogr. or Sea Miles.	
Sze-pa-kow (village) ...	17	
Hia-chay-wan (vill.)	40	
Shang-chay-wan (vill.)...	44	
Tiau-hien (open town)...	82	
Shi-show (hien)	120	
Ho-hia (open town)	143	
Quang-yin-shih (vill.) ...	161	
Sha-sze (open town)......	170	Port of KIN-CHOW (foo). From Hankow, 293.
Kiang-kow (open town)	190	
Tung-tsze (open town)...	197	
Point Grant	205	
Yang-chi (vill.).............	206	
Chi-kiang (hien)	210	
Pah-yang (vill.).............	218	
I-tu (hien)	221	Mouth of the Ching Kiang.
Tien-chow pagoda.........	238	{From Hankow, 363.
I-CHANG (foo)...............	240	{ „ Shanghai, 951. (1094 statute.)
Entrance of I-chang Gorge.......................	244	
First Rapid	256	
Shan-tow-pien (vill.)......	260	
Lu-kan Gorge	268	
Tsing-tan (vill.)	273	Mi-tan Gorge.
Kwei (chow)	279	
Yeh-tan Rapid	283	
Niu-kow-tan (vill.)	290	
Pa-tung (open town)......	294	
Kwan-du-kow (vill.)	300	Entrance of Wu-shan Gorge.
Nan-mo-yuen (vill.)	304	{Boundary between the provinces of Hoo-peh and Sz'chuan.
Pei-shih (vill.)	311	
Wu-shan (hien).............	324	
Tai-chi (vill.)...............	336	Near the entrance of Fung-siang Gorge.
QUAI-CHOW (foo)	342	From I-chang 102.
An-ping (vill.)	350	
Ku-liu-tu (vill.)............	361	
Tung-yan Rapid	364	
Yung-yan (hien)	370	
Siau-kiang (vill.)	382	{From Hankow, 522.
Wan (hien)...................	399	{ „ Shanghai, 1110.
Ta-chi-kow (vill.)..........	415	
Hu-lin (vill.)................	422	
Si-kia-tow (vill.)	428	
Shi-pow-chai (vill.)	430	Rock and Pagoda.

2 A

	Geogr. or Sea Miles.	
Shang-quan-chi (vill.) ...	439	
Chung (hien)	452	
Wu-yang (vill.)	457	
Sin-chan (vill.)	460	
Yang-tu-chi (vill.)..........	468	
Pa-ka-liang (vill.)	479	
Fung-tu (hien)	491	
Sou-mun-tsze (vill.)	500	
Lan-tu (vill.)	506	
Sun-chi (vill.)	511	
Sui-show (vill.)	520	
Fu (chow)	526	Mouth of the Kung-tan Ho.
Li-tu (open town)	532	
Lin-shih (vill.)	541	
Shi-kia-tu (vill.)	545	
Chang-show (hien)..........	554	
Pei-tu (vill.)	559	
Lo-shih (vill.)	566	
Hu-tung (vill.)	577	
CHUNG-KING (foo)	598	{From I-chang, 358. " Hankow, 721. " Shanghai, 1309.} Mouth of Ho-tow River.
Lo-whan-chi (vill.)	625	
Kiang-tsze (hien)	639	
Lung-mun (vill.)	649	
Yo-chi (vill.)	653	
Chung-pa-sha (vill.)	661	
Shi-mun (vill.)	666	
Ur-chi (vill.)	673	
Sung-chi (vill.)	676	
Chu-kia-tu (vill.)	678	
Yang-shi-pan (vill.)	684	
Ho-kiang (hien)............	693	Mouth of Chi-shui River.
Tow-pung-shih (vill.) ...	700	
Liang-tiow-nieu (vill.)...	706	
Lu (chow)	727	Mouth of the Fu-sung River.
Lan-tien-pa (vill.)..........	729	
Na-chi (hien)................	740	Mouth of the Yun-lin River.
Kiang-an (hien)	763	
Nan-ki (hien)................	776	
Li-chuang-pa (open town)	789	
Pa-ko-shan (vill.)	794	Coal Mines.
Tang-wan (vill.)............	797	Mouth of the Hu-nan River.
SÜ-CHOW (foo)	800	{From Hankow, 923. " Shanghai, 1511.} Mouth of the Min River.
Pa-shui-chi (vill.)	808	
An-pien (open town) ...	816	Mouth of the Whan Kiang.
Lo-fu (vill.)	823	
Lo-tung-chan (vill.)	826	
Fo-yien-chi (vill.)	832	
Ping-shan (hien)	838	From Sü-chow, 38. " Chung-king, 240. " I-chang, 600. " Hankow, 961. " Shanghai, 1550. (1782 statute.)

APPENDIX II.

TRADE OF CHUNG-KING.

The following statistics are from the information of a Chinese merchant, the prices being wholesale.

EXPORTS.

Raw silk	per catty,	2.4.4	taels.
White insect wax	„	0.3.1	„
Do. before the time of the rebels	„	0.2.8	„
Bees' wax (scarce)	„	0.2.5	„
Hemp (for grass-cloth)	„	0.0.9	„
Medicinal drugs, price unknown.			
Hung-qua (shoe-flower) for dyeing	„	0.3.2	„
Rhubarb	„	0.1.3	„
Seih (tin?)	in small pigs,	0.2.8	„
Lead (from Yu-nan)	per catty,	0.1.0	„
Salt	„	0.0.3	„
Sugar	„	0.0.5	„
Tobacco	„	0.0.7	„
Chuan-pin-ma (a drug)	„	0.7.5	„
Copper (from Yu-nan)	„	240	cash.
Coal (best quality) not much exported	per picul,	800	„
Silver	per tael,	1,500	„
Gold	„	16.0.0	taels.
Rice (said to be little exported)	per picul,	2.5.0	„
Opium	per tael,	380	cash.

Foreign opium sells at 680 cash per tael.
The price of silk is higher than before the rebel disturbances.
The iron seems to be consumed in the province.

IMPORTS.

Tea (best quality) from Ho-nan	per picul,	50.0.0	taels.
Do. (No. 2)	„	16.0.0	„
Do. (inferior) grown in Sz'chuan	„	3.3.4	„

Cotton is imported.

The following is a list of foreign goods imported from Canton; the figures prefixed to the colours signify the proportion in which each is in demand, 1000 being the maximum; the Chinese names are in brackets.

(Piki) Long Ells.

1,000 Scarlet	per piece,	11.0.0	taels.
150 Dark-blue	„	9.8.0	„
150 Light-blue	„	8.8.0	„
100 Black	„	8.0.0	„
80 Green	„	10.5.0	„
50 Foreign-blue	„	10.0.0	„

(Yu-mau) Dutch Camlet.

100	Dark-blue	per piece,	30.0.0	taels.
80	Sky-blue	,,	28.0.0	,,
10	Black	,,	19.0.0	,,
10	Scarlet	,,	27.0.0	,,
10	Foreign-blue	,,	25.0.0	,,
5	Green	,,	22.0.0	,,
5	Pale-yellow	,,	25.0.0	,,

(Yu-sho) English Camlet.

100	Dark-blue	,,	28.0.0	,,
80	Sky-blue	,,	18.7.2	,,
10	Black	,,	17.4.0	,,
10	Scarlet	,,	25.3.0	,,
10	Foreign-blue	,,	23.3.0	,,
5	Green	,,	19.8.0	,,
5	Pale-yellow	,,	23.5.0	,,

(Ki-tow) Fine Cloth.

100	Dark-blue	,,	10.3.0	,,
60	Sky-blue	,,	10.2.0	,,
10	Scarlet	,,	10.2.0	,,
10	Foreign-blue	,,	10.2.0	,,
5	Brown	,,	10.1.0	,,
5	Black	,,	10.1.0	,,

(Ma-kien) Common Cloth.

100	Dark-blue	,,	10.4.0	,,
50	Sky-blue	,,	10.3.0	,,
10	Scarlet	,,	10.3.0	,,
10	Foreign-blue	,,	10.3.0	,,
5	Brown	,,	10.2.0	,,
5	Black	,,	10.2.0	,,

(I-cho-ni) Broadcloth.

20	Black alone used	,,	20.0.0	,,

(Yu-ling) Lastings.

20	Dark-blue	,,	16.0.0	,,
100	Sky-blue	,,	17.0.0	,,
100	Foreign-blue	,,	17.0.0	,,
20	Black	,,	15.0.0	,,

Cotton goods packed in boxes of 20 pieces.

White prints		,,	3.7.0	,,
Coloured do.		,,	4.8.0	,,
Checks		,,	4.4.0	,,
White calico (1st quality)		,,	3.6.0	,,
Do. do. (2nd quality)		,,	3.4.0	,,
Do. do. (unbleached)		,,	3.3.0	,,
Printed chintz		,,	2.5.0	,,

Sundries.

Brass buttons	per gross,	3.2.0	,,
Telescopes	ea. about	10.0.0	,,
Pistols	,,	4.0.0	,,

APPENDIX III.

FORM OF PASSPORT REQUIRED BY BRITISH SUBJECTS
TRAVELLING IN CHINA.

Passport No. Three.

BRITISH CONSULATE, SHANGHAE,
2nd February, 1861.

The undersigned, Her Britannic Majesty's Consul at Shanghae, requests the Civil and Military Authorities of the Emperor of China, in conformity with the ninth article of the Treaty of Tien-tsin, to allow ——————————, British subject, to travel freely and without hindrance or molestation in the Chinese Empire, and to give him protection and aid in case of necessity.

——————————, being a person of known respectability, is desirous of proceeding to India viâ Tibet, and this Passport is given him on condition of his not visiting the cities or towns occupied by the Insurgents.

THOS. TAYLOR MEADOWS,

H. B. M.'s Consul.

This passport will remain in force for a year from the date thereof.

Signature of the bearer: ——————————.

NOTICE.—All passports must be countersigned by the Chinese Authority at the place of delivery, and must be produced for examination on the demand of the Authorities of any locality visited by the bearer. British subjects travelling in China without a passport, or committing any offence, are liable to be arrested and handed over to the nearest Consul for punishment.

FEE .. .. *One Dollar.*

APPENDIX IV.

FIRST LETTER RECEIVED BY EXPEDITION FROM M. J. P. VINÇOT, R. C. MISSIONARY AT CHUNG-KING. (See p. 219.)

A MONSIEUR LE MAJOR SAREL, 17th Lancers.

MONSIEUR LE MAJOR, 28 *Avril*, 1861.

Je viens d'apprendre de mes Chrétiens que les soldats Chinois ont projeté de vous *massacrer* en route, demain matin, quand vous irez voir les mandarins. Prenez vos précautions. J'ai fait dire aux mandarins de la ville de faire veiller à votre conservation. Je prie M. le Major de prendre son plus bel uniforme (épée, épaulettes), outrement les Chinois se moqueraient de leur tenue. Je vous attends, M. le Major, avec MM. vos compagnons de voyage, pour dîner. Je crois que ces bruits d'assassinat sont sérieux, et que vous devez prendre les précautions nécessaires pour votre sûreté personnelle.

J'ai l'honneur d'être, Monsieur,
Votre très humble et tout dévoué serviteur,
(Signed) J. P. VINÇOT,
Mis. Ap.

SECOND LETTER FROM M. VINÇOT, RECEIVED BY EXPEDITION SHORTLY AFTER THE FIRST. (See p. 219.)

A MONSIEUR LE MAJOR SAREL, 17th Lancers.

MONSIEUR LE MAJOR,

J'apprends que les soldats Chinois veulent certainement vous massacrer et piller vos barques. Ils ont déterminés de commencer l'attaque pendant le dîner; ils veulent creuser et détruire ma maison ; je crois donc prudent de remettre l'invitation à demain, jusqu'à ce que les mandarins n'aient pris leurs mesures pour notre sûreté. Si vous veniez aujourd'hui, il y aurait des massacres. Je vous prie donc de vouloir m'excuser. Mon dîner est déjà préparé, mais impossible de venir, il y va de la vie.

J'ai l'honneur, Monsieur le Major, de vous offrir mes respectueux et tous dévoués hommages.

(Signed) J. P. VINÇOT,
Mis. Ap.

# APPENDIX V.

GEOLOGICAL SPECIMENS FROM THE YANG-TSZE KIANG.

The following specimens were named through the kindness of Sir Roderick Murchison, at the Museum of Practical Geology, by Professor Ramsay; the coal has since been examined by Professor Morris; and Mr. Tennant has detected particles of gold in the samples of sand. The specimens are mostly but small fragments intended for overland carriage; they have been deposited in the Museum of the Royal Artillery Institution at Woolwich.

No.	Description.	Locality and Date.
1	Sandstone and felstone (?)	Chin-kiang. 20 Feb. 1861.
2	Red sandstone	Nanking. 26 „ „
3	Quartz rock	Between Hankow and King-kow, left bank. 28 June, 1861.
4	Pinkish limestone	Opposite Chi-kiang. 30 March, 1861.
5	Pebbles of quartz, jasper, and limestone from conglomerate.	Near I-chang. 1 April, 1861.
6	Calcareous sandstone.	Opposite I-chang. 4 April, 1861.
7	Limestone, and ribboned silicious rock and grit, or chert.	Six miles above I-chang. 5 April, 1861.
8	Granite, in boulders	Seven miles N.W. of I-chang. 5 April, 1861.
9	Gneiss	Below Lu-kan Gorge. 7 April, 1861.
10	Sandstone with green grains	Five miles below Kwei. 8 April, 1861.
11	Purple marly sandstone and silicious grit.	Kwei. 8 April, 1861.
12	Inferior coal and rock-like under clay.	Near Kwei. 8 April, 1861.
13	Sandstone, with exposed surface glossed.	Near coal. Two miles west of Kwei. 14 June, 1861.
14	Limestone (fine grained)	Village of Kwan-du-kow. 9 April, 1861.
15	Blackish limestone (very hard)	In Wu-shan Gorge, at the boundary between Hoo-peh and Sz'chuan provinces. 10 April, 1861.
16	Dark grey limestone, with veins of calcareous spar.	Quai-chow (foo). 13 June, 1861.
17	Coal (anthracite)	Between Quai-chow and Yung-yan. 14 April, 1861.

No.	Description.	Locality and Date.
18	Silicious sand, with spangles of white and yellow mica, iron, and small grains of gold.	Bed of the Yang-tsze near Wan (hien). 16 April, 1861.
19		
20	Rough calcareous sandstone	In blocks along the river near Wan. 16 April, 1861.
21	Lime, probably calcined, and which has afterwards, by exposure, reabsorbed carbonic acid.	Used for cement at Wan. 16 April, 1861.
22	Grey sandstone........................	Near Fung-tu. 23 April, 1861.
23	Grey sandstone........................	From a reef at Fu. 24 April, 1861.
24	Grey micaceous and felspathic sandstones.	Below Chung-king. 27 April, 1861.
25	Slag	Below Chung-king. 27 April, 1861. Supposed from an iron-smelting furnace.
26	Same as 21, with fragments of sandstone and limestone	Range of hills east of Chung-king, where coal is worked. 7 June, 1861.
27	Hard silicious grit	Above Chung-king. 4 May, 1861.
28	Soft micaceous and silicious grit	Do. Do.
29	Fine red calcareous sandstone ...	Near Kin-tin-tsze Island. 4 May, 1861.
30	Sandstone	Near village of Chung-pa-sha. 7 May, 1861.
31	Micaceous sandstone	Na-chi. 14 May, 1861.
32	Limestone, and red and grey sandstone.	Opposite Nan-ki. 17 May, 1861.
33	Bituminous coal, carbonaceous shale, and grey shale.	Mines of Pa-ko-shan, below Sü-chow. 18 May, 1861.
34	Dark purple micaceous sandstone	Sü-chow. 21 May, 1861.
35	Bituminous coal and sandstone ...	Ta-tan-pa Rapid above Sü-chow. 24 May, 1861.

APPENDIX VI.

SIR WILLIAM HOOKER'S LIST OF FERNS,

Collected on the Yang-tsze Kiang, in the Province of Sz'chuan,
by LIEUT.-COL. SAREL, 17th Lancers.

GLEICHENIACEÆ.

1. Gleichenia *dichotoma*, Hook. *Sp. Fil.* vol. i. p. 12; *Schk. Fil.* t. 148.

    A species abundant all over India, and found likewise in tropical Africa and America.

DAVALLIACEÆ.

2. Davallia *tenuifolia*, Sw. *Syn. Fil.* pp. 133 and 350; Willd. *Sp. Pl.* 5, p. 477; Hook. *Sp. Fl.* vol. i. p. 186.

    Perhaps the most common of all ferns in China and Japan, scarcely a collection of plants ever arriving which does not contain numerous specimens; yet it is singular that no figure of it has ever been published. Willdenow mistook the *Davallia venusta* (Schk. Fil. t. 128) for it, but that is a South American species (*D. clavata*, Sw.), peculiar to the tropical islands of the New World, as *D. tenuifolia* is peculiar to the tropical continents and islands of the Old World.

3. Davallia *Chinensis*, Sw. *Syn. Fil.* p. 138; Hook. *Sp. Fil.* vol. i. p. 187; Langsdorff and Fisch. *Fil.* p. 23, t. 27 (*excellent*); Trichomanes Chinense, *Osb. Voy. ed. Angl.* 2, p. 357, t. 2, t. 6 (*very good*).

    Our first knowledge of this species was derived from China, where it was detected, and first published, by Osbeck. It appears to be also sparingly found in the Malay Islands. It is always much larger, of a redder colour, and has much broader pinnules and segments than *D. tenuifolia*, which some, however, think is too closely allied to it.

ADIANTACEÆ.

4. Adiantum *caudatum*, Linn. *Mant.* p. 308; Sw. *Syn. Fil.* p. 122; *Schk. Fil.* t. 117; Hook. *Ex. Fl.* t. 104; *Sp. Fil.* vol. ii. p. 14.
Inhabits all India; but it appears to be rare in China. The same species has, however, been found in Arabia Felix, and in the Cape de Verdes.

5. Adiantum *Capillus-Veneris*, Linn. *Sp. Pl.* p. 1558; Sw. *Syn. Fil.* p. 124; Hook. *Brit. Ferns*, tab. 41.
This is the well-known "Maiden-hair Fern," found not only in Britain, but in all warm and temperate climates throughout the world.

6. Cheilanthes *tenuifolia*. Sw. *Syn. Fil.* p. 129 and 232; *Schk. Fil.* p. 117, t. 125; Hook. *Sp. Fil.* vol. ii. p. 82, tab. 87 C.
This is also a very abundant East Indian Fern, extending to the Malay Islands and those of Australia. The specimens of this collection are particularly fine and beautiful, and it is probably very common in the province.

7. Onychium *lucidum*. Spreng. *Syst. Veget.* 4, p. 66; Hook, *Sp. Fil.* vol. ii. p. 122; Hook. *Gen. Fil.* t. 11; Cheilanthes lucida, Wall. *Cat.* n. 69; Onychium Japonicum, Kunze, in *Schk. Fil. Suppl.* p. 11; Onychium Capense, Kaulf. *En. Fil.* p. 145, t. 1, f. 8 (*omitting the locality*, " *Cape of Good Hope* "); Trichomanes Japonicum, Thunb. *Fl. Jap.* p. 340; Cænopteris Japonica, Sw. *Syn. Fil.* p. 89.
A very delicate species, certainly first found in Japan, and imperfectly described by Thunberg, who referred it to *Trichomanes;* and Kaulfuss committed a further error by recording it as a native of the Cape of Good Hope. It is assuredly identical with the *Onychium lucidum* of the East Indies, where it abounds in the mountain regions bordering on the Western Himalaya, and in Khasya.

PTERIDACEÆ.

8. Pellæa *geraniifolia*, Fée, *Gen. Fil.* p. 130; Hook. *Sp. Fil.* vol. ii. p. 132; Pteris geraniifolia, Raddi, *Fil. Bras.* p. 110; Hook. *Ic. Pl.* 10, t. 915.
For a long time this well-marked species, with fronds a good deal resembling those of some Cape *Geranium*, was supposed to be peculiar to the New World, and even there to Brazil; but it has since been found in the Mauritius, at the

Cape, in the East Indies, in the islands of the S. Pacific, &c.; and it now proves to be an inhabitant of China.

9. Pteris (Eupteris) *longifolia*, Linn. *Sp. Pl.* p. 1531; Jacq. *Hort. Schœnbr.* t. 390, 400 (*excellent*); Hook. *Sp. Fil.* vol. ii. p. 157.

A Fern which is very general in the tropical and sub-tropical parts of the Old World, as far north as Spain. It is remarkable that, though our earliest knowledge of this species was from specimens found in the West Indies by Plumier, it is nowhere else found in America, except very sparingly in Mexico and Venezuela.

10. Pteris (Eupteris) *serrulata*, Linn. *fil. Suppl.* p. 425 (*excluding the synonyms*); Sw. *Syn. Fil.* p. 97; *Schk. Fil.* t. 91 (*excellent*); Hook. *Sp. Fl.* vol. ii. p. 167.

Common as this species undoubtedly is in China and Japan, we have no certain knowledge of its being indigenous to any other country of the globe. Swartz, indeed, gives Ceylon as a locality for it; but this statement has never been confirmed. It has long been cultivated in our Ferneries in Europe, and very successfully.

ASPLENIACEÆ.

11. Asplenium (Euasplenium) *elegantulum*, Hook. *Second Cent. of Ferns*, t. 28; *Sp. Fil.* vol. iii. p. 190; Asplenium lanceolatum? var. elegans, Hook. *Florula of Hong-Kong in Kew Gard. Misc.* 9, p. 342; Athyrium fontanum, Eaton, in *Asa Gray's Bot. of Japan*, vol. vi. New Series of *Mem. Am. Acad. of Arts and Sc. of Philad.*, pp. 421 and 436.

A perfectly distinct species, though variable in size, and in the more or less compound pinnæ. It was first discovered in Chusan, then at Hong-Kong, and since in several of the Japanese and Corean islands (Port Hamilton, Tsus-Sima, &c.), and will very likely be found to have an extensive range throughout China and Japan.

12. Asplenium (Euasplenium) *Sarelii*, Hook.; glabrous, stipes 3-4 inches long, green, compressed, herbaceous, slightly winged above; the base paleaceous, with dull black ovato-lanceolate acuminated scales; rachises everywhere compresso-alate and green; fronds subcoriaceous, 4-5 inches long; broad, ovate, acuminate, tripinnate; pinnæ primary and secondary, decurrently petiolate; pinnules about ¼ of an inch long, cuneato-lanceolate, laciniately pinnatifid, with sharp subulate segments or teeth; sori copious on nearly all the

pinnules, generally in opposite pairs parallel with the costule and margin, oblong soon confluent; involucres linear, membranaceous, white.—Asplenium Sarelii, Hook. in *Sp. Fil. Suppl. cum Ic. ined.*

The place of this species in the extensive genus *Asplenium* is undoubtedly near *A. varians*, Hook. and Grev. Ic. Fil. t. 172 (Spec. Fil. 3, p. 192), from which it is readily recognised by its larger size (a span long, including the stipes), broader and more cordate frond, the lowest pair of primary pinnæ being the longest, and an inch and a half broad; by the much narrower pinnules, so narrow, indeed, that the sori occupy the whole space between the costule and the margin, one quite parallel with them, and another very generally opposite: in this respect almost resembling an *Onychium*. It might be as correctly called a tripinnatifid as a tripinnate frond, for the compressed rachises are everywhere winged. The specific name is given in compliment to its discoverer, Lieut-Colonel Sarel, of the 17th Lancers.

ASPIDIACEÆ.

13. Aspidium (Polystichum?) *varium*, Sw. *Syn. Fil.* p. 51; Hook. *Sp. Fil.* vol. iv. p. 30, tab. 226; Polypodium varium, Linn. *Sp. Pl.* p. 1551; Aspidium setosum, Sw. *Syn. Fil.* p. 56; Langsd. et Fisch. p. 15, t. 17; Polypodium setosum, Thunb. *Fil. Jap.* p. 337; Lastrea opaca, Hook. *Florula of Hong-Kong in Kew Gard. Misc.* 9, p. 339; Aspidium opacum, Benth. *Fl. Hong-Kong*, p. 456.

First gathered in China by the Swedish naturalist Osbeck, a favourite pupil of Linnæus. Since found abundantly there and also in Japan. The specimens in this collection are peculiarly large.

14. Aspidium (Cyrtomium) *falcatum*, Sw. *Syn. Fil.* p. 43; Langsd. et Fisch. *Ic. Fil.* p. 13, t. 15; Benth. *Fl. Hong-Kong*, p. 454; Hook. *Fil. Exot.* t. 92; Cyrtomium falcatum, Pr. *Teut. Pterid*, p. 86; Hook. *Florula of Hong-Kong in Kew Gard. Misc.* 9, p. 340; Polypodium falcatum, Thunb. *Fl. Jap.* p. 336, t. 36.

This very fine Fern appears to be peculiar to China and Japan; especially common in the latter country, and in Loo Choo and Bonin. A very nearly allied species, the *Aspidium caryotideum*, Wall., is common in the mountains of Northern India, on the Neilgherries, and in Caffraria in Southern Africa.

15. Nephrodium (Eunephrodium) *molle*, Schott. *Gen. Fil. cum Ic.*; Hook. *Sp. Fil.* vol. iv. p. 68; Aspidium molle, Sw. *Syn. Fil.* p. 49; Polypodium molle, Jacq. *Ic. Pl. Rar.* t. 640.

I have had occasion to allude to this in my 'Species Filicum,' as perhaps the most cosmopolitan of all warm country Ferns. All the specimens here are characterized by their large size, 2-3 feet long including the stipes, loaded with fructifications, and, in that state, of a firm subcoriaceous texture.

16. Nephrodium (Lastrea) *decursivo-pinnatum*, Hook. Aspidium decursivo-pinnatum, Kze. *Bot. Zeit.* 6, p. 555; Phegopteris decursivo-pinnata, Fée. *Gen.* p. 242, t. 20. A. 1. (*fragments only*); Lastrea decurrens, J. Sm. in *Bot. Mag.* v. 72 : Comp. p. 33.

This again is peculiarly a Chinese and Japanese plant, as far as yet known. These specimens from Western China are much finer than any we have ever received from the coasts or the islands, and more firm and subcoriaceous in texture.

POLYPODIACEÆ.

17. Polypodium (Phegopteris) *tenericaule*, Wall. *Cat.* v. n. 335; Hook. in *Florula of Hong-Kong, in Kew Gard. Misc.* 9, p. 335; Polypodium trichodes, Reinw. Sm. in *Hook. Bot. Journ.* 3, p. 394; Lastrea leucolepis, Pr. *Epim.* p. 39; Aspidium religiosum, Kze. in *Linnæa*, 20, p. 6; *Bot. Zeit.* 6, p. 263; *Metten. Aspid.* p. 72.

Judging from the number of specimens of this Fern in the collection, it would appear to be very common in the province, and many of them, including the stipes, are 3-5 feet long. It abounds also in various parts of the East Indies, in the Malay Islands, and in Japan, as well as in China, and has been long cultivated in our gardens.

18. Polypodium (Dictyopteris) *membranaceum*, Hook.; caudex moderately creeping; paleaceous at the apex, with black subulate scales; stipites slender, a span long, brown glossy; fronds a span long, deltoid-ovate acuminate, membranaceous, glabrous, bipinnate at the base, pinnate in the middle, pinnatifid at the apex; primary basal pinnæ semi-ovate, falcate, their inferior pinnæ or pinnules much the longest : all of them, and the primary segments, oblong, acuminate, pinnatifid; the lobes also oblong, but obtuse,

subfalcate, entire, or the inferior ones serrated; veins anastomosing, costal areoles the largest, and in two series inappendiculate; the marginal veins always free; sori small (not very perfect), compital.

On the few specimens of this species the sori are sparse and young, but evidently those of a *Polypodium*, and the venation is quite that of *Dictyopteris*: but neither in my Herbarium nor in books does it accord with any described species of the genus.

19. Polypodium (Drynaria) *quercifolium*, Linn. *Sp. Pl.* p. 1547; *Schk. Fil. p.* 13, t. 13; *Bl. Fl. Jav.* p. 153; Phymatodes quercifolia, *Pr. Teut. Pterid,* p. 198; Drynaria quercifolia, J. Sm. in *Hook. Bot. Journ.* 3, p. 398.

A frequent inhabitant of the East Indies and the Malay Islands, North Australia, &c. The fronds are here all fertile, and, as is well known, are quite different in shape from the sterile ones.

LYGODIACEÆ.

20. Lygodium *Japonicum*, Sw. in *Schrad. Journ.* 1801, 2, p. 305; Sw. *Syn. Fil.* p. 154; Hydroglossum Japonicum, Willd. *Hort. Berol.* 2, p. 84, t. 84; *Sp. Pl.* 5, p. 81; Lygodium pubescens, Kaulf. *En. Fil.* p. 47; Ophioglossum Japonicum, Thunb. *Fil. Jap.* p. 328.

This species is probably peculiar to China and Japan.

LYCOPODIACEÆ.

21. Lycopodium *clavatum*, Linn. *Sp. Pl.* p. 1566; Sw. *Syn. Fil.* p. 178; Dillenius, *Musc.* t. 63, f. 10; Spring, *Monogr. Lycop.* Part I. p. 79, Part II. p. 37.

Spring justly observes of this plant, "Intra tropicos undique communissimum."

22. Selaginella *uncinata*, Spring, *Monogr. Lycopod.* Part II. p. 109; Lycopodium uncinatum, Desv. in *Encycl. Bot.* 3, p. 558; Lycopodium dilatatum, Hook. et Grev. *Enum. Fil.* n. 149; Dillenius, *Hist. Musc.* t. 65, f. 7.

Since the time of Dillenius this has been described as a native of China, and has also been found by Messrs. Lay and Collie and Mr. Fortune. It is, I believe, too, a native of Japan.

23. Selaginella *radicata*, Spring, *Monogr. Lycopod.* Part II. p. 114;

Lycopodium radicatum, Hook. et Grev. *Enum. Fil.* n. 160;
Lycopodium cupressinum, Bory, in *Belang. Voy. Bot.* p. 9.

This has been previously found in several parts of India, and in the mountains of Ava and Mergui.

24. Selaginella *fulcrata*, Spring, *Monogr. Lycop.* Part II. p. 171; Lycopodium fulcratum, Hamilt. in *Don Prod. Fl. Nepal.* p. 17; Hook. et Grev. *Enum. Fil.* Part II. n. 102; Lycopodium pectinatum, Wall. *Cat.* n. 125; β. *rubricaulis;* stem of an orange-red colour.

If I am correct in referring this handsome species to the Selaginella fulcrata, it is also a native of the mountains of Nepal; and it is a species nearly allied to S. Pervillei of Madagascar, and to S. Vogelii of tropical Western Africa, figured in Hook. *Second Century of Ferns,* t. 86.

APPENDIX VII.

UPPER YANG-TSZE.—GEOGRAPHICAL POSITIONS.
From Observation.

Station.	Place.	Date.	Latitude, N.	Longitude, E.	Mag. Variation.
		1861.	° ′ ″	° ′	° ′
*1	"Red Cliffs," Tung-ting outlet.	25 June	29 27 53		
2	Near village Sze-pa-kow	23 ,,	29 36 28		
3	4½ miles below Hia-chay-wan.	19 Mar.	29 40 2		
4	Near Chay-wan	June			0 1 East.
5	8 miles below Tiau-hien	21 Mar.	29 48 29		
6	North bank of Attalante Bend.	22 ,,	29 61 59		
7	Below Shi-show	{ 22 ,, { 23 ,,	.. ..		0 21 E. 0 25 ,, } 31′
8	Do. do.	21 June	..		0 49 ,,
9	"Point Grant"	18 ,,	30 17 30		
10	3 miles above I-tu	31 Mar.	30 27 48		1 15 E.
11	7 miles below I-chang	1 April	30 36 41		0 67 ,, } 1°
12	Near I-chang	2 ,,	30 40 52		1 16 ,, 23′ 2 4 ,,
*13	Opposite I-chang	16 June		{ 112 12·0 } 111° { 111 34·6 } 53′	
14	2 miles west of Kwei	14 ,, {	31 0 22 31 0 13 } 31° 0′ 18″		
15	Tung-yan Rapid	14 April	30 56 54	{ 109 6·0 } 109° { 109 45·0 } 25′	
16	3 miles below Yung-yan	12 June	30 66 33		
*17	Wan	17 Apr.	..	109 1·0	
18	Ta-chi-kow	18 ,,	30 36 26		
*19	3 miles above Shih-pow-chai.	21 ,,	30 6 16 (?)		
20	St. George's Island (upper end).	23 ,,	29 51 10	{ 107 46·7 } 107° { 107 33·4 } 40′	
21	Chang-show (right bank)	25 ,,	29 49 36		
22	2 miles below Hu-tung	26 ,,	29 36 24		
*23	Chung-king	{ 30 ,, { 3 May { 2 ,,	29 33 50	{ 106 60·0 } 107°2′ { 107 15·0 } ..	2 45 E. } 2° 2 7 E. } 26′
24	3 miles below Chung-pa-sha.	8 ,,	29 7 49		
*25	Sü-chow	18 ,,	28 45 35	{ 104 68·0 } 104° { 104 61·6 } 55′	2 25 E.

* *Notes.*— 1. The longitude of this station, deduced from the latitude cutting the naval chart, is 113° 14′.
13. The latitude of this station was obtained by cross bearings.
17. The latitude of this station was obtained by dead reckoning back and forward between Stations 16 and 18.
19. The latitude of this station is probably 30° 26′ 15″.
23. The station at Chung-king is the "Taiping" gate.
25. The station at Sü-chow was on the right bank of the Yang-tsze, immediately opposite the mouth of the Min.

General Note—The latitudes are all from meridian altitudes, except at Station 15, where it was determined by double altitudes.

The longitudes are by lunar distances usually both east and west—a pocket chronometer which was taken proving useless. In compiling the chart, Mr. Arrowsmith has adopted the following:
I-chang, 111° 29′; Tung-yau Rapid, 109° 31′; Wan, 108° 56′; St. George's Island, 107° 48′; Chung-king, 106° 60′; Sü-chow, 104° 56′; Ping-shan, 104° 24′.

The "stations" of observation have been marked on the chart.

All the lunar observations have been re-computed at the Royal Nautical School, under the superintendence of Mr. John Riddle and Mr. H. Mugridge.

THOS. BLAKISTON.

APPENDIX VIII.

METEOROLOGICAL REGISTER FOR FIVE MONTHS ON THE YANG-TSZE KIANG.

EXPLANATION.—*Temperature of the Air* is Fahrenheit in the shade. *Barometer* is the reading of an Aneroid found to be ·03 lower than a well-tested Mercurial Barometer, the lower numbers being the attached thermometer. *Force of the Wind* in comparison to the numbers usually applied is,—Very light, 1-2; Light, 3-4; Fresh, 5-6; Strong, 7-8; Gale, 9-10. *Weather.*—"Cloudy" signifies detached clouds; "Clouded over," distinct clouds covering the sky; "Overcast," sky covered with one mass of cloud.

PLACE.	Date.	Thermometer.				Barometer.				Wind.			Weather.			REMARKS.
		Sun-rise.	a.m. 7 30	Noon.	p.m. 8 0	a.m. 7 30	Noon.	p.m. 8 0		Morning.	Mid-day.	Evening.	Morning.	Mid-day.	Evening.	
Shanghai River.	1861. Feb. 11	°	°	°	°											
	12	Slight frost.	..	..	..	..	..	..		Light. N.E.	Light. N.	..	*Rain.*	*Rain.*	Clouded over.	Ther. 10 P.M. 28°.
	13	Sharp frost.	..	..	..	..	..	..		Fresh. N.	..	Strong. N.	Clear.	Cloudy.		Ther. Max. 32°.
	14	..	..	35	..	30·33	30·37	..		Light. N.E.	Light. N.E.	Calm.	Clear.	Dull and threatening.	Thick.	
	15	..	..	37	..	48	46	..								
	16	..	37	39	..			..								
	17	..	35	39	..	30·48	30·49	..		Light. N.W.	Very light. N.W.	Light.	Overcast. *Rain and snow.*	Overcast. *Light rain.*	Cloudy.	
						48	46									
	19	..	34	40	..	30·67	30·72	..		Light. N.	Fresh. N.	Light. N.	Overcast and thick.	Cloudless, but hazy.	Cloudless, but hazy.	Min. Ther. 28°. Ther. 10·30 P.M. 34°.
						45	42									
	19	..	32	40	..	30·78	30·80	..		Very light. N.	Very light and calm.	Light. S.S.E.	Cloudless, but hazy.	Cloudless, but hazy.	Clear.	
						44	41									
	20	..	28	..	..	30·71	..	..		Very light. S.	Very light. S.E.	..	Clear.	Clear.	Clear.	Min. Ther. 32°. Max. 46°.
						42										
Chin-kiang	21	..	32	47	..	30·67	30·58	..		Light. S.S.E.	..	..	Clear.	Cirri strata.	Clear.	
						46	46									
	22	..	34	..	..	30·62	30·37	..		Light. S.S.E.	Fresh. S.E.	Very light. N.W.	A few cirri.	Few cumuli.	Clouded over.	*Rain* during the night following.
						44	46									
	23	..	42	45	..	30·40	30·37	..		Calm.	Calm.	..	Overcast.	Overcast and light *rain.*	*Rain.*	Min. Ther. 42°.
						52	52									

2 B

370 METEOROLOGICAL REGISTER. App. VIII.

PLACE	Date	Thermometer			Barometer			Wind			Weather			REMARKS
		Sun-rise	a.m. 7 30	Noon	p.m. 8 0	a.m. 7 30	Noon	p.m. 8 0	Morning	Mid-day	Evening	Morning	Mid-day	Evening	
Nanking	1861 Feb. 24	..	41	44	..	30·54	30·45	..	Light. N.W.	Light. N.W.	Very light. S.E.	Clouded over.	Clouded over.	Clouded over.	Min. Ther. 40°.
	25	..	41	..	..	49	46	..	Very light. S.E.	Calm.	Fresh. N.E.	Cloudy.	Cloudy. Hot sun.	Clouded over.	Min. Ther. 40°.
	26	..	34	37	..	30·35	30·61	..	Gale. N.	Gale. N.	Fresh. N.N.E.	Rain and snow.	Clouded over.	Clouded over.	
	27	..	30	36	..	49	47	..	Light. N.	Light. N.	..	Clear.	Few cirri.	..	Min. Ther. 29°.
	28	..	29	..	..	30·56	30·67	..	Light. E.	Very light. E.	..	Cloudy.	Clear.1	Clouded over.	Min. Ther. 29°.
Wu-hoo	Mar. 1	..	37	40	..	53	44	..	Light. N.	Light. N.E.	Strong. E.	Overcast.	Overcast.	Overcast and raw.	
	2	..	37	42	..	30·68	..	..	Very light. S.E.	Fresh. E.	Light. N.W.	Clouded over.	Hail and rain.	Overcast and rain.	
	3	..	40	42	..	30·59	30·55	..	Light. N.	Very light. N.W.	Light. N.	Overcast and light rain.	Overcast and rain.	Hail.	
	4	..	38	39	..	43	47	..	Very light. S.E.	Light. N.	Light. N.	Clouded over.	Clouded over. Rain.	Clouded over.	
	5	..	38	42	..	30·54	30·61	..	Light. N.	Very light. N.E.	Calm.	Clouded over.	Clouded over.	Clear.	
	6	..	39	50	..	30·67	46	..	Very light. N.	Light. N.	Very light. N.E.	Clear.	Few cirri.	Clear and bright.	
Outlet of Poyang Lake	7	..	41	..	..	45	30·42	..	Calm.	Calm.	Calm.	Clear and bright.	Cloudless, but hazy.	..	Ther. 4 p.m. 54°.
	8	..	..	..	..	30·47	45	..	Very light. E.	Fresh. N.E.	..	Clouded over. Light rain.	Clear.	..	Ther. 2·15 p.m. 60°.
						30·47	30·47								
						30·30	30·44								
						51	49								

APP. VIII. METEOROLOGICAL REGISTER. 371

Location	Day	Temp Sunrise	Temp 8 A.M.	Temp Noon	Temp 8 P.M.	Bar./Th. 8 A.M.	Bar./Th. Noon	Bar./Th. 8 P.M.	Wind Sunrise	Wind 8 A.M.	Wind Noon	Wind 8 P.M.	Sky Sunrise	Sky 8 A.M.	Sky Noon	Sky 8 P.M.	Remarks
Wu-chang (hien)	9	..	..	..	50°5	30°42 / 45	30°40 / 47	..	Very light E.	Fresh. E.	..	..	Cloudy and thick.	Clouded over and dull.	Overcast and thick.	..	Rain during night following.
	10	..	..	..	..	30°27 / 49	30°25 / 47	..	Light. S.E.	Light. S.	..	..	Cloudy.	Overcast and hazy.	..	..	Sun powerful.
	11	..	..	..	..	30°29 / 50	30°26 / 55	..	Very light W.	Calm.	Very light. W.	..	Cloudy.	Few cir. cum. Hazy.	Fine.	..	
Hankow	12	..	..	..	..	30°17 / 53	..	..	Light. E.	Calm.	Very light. N.N.E.	..	Clear.	Clouded over.	Overcast. Light rain.	..	
	13	..	..	53	..	30°07 / 55	30°09 / 53	8 P.M.	Calm.	Very light. N.E.	Calm and light E.N.E.	Light. N.E.	Overcast and light rain.	Overcast and rain.	Overcast.	..	
	14	..	47°5	53	51	30°09 / 53	30°17 / 55	29°93 / 56	Light. N.E.	Calm and variable.	Light. N.E.	Light. N.E.	Overcast.	Clouded over. Rain.	Clouded over.	..	
	15	..	53	54	..	29°98 / 55	29°98 / 56	30°04 / 53	Very light. E.	Light. N.E.	Calm.	Very light. N.E.	Few cumuli.	Clouded over.	Cloudy.	..	
	16	..	53	53°5	53	30°14 / 55	30°12 / 56	30°15 / 55	Light. N.E.	Light. N.	Very light. N.E.	Calm.	Clouded over.	Overcast. Rain.	Overcast. Light rain.	..	
	17	53	54	64	..	30°13 / 54	30°12 / 55	..	Very light. N.E.	Light. N.E.	Calm.	Calm.	Overcast.	Rain.	Overcast.	Rain.	
	18	50	56	57	56	30°16 / 54	30°06 / 55	30°13 / 58	Calm.	Very light. N.E.	Calm.	Calm.	Clear.	Overcast. Rain.	Very light rain.	..	
Yo-chow	19	49°5	57	58	..	30°07 / 56	30°10 / 57	..	Light. N.N.E.	Fresh. N.N.E.	Calm.	Calm.	Cirri strati.	Clouded over.	Clouded over.	..	9h 20 p.m. 59°, 30°06
	20	57	52	54	52°5	30°16 / 51	30°13 / 54	30°10 / 57	Very light. E.N.E.	Very light. N.N.W.	Light. W.S.W.	Fresh. N.E.	Clouded over.	Cloudy and hazy.	Overcast and rain.	Clouded over.	
	21	48°5	52	..	..	30°10 / 51	30°07 / 54	30°00 / 60	Light. S.S.W.	Light. S.	Calm.	Light. W.S.W.	Overcast.	Clouded over.	Clouded over.	Cloudy.	61, Solar halo at 10·30 A.M.
	22	47	51	..	52°5	.. / 53	.. / 38	..					Few cirri.	Clear.	Clear.	Clear.	

2 B 2

METEOROLOGICAL REGISTER.

PLACE.	Date.	Thermometer.				Barometer.				Wind.			Weather.			REMARKS.
		Sun-rise.	a.m. 7 30	Noon	p.m. 8 0	a.m. 7 30	Noon.	p.m. 8 0		Morning.	Mid-day.	Evening.	Morning.	Mid-day.	Evening.	
Shi-show	1861. Mar. 23	46·5	56	63	57	30·00	29·96	29·90		Very light. S.E.	Light. S.	Very light. W.	Cloudy.	Cloudy.	Cloudy.	
	24	54	58	65	62·5	56	59	61		Very light. S.	Light. S.	Calm.	Cloudy.	Overcast.	Clouded over.	
	25	59·5	59	58	60	29·93	29·92	29·93		Calm.	Fresh. N.	Strong. N.	Overcast. Rain.	Overcast. Rain.	Rain.	* Aneroid moved with a jump to this point. Afternoon very boisterous.
Storm Island	26	...	46	50·5	48·5	29·94	29·80	29·82		Gale. N.	Strong. N.	Strong. N.	Overcast and thick.	Overcast and thick.	Overcast and thick.	
	27	46	47·5	53	54	62	61*	55		Fresh. N.	Light. N.N.E.	Calm.	Overcast.	Overcast.	Overcast.	
Kin-chow	28	50	54	66	59	29·93	29·80	30·09		Very light. S.	Variable.	Very light. E.	Cloudy.	Overcast.	Overcast.	Heavy rain night following.
	29	54·5	55·5	57·5	58·5	30·17	30·15	30·13		Very light. N.E.	Very light. N.E.	Fresh. N.E.	Overcast. Light rain.	Clouded over. Showers.	Overcast.	High wind during night, followed with heavy rain.
	30	47	48·5	53	52	30·14	30·10	30·05		Fresh. N.N.E.	Fresh. N.N.E.	Calm.	Clouded over. Rain.	Showers.	Overcast.	
	31	49·5	51	57	55·5	29·99	30·03	30·07		Calm.	Light. S.S.E.	Very light. N.W.	Overcast.	Clouded over.	Overcast.	
April. 1		47	53·5	57	58·5	30·17	30·13	30·14		Calm.	Very light. S.	Light. S.E.	Misty.	Cloudy.	Cloudy.	
	2	55	56·5	58	65	30·18	30·10	30·17		Calm.	Light. S.E.	Very light. S.E.	Overcast.	Cloudless but hazy.	Clouded over.	A warm day.
I-chang	3	60	54	...	62·5	62	58	53		Calm.	Calm.	Calm.	Cloudy.	Overcast. Heavy rain.	Overcast.	
	4	60	62·5	69·5	63	29·86	29·84	29·96		Calm.	Very light. S.E.	Calm.	Overcast.	Clouded over.	Clouded over.	
						59	66	60								
						29·85	29·83	29·75								
						63	65	67								
						29·83	29·75	29·80								
						64	63	64								

METEOROLOGICAL REGISTER.

5		58·5	61	63	29·69	29·28	29·80	Very light. E.	Light. E.	Light. E.	Overcast. Light Rain.	Overcast.	Overcast.	Heavy thunderstorm at 6 A.M.
6	59	58			29·83	61	60	Light. S.E.			Clouded over.	Clouded over and rain.	Overcast.	
7	58	60·5	58	60	60		60	Very light. E.	Light. N.E.		Overcast. Rain.	Cloudy and light rain.	Clear.	
8	56	63·5	70	68	29·87	29·62	29·67	Very light. S.E.	Calm.	Fresh. S.E.	Cloudy.	Clear.	..	Oppressive weather. Rain during following night.
9	59		71·5	74	62	53	63	Calm.	Very light. E.	Very light. S.E.	Cloudy.	Few cirri.	Clouded over.	
10	64	63·5	65	66	29·87	29·76	29·76	..	Light. E.	Fresh. E.	Clouded over. Rain.	Overcast.	Clouded over.	
11	64	65·5	70·5	69	62	64	70	Light. E.	Light. E.	Very light. E.	Clouded over.	Clouded over.	Clouded over.	
12		62·5	64·6	63·5	29·87	29·70	29·66	Light. S.E.	Fresh. S.E.	Fresh. E.	Clouded over. Rain.	Clouded over. Showers.	Clouded over.	
13	..		62	66·5	66	68	73	..	Light. E.	Light. E.	Clouded over.	Overcast. Rain.	Overcast.	
14	56	59·5	68	..	29·83	29·67	29·83	Light. E.	Light. N.E.	Light. E.	Clear.	Few cumuli.	Clouded over.	
15	57·5	62·5	67·5	61·5	69	63	66	Light. S.E.	Fresh. E.	Fresh. E.	Cloudy.	Clear.	Clear.	Heat becoming oppressive.
16	56	64	71·5	68	29·78	30·00	29·74	Very light. N.E.	Calm.	Very light. N.	Cloudy.	Few cumuli.	Cloudy.	Sun very powerful.
17	60	63	71	65·5	64	61	65	Light. E.	Very light. N.E.	Variable.	Overcast and fog.	Overcast and hazy.	Cloudy and hazy.	
18	62·5	66·5	71·5	66	29·73	29·69	29·33	Light. E.	Calm.	Very light. S.	Cloudy and hazy.	Clouded over. Few drops of rain.	Hazy and light clouds.	Threatening sky at noon.
19	62	68	76	70	29·71	29·64	29·52	Calm.	Light. S.	Very light. N.	Cloudy and hazy.	Cloudy and hazy.	Lightly overcast.	Oppressive weather.

In the Gorges.

Quei-chow.

Wan.

METEOROLOGICAL REGISTER.

PLACE	Date	Thermometer			Barometer			Wind			Weather			REMARKS
		Sun-rise	Noon	p.m. 8 0	a.m. 7 30	Noon	p.m. 8 0	Morning	Mid-day	Evening	Morning	Mid-day	Evening	
Fu	1861, April 20	65	77·5	76	29·62 68	29·54 73	29·48 78	Light, N.	Calm.	Very light. W.	Overcast.	Lightly overcast. Hazy.	Overcast. Hazy.	Very hot.
	21	71	79	68·5	29·67 70	29·58 74	29·47 74	Light, N.E.	Calm and fresh. W.	Calm.	Overcast.	Thunderstorm and rain.	Cloudy.	Thunderstorm at 3 P.M.
	22	66	72	68	29·48 69	29·43 71	29·44 76	Calm.	Calm.	Very light. S.W.	Clouded over.	Overcast. Heavy rain.	Cloudy.	Rain from 1·10 to 3 P.M.
	23	65	74·5	73	29·60 67	29·53 70	29·40 77	Calm.	Calm.	Very light. S.E.	Overcast and fog.	Lightly overcast.	Clear.	Solar halo at 9·30 A.M.
	24	64	68	75	29·56 68	29·41 74	29·22 81	Calm.	Light. N.	Calm.	Clear.	Clear.	Clear.	Noon observation 25 m. late.
	25	66·5		76·5	29·43 71	29·23 77	29·09 84	Calm.	Calm.	Very light. E.	Cloudless but hazy.	Clear.	Clear.	1 P.M. 86·5.
	26	71·5	68	87·5	29·20 75.	29·06 81	28·81 87	Calm.	Light. N.	Very light. S.	Cirri-strata.	Few cumuli.	Cloudy.	Oppressively hot, and sun very powerful.
Fu	27	76	86·5	71	28·95 80	28·98 84	29·12 77	Very light. N.	Fresh to strong. N.E. and	..	Clear.	Thunderstorm with heavy rain.	Clear.	Thunderstorm cleared the air.
	28	70	80	74	29·30 72	29·24 75	29·13 80	Very light. N.E.	Very light. N.E.	Calm.	Clouded over. Rain.	Cloudy.	Overcast. Rain.	
	29	68	73·5	67·5	29·38 72	29·38 74	29·48 71	Calm.	Calm and fresh. N.E.	Light. N.E.	Overcast. Rain.	Overcast. Rain.	Overcast.	
	30	66		73·5	29·57 69	..	29·40 77	Very light. S.W.	..	Calm.	Overcast.	Cloudy.	Clear.	
Chung-king	May 1	67	80·5	77	29·44 69	29·33 76	29·23 80	Calm.	Light. N.E.	Very light. N.E.	Cloudless but hazy.	Clear.	Clear.	Noon observation 40 m. late.
	2	66·5	81	76	29·34 73	29·17 78	28·96 88	Calm.	Very light. N.E.	Calm.	Cloudless but hazy.	Clear.	Clear.	

App. VIII.   METEOROLOGICAL REGISTER.   375

Chung-king	3	69	77	92.5	78	29.11	28.96	28.93	Calm.	Very light. W.	Calm.	Cirri-strata and haze.	Clear.	Cloudy.	Oppressive at night.
	4	73.5	79.6	88.5	81	29.08	28.98	28.95	Calm.	Calm.	Calm.	Cloudy and thunder.	Cloudy.	Cloudy.	8 A.M. Observation 15 m. late. Very oppressive.
	5	74.5	80.5	90	84	28.96	28.95	28.94	Calm.	Very light. S.E.	Calm.	Cloudy.	Cloudy.	Cloudy with distant lightning.	Very close and oppressive in evening.
	6	77.5	79	85	80	79	82	87	Very light. E.	Light. N.	Light. N.E.	Clouded over.	Clouded over.	Cloudy.	Following night. Clear.
	7	74	74	84.5	73.5	28.92	28.91	28.88	Light. N.E.	Calm and fresh. N.	Light. S.W.	Cloudy.	Thunder-storm and heavy rain.	Clear.	Storm 2 to 7 P.M.
	8	..	..	67.5	67.5	80	81	84	Calm and fresh. N.W.	Light. N.W.	Light.	Heavy rain and distant thunder.	Rain in showers.	Overcast. Heavy rain.	
	9	68.5	66.5	77.5	71	29.01	28.99	28.99	Light. N.W.	Calm.	Calm.	Rain.	Clouded over.	Overcast. Light rain.	
	10	68	73	69.5	67	29.00	29.18	29.19	Calm.	Calm.	Light. N.	Overcast. Rain.	Overcast. Rain.	Overcast.	Night following. Heavy thunderstorm with rain. Fresh N. and E.
La	11	70	63.5	79	76	29.26	29.18	29.07	Fresh. N.N.W.	Light. E.	Calm.	Clouded over. Rain.	Cloudy.	Clouded over.	Night following. Rain in showers.
	12	65	69	65	64	29.17	29.20	29.20	Very light. N.E.	Very light. S.	Light. W.S.W.	Clouded over. Rain.	Overcast. Rain.	Overcast.	
	13	63	64	74	68	29.12	29.12	29.06	Calm.	Calm.	Calm.	Overcast. Rain.	Cloudy.	Clouded over.	Night following. Rain, and fresh W. breeze.
	14	63	54.5	67	67	29.37	29.40	29.42	Very light. S.W.	Light. W.S.W.	Light.	Overcast. Rain.	Overcast. Rain.	Overcast.	
	15	65.5	68.5	..	70	29.40	29.30	29.24	Calm.	Very light. S.W.	Calm.	Clouded over. Rain.	Rain in showers.	Clouded over.	Noon observation 25 m. late. Rain at night.
Nan-ki	16	70	73	77.5	73	29.39	29.30	29.22	Very light. W.	Very light. E.	Calm.	Overcast.	Overcast. Rain.	Cloudy.	8 P.M. Observation 25 m. late.
	17	..	..	82.5	73	29.05	29.00	29.00	..	Very light. S.W.	Calm:	Overcast.	Cloudy and close.	Lightly overcast.	Solar halo at noon.

METEOROLOGICAL REGISTER.

App. VIII.

PLACE	Date.	Thermometer.				Barometer.			Wind.			Weather.			REMARKS.
		Sun-rise.	a.m. 7.30	Noon.	p.m. 3.0	a.m. 7.30	Noon.	p.m. 3.0	Morning.	Mid-day.	Evening.	Morning.	Mid-day.	Evening.	
Sï-chow	1861. May 18	65	...	84	90	28·30	28·78	28·82	Very light. S.W.	Calm.	Calm.	Cloudy and hazy.	Clear.	Lightly overcast.	Noon observation, 25 m. late.
	19	73	...	...	82·5	28·83	77	83	Calm.	Light. E.	Very light. W.	Light clouds.	Clear.	Lightly overcast.	Night following. Clouded over, and fresh W.
	20	73·5	74	78	66·5	28·88	28·78	28·82	Fresh. W.	Fresh and Light. N.E.	Light. N.E.	Clouded over.	Rain in showers.	Clouded over. Rain.	Night following. Rain.
	21	65·5	76	78	78	28·83	81	28·90	Calm.	Light. Variable.	Calm.	Clouded over.	Cloudy.	Overcast.	8 A.M. Observation 15 late.
	22	70	72·5	79·5	78	28·88	77	76	Very light. N.	Calm.	Calm.	Cloudy.	Few cumuli.	Cloudy.	Evening very close.
	23	74	80	86·5	83·5	73	76	28·79	Calm.	Calm.	Calm.	Clear.	Cloudy.	Clouded over.	
	24	76·5	81	90	71·5	28·78	28·78	78	Calm.	Very light. E.	Fresh. W.	Clouded over.	Clouded over.	Clouded over. Rain.	Night following, heavy rain.
	25	...	71	79	74·6	28·72	28·82	28·67	Calm.	Very light. N.E.	Very light. W.	Clouded over. Rain.	Overcast.	Overcast.	Noon observation 15 m. late.
Ping-shan	26	70·5	78	84·5	76	77	81	82	Fresh. W.	Light. S.E.	Calm.	Overcast and thick.	Clouded over.	Clouded over.	Night following, light rain.
	27	72	74	77·5	70	28·50	28·46	28·60	Calm.	Calm.	Very light. W.	Clouded over.	Overcast. Rain.	Overcast.	
	28	71	76·5	84·5	77·5	28·95	28·94	28·83	Calm.	Light. S.E.	Very light. W.	Overcast and thick.	Cloudy.	Cloudy.	Noon observation 15 m. late.
	29	...	71	81·5	71	73	75	73	Calm.	Calm.	Calm.	Clouded over. Rain.	Overcast. Rain.	Clouded over.	3 P.M. observation 45 m. late.
	30	...	72·5	77·5	74	28·93	28·85	28·72	Very light. S.W.	Very light. N.	Very light. E.	Clouded over. Rain.	Cloudy.	Cloudy.	Noon observation 25 m. late. Night following, rain and strong W. breeze.
						28·70	28·67	28·80			Very light. W.	Overcast.	Clouded over.	Clouded over.	
						74	76	77							

METEOROLOGICAL REGISTER.

Location	Date								Wind 1	Wind 2	Wind 3	Obs 1	Obs 2	Obs 3	Remarks
Sü-chaw	31	67·5	69·5	80	73	28·97	70	28·89	Fresh. W.	Very light and calm.	Very light. S.E.	Clouded over. Rain.	Cloudy.	Overcast.	Night following, rain.
	June 1	67	72	78·5	73·5	29·06	74	28·92 74	Calm.	Calm.	Very light. S.E.	Clouded over.	Cloudy and hazy.	Overcast.	Noon observation 15 m. late.
	2	71	70·5	72·5	71	28·98	75	28·90 76	Calm.	Very light. E.	Calm.	Rain.	Overcast.	Overcast.	
	3	67	69	80·5	69·5	28·98	72	28·90 73	Very light. S.	Calm.	Calm.	Rain.	Rain.	Clouded over.	
	4	68·5	68·5	68	67	29·09	70	29·10 73	Light. E.S.E.	Very light. S.	Very light. S.E.	Clouded over.	Heavy rain.	Heavy rain.	Night following, rain.
Chung-king	5	67	71	75·5	75	29·36	71	29·23 71	Light. S.W.	Light. W.	Calm.	Rain.	Cloudy.	Overcast.	Noon observation 15 m. late.
	6	71	73	76·5	74	29·30	73	29·21 77	Calm.	Calm.	Calm.	Rain.	Heavy rain.	Cirri-strata.	8 A.M. observation 15 m. late.
	7	69	76	84	76	29·34	74	29·00 80	Calm.	Very light. W.	Calm.	Clouded over.	Cloudy and hazy.	Overcast.	Solar halo at noon.
	8	72·5	76	83	77	29·23	74	28·94 84	Calm.	Very light. W.	Calm.	Overcast and fog.	Cloudy.	Cloudy.	Water of the river, 73·5.
Wan	9	75	76·5	79·5	76	29·13	78	29·00 78	Calm.	Very light. E.	Fresh. E.	Cloudy.	Overcast. Rain.	Overcast. Rain.	
	10	72	77·5	78	80·5	29·05	77	29·07 82	Calm.	Fresh. N.N.E.	Calm.	Thick mist.	Cloudy.	Cloudy.	Afternoon, thunder and lightning. Squall from S.W.
	11	71·5	71·5	83	72·5	29·21	77	29·26 79	Light. E.	Light. N.N.E.	Fresh. E.	Overcast. Hazy.	Overcast. Hazy.	Heavy rain.	Ther. 1·10 P.M. 74°.
Quai-chow	12	74	74	—	70	29·42	79	29·36 76	Calm.	Fresh. E.S.E.	Calm.	Cloudy and hazy.	Rain in showers.	Cloudy.	
	13	71·5	76	79	75	29·39	75	29·30 76	Light. E.	Very light. S.W.	Fresh. E.	Clouded over. Rain.	Cloudy.	Cloudy.	
	14	71	76	86	81	29·45	78	29·25 83	Calm.	Light. W.	Strong. E.	Clouded over.	Cloudy and showers.	Few cumuli.	Ther. exposed 12·30 P.M. 116°. Water of river, 73°.

2 c

METEOROLOGICAL REGISTER.

PLACE.	Date.	Thermometer.				Barometer.			Wind.				Weather.			REMARKS.
		Sun-rise.	a.m. 7.30	Noon.	p.m. 8.0	a.m. 7.30	Noon.	p.m. 8.0	Morning.	Mid-day.	Evening.		Morning.	Mid-day.	Evening.	
	1861. June 15	° 72	° 75	° 85	° 77	29·43	29·33	29·33	Very light. E.	Fresh. S.E.	Calm.		Clear.	Few cumuli.	Overcast.	Evening oppressive.
I-chang....	16	78	81	88	78	77	81	83	Calm.	Light. S.E.	Calm.		Overcast.	Thunder-storm and shower.	Cloudy.	
	17	..	81	88	81	29·34	29·30	29·22	Calm.	Fresh. S.S.E.	Very light. N.W.		Cloudy.	Clear.	Cloudy.	Ther. 2 P.M. 90°.
	18	75	81	91	82	81	83	84	Calm.	Strong. S.S.E.	Light. S.S.E.		Clouded over.	Cloudy.	Clear.	Night following, rain.
	19	73	82	93	66·5	29·38	29·33	29·14	Calm.	Gale. W.N.W.	Strong. N.		Clouded over. Rain.	Rain and thunder.	Clouded over. Rain.	Noon observation 15 m. late.
	20	84	84	70	69	79	85	69	Light. S.S.E.	Fresh. N.	Very light. N.		Overcast. Rain.	Clouded over.	Clear.	Water of river, 74°. Noon observation 25 m. late.
	21	..	71	80	72	29·41	29·33	29·24	Fresh. N.E.	Light. N.	Very light. E.S.E.		Cloudy.	Clouded over.	Clear.	Water of river, 71°. Noon observation 15 m. late. 8 P.M. obs. 15 m. late. Ther. 1 P.M 66°.
	22	71	77	80	77	80	84	69	Very light. N.E.	Very light. S.W.	Light. E.		Clear.	Cloudy.	Clear.	
	23	76	80	84	70	29·34	29·21	29·44	Calm.	Light. S.	Very light. W.S.W.		Clear.	Cloudy.	Cloudy.	Noon observation 35 m. late.
	24	79	82	85	68	81	66	81	Very light. S.E.	Strong. S. by W.	Fresh. S.		Cloudy.	Cirri-strata.	Cloudy.	Solar halo at noon, lunar halo at 8 P.M. Wind fell during night.
Near Tung-ting L.	25	75	76	78	76	29·62	29·60	29·30	Light. S.	Fresh. N. by E.	Light. N.		Cloudy.	Overcast.	Clear.	Noon observation 15 m. late. Temperature of water, 77·5° and 80°.
	26	76	79	82	80	72	70	75	Light. N.E.	Light. N.E.	Light. N.E.		Clouded over.	Clouded over.	Clouded over.	Water of river, 80°.
	27	78	87	81	66	29·53	29·47	29·50	Light. N.E.	Fresh. W.	Strong. N.		Cloudy.	Cloudy.	Clouded over. Rain.	Wind hauled to N.W. and N.N.W. blowing a gale. Wind sending clouds.
Hankow....	28	69	72	..	..	73	76	73	Fresh. N.				Cloudy.			

APPENDIX IX.
Specimen Page of Log-Book.

25th *April*, 1861. Thursday,   *Yang-tsze River*.
Station.—Chang-show (hien), 1265 geographical miles from Shanghai.
677 geographical miles from Hankow.
Lat. by observation 29° 49' 36" N.
Long. D. R. 107° 22' E.

Time.	Course.	Miles.	Place.	Nature of the Country.	Reference.
A. M. 5·0 (20″ m. delay.)	W.S.W.	¾	⚓ Left bank.	Country hilly, particularly around village of *Lin-shih*, where the hills were to a great extent clothed with trees of small growth. River in some places strong, with one rapid. Some more fortified camps or redoubts on the hills, of late construction. Coal near *Hwang-pin-ma* rapid.	
7·10	W. by S.	3			
8·35	S.W. by W.	2¼			
9·0 (20 m. delay)	{ N.W. by W. }	2½	Village *Lin-shih* (right).		
11·15	N. ½ W.	1¼			
12·10					
12·50	N.W.	3	Village *Shih-kia-tu* (right). Small village (left). Rapid *Hwang-pin-ma*		
2·30	N.W. N. by E.	1½			
4·25	N.W.	1	Small village (left).		
7·0	N.N.W.	2	⚓ { Opposite *Chang-show* (station).		
		18			

	Ther.	Bar.	Wind	Weather.	
Sunrise	66½		Calm	Clear.	
8·0	72	29·43 / 71	Calm	Hazy, but no cloud.	
Noon		29·23 / 77	Calm	Clear.	
1·0 8·0	86½ 78¾	29·09 / 84	Very light—East .	Clear.	

(*From the back of the Page.*)
Soundings.—7·30 From right to left bank   2½   6½   1⁄10   2
   Noon   ,,   left   ,,   right   1⁄10   1⁄13 ·18   15
   1·5   ,,   right ,,   left   1⁄13   1⁄17   1⁄13   13

APPENDIX X.
Specimen Page of Field-Book.

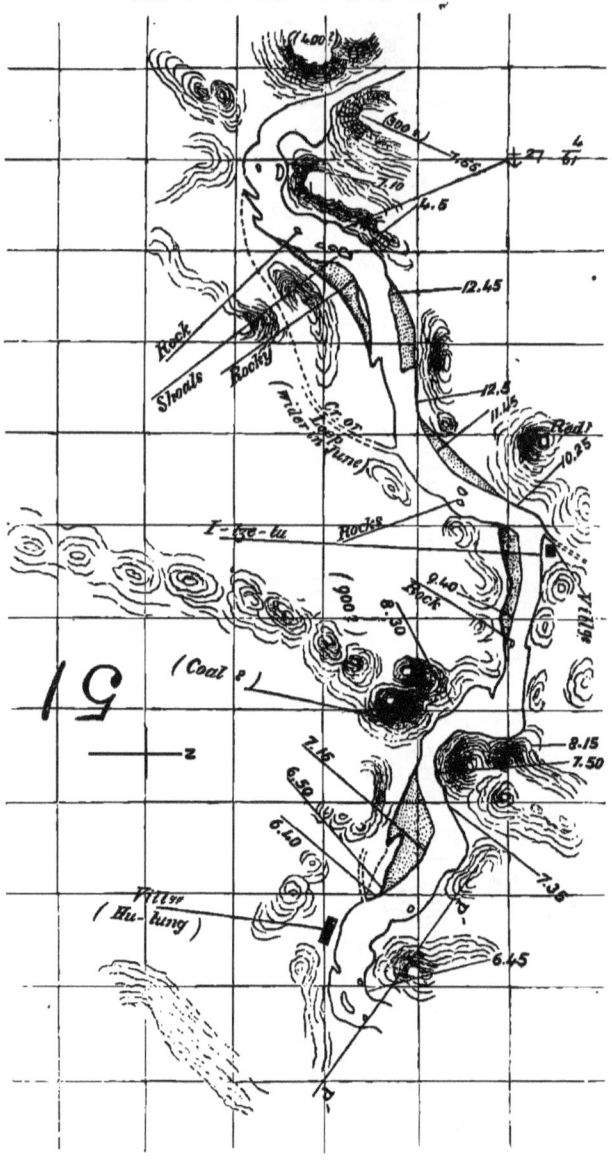

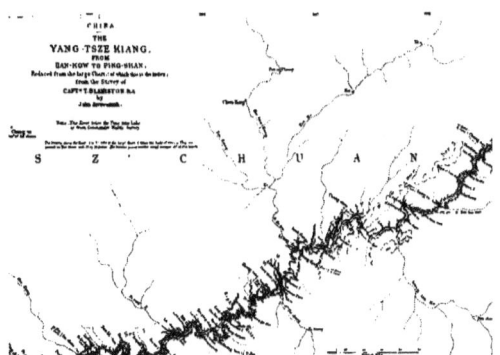

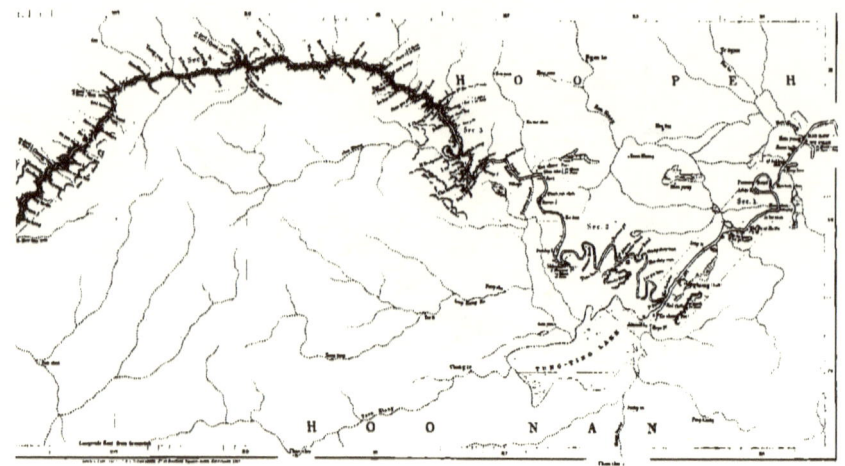

ALBEMARLE STREET,
November, 1861.

MR. MURRAY'S
LIST OF NEW WORKS.

LIVES OF ENGINEERS;
WITH AN ACCOUNT OF THEIR PRINCIPAL WORKS,
AND A HISTORY OF INLAND COMMUNICATION IN BRITAIN.

By Samuel Smiles,
Author of "Life of Stephenson," &c.

Portraits and numerous Woodcuts. Vols. 1 and 2. 8vo. 42s.

AIDS TO FAITH;
A SERIES OF THEOLOGICAL ESSAYS BY THE FOLLOWING WRITERS.

REV. E. HAROLD BROWNE	On Inspiration.
REV. F. C. COOK	Ideology and Subscription.
BISHOP OF CORK	Christian Evidences.
DEAN OF EXETER	Scripture and its Interpretation.
REV. H. L. MANSEL	On Miracles.
REV. DR. McCAUL	Mosaic Record of Creation—and On Prophecy.
REV. GEORGE RAWLINSON	The Pentateuch.
BISHOP OF GLOUCESTER AND BRISTOL	Doctrine of the Atonement.

One Volume. 8vo.

A NEW HISTORY OF MODERN EUROPE;
FROM THE TAKING OF CONSTANTINOPLE BY THE TURKS TO THE CLOSE
OF THE WAR IN THE CRIMEA.

By Thos. H. Dyer.

Vols. 1 and 2. 8vo.

MANUAL OF METALLURGY;

THE ART OF EXTRACTING METALS FROM THEIR ORES, AND ADAPTING THEM TO VARIOUS PURPOSES OF MANUFACTURE.

By John Percy, F.R.S.

First Division.—FUEL, REFRACTORY MATERIALS, COPPER, ZINC, BRASS.

With numerous Illustrations. 8vo.

EXPLORATIONS AND ADVENTURES IN EQUATORIAL AFRICA;

WITH ACCOUNTS OF THE MANNERS AND CUSTOMS OF THE SAVAGE TRIBES, AND THE CHASE OF THE GORILLA, NEST-BUILDING APE, CHIMPANZEE, &c.

By Paul B. Du Chaillu.

Tenth Thousand. With Map and 80 Illustrations. 8vo. 21s.

ICELAND:
ITS VOLCANOES, GEYSERS, AND GLACIERS.

By Commander C. S. Forbes, R.N.

With Map and Illustrations. Post 8vo. 14s.

LECTURES ON THE HISTORY OF THE EASTERN CHURCH;

WITH AN INTRODUCTION ON THE STUDY OF ECCLESIASTICAL HISTORY.

By Rev. A. P. Stanley, D.D.,

Regius Professor of Ecclesiastical History, and Canon of Christ Church, Oxford.

8vo. 16s.

LIFE OF THE RIGHT HON. WILLIAM PITT.

WITH EXTRACTS FROM MSS. PAPERS.

By Earl Stanhope,

Author of the "History of England from the Peace of Utrecht."

Portrait. Vols. 1 and 2. Post 8vo. 21s.

ADDRESS AT THE SOCIAL SCIENCE ASSOCIATION, 1861.

By Henry Lord Brougham.

Revised, with Notes. 8vo, 1s.

HISTORY AND THE HEROES OF MEDICINE;

By J. Rutherfurd Russell, M.D.

With Portraits. 8vo. 14s.

SUNDAY—ITS ORIGIN, HISTORY, AND PRESENT OBLIGATIONS.

By Rev. J. A. Hessey, D.C.L.,

Head Master of Merchant Taylors' School, Prebendary of St. Paul's, and Preacher to the Hon. Society of Gray's Inn.

Second Edition. With Index. 8vo. 16s.

TWO YEARS' RESIDENCE IN JUTLAND, THE DANISH ISLES, AND COPENHAGEN.

By Horace Marryat.

With Map and Illustrations. 2 Vols., 8vo. 24s.

SCEPTICISM;

A RETROGRESSIVE MOVEMENT IN THEOLOGY AND PHILOSOPHY;

By Lord Lindsay.

8vo. 9s.

THE ENGLISH CATHEDRAL OF THE NINETEENTH CENTURY.

By A. J. Beresford Hope.

With Illustrations. 8vo. 12s.

THE STORY OF DR. LIVINGSTONE'S TRAVELS IN SOUTH AFRICA.
Illustrations. Post 8vo.

THE MESSIAH:
HIS LIFE AND MINISTRY, SUFFERINGS, DEATH, RESURRECTION, AND ASCENSION.
Map. 8vo.

HANDBOOK OF DESCRIPTIVE AND PRACTICAL ASTRONOMY.
By George F. Chambers.
Illustrations. Post 8vo.

ARREST OF THE FIVE MEMBERS BY CHARLES I.
A CHAPTER OF ENGLISH HISTORY RE-WRITTEN.
By John Forster.
Post 8vo. 12s.

THE GRAND REMONSTRANCE, 1641.
WITH AN INTRODUCTORY ESSAY ON ENGLISH FREEDOM UNDER PLANTAGENET AND TUDOR SOVEREIGNS.
By John Forster.
Second Edition. Post 8vo. 12s.

BIOGRAPHICAL ESSAYS.
CROMWELL, DEFOE, STEELE, CHURCHILL, AND FOOTE.
By John Forster.
Third Edition. Post 8vo. 12s.

SUGGESTIONS ON POPULAR EDUCATION.
By Nassau William Senior.
8vo. 9s.

PRIVATE DIARY OF TRAVELS, PERSONAL ADVENTURES, AND PUBLIC EVENTS,

Of the late General Sir Robert Wilson.

DURING MISSIONS AND EMPLOYMENTS ABROAD.

Edited by Rev. Herbert Randolph, M.A.

With Map. 2 Vols. 8vo. 26s.

THE DIARY AND CORRESPONDENCE OF CHARLES ABBOT, FIRST LORD COLCHESTER,

SPEAKER OF THE HOUSE OF COMMONS, 1802—1817.

Edited by his Son.

With Portrait. 3 Vols., 8vo. 42s.

ANCIENT LAW:

ITS CONNECTION WITH THE EARLY HISTORY OF SOCIETY, AND ITS RELATION TO MODERN IDEAS.

By Henry Sumner Maine,

Reader in Jurisprudence and the Civil Law at the Middle Temple.

8vo. 12s.

THE STUDENT'S MANUAL OF THE ENGLISH LANGUAGE.

BEING LECTURES

By George P. Marsh.

WITH A RECOMMENDATORY PREFACE

By Dr. Wm. Smith.

Post 8vo. Uniform with the "Student's Hume."

PROVINCE OF JURISPRUDENCE DETERMINED.

BEING THE FIRST PART OF A SERIES OF LECTURES ON JURISPRUDENCE, OR THE PHILOSOPHY OF POSITIVE LAW.

By the late John Austin,

Barrister-at-Law.

Second Edition. 8vo. 15s.

THE GREAT SAHARA.
WANDERINGS SOUTH OF THE ATLAS MOUNTAINS.

By Rev. H. B. Tristram,
Master of Greatham Hospital.

With Maps and Illustrations. Post 8vo. 15s.

A DICTIONARY OF THE BIBLE;
ITS ANTIQUITIES, BIOGRAPHY, GEOGRAPHY, AND NATURAL HISTORY.

Edited by William Smith, LL.D.,
Classical Examiner in the University of London.

Second Edition. With Plans and Woodcuts. Medium 8vo. 42s.

A THIRD SERIES OF PLAIN SERMONS.
By Rev. J. J. Blunt, B.D.,
Late Margaret Professor.

Post 8vo.

ANTIQUE GEMS;
THEIR ORIGIN, USES, AND VALUE,

AS INTERPRETERS OF ANCIENT HISTORY, AND AS ILLUSTRATIVE OF ANCIENT ART.

By Rev. C. W. King, M.A.

With Plates and numerous Illustrations. 8vo. 42s.

A FIRST LATIN DICTIONARY AND VOCABULARY.
APPLICABLE FOR THOSE READING PHÆDRUS, CORNELIUS NEPOS, AND CÆSAR.

By Dr. Wm. Smith.

12mo. 3s. 6d.

Uniform with Smith's " PRINCIPIA LATINA."

THE DUKE OF WELLINGTON'S SUPPLEMENTARY DESPATCHES.

INDIA—IRELAND—THE PENINSULA—WATERLOO—PARIS—PENINSULA AND SOUTH OF FRANCE.

Edited by his Son, the Present Duke.

Volumes 1 to 8. 8vo. 20s. each.

SERMONS PREACHED BEFORE THE UNIVERSITY OF OXFORD.

By Rev. Robert Scott, D.D.

Master of Baliol College, Oxford.

Post 8vo. 8s. 6d.

THE SOUTHERN CATHEDRALS OF ENGLAND;

WINCHESTER, SALISBURY, EXETER, WELLS, CHICHESTER, CANTERBURY, AND ROCHESTER.

With 200 Illustrations. 2 Vols. Crown 8vo. 24s.

MANNERS AND CUSTOMS OF THE MODERN EGYPTIANS.

By Edward Wm. Lane.

Fifth Edition. With Additions and Improvements, and numerous Woodcuts.

Edited by Stanley Poole.

8vo. 18s.

THE GLACIERS OF THE ALPS.

BEING

A NARRATIVE OF EXCURSIONS AND ASCENTS; AN ACCOUNT OF THE ORIGIN AND PHENOMENA OF GLACIERS;

AND AN EXPOSITION OF THE PHYSICAL PRINCIPLES TO WHICH THEY ARE RELATED.

By John Tyndall, F.R.S.,

Professor of Natural Philosophy in the Royal Institution of Great Britain and in the Government School of Mines.

With Illustrations. Post 8vo. 14s.

STUDENT'S MANUAL OF ANCIENT GEOGRAPHY
BASED ON THE "DICTIONARY OF GREEK AND ROMAN GEOGRAPHY."

Edited by Wm. Smith, LL.D.

With Plans and Woodcuts. Post 8vo. 9s.

AUTOBIOGRAPHICAL RECOLLECTIONS OF CHARLES ROBERT LESLIE, R.A.
WITH SELECTIONS FROM HIS CORRESPONDENCE, AND AN ESSAY ON HIS CHARACTER AS AN ARTIST.

Edited by Tom Taylor.

With Portrait. 2 Vols., post 8vo. 18s.

AN ESSAY ON THE ORIGIN OF LANGUAGE.
BASED ON MODERN RESEARCHES, AND ESPECIALLY ON THE WORKS OF M. RENAN.

By Rev. F. W. Farrar, M.A.,
Late Fellow of Trinity Coll., Cambridge.

Fcap. 8vo. 5s.

THE HORSE AND HIS RIDER.
By Sir Francis B. Head, Bart.

Fourth Thousand. With Woodcuts. Post 8vo. 5s.

MEMOIR OF THE LATE ARY SCHEFFER.
By Mrs. Grote.

Second Edition. With Portrait. Post 8vo. 8s. 6d.

MR. MURRAY'S LIST OF NEW WORKS. 9

LIFE OF DANIEL WILSON, D.D.

LATE LORD BISHOP OF CALCUTTA AND METROPOLITAN OF INDIA.

WITH SELECTIONS FROM HIS LETTERS AND JOURNALS.

By Rev. Josiah Bateman, M.A.,

Rector of North Cray.

Second and Condensed Edition. With Portrait and Illustrations. Post 8vo. 9s.

ON THE ORIGIN OF SPECIES BY MEANS OF NATURAL SELECTION.

OR, THE PRESERVATION OF FAVOURED RACES IN THE STRUGGLE FOR LIFE.

By Charles Darwin, M.A., F.R.S.

Seventh Thousand. Third Edition, with Additions and Corrections. Post 8vo. 14s.

THE GERMAN, FLEMISH, AND DUTCH SCHOOLS OF PAINTING.

BASED ON THE HANDBOOK OF KUGLER.

By Dr. Waagen,

Director-General of the Berlin Gallery.

With Illustrations. 2 Vols., post 8vo. 24s.

HISTORICAL EVIDENCES OF THE TRUTH OF THE SCRIPTURE RECORDS, STATED ANEW,

WITH SPECIAL REFERENCE TO THE DOUBTS AND DISCOVERIES OF MODERN TIMES.

By Rev. George Rawlinson, M.A.,

Late Fellow and Tutor of Exeter College, Oxford.

Second Edition. 8vo. 14s.

HISTORY OF THE UNITED NETHERLANDS;

FROM THE DEATH OF WILLIAM THE SILENT TO THE SYNOD OF DORT;

Including the Struggle of the English and Dutch against Spain; and the Origin and Destruction of the Spanish Armada.

By John Lothrop Motley, D.C.L.,
Author of " The Rise of the Dutch Republic."

Fourth Thousand. With Portraits and Plans. 2 Vols. 8vo. 30s.

CLERICAL AND LITERARY ESSAYS.

By Rev. J. J. Blunt,
Late Margaret Professor of Divinity at Cambridge.

8vo. 12s.

THE DANGERS AND SAFEGUARDS OF MODERN THEOLOGY.

CONTAINING "SUGGESTIONS TO THE THEOLOGICAL STUDENT UNDER PRESENT DIFFICULTIES."

By Archibald Campbell Tait, D.D.,
Lord Bishop of London.

8vo. 9s.

SERMONS PREACHED IN LINCOLN'S INN CHAPEL.

By Rev. Wm. Thomson, D.D.,
Bishop of Gloucester and Bristol.

8vo. 10s. 6d.

RECOLLECTIONS OF THE DRUSES,

AND SOME NOTES ON THEIR RELIGION.

By Lord Carnarvon.

Third Edition. Post 8vo. 5s. 6d.

A RE-ISSUE
OF
MURRAY'S
HOME AND COLONIAL LIBRARY,
AT A REDUCED PRICE.

THE object of MR. MURRAY'S COLONIAL LIBRARY, when first published, was to furnish the highest Literature of the day, at a very low price. The great success which has attended its publication shows how well suited it was to the wants of the reading public at that period. Since then a fresh class of readers has arisen, and the establishment of Literary Institutions, School and Village Clubs, Book Hawking Societies, Parochial and Lending Libraries, has become so general, that it appears to the Publisher a good opportunity to disseminate these Volumes, at a rate which shall place them within reach of the less wealthy classes. By removing the impediment of price, he hopes to throw open these attractive and useful Works to the Million; so that having hitherto been the delight of the Parlour and Drawing-room, they may now do equally good service in the Factory and Workshop—in the Cottage of the Peasant and Log-hut of the Colonist—in the Soldier's Barrack and the Sailor's Cabin.

The Works composing the "Colonial and Home Library" have been selected for their acknowledged merit, the ability of their authors, and are exclusively such as are calculated to please all classes and circles of readers. The character of the work is made. It is so well known and esteemed as no longer to require expensive advertising, so that the publisher is enabled to circulate it at a great reduction in price.

The attention of the Clergy, of Secretaries of Village Reading-Clubs, of Masters of Factories and Schools, is especially invited to the above announcement and the lists which follow, in which the various Works have been arranged under two distinct heads.

CLASS A.
BIOGRAPHY, HISTORY, AND HISTORIC TALES.
CLASS B.
VOYAGES, TRAVELS, AND ADVENTURES.

Each Work will be complete in itself, and may be obtained separately, neatly bound in cloth.

₊ *For List of Works see next page.*

MURRAY'S
HOME AND COLONIAL LIBRARY.

CLASS A.
Biography, History, and Historic Tales.

I. HISTORY of the SIEGE of GIBRALTAR, 1779—83. With a Description and Account of that Garrison. By JOHN DRINKWATER. 2s.

II. The AMBER WITCH—the most interesting Trial for Witchcraft ever known. By Lady DUFF GORDON. 2s.

III. LIVES of CROMWELL and BUNYAN. By ROBERT SOUTHEY, LL.D. 2s.

IV. LIFE, and EXPLOITS of Sir FRANCIS DRAKE. By JOHN BARROW. 2s.

V. CAMPAIGNS of the BRITISH ARMY at WASHINGTON. By the Rev. G. R. GLEIG. 2s.

VI. The FRENCH in ALGIERS. Translated by Lady DUFF GORDON. 2s.

VII. HISTORY of the FALL of the JESUITS in the 18th CENTURY. 2s.

VIII. LIVONIAN TALES. By A LADY. 2s.

IX. LIFE of CONDÉ. By Lord MAHON. 3s. 6d.

X. SALE'S BRIGADE in AFFGHANISTAN. By the Rev. G. R. GLEIG. 2s.

XI. The SIEGES of VIENNA. Translated by Lord ELLESMERE. 2s.

XII. The WAYSIDE CROSS. A Tale of the Carlist War. 2s.

XIII. SCENES from the WAR of LIBERATION in GERMANY. By Sir ALEXANDER DUFF GORDON. 3s. 6d.

XIV. The STORY of the BATTLE of WATERLOO. By Rev. G. R. GLEIG. 3s. 6d.

XV. ADVENTURES. From the Autobiography of HENRY STEFFENS. 2s.

XVI. LIVES of the BRITISH POETS: with an Essay on English Poetry. By THOMAS CAMPBELL. 3s. 6d.

XVII. HISTORICAL and CRITICAL ESSAYS. By Lord MAHON. 3s. 6d.

XVIII. LIFE of LORD CLIVE. By the Rev. G. R. GLEIG. 3s. 6d.

XIX. STOKERS and POKERS; or, The North-Western Railway. By Sir FRANCIS B. HEAD. 2s.

XX. LIFE of Sir THOMAS MUNRO. By Rev. G. R. GLEIG. 3s. 6d.

CLASS B.
Voyages, Travels, and Adventures.

I. The BIBLE in SPAIN; or, The Adventures of an Englishman in an Attempt to Circulate the Scriptures. By GEORGE BORROW. 3s. 6d.

II. The GIPSIES of SPAIN; their Manners and Customs. By GEORGE BORROW. 3s. 6d.

III. IV. A JOURNEY through INDIA, from Calcutta to Bombay, Madras, and the Southern Provinces. By Bishop HEBER. 2 vols. 7s.

V. TRAVELS in the HOLY LAND. By Captains IRBY and MANGLES. 2s.

VI. WESTERN BARBARY, its Wild Tribes and Savage Animals. By J. DRUMMOND HAY. 2s.

VII. LETTERS from the SHORES of the BALTIC. By a LADY. 2s.

VIII. NOTES and SKETCHES of NEW SOUTH WALES. By Mrs. MEREDITH. 2s.

IX. The WEST INDIES. From the Journal of M. G. LEWIS. 2s.

X. SKETCHES of PERSIA. By Sir JOHN MALCOLM. 3s. 6d.

XI. THIRTEEN YEARS at the COURT of PEKIN. By FATHER RIPA. 2s.

XII. XIII. TYPEE and OMOO; or, The Marquesas Islanders. By HERMAN MELVILLE. 2 vols. 7s.

XIV. MEMOIRS of a MISSIONARY in CANADA. By Rev. J. ABBOTT. 2s.

XV. LETTERS from MADRAS. By a LADY. 2s.

XVI. The WILD SPORTS of the HIGHLANDS. By CHARLES ST. JOHN. 3s. 6d.

XVII. RAPID JOURNEYS ACROSS THE PAMPAS. By Sir FRANCIS HEAD. 2s.

XVIII. GATHERINGS FROM SPAIN. By RICHARD FORD. 3s. 6d.

XIX. A VOYAGE UP THE RIVER AMAZON. By WILLIAM EDWARDS. 2s.

XX. A POPULAR ACCOUNT of INDIA. By Rev. CHARLES ACLAND. 2s.

XXI. MEXICO and the ROCKY MOUNTAINS. By GEORGE F. RUXTON. 3s. 6d.

XXII. PORTUGAL and GALICIA. By Lord CARNARVON. 3s. 6d.

XXIII. BUSH LIFE in AUSTRALIA. By Rev. H. W. HAYGARTH. 2s.

XXIV. ADVENTURES in the LIBYAN DESERT. By BAYLE ST. JOHN. 2s.

XXV. LETTERS from SIERRA LEONE. By a LADY. 3s. 6d.

www.ingramcontent.com/pod-product-compliance
Lightning Source LLC
Chambersburg PA
CBHW020532300426
44111CB00008B/632